BOOKS BY
THOMAS J. WERTENBAKER
★
PRINCETON, 1746-1896
THE FOUNDING OF AMERICAN CIVILIZATION:
THE MIDDLE COLONIES
THE OLD SOUTH
THE PURITAN OLIGARCHY

★

CHARLES SCRIBNER'S SONS

THE PURITAN OLIGARCHY

The Founding of American Civilization

THE
PURITAN OLIGARCHY

The Founding of American Civilization

By
THOMAS JEFFERSON WERTENBAKER

ILLUSTRATED

CHARLES SCRIBNER'S SONS · NEW YORK

CHARLES SCRIBNER'S SONS · LTD · LONDON

1947

PREFACE

THIS VOLUME is devoted to the study of the Massachusetts Bible State. It traces the origins of this State in England, follows it to the wilderness of America, describes its chief features—the close relationship of the Churches and the government, the stern code of morals, the expression of the Puritan spirit in architecture, literature and music, the educational system—and then turns to the forces of disintegration—the development of commerce, the shift from the agricultural village to the farm, the growth of rationalism, the failure to exclude religious "error," the loss of political autonomy.

Massachusetts has been chosen because it affords the best opportunity for a study of the Puritan experiment. In the Bay Colony the Puritan leaders had a free hand in building their Zion exactly after the blue print which they were confident God had made for them. For a full half century they were permitted to shape their government as they chose, they could legislate against heresy and Sabbath-breaking, they could force attendance at worship, they could control the press, they could make education serve the ends of religion.

In England the Puritan experiment was never made, because the Puritans at no time had the necessary power, not even under Oliver Cromwell. Neither Rhode Island nor Connecticut are appropriate for our study since both, so far from being modeled on the ideals of the great majority of Puritans, were founded in protest against some of the most important of them. As for New Haven, though it followed closely the "correct" model, its annexation to Connecticut brought its career as a true Bible State to a premature end.

When the historian seeks a name for the Massachusetts type of State he encounters difficulties. The use of the word "theocracy" has been criticized. In a theocracy, it is argued, the clergy are rulers, whereas in Massachusetts the ministers, even though they had a deciding voice in picking the electorate, did not themselves hold civil office. The word "commonwealth" is also open to objection, since it is defined as "a State especially viewed as a body in which the people have a voice" or as "a State in which the sovereignty is vested in the people," or "a government chosen directly by the people," and none of these definitions fits the society established in Massachusetts. It is more accurate to call it an oligarchy, since from its inception it was the government of the many by the few, a government by the comparatively small body of Church members.

John Winthrop, William Bradford, Cotton Mather and others have given us contemporaneous accounts of early Massachusetts history; more recent writers have repeated and added to their narratives; modern scholars have presented new points of view, new interpretations. But so far as I know, no one has before made a study of the history of the Puritan State in Massachusetts as an experiment in a unique and interesting civilization.

The task of the historian is not so much to praise or condemn as to analyze and interpret. It should be less his concern that the men with whom he deals were pious or intolerant or kind or bigoted than to explain why. Logically they should be in the laboratory of history as impersonal as are atoms to the physicist and the chemist. Actually this is impossible. The historian is a human being with his own beliefs, prejudices and dislikes, who writes about other human beings who have their own beliefs, prejudices and dislikes. If he tries to describe a civilization which flourished three centuries ago, he inevitably judges it from the point of view of his own age.

I make no pretense of divorcing myself from the twentieth century. Like most Americans I dislike the fettering of men's minds and the denial of the right of the people to rule themselves, and this no doubt makes itself apparent in these pages. But I have tried to be fair to the leaders of the Massachusetts Bible State by presenting their ideals, their points of view, their defense of their conduct in their own words. Among the chief sources for this book are the writings of John Winthrop, Cotton Mather, Increase Mather, Urian Oakes, William Hubbard, John Norton, John Higginson, Samuel Torrey, John Hull and Samuel Sewall. At the

same time a fair hearing has been given to the enemies of the
established order—to the Quaker pamphleteers, to Roger Williams, to Robert Calef, to Robert Child, to Edward Randolph,
even to Sir Edmund Andros.

The historian should beware of emphasizing too strongly any
one interpretation of history. History is vastly complex and so is
open to many interpretations. Yet in view of the great interest in
the Salem witchcraft episode and the vast amount that has been
written about it, it is strange that the fact that it becomes intelligible
only when considered as an incident in the battle of the clergy
against rationalism seems to have escaped attention. Neglected,
also, has been the shift from the agricultural village to the farm,
a movement which revolutionized rural life, tended to lessen the
influence of the clergy and changed the structure of the town. This
matter offers a fruitful field for further examination. The effect
upon religion of the growth of commerce, of the accumulation of
wealth, of the liberalizing of the educational system, the inability
of the Churches and the State to enforce the rigid code of morals,
the revolt against mental fetters has not received the study it
deserves.

In conclusion I should like to acknowledge my indebtedness to
the American Philosophical Society and to the Committee on
Research of Princeton University, for grants to aid in the preparation of this book. May I express my appreciation, also, to Dr.
Nelson R. Burr, of the Library of Congress, for reading the manuscript and making valuable suggestions.

T. J. W.

CONTENTS

ILLUSTRATIONS

xiii

THE PURITAN OLIGARCHY

The Founding of American Civilization

Chapter I

EAST ANGLIA

THE TRAVELER who made his way through the English shires of Norfolk, Suffolk and Essex during the reign of James I viewed a fair and interesting region. If he were a west of England man he would have missed the mountains of Cumberland or Lancaster, for on all sides were low-lying fenlands or broadlands or gently rising hills overlooking shallow dales. The country abounded in rivers, which flowed peacefully on to the North Sea—the Great Ouse, the Yare, the Waveney, the Orwell, the Stour, the Crouch, the Thames. Many and beautiful were the scenes along these streams—here silent waters bordered by reeds, willows and green pastures, here a tiny village of thatched cottages, here a weather-boarded sawmill, here a bevy of fishing boats tied up at a wooden landing, here a commercial town with its warehouses, wharves and fortifications.

In crossing the heaths of the breckland or the flat plains of the fenlands, the traveler had to be on his guard, for they were infested with robbers. The prospect, though wild and dreary, was picturesque—wide spaces unbroken by roads or hedges, a few wind-swept trees, an occasional house, the misty horizon. It was with relief that the wayfarer left this region to find himself on slightly higher ground given over to agriculture. As he journeyed on he noted here a noble mansion, the residence of some landed gentleman, its curving gable ends revealing the influence of the Flemish architects; here an enclosed field with a flock of grazing sheep; here a manor with its lowly cottages, its mill, its chapel and its open fields; here a deserted abbey, its Romanesque architecture revealing its antiquity, its broken roof and empty halls proclaiming the thoroughness with which it had been pillaged by King Henry VIII.[1]

[1] W. G. Clarke, *Norfolk and Suffolk.*

The traveler found that the region, though chiefly agricultural, was not without prosperous towns, some industrial, some commercial, some dependent on fishing. Norwich, picturesque with its flint and lime houses, its Strangers' Hall, its Music House and its Bishop's Palace, was a center of cloth manufacture, as were Colchester, Bury St. Edmunds, Ipswich and quaint little Lavenham. Harwich, at the mouth of the Stour, was a commercial center; Ipswich resounded to the saws and the hammers of shipwrights; Orford, Aldeburgh, Yarmouth and other coastal towns sent out each year their fleets of fishing boats to Iceland or the North Sea; Waldon, in northwest Essex, became so dependent upon the culture and manufacture of saffron, that it became known as Saffron Waldon.

This beautiful region, which now seemed so peaceful, had during past centuries been the scene of fierce battles, of massacres, of ruthless pillaging and burning. Here the ancient Britains struggled fiercely against the disciplined legions of Julius Caesar; here the invading hosts of Saxons, Jutes and Angles in the sixth century swept the countryside almost clean of its inhabitants and established their own kingdoms and their own civilization; here several centuries later the Danes poured in from across the North Sea to plunder, kill and burn, and finally to conquer; here Alfred the Great defeated the newcomers at Beamfleet, destroyed their fortifications and brought many of them as prisoners to London; here the conquering Normans built their castles, divided up the land and reduced many of the people to the condition of serfs.

Thus eastern England was the product of the melting pot. Into the Anglo-Saxon population came a host of Danes; hardly had this amalgamation been effected than the Normans added still another strain; when they too had been assimilated, a new element was added with the migration from across the North Sea of Flemings, Dutch and Huguenots. And each of these peoples has lent something to the region—not only of their blood, but of their tongue, their institutions, their achitecture, their psychology, their industry.

During the Middle Ages the life of this mixed people centered in the manor. And in the manor, of first importance was the village. Here, clustered around a central square or stretched out along a street or overlooking a brook or rivulet, were the humble cottages of villeins, cotters and free tenants. Here was the gristmill with its wings spread ready to catch the breeze, here perhaps the water-driven sawmill, here the parish church, its Gothic or Roman-esque tower rising above the surrounding trees and thatched roofs, the blacksmith shop, the little vegetable gardens, the tiny orchards. Nearby was the residence of the lord of the manor. In the first centuries after the Conquest the manorhouse was usually a minor fortress, with sturdy stone walls, battlements and perhaps moat, but in later times military considerations gave way to the demands of comfort.[2] Friston Hall, the residence of Thomas Bacon, which was typical of the smaller manorhouses of the early seventeenth century, contained twenty or more rooms, with barns, stables, outhouses, a dovehouse, orchards and courtyards nearby.

In the immediate vicinity of the village were the open fields devoted to agriculture, usually three in number and known as the South Field, or the East Field or the North Field. Although each of these was comparatively small, seldom embracing more acreage than the average eastern United States farm, it was subdivided into many narrow strips, an acre or half acre in extent, and separated from each other, not by hedges, but by little mounds of earth. Every cultivator held a number of strips, usually about thirty, not grouped to form a compact block, but scattered throughout the various fields. The lord's land, known as the demesne, which con-stituted from a third to a half of the cultivated area, was also divided into strips and lay alongside those of the peasants.[3]

The open field was not, as might be imagined, a crazyquilt of cultivation, with here a strip of wheat, there of rye, there of barley, but a solid mass of waving wheat, or oats, or rye. The cooperative system, in which a field was devoted entirely one year to a desig-nated crop, the next year to another crop and the third allowed to lie fallow, was well suited to the method of plowing in vogue at the time, in which the cultivator combined with his fellows to provide a team of from six to eight oxen. It also made it possible to graze the cattle over the field after the crop had been harvested,

[2] Arthur Birnie, *An Economic History of the British Isles,* p. 48.
[3] William Page (ed.), *The Victoria History of the County of Suffolk,* Vol. I, p. 639.

not only to provide food for the beasts, but to enrich the soil with manure.

The yields were small, usually not more than five or six times the amount sown—for wheat ten bushels an acre; for oats and barley from ten to twelve bushels, for vegetables from six to ten bushels. Had only the more fertile land been cultivated the average returns would have been larger, but the pressure of population forced under the plow large areas better suited to sheep grazing. Nor could one hope for the best results from the primitive agricultural implements and the still cruder husbandry of that day.

The workers of the manor comprised villeins, cotters and free tenants. The strips of the villein, which he held in return for labor on the demesne or for payments in kind or in money, usually aggregated thirty acres. Not only did he have to plow or hoe on the lord's land two or three days a week, but perform boon-work at especially busy seasons such as planting time and harvests. At Christmas he must deliver his best chickens; at Easter, a specified number of eggs; at Martinmas, grain; while additional payments of money were required for permission to fish in the pond, or to grind his grain at the mill or gather timber in the woods.

Less numerous than the villeins, holding less land and performing smaller services, were the cotters. Formerly slaves, they had acquired a large degree of freedom through the gradual realization of the lords that free labor is more efficient and less costly than the labor of bondsmen. The tenants of the manor, holding scattered strips like the villeins, made money payments to the lord and performed boon-work, but not week work. And unlike the villeins, they enjoyed security of tenure and could appeal to the courts in case they were threatened with ejection. Since the free tenants were most numerous in the parts of England formerly held by the Danes, it has been suggested that they had belonged to the invading hosts and had been accorded especial privileges as a reward for their services.

Life on the manor for all save the lord was hard. The villein's fare was coarse and scanty and only too often unwholesome, his clothes were of the roughest, his residence was a thatched cabin with earthen floor. Though he toiled year in and year out, from dawn to dark, it sufficed only to keep breath in his body, for the major part of what he produced went to the lord. It must have been with bitter resentment that he turned over his best animal

PLAN OF AN ENGLISH MANOR

when he succeeded to his father's position, or a heavy fine when his daughter was married.

The manor was a little world to itself. Not only did its inhabitants supply their own grain and raise their own cattle for meat and milk, but they spun and wove their own wool, tanned their own leather, made their own shoes, brewed their own beer, hammered out many of their own implements at the village smithy, hewed their own timbers, constructed their own houses. From the outside came only wines, spices and armor for the lord, and salt for preserving meat, iron for hoes and scythes, stones for the gristmill. To the villein or the cotter a neighboring manor was like a foreign country, an adjacent shire seemed as remote as Palestine or even China.[4]

In time, however, the horizon of the workers widened, their condition became better. It was in 1349 that the Black Death swept over England, leaving a trail of suffering, death and desolation. Ignorant of the cause of the plague and so not knowing how to combat it, the people succumbed by the tens and hundreds of thousands. Many manors were denuded of workers and the lords viewed disconsolately their empty villages and their fields grown over with weeds. But for the peasants who escaped with their lives the terrible epidemic proved a boon. In order to keep them from deserting, the lord was forced to grant many villeins and cotters the status of free tenants, to lessen the burdens of the workers and to pay higher wages.[5]

Unfortunately for the peasants, in the sixteenth century the trend toward higher wages was reversed, chiefly because of the conversion of large tracts of arable land into pasture. The expansion of cloth-making and the consequent demand for wool made it profitable for the lords of the manor to dispossess their tenants and enclose the land with hedges so that it could be devoted to sheep raising. In Norfolk this movement lagged, but in Suffolk and Essex large areas were enclosed even before the Tudor period. At the manor of Wigborough, for instance, we are told "that there was wont to be kept in it a farmer and his wife and eighteen or twenty persons . . . and now it is returned to pasture and grazing." [6]

---

[4] Arthur Birnie, *An Economic History of the British Isles,* pp. 55–57.
[5] William Page and J. Horace Round (Eds.), *The Victoria History of the County of Essex,* pp. 316, 317, 320. In Norfolk, Suffolk and Essex the cost of threshing doubled. At Hadleigh, a typical Essex manor, the proportion of free tenants to villeins after the Black Death was nine to one.
[6] *Ibid.,* p. 322.

The dissolution of the manors was accelerated by the growing custom of converting the open fields into farms which were let out to tenants. We may follow this process in the records of Friston, in Suffolk. Sir Henry Johnson, who purchased it from Thomas Bacon, himself held the manorhouse with its chapel, barns, gardens, etc., as well as a demesne of woodland and arable and pasture ground; but he leased most of the land, formerly open but now enclosed, as farms or sheepfolds—Friston Hall farm for £115, Smart's farm for £100, Little Borrough Marsh farm for £32, one shepherd's farm or sheepwalk for £60, another for £50, a smith's shop for £3. His rentals from copyhold tenants and the returns from the manorial court, fishing rights, fairs and tolls were estimated at £30. Even before the sixteenth century had come to a close the manorial system had so declined that the larger part of the countryside, especially in Suffolk and Essex, was cut up into enclosed farms and sheep pastures.[7]

Although many of the dispossessed peasants were reduced to beggary, some no doubt found employment in the cloth industry for which the eastern shires had long been noted. That spinning was carried on at Bury St. Edmunds as early as the end of the twelfth century we may conclude from the story told by Jocelyn of the old women who rushed out to brandish their distaffs in the face of the monastic tax-gatherers, while his further assertion that the fullers of the town were forced to furnish cloth for the abbey indicates that weaving was also common.[8] Colchester, too, was an ancient "cloth town," boasting in 1301 of sixteen weavers, eleven dyers and fullers and eighteen clothiers and tailors.[9]

Varied and tedious were the tasks required before the finished cloth was ready for the market. After the sheep had been sheared, the wool was gathered by middlemen and sold to the clothiers who distributed it to cottage homes over the countryside, where women and children did the carding and spinning. At intervals riders were sent out to collect the yarn and in turn deliver it to the weaver. Even when the cloth left the loom it was not ready for sale, for it must now be dyed violet or purple or green with woad

[7] British Museum, *Additional MSS.* 22249.
[8] *The Victoria History of the County of Suffolk*, II, p. 254.
[9] *The Victoria History of the County of Essex*, p. 382.

or indigo and then turned over to the fuller for scouring, pressing and thickening. At last all was ready for home consumption or for export from Ipswich or Harwich to Flanders or other European countries. So large had this trade become at the time of James I that no less than 30,000 cloths were shipped out annually, "wherein is maintained 400 mariners continually."

The clothmakers of the eastern shires acquired much of their skill from Flemish workers who from time to time crossed the North Sea to set up their looms in Norfolk, Suffolk and Essex. One group from Bruges landed in 1304 at Harwich, where they spread out to Worstead, in Norfolk, and Bocking, Shalford, Braintree, Dedham and elsewhere. They were powerfully reinforced a third of a century later when Edward III forbade the exportation of wool or the wearing by Englishmen of cloth made abroad, and Flemish weavers, combers, fullers and dyers flocked in to save their ancient market.

These foreigners brought to East Anglia and Essex a new period of industrial prosperity. In many a town and village even today the long, low windows of the second story of the older houses proclaim that their former occupants had busied themselves with the spinning wheel or the loom. Sudbury was "populous and wealthy by reason of" its baize, bunting and shrouds; at Colchester fifty-one Flemish families were kept busy at the loom; while Lavenham became a town of weavers whose prosperity is attested by the imposing church, the quaint old wool hall and the charming, half-timbered guildhall. That the acquiring of fortunes through "big business" is not a phenomenon unique with modern times is shown by the history of the Spring family of Lavenham. Thomas Spring II who died in 1486 left 100 marks to be divided among his workmen, 300 for building the church tower and 200 for the repair of roads; his son, Thomas Spring III, left money for 1,000 Masses and £200 for the work on the church.[10]

The Flemish workers of the early migrations had long been assimilated by the English through intermarriage, when a fresh stream began to pour over from the Continent—skilled weavers fleeing the Spanish Fury at Antwerp, Walloons who had eluded the Inquisition, Huguenot refugees from France. Many of the

---

[10] *The Victoria History of the County of Suffolk*, II, p. 256.

Flemings settled in Colchester where at first they received a hearty welcome and were granted permission to worship in St. Giles' Church.[11] They soon made the place one of the chief industrial centers of eastern England. The cloth trade employed "not only the poor inhabitants of the town . . . but also most part of the country round about for the space of ten miles," and sent to London weekly great quantities of cloth, "besides the great trade it hath by sea."

For commerce the eastern shires, almost surrounded by water as they are, would seem to be admirably suited. Were not the country so flat there would hardly be a village from which the North Sea would not be visible. The plowman, as he rested from his labor, or the weaver as he looked out from his window to the distant waters, must at times have longed to take up the adventurous life of the sailor. Yet there is an obstinate barrier to trade in the belt of sand which shuts in the coast, through which the scour of the rivers has cut a few inlets navigable only for ships of moderate burden. The passage to the eastern ports even today, when the pilot has the aid of charts and lighthouses, is dangerous; to the seafarers of four centuries ago it must have been a death-trap.[12]

Nonetheless, Harwich, Colchester, Leigh, Maldon, Ipswich and other towns carried on a lively trade with the Continent. Leigh was described in 1565 as "a very proper town, well furnished with good mariners, where commonly tall ships do ride, . . . a special landing place for butter, all manner of grain and other things." On the other hand, Ipswich, before the end of the sixteenth century, was threatened with decline, because the Orwell had become too shallow for the passage of large vessels. Had not the current in time again scoured out a deeper channel, this important port would have been permanently sealed up. Yet in 1629 Suffolk alone could boast of 1,129 mariners, of whom 250 lived in Ipswich and 256 in Aldeburgh. Maldon, however, once a port of some importance, was "in much decay" because the creek on which it was situated had

[11] In 1622 Colchester householders of foreign birth or born of foreign parents numbered 613. Their children born in England numbered 798. *British Calendar of State Papers, Domestic, 1619–23*, p. 381.

[12] *The Victoria History of the County of Essex,* II, p. 259.

become choked with "sand and great quantities of sea ooze" and diverted from its former course.[13]

It was a bold and hardy group of navigators that the eastern counties developed, men trained in the hard school of the North Sea, where endurance, skill and courage were requisite for the ceaseless struggle with the winds and waves. From Harwich hailed Christopher Newport, who in 1606 commanded the little squadron which carried to Virginia the men who made the first English beachhead of settlement in the New World. This veteran navigator made in all five voyages to Virginia, one to the West Indies and three to the Far East. He died in the Philippines in 1617. John Foxe, of Woodbridge, won acclaim by his daring exploit of liberating himself and 266 other Christian slaves from the Turkish galleys. Thomas Thompson became equally famous when he dropped anchor in Harwich harbor, his vessels laden with the plunder of the great carrack, the *Madre de Dios*.[14]

Not a little of the credit for the exploits of these navigators is due to the sturdiness of the vessels turned out from the shipyards of Ipswich, Aldeburgh and Woodbridge.[15] Nowhere could better oak be found than in Suffolk, and nowhere shipwrights more skilled than those in the employ of Zephonias and Saphire Ford, Robert and Jeremiah Cole, Henry Dancke and William Cary. In 1626 it was stated that for thirty years past Ipswich had built annually no less than twelve ships, while from 1625 to 1638 the town delivered to London alone 59 vessels. When the *Henry Grace de Dieu* was laid down in the dockyard at Woolwich, Ipswich was among the first in supplying the needed shipwrights, caulkers, sailmakers and blacksmiths. From Harwich, too, came many sturdy vessels, especially from the yards of the famous Pell family.[16]

Some of the vessels which slid down the ways into the Orwell or Stour were used in the trade to the Continent, but others did service in the fishing expeditions to Iceland, the Faroes or the North Sea. Daring indeed were the men who pointed the prows of their little fifty-ton boats northward past the eastern coast of Scotland, the Orkneys and the Shetlands to the icy waters of the

[13] *Ibid.*, p. 274.
[14] *Ibid.*, p. 273.
[15] *British Calendar of State Papers, Domestic*, 1581-90, p. 544.
[16] *The Victoria History of the County of Suffolk*, p. 211.

North Atlantic for their catches of cod and herring. In 1528 the Iceland fleet, which numbered no less than 149 vessels, brought back such quantities of fish that the king claimed a part of their catch under the right of purveyance. The Danes encouraged the Iceland trade, but the Scotch, who resented the intrusion of the English fishermen, threatened to fit out a squadron to intercept them.[17]

With the extension of the northern voyage to new fisheries off the coast of Greenland, the need for protection for the fleet became even greater, so that the government chartered the Greenland Company. But with the usual English hatred of monopoly the independent fishermen resented the creation of this corporation and habitually ignored its rights.

In 1634 when the company's fleet, under Captain Goodlad, arrived at Horneslound, they found two Yarmouth vessels in possession of the best fishing site. One of these ships was the *Mayflower*, possibly the same *Mayflower* which fourteen years previously had taken the Pilgrims to New England.[18] On this occasion her commander showed a decidedly belligerent spirit, and so far from yielding was he, that he "resisted with fire arms and pieces of great ordnance charged with barr shot." [19]

The visitor who today stops at one of the resorts of the east of England will find at intervals along the shores scores of fishing villages, some of them centuries old, all picturesque with their quaint cottages and long streets. Yarmouth is remarkable for its narrow lanes which mark the lines along which in former days the fishermen had spread their nets, and which in time were utilized for building lots. Kitty Witches Row is said to have received its name from one of its residents who was tried and executed for witchcraft. Dunwich, Walberswick, Ipswich, Harwich, Aldeburgh and other towns also contributed their quotas to the fishing fleet.

Although agriculture, sheep-raising, cloth-making, commerce, shipbuilding and fishing were the most important occupations in the eastern shires, a part of the people devoted their attention to

[17] *Ibid.*
[18] The famous *Mayflower* "was of Yarmouth." Azel Ames, *The Mayflower and Her Log,* p. 97.
[19] *British Calendar of State Papers, Domestic,* 1634–35, p. 231.

other activities. In northwest Essex field after field of waving saffron, with their purple flowers and vivid orange trifid stigma giving a touch of beauty to the countryside, attested that the prosperity of the region was largely based upon that plant. When dried by artificial means saffron commanded a ready sale as medicine, condiment, perfume or dye. "About the town of Walden groweth great store of saffron," declared one writer, in 1594, "whose nature in yielding her fruit is very strange and bindeth the laborer to great travail and diligence, and yet at length yealdeth no small advantage to recomfort him again." [20]

The visitor to Roydon, Great Hallingbury and other towns in the east of England, notes that the "Sign of the Hop-pole" is a favorite designation for inns, and that in the surrounding countryside numerous fields or enclosures are known as the hop-field or the hop-garden or the hop-ground. These all bear out the statement made by a group of Essex men in 1621 that "hop planting has long been a great advantage to . . . farmers and laborers." [21] "The Essex hops are not, I believe, esteemed altogether as strong as the Kentish, but in flavor they are, to my mind, by no means inferior," declared one writer.[22] "The need for poles to support the growing plants was at one time so great as to make extensive inroads upon the woodlands, and at Castle Hedingham a plot of forty acres was set aside as a nursery of ash and chestnut trees to supply the growing demand.

As the "Sign of the Hop-pole" is a survival of the days of hop-raising, so the recurrence of the word "wick" along the coast is an indication of the extent of the manufacture of cheese from ewes' milk. The "wickes" or "wiches" were the dairies in which the cheese was made, and wherever there are extensive marshes, formerly the grazing ground for flocks of sheep, the name has survived, as North Wick, or West Wick, or Monk's Wick, or Knight's Wick. The industry was carried on without interruption for six centuries, but in Queen Elizabeth's reign it began to wane, because, if we may credit Thomas Cox, an Essex minister, ewes' "milk makes the cheese strong." [23]

[20] *The Victoria History of the County of Essex*, II, pp. 360–363.
[21] *British Calendar of State Papers, Domestic*, Addenda, 1580–1625, p. 638.
[22] *The Victoria History of the County of Essex*, p. 368.
[23] *Ibid.*, p. 369.

Even more important was the production of potash from the ashes of burnt wood, weeds and other vegetable matter. Useful in washing clothes, dyeing, glass-making, linen-bleaching and soap-making, the product was always in lively demand. It was in no small degree the decline of this industry, because of the shrinkage of the forest areas, which convinced English economists of the advisability of making settlements in America.

The diversified industry of the eastern shires stood in good stead the thousands who were to leave their native fields or towns to create for themselves a new life in the wilds of America. If conditions in the localities where they were to settle called for agriculturalists, there were many among them who were familiar with the plow, the hoe and the sickle; if they found themselves near new fishing fields, some who had long been accustomed to the trawl or the line and hook were at hand to instruct them; if the presence of deep harbors lured them to a life at sea, there was a group of hardy sailors among them to point the way; if they found wood and other materials for shipbuilding, some who had worked in the yards of Ipswich or Harwich were ready to practice and teach the shipwright's art.

The life and the history of the eastern shires were reflected in the architecture of the region. Waltham Abbey Church, in Essex, its heavy columns and rounded arches denoting the Romanesque influence, dated back to the time of Edward the Confessor; Castle Rising, in Norfolk, its walls and towers surrounded by huge earthworks, was built in 1176 by the Norman William d'Albini; Eastbury House, near Barking, is in the Tudor style; Little Warby Hall, Essex, is almost as Flemish as though it had been transplanted from Bruges. As for the cottages of the middle class—cloth workers, farmers, fishermen, shipwrights—they varied with the building materials of the different localities, the period in which they were erected and the economic status of the families who lived in them. There was a wide divergency between the medieval half-timber cottage of Lavenham and the Flemish brick cottage of near-by Cottenham; between the flint houses of Norwich and the plastered buildings of Cambridge or Grantchester.

The medieval house was usually two stories high, the second story projecting over the lower, with a frame of heavy timbers filled in with wattle and daub, or with brick, or covered with plaster or weatherboarding; the roof perhaps thatched and broken by dormers, the chimneys often centrally located, the walls pierced by casement windows glazed with tiny, greenish leaded panes. At quaint old Lavenham, nestling sleepily on the banks of the Brett River and formerly one of the chief wool centers of Suffolk, many examples of this style of house have survived. The old wool hall, with its pronounced overhang, its vertical timbering and its steep roof, is typical. The fine guildhall stands on the south side of the market place, guarded by a small figure of John, fifteenth Earl of Oxford, carved on the cornerpost. Tradition has it that Dr. Rowland Taylor was imprisoned in one of the cellars of this building while waiting for his execution at Aldham Common.

Even in Cambridge, where modern buildings have encroached upon many of the ancient streets, we find numerous examples of the two-story house, their plastered upper stories projecting over the sidewalks, their signs swaying in the breeze. Interesting are the medieval houses at Sudbury, especially the ancient moot-hall with its vertical half-timbering, its overhang and its oriel window; at Dedham, Essex; Kingsbury Green, Middlesex; Cockfield, Hawkedon and many other places. At Cockfield brick nogging in many cases replaces the usual clay and straw filling between the studs, while at Framlingham there is a fine example of brick laid in the herringbone pattern.

The half-timber house was obviously devised to save wood at a time when the forests were suffering from the inroads of the farmer, the shipbuilder, the carpenter and the potash burner. When wood became expensive, although it still constituted the framework of the house, it was only in restricted areas that it could be used for wall coverings as well. Yet the survival today of a handful of old weatherboarded buildings attests to the fact that the migrants to New England were well acquainted with that type of structure. At Kingsbury Green, Essex, stands an old weatherboarded house which, with its overhang, its central chimney, its wide expanse of roof, would fit perfectly into the scene at Salem or Ipswich or some other Massachusetts village. The boards were usually of oak or elm, six to eight inches wide with a lap of one to one and a half inches, and were fastened to the studs with rough wrought-iron nails at intervals of from fifteen to twenty inches.²⁴

The little one-and-a-half-story Flemish cottage was not less common in the eastern shires than the medieval house, though rare in other parts of England. When the foreign workers came over at the invitation of Edward III in the fourteenth century, they brought not only their looms, but their architecture as well. One has only to note the stepped gables of Woodham Walter Church, Essex, or parts of Horeham Hall or the elbowed gable ends and finials of Eastbury House, near Barking, or the constant use of the mouse-tooth motif in small brick houses, to realize the extent of this influence. The Flemish cottage is a long, low structure, one story in height with a loft, the chimney sometimes in the center, in other cases at the gable end, the sharply rising roof pierced by dormers. In Flanders the walls are often made of clay mixed with lime and straw, and protected from the rains which sweep in from the North Sea by "flying gutters," or projections at the eaves which curve out for two feet or more over the front and rear walls. In England the flying gutter was discarded, since the use of brick or stone, or in some cases weatherboarding, made it unnecessary. The traveler in the eastern shires finds these charming little cottages everywhere; they smile at him from the midst of the fields, they snuggle beside the narrow country roads, they peep out from the lanes and squares of villages and towns.²⁵

The thatch of the roof, which often hangs over eaves and dormers like half-melted snow, adds a softness of outline; the little casement windows with small diamond-shaped leaded panes look out on garden or street. The ancient porch, that two-story projection with entry below and tiny chamber above which graces so many old houses in Sussex and elsewhere in England, is rare in East Anglia and Essex.

The medieval two-story frame house and the Flemish cottage are of especial interest since they were both transplanted to America and became the basis for a distinctive New England architecture. On the other hand, the mansions of the great—such stately

²⁴ Martin S. Briggs, *The Homes of the Pilgrim Fathers*, etc., pp. 77–80.
²⁵ T. J. Wertenbaker, *The Founding of American Civilization. The Middle Colonies*, p. 69.

piles as Audley End or Easton Lodge—do not concern us, since they have no counterparts on the shores of Massachusetts. Even the little parish churches, with their buttresses and pointed arches and their ancient towers, had no effect on New England architecture, because the Puritans associated them with high-church Anglicism or even Catholicism and so would have none of them.

Against the windmill, however, they had no inhibition, so that these interesting as well as useful structures became common in their new homeland. In the east of England there are two types of windmill: the postmill, which seems to have been imported from the Netherlands where it is still in common use, and the tower or smock mill. In the former type the main structure together with its wings revolves on a great central post; in the latter the mill is stationary and only the roof cap rotates when it becomes necessary to change the direction of the sails. In both types a long tail-tree which stretches from the rear of the sail axle to the ground gives support to the structure. In the low-lying regions of Norfolk and Suffolk the many mills, visible often for miles, give to the landscape a character not unlike that of Holland.

In evaluating the civilization of the eastern English shires one must emphasize the influence of the continent of Europe. Harwich lies less than a hundred and fifty miles from Rotterdam; it is but little more than a hundred miles from Flushing. Across the intervening waters of the North Sea have come not only physical products but cultural and spiritual forces. We have seen that Denmark, Normandy and the Netherlands sent their emigrants to mingle with the Anglo-Saxons, and that the Flemings influenced profoundly the industrial life of the region and even left their imprint upon its architecture. But stronger, more lasting in their effects upon the mentality of the people, were the religious ideals and tenets imported from the Continent.

If Martin Luther defied the Pope and nailed his ninety-five theses on the door of the church at Wittenburg, it would not be long before the East Anglians heard of it; if Zwingli pronounced against transubstantiation, it would influence the trend of thought in Ipswich or Colchester long before the news reached Cornwall or Wales. The Flemings who fled the Inquisition brought with them

LAVENHAM, SUFFOLK, ENGLAND, SHOWING OVERHANG AND FRONT GABLES

CAMBRIDGE, ENGLAND, SHOWING TYPICAL EAST ANGLIAN HOUSES

to Suffolk and Essex, not only their looms, their skill and their culture, but an invincible devotion to the doctrines of Calvin, which was important in making the east of England the stronghold of Puritanism.

It was in 1525 or 1526 that vessels entering Ipswich or Harwich brought in, perhaps concealed by members of the crew among their private effects, perhaps mingled with the barrels and crates of the regular cargoes, perhaps in the luggage of weavers coming in to join the foreign colony at Colchester, a number of copies of Tyndale's translation of the New Testament. Soon after, it was bruited abroad that the "Word of God" was being read aloud at secret meetings, and in 1527 came news of the arrest of about forty persons in Colchester, Witham and Braintree. When a certain Edward Freese showed his familiarity with the Bible by painting sentences from it on some cloths he was preparing for an inn at Colchester, he was arrested and lodged in the Lollards' Tower. Devout Catholics were shocked at the spirit of hostility to images, the cross and other sacred objects, which manifested itself in a series of violent acts. At Coggeshall as early as 1532 a "crucifix was cast down and destroyed in the highway," the image of St. Parnel which stood in the church at Great Horkesley was broken, and the rood of Dovercourt was burnt to ashes with its own tapers.[26]

Henry VIII, who had no liking for Protestant doctrines even though he broke with the Papacy, was active in prosecuting those who held Lutheran or Zwinglian views, and during his reign at least thirty heretics, many of them from the eastern shires, were tried and burnt at the stake.[27] It was not only with intense relief but with a sense of triumph that the reformers greeted the news in 1543 of Henry's death and the succession to the throne of the youthful Edward VI. Immediately a new wave of iconoclasm swept over Essex and Suffolk, marked by the smashing of stained-glass windows, the whitewashing of murals, the taking down of altars and the destruction of images. Many church ceremonies were abrogated; and with the approval of the Convocation of 1547 and of Parliament scores of priests married.

But the death of Edward and the accession of the Roman

[26] *The Victoria History of the County of Essex,* pp. 20, 21.
[27] *The Victoria History of the County of Suffolk,* II, p. 27.

Catholic Mary came like a sentence of doom. The Queen at first seems not to have contemplated a violent persecution and contented herself with the restoration of the power of Rome and with depriving married clergymen of their cures. But with her marriage to the bigoted Philip of Spain, the iron hand of repression fell heavily upon the eastern shires. Thomas Hawkes, of Coggeshall, was taken to London, examined before Bishop Bonner, and burned at the stake; Dr. Rowland Taylor was burned at Hadleigh; in June, 1555 alone, seven men were led out of Newgate to different places in Suffolk and Essex that their fellow townsmen might witness their martyrdom. So abhorrent were these executions to the people that it was extremely difficult to have the burnings carried into effect, and had a leader of distinction appeared among them the whole east would probably have burst into rebellion.

Mary would have been incredulous had one told her that these persecutions, so far from rooting Protestantism out of Norfolk, Suffolk and Essex, would be instrumental in fixing it there permanently. As one human torch after another lit up the little squares of the eastern towns, many of the most ardent religious zealots fled, some of them to Geneva, where they fell under the spell of Calvin. Then, when death claimed the unhappy Mary, they returned to their native land fired with the spirit of the crusaders, to spread the gospel of Calvinism.

In ardent sermons they warned the people that God had chosen His own from the mass of those predestined to damnation, that He would not tolerate the breach of His Commandments, that His delight was a contrite soul rather than church ornaments and ceremonials, that the one sure guide for the State as well as for the individual was the Bible, that the civil government, while separate from the Church, should be in the hands of godly men who would give religion their hearty support and suppress error.

These Calvinist missionaries were far from being satisfied with the Elizabethan middle-course policy, especially the famous Thirty-Nine Articles, in which the episcopal organization was retained, the ritual borrowed from the Medieval Church and the creed in large part from Lutheranism. They demanded the "completion" of the Reformation. By this they meant the acceptance by the established Church of all of Calvin's doctrines, the abolition of ceremonial in worship, and the ousting from their cures of clergymen who were not in accord with their views.

Throughout Elizabeth's long reign the Calvinist movement gained headway, especially in Essex, which has been called the "headquarters of Puritanism." Once more images and shrines were removed, the minister held services "in the body of the church with his face towards the people," the Book of Common Prayer was often neglected. Elizabeth was tolerant of these proceedings, so long as they were carried on within the structure of the Anglican Church, but she took repressive measures against separatists, and in 1583 sent three of them to the gallows at Bury St. Edmunds.

The prophet of separatism was Robert Browne, an eccentric but able preacher and writer and a relative of Cecil, Lord Burghley. Coming to Norwich, he joined with Robert Harrison in gathering a congregation, to whom he poured out his revolutionary views. When complaints of his heresy began to pour in to the bishops, he, together with the body of his followers, fled to Middleburg. Though a few years later he returned and completed a long life as a school teacher, the influence of his writings continued to grow until they had affected the religious thought of thousands.

In the final analysis Browne was an opportunist. Contending that the Anglican Church was filled with corruption and ruled by an unscriptural hierarchy, he exhorted all true Christians to strive for its reformation, or failing in this, to separate from it in order to establish independent congregations. It was the assertion of local autonomy as a shield against a hostile central power, a kind of ecclesiastical "States' rights." The essence of the system he proposed is found in his statement that "magistrates have no ecclesiastical authority at all, but only as any other Christians."

The congregation should derive its authority not from an established Church, but directly from God, Browne held. Any company of true believers associating themselves together could constitute a Church of Christ by making a solemn covenant with God and with each other. Nor was ordination of ministers necessary, since each congregation was fully empowered by Scripture to elect its own pastor. The weakness of organization which Browne's plan of extreme decentralization entailed he sought to remedy by a close fellowship of congregations. Just as England and Scotland later were bound together by having the same king, so the various local Churches were to be united by the leadership of Christ. And though they exercised no control one over the other, friendly advice or even admonition was welcomed. For this end it might be necessary to hold a joint meeting of representatives from the various congregations. "There be synods, or the meeting of sundry churches," Browne declared, "which are when the weaker churches seek help of the stronger for deciding or redressing of matters." This he explained as the "joining or partaking of the authority of many churches met together in peace." [28]

Browne believed that the Bible sanctioned several officers whose duties within the congregation were clearly defined—a pastor "having office and message of God for exhorting and moving especially and guiding"; a teacher of doctrine; one or more elders "for oversight and counsel and redressing things amiss"; one or more relievers "to gather and bestow gifts and liberality"; one or more widows "to pray for the church and to visit and minister to those which are afflicted."

Browne proved apostate to his own views by accepting a cure in the established Church, but his ideas lived on through the words and writings of new and more determined leaders. First among these were Henry Barrowe and John Greenwood. Beginning life as a dissolute young lawyer, Barrowe was changed into a religious zealot by a passing whim which led him to enter a church where the minister's earnest exhortations sank deep into his soul. Before long his own teachings, which followed close in the steps of Browne, brought upon him the wrath of Archbishop Whitgift, John Aylmer, Bishop of London, and other prelates. Whitgift had already had Greenwood arrested, and when Barrowe visited him in prison, the jailor, though without legal warrant, detained him also.

Now followed years of captivity, interspersed with visits to Lambeth Palace for questioning before "goodly synods of bishops, deans, civilians, etc." But the two zealots stood steadfast, not only refusing to recant, but stoutly defending their beliefs. The rites, sacraments and government of the Church of England were not as

[28] H. M. Dexter, *The Congregationalism of the Last Three Hundred Years,* pp. 106–09.

Christ had directed, Barrowe told his listeners; its all-inclusive membership was unscriptural; Christ alone, and not the Queen, was its true head. In the last of these hearings Whitgift, losing his temper, cried out: "Where is his keeper? You shall not prattle here. Away with him. Clap him up close. Let no man come at him!" If the bishop imagined that in this way he could silence the two reformers, he was greatly mistaken. During the years of their confinement they wrote no less than eight treatises, aggregating more than nine hundred printed pages, working under the greatest difficulties and smuggling their manuscript out of prison page by page, so that they could not have one sheet in hand while writing the next.[29]

Barrowe and Greenwood agreed with Browne that since there was little hope of reforming the national Church each congregation should be independent of all others. But within the congregation they thought that authority should reside, not with the body of members, but with the pastor, elders and teachers, who would be "able to discern between cause and cause, between plea and plea." These officers must see to it that the ordinances of God be "truly taught and practiced," and that the people obey "willingly and readily." Thus they substituted for Browne's congregational democracy an aristocracy of the eldership, borrowed from Presbyterianism.[30]

When Whitgift, discovering that prison walls had not silenced the two reformers, put them on trial at Old Bailey on the charge of writing with malicious intent, he was too late, for hundreds had already read their treatises. Nonetheless, they were sentenced to death and on April 1, 1593, hanged at Tyburn.

John Cotton many years later denied that New England Congregationalism owed anything either to Browne or to Barrowe, condemning the former for his "inconstancy" and the latter for "the unsoundness of his judgment" and "the bitterness of his style."[31] Yet it is obvious that Cotton's own Church, as well as the other Churches of Massachusetts, were in part founded on the conception of the congregational covenant with God, which Browne

[29] Williston Walker, *A History of the Congregational Churches,* etc., p. 44.
[30] Henry M. Dexter, *The Congregationalism of the Last Three Hundred Years,* pp. 260, 261.
[31] John Cotton, *The Way of the Congregational Churches Cleared,* p. 5.

so clearly enunciated, and upon Barrowe's aristocracy of the eldership.

It is true, however, that the rank and file of Puritans in England could never bring themselves to turn their backs upon the national Church. Though it might be corrupt, though among its members were many who led dissolute lives, though it adhered to unscriptural forms of worship, it was still God's Church and so could not be cast aside nor ignored. On the contrary, all good men should labor mightily for its reformation by agitating, arguing, explaining, and especially by themselves setting an example of godly living.

The acknowledged leader of this crusade was the distinguished scholar, preacher and writer, Thomas Cartwright. With Browne's conception of the independent congregation, Cartwright had no sympathy. No doubt when Barrowe and Greenwood perished on the scaffold, he believed they were receiving their just deserts. Even in his old age he wrote Mrs. Stubbe, his sister-in-law, that abuses in the Church did not justify separation. He would not face the possibility that the reformers might never gain control and that his own rule of conformity could be turned against the Puritans to deprive their ministers of their cures or even to drive them into exile. He had witnessed the overthrow of Catholicism in England and the rapid growth of Calvinism, and there seemed no reason to fear the ultimate triumph of reaction.

Yet the fact that the triumph of the reform movement had been delayed, and that the national Church was still governed from the throne through archbishops and bishops, forced Cartwright into what may be described as semi-Congregationalism. Each congregation should have a voice in the selection of their minister, he thought, so that the legates could not force upon them one who was unfit for the office or who was out of sympathy with them in matters of worship. Discipline, also, should be left largely in the hands of the congregation, so that the pastor and elders could search out unregenerate members for training and purifying.[32]

The crisis came in 1603 with the death of Elizabeth, but Cart-

[32] Williston Walker, *A History of the Congregational Churches,* etc., pp. 19, 20.

wright did not live to see it, for within a few months he followed
the Queen to the grave. Other Puritan leaders, rejoicing in the
accession to the throne of James I, who had been educated in
Scotland under Presbyterian divines, prepared to make use of the
royal power to carry out their ends. But they were doomed to disappointment. At the famous Hampton Court conference, Andrew
Melville's suggestion that the King should call a General Church
Assembly brought an emphatic refusal. "If you aim at a Scottish
Presbytery, it agreeth as well with monarchy as God with the
devil." If the Puritans had nothing better to offer than this, he was
determined to make them conform, or he would "harry them out
of the land."

As the Puritan ministers returned sadly to their parishes, they
must have realized that there was now little hope of reforming
the Church through governmental action. Something might be accomplished by bringing a majority of the English people over to
their views and, through a majority in the House of Commons,
forcing the king to yield. But this would entail a long and bitter
struggle, with the outcome uncertain. So, gradually, even reluctantly, they were forced to fall back upon the protection of Congregationalism. It was so easy to declare that the bishop was
infringing upon the rights of the congregation when he ordered
them to observe the saints' days, or place the altar at the east end
of the church, or to use the Book of Common Prayer.

It was but one step further, perhaps an inevitable step, for the
congregations to deny that they existed by the authority of the
national Church. Turning to Browne, Barrowe and Greenwood
for their inspiration, though openly disavowing Separation or
Independency, some of them drew up covenants placing themselves under the direct leadership of God. "There were some scores
of Godly persons in Boston, in Lincolnshire, whereof some are
there still and some are here, who can witness that we entered
into a covenant with the Lord and with one-another to follow after
the Lord in the purity of his worship," John Cotton declared after
his migration to New England. He had learned from the writings
of Parker, Paul Baynes and William Ames "that the ministers of
Christ and the keys of the government of his Church are given to
each particular Congregational Church respectively. And therefore

neither ministers nor Congregations are subject to the ecclesiastical jurisdiction of cathedral churches." [33]

So great was the influence of William Ames in shaping Puritan opinion during the first third of the seventeenth century that he may be considered the father of New England Congregationalism. Scion of an ancient Norfolk family, a learned theologian, he would probably have been made Master of Christ College, Cambridge, had he not given offense by refusing to wear the surplice and by a violent attack from the pulpit upon the prevalent custom of card playing. Forced to resign as a Fellow of Christ College, and forbidden by the Bishop of London to preach, he finally took refuge in Leyden. In 1622 he went to the University of Franeker, in Friesland, where he won for himself a reputation for scholarship so great that students flocked to him, not only from all parts of the Netherlands but from Hungary and even from Russia.

But it was through his writings that he exerted his greatest influence upon religious thought in England. His *Medulla Theologiae,* in which he set forth his views on Calvinist theology, was frequently reprinted, while his *De Conscientia, ejus Jure et Casibus* was familiar to every Puritan divine. His translation into Latin and publication of William Bradshaw's manuscript on the *English Puritans* gave that important work wide circulation. How greatly the New England clergy were guided by him is shown by a statement of Thomas Hooker that "if a scholar was well studied in Dr. Ames his *Medulla Theologiae* and *Casus Conscientiae* so as to understand them thoroughly, they would make him, supposing him versed in Scriptures, a good divine, though he had no more books in the world." [34]

Ames reduces the national Church to a loose federation of sovereign congregations. "The Church . . . is not one Catholic Church," he states in his *The First Book of Divinity,* "but there are so many churches as there are companies, or particular congregations, of those that profess the faith, who are joined together by a special band for the constant exercise of the communion of the Saints."

[33] John Cotton, *The Way of the Congregational Churches Cleared* (1648), p. 17.
[34] Quoted by Cotton Mather, *Magnalia* (Hartford, 1820), II, p. 308.

PORTRAIT OF THE REVEREND
WILLIAM AMES, ARTIST UNKNOWN

JOHN WINTHROP, COPY FROM
VAN DYCK

The Greek word signifying Church refers not to a "national, provincial or diocesan" body, but only to one congregation, he maintains. "Hence divers fixed congregations of the same country and province are always called Churches in the plural number, not one Church. . . . Neither is there anything in all the New Testament of the institution of any larger Church upon which lesser congregations should depend. . . . Yet particular Churches, as their communion doth require . . . may and oftentimes also ought to enter into mutual confederacy and fellowship among themselves in classes and synods, that they may use their common consent and mutual help as much as fitly may be, . . . but that combination doth neither constitute a new form of a Church, neither ought it to take away . . . that liberty and power which Christ hath left to his Churches."

As for the appointment of a minister, it should belong solely to the congregation he was to serve. "The episcopal ordination of a minister without title, that is without a Church to which and in which he should be ordained, is as ridiculous as if any should be fained to be a husband without a wife." Thus, the ordination of a minister properly followed election by a congregation and was "nothing else than a certain solemn entrance" into the exercise of the clerical duties.[35]

From Cartwright to Ames, from the theories of the Puritans of Queen Elizabeth's day concerning the organization of the Church to those of the Puritans of the time of James I and Charles I, was a long cry. To Cartwright the Church of England was the Church of God, to Ames it was no more than a loose confederation of many Churches of God. But they were in agreement in contending that coherence and strength should be attained through the civil government whose duty it was "to suppress and root out by their authority all false ministers, voluntary religions and counterfeit worship of God, and establish and maintain by their laws every part of God's word."

The earlier and later Puritans were in accord also, in demanding that none be admitted to the ministry save pious, learned and able men. Without a good example from the spiritual leaders it would be difficult indeed to raise the standards of morality among

[35] William Ames, *The First Book of Divinity*, pp. 178–180.

the people; without inspiring, scholarly sermons, the congregations would grope in darkness and might fall into fatal error. So
it was with indignation and horror that the reformers saw unworthy men, many of them unlettered, some known for their
scandalous lives, appointed to important cures. There were cases
in which the patrons of a parish forced the candidate to pay for
his appointment, which not only impoverished the incumbent by
"scraping the wool from his cloak," but excluded the able and
the conscientious.[36]

In 1584 it was charged that of 335 benefices in Essex 173 were
held by "ignorant and unpreaching" ministers, and twelve by men
of "scandalous life." The walk of life from which several came
is indicated by such entries against their names as "sometime a
tailor," "sometime a grocer," "sometime a weaver," "sometime an
apothecary," "sometime a sow-gelder."[37] That conditions had not
improved two decades later we gather from the statement that
some ministers were drunkards, some were incontinent, some
hunted on Sunday. One parson was stigmatized as "an unprofitable preacher, a notorious swearer, a haunter of lewd company,
full of filthy behavior, a quareller."[38]

Thus before the end of the reign of James I, English Congregationalism, the Congregationalism which was transplanted in
New England, had assumed its final form. It was based upon the
assumption that each congregation in itself was a Church, receiving its authority, not from any national or international body, but
direct from God. And though it recognized the Church of England, it reduced it to a loose federation of congregations, who
might and should from time to time send representatives to synods
to give and receive support and advice. This loosely knit body was
to attain unity, however, through the support of the civil government, through pious and orthodox magistrates, whose duty it was
to support the true faith and to suppress all others. Not only
Church law, but civil law, must be based upon the Bible, since the
word of God should supersede the word of man in every decision,
large or small. Essential to the true Church was a devout, learned

[36] *The Victoria History of the County of Essex*, II, p. 36.
[37] *Ibid.*, p. 40.
[38] *Ibid.*, p. 48.

ministry who would serve as fathers to their flocks in guarding them and in admonishing them if in their daily lives they strayed from the strict path of duty. There should be no hierarchy, since this had no sanction in the Bible, while ceremonial in worship, the use of images, the observance of saints' days, the wearing of the surplice should be abandoned.

But as the Congregational program became thus clearly defined, the more uncertain appeared the prospect of putting it into effect. The weak link was the need for the cooperation of the government. So long as the King set himself in opposition, so long as bishops and archbishops held sway within the Church, so long as the patrons and not the congregations selected the ministers, so long as the hand of the law was raised against the Puritan ministers to force them to use the Book of Common Prayer, or to rail in the altar, or to use the prescribed vestments, the reformers could see no hope of ultimate victory.

Wherever the leaders met together the chief topic of conversation was the "darkness" of the times. On the continent of Europe Protestantism seemed doomed. In Germany the forces of Tilly and Wallenstein were marching from victory to victory; in France the Huguenots had been crushed by the forces of Richelieu; while at home Charles I was proving even less tolerant of the Puritans than James. "All other Churches of Europe are brought to desolation," said the pious English gentleman, John Winthrop, "and our sins for which the Lord begins already to frown upon us and to cut us short, do threaten evil times to be coming upon us." [39] "Danger enlarges itself in so great a measure that nothing but Heaven shrouds us from despair," echoed Sir John Eliot.

The outlook became even blacker with the appointment in 1628 of William Laud as Bishop of London. This sincere, devout, learned man had risen from the body of court prelates to become the champion of the Anglican Church and the defender of the hierarchy, ceremonial in worship and Church unity. To the Puritans, who could now anticipate stern repression in Essex and other parts of his see, he loomed as the veritable anti-Christ.

It was at this moment that some of the Puritan leaders conceived the idea of migrating to New England to establish there a

[39] *Winthrop Papers*, II, p. 138, Massachusetts Historical Society, 1931.

Wilderness Zion, in which Church and State would unite to uphold the congregationalism of Baynes and Ames and the fundamental tenets of Calvin. On those distant shores they would be free from the restrictions of King and bishops, there the ministers could expound the Word of God without fear of losing their cures; there they could turn to magistrates of like mind with themselves to stamp out error, there the hated surplice could be cast aside and religious services be held within walls bare of images. "What can be a better work and more honorable and worthy of a Christian than to help raise and support a particular Church while it is in its infancy?" wrote Winthrop.[40]

There can be no doubt that Winthrop, Thomas Dudley, Isaac Johnson and the other movers in this project were inspired by the example of the small group of Separatists who in 1620 had planted themselves on the shores of Cape Cod Bay. This settlement had its origins in a congregation at Scrooby, in Nottinghamshire, who had attracted the attention of the bishops through the writings of one of their teachers, the gentle and learned John Robinson. To escape persecution some of the more earnest members fled with Robinson to Holland, the lone European refuge in the stormy sea of intolerance. Here they lived in peace for twelve years. But fearing that they might be absorbed into the Dutch population or that their children would become lost in the maze of religious beliefs which surrounded them, they sought a new refuge across the Atlantic.

The London Company had already established a beachhead in the American wilderness, so the Scrooby exiles sought permission from its pious secretary, Sir Edwin Sandys, to make a new settlement under its jurisdiction. King James gave his approval and promised not to molest the colonists. The little Pilgrim band sailed from Holland for Southampton in July, 1620, where recruits and supplies were awaiting them. Early in August they cleared for America and three months later came in sight of the high sand bluffs of Cape Cod. As they had no license to settle outside the territory of the London Company, they tacked about and sailed south. But when they fell among the shoals off Monomoy Point, they returned to Provincetown harbor and later established themselves across Cap Cod Bay at Plymouth.

[40] *Ibid.*, p. 139.

The Pilgrim movement is important because it led to other and greater migrations. "Let it not be grievous to you that you have been but instruments to break the ice for others, the honor shall be yours till the world's end," their friends wrote them. But from the time of Winthrop and Cotton to the present day there has been a tendency to exaggerate the influence of Plymouth in shaping the religious and civil structure of Puritan Massachusetts. It was as early as 1645 that Robert Baillie stated in his *Dissuasive from the Errors of the Time* that "the most who settled their habitations in the land, did agree to model themselves after Robinson's pattern." To this John Cotton replied, "I do not know that they agreed upon it by any common consultation. But it is true they did as if they had agreed, by the same spirit of truth and unity, set up by the help of Christ the same model of Churches, one like to another. But whether it was after Mr. Robinson's pattern is spoken gratis, for I believe most of them knew not what it was, if any at all." [41]

The Church covenant, so fundamental in the New England Church system, did not come from Plymouth, Cotton insisted, but from the Bible through Ames and other English Congregational leaders. As for episcopacy, the Word of God, explained by nonconformist scholars in England, had commanded them to reject it. "That we laid aside the Book of Common Prayer," Cotton continued, "we received from the . . . second commandment and not . . . from the Separatists." It is clear that the Puritan migrants not only came to Massachusetts with a definite order which they were ready to establish, but they came there for the purpose of establishing it. To imply, as certain historians have done, that they left their homes in England and plunged into the wilderness without knowing their minds, so that upon their arrival they were forced to turn to the Pilgrims for advice and direction, is an indictment of their foresight and fixity of purpose.

In 1623 a group of businessmen of Dorchester organized a company for fishing in American waters and sent out Roger Conant to establish a base at the site of the present Gloucester. When the venture proved unprofitable, most of the stockholders withdrew. But the Dorchester minister, John White, a moderate

[41] John Cotton, *The Way of the Congregational Churches Cleared*, p. 16.

Puritan, greatly beloved by his flock, conceived the idea that the infant settlement might be of use as a retreat for the poor and a missionary base.[42] So he sought and secured the support of some "gentlemen of London," among them several prominent Puritans. The new group organized the New England Company, secured a large grant of land from the Council of New England, took over the defunct Dorchester concern and dispatched the pious John Endicott to replace Conant.

In the meanwhile some of the leading Puritans of the eastern shires, who had become interested in the new company through White's efforts, now began to think of sending thousands of godly men and women to New England as the basis of a new Puritan State. Though the King turned his back upon the Calvinistic reformers, though the bishops thwarted their efforts, though there was no longer hope of "purifying" the English congregations and uniting them through the medium of a sympathetic civil government, might not the "chosen people" migrate to the American wilderness, there to carry out the plans which they deemed so necessary to their salvation?

Foremost among this group was John Winthrop, a country squire of the Manor of Groton, Suffolk, and a man of piety, learning, judgment and powers of leadership. Associated with him was the austere, intolerant Thomas Dudley, steward of the Puritan noble, the Earl of Lincoln; William Pynchon, of Springfield, Essex, whose wealth and distinguished connections lent strength to the movement; and Isaac Johnson, son-in-law of the Earl of Lincoln.

In March, 1629, the New England Company secured a royal charter from Charles I, incorporating them into the Massachusetts Bay Company and granting large powers of government within their territories. Events now moved rapidly to a climax. It would obviously be dangerous and perhaps fatal to establish a godly state in America if its fate rested in the hands of a group of gentlemen residing in England. Even though the stockholders might be Puritans in hearty sympathy with the principles of Ames, Parker and Cotton, they would be under the direct authority of the King and so might find it necessary to modify their policies in conformity

[42] Frances Rose-Troup, *John White.*

with his wishes. Moreover, the stock might in time fall into hostile hands, in which case the very purposes of migration would be defeated. In other words, unless the control both of Church and State in the projected colony resided in the colonists themselves, the venture would be futile.

With this in view, the Winthrop group effected a maneuver which was as clever as it was unexpected. In the latter part of July, 1629, Winthrop, Johnson, Dudley, John Humphrey and several others met at the residence of the Earl of Lincoln at Sempringham. Here, it seems, a plan was put forward for such stockholders as desired to go to New England to buy up the shares of all who remained in England, so that the founders of the new colony would have complete possession of the charter and could take it with them as a safeguard of their liberties and of the Churches. They were careful that no hint of their purpose should reach the ears of King Charles, for well they knew that he would never knowingly consent to the establishment of a semi-independent State under his nominal jurisdiction. So it was in secret that four weeks later twelve men met at Cambridge, possibly within one of the rooms of Emmanuel College, to make a momentous agreement. "We bind ourselves to embark with our families for New England," they said in effect, "there to inhabit, provided that the government of the colony, together with the patent, be first transferred to us."

Eight months later an armada of four little vessels—the *Arbella,* named for the daughter of the Earl of Lincoln, the *Ambrose,* the *Jewel* and the *Talbot*—hoisted sail at Southampton and headed for New England. It was the beginning of the great Puritan exodus. On board were Winthrop, Dudley, Saltonstall, William Coddington, and several hundred other settlers. Despite a stormy voyage, in which cold and rain were faced without "fear or dismayedness," the company at last came in sight of the highlands of Maine. Tacking to the south, they ran along the New England coast, enjoying "a smell off the shore like the smell of a garden," until, a week later, they cast anchor in Salem harbor.

There is always a temptation to simplify history by assigning a sole reason for every great movement—to explain American democracy by the frontier, or the American Revolution by economic determinism, or the War between the States by the abolitionist crusade. But men in the mass, as well as men as individuals, are usually moved, not by one single motive, but by mixed motives. It is usually the integrating of complex forces which produces major changes in society; just as the uniting of certain chemicals causes an explosion, or the joining of many tiny streams creates a river or a lake.

There can be no doubt, however, that the chief motive for the founding of Massachusetts was religious. Winthrop and the others of his group believed that their only safeguard against the forces of evil lay in establishing a society after the concept of Baynes and Ames, with a confederation of congregations buttressed by a sympathetic government. This alone, they thought, would cleanse the Churches of unworthy ministers and immoral communicants, remodel worship upon the Biblical model and dethrone the bishops. Since this seemed impossible of accomplishment in England, they proposed to bring it about in distant America by founding there a Wilderness Zion. "We came hither because we would have our posterity settled under the pure and full dispensations of the gospel, defended by rulers that should be of ourselves," wrote Cotton Mather.[43]

It is erroneous to suppose that fear of persecution was a prime cause for the original movement. Prior to the Cambridge conference the large body of the Puritan clergy had been left undisturbed in their cures, there had been very few cases of imprisonment, the efforts to enforce the use of the Book of Common Prayer had been half-hearted. It is true that with the appointment of Laud as Bishop of London it was obvious that a period of persecution was at hand, but it was later comers, not the original founders, who felt the full weight of Laud's harsh rule.

Nor did the Puritans desert their homes for a strange land for the sake of religious freedom. They did not believe in toleration. Had they gained control of the civil government in England they would certainly have rooted out "error" without compromise. " 'Tis Satan's policy to plead for an indefinite and boundless toleration," declared Thomas Shepard,[44] while Urian Oakes denounced

---

[43] Cotton Mather, *Magnalia* (Hartford, 1820), I, p. 219.
[44] Lindsay Swift, "The Massachusetts Election Sermons," Colonial Society of Massachusetts *Publications,* I, p. 400.

freedom to worship as one chose as the "first born of all abominations." After their arrival in New England they insisted upon orthodoxy, even though it entailed the imprisonment, whipping and even hanging of those whose religious views differed from their own.

Hardly had the sails of Winthrop's little squadron vanished over the western horizon than the threatened storm broke over the heads of the Puritans in England. Even before his elevation to the see of Canterbury, Laud, as Bishop of London, had set himself the task of enforcing uniformity. Visitations were held in every parish to investigate the orthodoxy of the ministers, and those who continued to defy the bishop were warned or perhaps suspended. With his appointment to the primacy, Laud's efforts were redoubled. Chief among his victims was John Bastwick, a Colchester physician and a graduate of Emmanuel, whose violent advocacy of Calvinism had brought on him the anger of the bishops. The High Commission clapped him in prison, and when he steadfastly refused to recant, placed him in the pillory, where his ears were cut off.[45] The chief result was to make him a popular hero in the eastern shires. Samuel Ward, one of the ablest of the Puritan divines and long the "town preacher" of Ipswich, was convicted of nonconformity, suspended and placed in jail. In a preface to a volume of his sermons, with admirable good humor, he describes his imprisonment as "a little leisure occasioned against my will." [46]

Shocking to the Puritans was the encouragement which some clergymen gave to their flocks to indulge in recreations on the Lord's Day. Laud himself ordered every minister to read from the pulpit a declaration in favor of Sunday sports which had been issued by the Crown under James I. One minister, although obeying, dared to close the reading with the significant hint: "You have heard read, good people, both the commandment of God and the commandment of man. Obey which you please." The wisdom of this minister's course became obvious when others who refused to read the declaration were cited before the High Commission, silenced or deprived of their cures.

[45] *The Victoria History of the County of Essex,* II, p. 53.
[46] *The Victoria History of the County of Suffolk,* II, p. 40.

Not only did Laud in this way rid the Church of many Puritan ministers, but he was careful in filling vacancies to appoint none but avowed high churchmen. The reformers countered by buying up the endowments of various parishes so that they themselves could appoint whom they pleased. But the archbishop cited them before the Court of Exchequer, which promptly deprived them of the right of patronage.

Similar action was taken against the so-called lectureships, endowed by Puritan gentlemen or by municipalities to support independent preachers. Typical were the lectureships at Colchester, founded in the sixteenth century, which had at first been supported by popular subscriptions, and later by the town government; at Dedham, Wethersfield, Chelmsford, Bury St. Edmunds, Ipswich and elsewhere. In some cases Puritan country gentlemen employed able divines as chaplains, in order to shelter them from persecution.

Against lecturers and dissenting chaplains alike Laud launched an offensive. John Rogers, known as "roaring Rogers" because of his "awakening preaching," who had been lecturer at Dedham for more than thirty years, was suspended for nonconformity. Soon after this all eastern England was aroused by an attack on Thomas Hooker, the lecturer at Chelmsford. When this learned, godly, eloquent man was threatened by Laud in 1629, no less than forty-nine ministers of Essex wrote "begging him not to silence or remove him" and "pledging themselves that he was an orthodox, honest and peaceable man." But when a counter-petition arrived the bishop seized the opportunity to summon Hooker before him. The lecturer, forfeiting his bail, fled to Holland, whence he made his way to New England to become a leader in the Massachusetts Bay Colony and later the founder of Connecticut.[47]

From Essex came also to New England John Eliot, assistant to Hooker in his school at Little Baddow; Thomas Shepard, a Fellow of Emmanuel, who was deprived of his lectureship at Earl's Colne in 1630; John Wilson, one of the ablest of the Puritan divines; John Norton, chaplain to Sir William Masham at High Laver; John Rogers, son of John Rogers of Dedham; Giles Firmin, Ezekiel Rogers, and many others. From Suffolk, too, Laud's sever-

[47] *The Victoria History of the County of Essex,* II, pp. 52, 53.

ity drove scores of devout persons to Massachusetts. When he ordered a visitation in that county, the inquisitors reported that nonconformist lecturers abounded, preaching on the bowling greens or in inns and living in the homes of private gentlemen under the guise of tutors. Instantly the machinery of persecution was put in motion against them, and many were silenced. When Samuel Ward, the great Puritan divine whose influence was felt far beyond the confines of the shire, was haled before the Court of High Commission, no less than 600 of his followers made ready to leave for New England.[48]

Nor were Essex and Suffolk alone in giving their sons and daughters to New England. Enfield, Hadley, Acton, Chelsea and other names suggest the influence of Middlesex; Chatham, Dover, Rye, Sandwich, Canterbury and Greenwich were no doubt founded by men from Kent; Hingham, Lynn, Norwich and Yarmouth by Norfolk settlers; Boston and Lincoln by Lincolnshire families. In short, although the eastern shires provided the major part of the settlers, their sons were joined by fellow Puritans from all parts of England.[49]

In evaluating the motives for the Puritan exodus it would be erroneous to ignore economic factors. Even Winthrop hoped to better his financial condition. "His means here are so shortened, now three of his sons being come to age have drawn away the one half of his estate, as he shall not be able to continue in that place and employment where he now is, his ordinary charge being still as great almost as when his means was double." [50]

Winthrop emphasized hard times and unemployment as important reasons why others also should join in the movement. "This land grows weary of her inhabitants, so as man, who is the most precious of all creatures, is here more vile and base than the earth we tread upon and of less price among us than a horse or a sheep. . . . All towns complain of the burden of their poor . . . and it has come to pass that children, servants and neighbors, especially if they be poor, are counted the greatest burdens, which, if things were right, would be the chiefest earthly blessings. The

---

[48] *The Victoria History of the County of Suffolk*, II, p. 188.
[49] Martin S. Briggs, *The Homes of the Pilgrim Fathers in England and America*, p. 43.
[50] *Winthrop Papers*, II, p. 148, Massachusetts Historical Society.

whole earth is the Lord's garden and he hath given it to the sons of
men with the general commission (Gen. 1:28) increase and multiply and replenish the earth and subdue it. . . . Why then should
we stand striving here for places of habitation, etc., many men
spending as much labor and cost to recover or keep sometimes an
acre or two of land as would procure them many hundred as
good or better in another country, and in the meantime suffer a
whole continent as fruitful and convenient for the use of man
to lie waste without any improvement?" [51]

Thus did Winthrop advance the argument which was to be
made over and over again for every American colony and which
in the centuries which followed sent millions of poor families
across the Atlantic. It is reasonable to infer, then, that many who
followed the Puritan leaders into the wilderness did so, in part at
least, to better their economic condition in a land where men were
few and natural resources abundant. No doubt the Puritan tenant
farmer, or shipwright, or fisherman, as he listened to the earnest
pleas of his minister, was convinced that he could remain in
England only at the peril of his soul; but in the quiet of his own
home, or in conversation with his neighbors he must have given
consideration, also, to the opportunities held out for a larger income and the acquisition of property. To him a hundred acres of
arable and fifty acres of pasture in New England, for whose
ownership he had good reason to hope, must have seemed like a
dream of riches.

Especially alluring were the promises held out by Winthrop,
since they came in the midst of a protracted depression. In 1622
conditions were so critical that there was fear of open rebellion
in the eastern shires. "The poor have assembled in troops of forty
or fifty and gone to the houses of the rich and demanded meat
and money, which has been given through fear," it was reported to
the government. "They have also taken provisions in the
markets." [52] On all sides there were sturdy beggars, the support of
the poor became a heavy burden on the taxpayers, many towns
formerly the scene of bustling activity were now "decayed."

Chief among the causes of distress was the decline of the cloth

[51] *Ibid.*, p. 139.
[52] *Calendar of State Papers, Domestic,* 1619–23, pp. 346, 382.

trade. The clothiers of Suffolk reported that they had been compelled to discharge their workmen because they could not dispose of the stocks of cloth on hand. In twenty towns alone, unsold goods totalled £39,282, while in twelve towns the clothiers had lost £30,415 in bankruptcies.[53] Altogether some 8,000 cloth workers were out of work.[54] The number of cloths exported from Ipswich, which in 1626 was 3,340, the very next year dropped to 728. One clothier who had formerly used a hundred workmen now could employ only twenty.

The reasons advanced for this situation are many. The drapers thought that the decline of their trade was caused by the "deceitful making of cloth," the employment of inexperienced workers, the wearing of "stuffs which hinder the sale of cloth" and "night funerals." They suggested that it might make work if "dyers, weavers, tuckers" and others would stick to their own distinctive tasks.[55] A committee for the cloth trade blamed the depression upon "the increased manufacture of cloth abroad; deceits in making or dyeing English cloth and the heavy burdens of it; foreign wares; the close policy of the Merchant Adventurers; scarcity of coin; want of returns for cloth exported; and the general wearing of silks and foreign stuffs instead of cloth."[56]

Of first importance in explaining the situation was the granting of patents of monopoly as a part of a general scheme of industrial planning. Abuses had crept into this system even in Elizabeth's reign, and Charles I converted it into a source of revenue by selling patents to the highest bidder.[57] It was James I, however, who sanctioned a large grant of monopoly which required the dressing and dyeing of all cloth before exportation. Since by far the larger part of the cloth which went to the Continent had hitherto been undressed, this restriction proved disastrous. Of like kind was the monopoly given the merchant adventurers and to the drapers in London of selling woolen cloths either by wholesale or by retail. This brought bitter complaints from the Suffolk clothiers. "One hundred thousand pounds' worth of cloth lies pawned for

[53] *Ibid.*, p. 362.
[54] *Ibid.*, p. 382.
[55] *Ibid.*, p. 400.
[56] *Ibid.*, p. 410.
[57] Arthur Birnie, *An Economic History of the British Isles*, p. 191.

want of buyers and in storehouses. . . . The merchant buys generally only against shipping time. The clothiers at all times of the year are driven to repair to London to sell their cloths to pay the wool-growers and the poor whom they set to work." [58]

Since the making of cloth was the principal industry of the east of England, it is reasonable to suppose that its decline played an important part in the settlement of Massachusetts. But there were other causes of bitter discontent. In 1626 Charles I, in desperate need of money for the prosecution of war against France, Spain and the Catholics of Germany, and unable to secure it from a recalcitrant House of Commons, resorted to the illegal expedient of forced loans. This differed from taxation only in name, and those who refused when the collector knocked at the door were promptly put in jail. No less than eighty gentlemen suffered in this way, while hundreds of poor men were forced into the army, leaving their families to beg for bread or to starve.[59]

Not less objectionable than the forced loans was the billeting of soldiers. These ruffians not only ate their hosts out of house and home, but often robbed them. Flouting the authority of their officers, or egged on by them, they roamed over the countryside to pillage and murder. From Essex came bitter complaints of a regiment quartered at Chelmsford who had been guilty of such violence that householders found it necessary to remain away from church or business to guard their houses and protect their daughters.[60]

The proclaiming of martial law, even though ostensibly done for the protection of the people, far from diminishing the discontent, actually added to it. "When a countryman, who had seen his thatch fired and his horses carried off by a company of pikemen, appeared before the Court Martial with the tale of his wrongs, and was dismissed with scant courtesy by a harassed colonel whose troops had disappeared and who did not understand his dialect, he went home in no humor to regard Martial Law as a necessity, nor billeting as a privilege." [61]

To the injuries of the Forced Loan, Billeting and Martial Law

---

[58] *The Victoria History of the County of Suffolk,* II, p. 266.
[59] George M. Trevelyan, *England under the Stuarts,* pp. 138, 139.
[60] *The Victoria History of the County of Essex,* II, p. 226.
[61] George M. Trevelyan, *England under the Stuarts,* p. 143.

was added the legal fiction of Ship Money, which revived and extended an obsolete power of the government to draft merchant-men in time of war. It was in October, 1634, that writs were issued to the bailiffs of certain towns in Essex and Suffolk to provide one warship of 700 tons, manned by a crew of 250. Everyone knew, of course, that the King intended to use the money raised under this pretext not for the actual construction of the vessel, but for the expenses of his government. In other words, like the Forced Loan, Ship Money was merely an excuse for taxing the people without the consent of their representatives in Parliament. On the whole it was successful in its immediate end, for it brought large sums into the royal exchequer, but it aroused bitter opposition, convinced many that the King was bent on overthrowing constitutional government and prepared the way for the Civil War.

How important Ship Money was in the settlement of New England is evident from the report of Edward Duke, Sheriff of Suffolk, in October, 1637: "Hundred of Wangford, Garrett, the tanner, gone into New England: . . . St. Michael's, George Barrell, gone into New England. Hundred of Lothingland, Bradwell, William Ballard, the like. . . . Weentham, Henry Chickren, the like. . . . The parsonage is rated 145, and since that time the incumbent was deprived of his living and is gone into New England. Hundred of Loes, Framlingham, Francis Baylie, gone with his family to New England." [62] So many of the demands of 1638 and 1639 were not paid because the defaulters had fled that Sir John Clench, the new sheriff, was practically ruined.

In evaluating the forces which were responsible for the founding of Massachusetts, it is obvious that the most important was the crisis which confronted the English Puritans in the early years of the reign of Charles I. Certainly this it was which induced the leaders to plan a colony across the Atlantic based upon their own conception of what the Biblical commonwealth should be. Men of education, some of them distinguished scholars, earnest, sincere, determined, they not only created the framework of the new society into which the mass of the settlers fitted themselves, but also exerted a powerful and continuing influence upon the lives, thoughts and everyday existence of the people.

[62] *Calendar of State Papers, Domestic*, 1638–39, p. 64.

The humbler settlers, too, were influenced chiefly by religious considerations. They left their homes, most of them, to live in a society where they would be free of the danger of error which might lead to damnation. It was not only that they found it difficult to worship in England after the way God had directed; they wished to flee behind impregnable walls erected against heresy. Even when actually forced to come to a decision as to whether they would or would not migrate by unemployment, or by the Forced Loan or by Ship Money, or by the pillaging of their little estates, it was to New England that they turned since it offered a religious as well as economic haven. Some there were, no doubt, who took passage on the crowded vessels which set sail for Massachusetts, who were not in full sympathy with the views of the leaders. Some were actually irreligious. But the majority were God-fearing, devout Puritans, who risked not only their property but their lives in the experiment of a religious Utopia under the direct kingship of the Maker.

Chapter II

THE BIBLE STATE

THE GREAT migration to Massachusetts, which began with the arrival of John Winthrop and his company, continued without interruption for thirteen years, scores of little vessels making the dangerous voyage to discharge their human freight upon the wild New England shores. Crowded below deck where the ceilings were so low a man could not stand erect, often ill from eating tainted beef or cheese or butter, terrified at the pitching of the vessel, the voyagers found the passage a severe ordeal. Francis Higginson, who came over on the *Talbot,* relates how "the wind blew mightily, the sea roared and the waves tossed us horridly; besides it was fearful dark and the mariners made us afraid with their running here and there and loud crying one to another to pull at this and that rope."[1] It was only in prayer and in the thought that they were following God's command that the people found consolation.

Humble thanks went up when at last the port was sighted and the vessels headed in to draw up beside the crude wharves. The chief dangers were now passed; there remained only to secure a grant of land, make for themselves new homes and enjoy the safety from error which they regarded as so vital to the salvation of their souls. A busy scene it was as the passengers came ashore, some still sick from the voyage, some grieving over the loss of relatives or friends. After them came the domestic animals which had been penned in the hold—cattle, horses, sheep, fowls, etc.; then clothing of all kinds, seed and food sufficient for one year; next the supplies which the newcomers had been warned were necessary for life in a pioneer region—felling axes for clearing away trees; hoes and plows with which to till the soil; saws, hammers, augers, nails, locks, tiny panes of glass to facilitate the erection of the first crude

[1] Francis Higginson, *New England's Plantation.*

41

houses; household equipment such as kettles, pans, gridirons, wooden dishes, buckets; perhaps a few branding irons, cart wheels, ladders, wheelbarrows, lanterns and bellows.[2] That the settlers came as an armed host, ready to defend their new colony against possible attack not only by Indians or the Spaniards, but by England itself, was evident from the military equipment which they brought with them—armor, long pieces, swords, ammunition.

Enjoying the hospitality of the good people of the port where they arrived, or camping out in improvised shelters, the immigrants waited until they had secured a grant of land from the General Court. So their leaders pored over some crude map of the region or listened with intense interest to the descriptions of hunters or of Indians, in search of a site where there would be running fresh water, meadows and fertile arable. Having made their choice, they handed in their petition and in good time received the charter for a new town. There must have been rejoicing among the group when they were told that they were now the proprietors of a tract of land perhaps ten miles square, or large enough to embrace a hundred manors. If divided equally, each head of family would own hundreds of acres, enough not only for his own needs, but for the needs of his sons and his grandsons.

Now ensued prolonged conferences with the older settlers, for instruction in the clearing of fields, the erection of houses, dealing with the Indians, planting their crops, caring for the cattle and a hundred other matters. Above all they needed advice in the organization of their town, so that there would be close coordination between religion and government, and between religion and economic life.

It could not have been by chance that each group of settlers turned to the English manor as the model for their town, not in political or religious matters, but in its agricultural, industrial and, to some extent, social features. The manor was a dying institution in England, especially in the part of England whence most of them had come, and it is improbable that many of the settlers had lived on a manor, since most of them seem to have been tenant farmers, or weavers, or shipwrights, or tanners, or shopkeepers. Their natural impulse would have been to ignore this relic of medieval

[2] George F. Dow, *Every Day Life in the Massachusetts Bay Colony*, pp. 10, 11.

times, and divide their land into farms. But against this, it seems certain, their advisors warned them in the most emphatic terms, pointing out that to scatter themselves throughout their town would not only militate against the unity so essential to a new community, but might so discourage the advancement of religion as to defeat the chief purpose of their migration.

In 1705 Francis Makemie, the noted Presbyterian divine, wrote a pamphlet entitled *A Plain & Friendly Perswasive to the Inhabitants of Virginia and Maryland for Promoting Towns,* in words which echoed the arguments of the first Puritan settlers. "Towns and cohabitations would highly advance religion . . . for in remote and scattered settlements we can never enjoy so fully, frequently and certainly those privileges and opportunities as are to be had in all Christian towns and cities, for by reason of bad weather or other accidents ministers are prevented and people are hindered to attend and so disappoint one another. But in towns congregations are never wanting, and children and servants never are without opportunity of hearing, who cannot travel many miles to hear and be catechised." Education, too, "flourishes only in such places, for the smallest and meanest of schools cannot be maintained . . . where the number to be entertained together are too few to maintain any master or mistress." [3]

So the new settlers were advised to found as the focal point in their town a village in which all should have their dwellings, and so live under the watchful eyes of the minister and the elders, within walking distance of the meeting-house, the school and the parsonage. To make it practicable for each villager to go out to his fields in the morning and return in the evening, he had to have his land as near the village as possible. But here the imitation of the English manor ceased. There must be no lord, of course; no demesne, no manorial court, no villeins and cotters, no chevage, no boon work. In other words, the settlers were to borrow from the manor only the feature which fitted in with their plans for a religious commonwealth.

The creation of the agricultural village is a tribute to the foresight of Winthrop, or Dudley, or Endicott, or whoever it was that thought this matter through, for it became the corner stone of

[3] *Virginia Magazine of History and Biography,* IV, pp. 264, 265.

Puritan New England. Not only did it keep the flock under the
minister's wing, but it facilitated the town meeting, knit together
congregation and town to a degree unknown elsewhere, even at
Geneva itself, tended toward economic independence, influenced
every phase of social life, prevented the intellectual stagnation
which isolation breeds, gave a measure of protection from attacks
by the Indians. The great mistake of the founders lay in making
the average town too large for the village, which was the center of
gravity, to hold it together, so that in time it tended to disinte-
grate.

When the group of settlers had perfected their plans and
received their instructions, they gathered their belongings around
them, said good-bye to their friends and set out through the
wilderness. To guide them along the forest trails they often had a
trusted Indian. Trudging behind him came the men and women,
driving before them the cows, sheep, swine and other domestic
animals upon which they must in part depend for sustenance during the first year of the settlement; the children, together with
household utensils and farm implements, in the crude carts that
they had brought from England in separate parts and put together
at the port.

It was with mixed emotions that they arrived at the site of their
future home—dismay at the wildness of the country, the huge
trees, the dense undergrowth, the lack of all facilities for civilized
life; hope at the thought that the land was theirs, hundreds of
acres of land, which their labor could convert into fields of waving
Indian corn, or wheat or rye; sadness at the memory of England
with its comfortable houses, its fertile farms, its villages and towns.
But it was not a time for repining, for there was work to be done
and without delay.

By an act of the Massachusetts General Court, 1635, a large
degree of autonomy was accorded each town. "Whereas particular
towns have many things which concern only themselves," declares
the act, "it is therefore ordered that the freemen of every town, or
the major part of them, shall only have power to dispose of their
own lands and woods, with all the privileges and appurtenances
of the said towns to grant lots and make such orders as may concern the well ordering of their own townes . . . to levy and dis-

train, . . . also to choose their own particular officers, as constables, surveyors of highways and the like." [4]

Under this act the town became to the State what the congregation was to the Church. Localism in religion, which had become so vital a feature of Puritanism, was to be matched in New England by localism in government. Scholars, pointing out that the town was rooted in English custom and traditions, trace its origin to Anglo-Saxon institutions. Yet it seems obvious that the founders of New England shaped it and gave it unusual powers for the purpose of aiding and buttressing the individual congregation. They realized that it was not enough for the provincial government to be the handmaiden of the Churches; if their experiment in the New World was to succeed it was vital that the civil officers of each community be accorded large powers so that they could uphold the hands of the individual ministers, the elders and the congregation.

So the first act of the freemen was to gather, perhaps in some open space in the woods, in order to elect a committee to decide upon the location of the village, to plot its streets and lots, to supervise the surveying and to conduct the division of land. There must have been prolonged discussions as to where to place the village, since it was to be the center of religious, political and economic activities. If there were a body of navigable water at hand, some spot along its shores was usually chosen, so that transportation would be convenient and cheap. The village of Enfield was built on the east bank of the Connecticut; Cambridge, as near to the Charles as the marshy banks permitted; Milford, on the Mill and West rivers. In case navigable water was lacking, the village was usually laid out in the center of the town, so that as much of the surrounding arable, woodland and pasturage as possible would be within a short compass. It was of the utmost importance that the distance from residence to field be not too great for the owner to go out in the morning with his hoe or his ox team and return at the close of the work day.

In planning the village it was customary, if the lay of the land permitted, to have one long main street, with long, narrow home lots which abutted upon it on either side. The motorist who today

[4] James D. Phillips, *Salem in the Seventeenth Century*, p. 80.

passes through the quaint New England village with its old houses seldom realizes that the lots on which they are built formerly often stretched out behind for a mile or more.[5] Thus the Enfield home lots, which had a frontage of 198 feet, were 1,920 feet in length.[6] They constituted what must have seemed to their proprietors little farms in themselves, with ample space, not only for a residence, a barn, an orchard and a vegetable garden, but for fields of Indian corn or of English grain. In many cases the settlers contented themselves with their home lots for several years, before asking for additional land lying beyond.

In the distribution of lots, the settlers displayed a decided leaning toward economic democracy. There must be no aristocracy of wealth to vie with the aristocracy of religion, to dispute its authority and magnify the things of this world in comparison with the things of the next. In the words of Urian Oakes they hoped never to see the day when "houses and lands, lots and farms and outward accommodations are of more value . . . than the Gospel and Gospel ordinances. . . . Sure there were other and better things the People of God came hither for than the best spot of ground, the richest soil." [7] So the leaders not only were very temperate in demanding land for themselves, but they would not permit others to monopolize the choice spots or to hold large areas for speculative purpose or to build up great estates. There should be no landed aristocracy in New England if they could prevent, no Van Rensselaers, no Dulaneys, no "King" Carters.

Yet the Puritans did not carry economic democracy to the extreme of making every lot exactly equal in size and value so that no man would have any advantage over his neighbor. In Milford, for instance, they determined each man's share of the common land by "the rule of persons and estates," by which was understood the relative amount of a man's property and of his contributions to the undertaking, the size of his family and his powers of leadership.[8] But inequalities were never carried to an extreme, and

---

[5] William Cothren, *History of Ancient Woodbury, Conn.*, p. 65.

[6] *History of Enfield, Conn.*, I, p. 69.

[7] Urian Oakes, *New England Pleaded With* (Election sermon for 1673), pp. 30, 33.

[8] Leonard W. Labaree, "Milford, Conn.," Tercentenary Commission, *Historical Publications*, No. 1–10, p. 4.

always great care was taken that injustice be done no man. In Enfield the Committee was empowered to determine "where and in what order men's lots and land" should lie; "the Committee

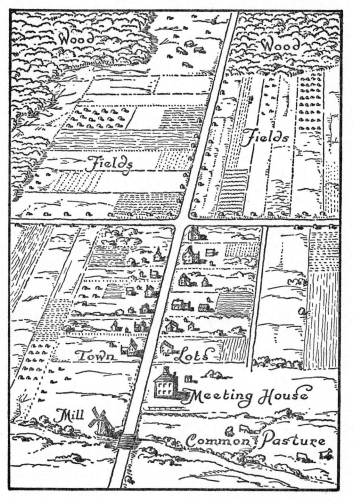

PLAN OF A NEW ENGLAND TOWN

laboring the best they can to suit and accommodate . . . and when a man lies bad in the first field to endeavor to mend him in the next." [9]

[9] *History of Enfield, Conn.,* I, p. 66.

Once the proud owner had taken possession of his home lot, he faced the arduous tasks, not only of erecting his house and barn, setting out his orchard and planting grain and vegetables, but of clearing away the trees and underbrush. In Enfield it was ordered "that every man cut up and clear the brush and bushes in the highway . . . all the breadth of his home lot from front of it for the one half of the highway or street."[10] Time-consuming also, was the constructing of a fence around his lot to protect the precious crops from the depredations of cattle and swine. In some cases the fence was made of rails closely spaced, in others of paling.[11] The Boston common was paled, each of forty-two persons erecting and keeping up his share.[12]

Had one been able to fly over a New England village of three centuries ago, an interesting view would have presented itself. On either side of the main street were the houses of the freeholders, with the barns, the orchards and the gardens behind them. Here was the meeting-house, its simple lines and the absence of a steeple giving it more the appearance of a large residence than a church.[13] Here was the gristmill, its fans spread to catch the breeze; here the schoolhouse; here the smithy; here the sawmill. Stretching out on all sides were the fields; the strips, planted some in Indian corn, some in wheat, some in rye, some in barley, giving the appearance of a crazy quilt. The broad bands of green on either bank of a small stream one recognized as the common pasture. And in the distance were the woods, awaiting the day when a new division would bring them under the axe.[14]

The town imitated the manor, not only in its agricultural life, but in its economic semi-independence. It is true that the typical town was by no means completely cut off from the rest of the world; it shipped out its surplus of Indian corn, wheat, rye, hides, etc., and received in return the finer grade of manufactured goods —clothing, firearms, household utensils, farm implements. But many of the articles of everyday use were made in the village itself by the local shoemaker, carpenter, cooper, weaver or black-

---

[10] *Ibid.*
[11] *Records of the Town of Cambridge, Mass.,* 1630–1703, p. 3.
[12] *Second Report,* Record Commissioners of City of Boston, p. 12.
[13] Noah Porter, *The New England Meeting House,* p. 5.
[14] William Cothren, *History of Ancient Woodbury, Conn.,* p. 39.

smith. There was no need to train artisans to serve the infant community, for there were many skilled workers among the immigrants. These men brought their tools with them and had only to begin in their new homes where they had left off in the old. The "mystery" of their trade, as it was customary to call it, they passed on to their sons or to apprentices.

Vital to the town was the blacksmith, for there was constant need of repairing hoes, plows, kettles, saws, sickles, and of making hinges, locks, branding irons and many other useful articles. It was not unusual to hold out special inducements to a smith to settle in a town and open shop. In 1658 Haverhill offered John Johnson a house and lands valued at twenty pounds if he would ply his trade there for seven years.[15] Enfield, "for the encouragement of a smith," granted Andrew Miller of Southold a choice home lot, together with fifty acres of land "with a proportion of meadow," upon condition that he should come and live upon it "and do the work of a smith for the town" for seven years.[16]

Concessions were also made to any who would set up either gristmills or sawmills, since the former were necessary for grinding the villager's grain, while the latter saved him infinite labor in hewing out timbers for his house or barn. Soon after the founding of Enfield the town granted to three of its citizens the privilege of setting up a sawmill on Scantic Creek, with the right to cut wood in the common, provided "they afford boards which the inhabitants need." [17] Milford agreed with one William Fowler for a gristmill, which, though erected at his own expense, was always regarded as a community project. When freshets injured the machinery, each inhabitant contributed a day's labor to aid in repairing it, and when Fowler imported a new pair of stones from England, the town rewarded him with a grant of land.[18]

The visitor who came to Enfield during the first third of the eighteenth century would have found a number of artisans plying their trades. Here was Phineas Felt, the cordwainer, busy at his bench, fashioning the leather supplied from the local tannery into

---

[15] W. B. Weeden, *Economic and Social History,* I, p. 81.
[16] *History of Enfield, Conn.,* I, p. 288.
[17] *Ibid.,* p. 128.
[18] Leonard W. Labaree, "Milford, Conn.," Tercentenary Commission, *Historical Publications,* No. 1–10, p. 15.

rough but lasting shoes; here Benoni Gains, making barrels in which the townsmen were to store or ship their grain; here John Pasco at work with his noisy loom to turn out the linens and woolens so highly valued by the people; here Benjamin Terry plying the bellows in his smithy; here Ephraim Terry tanning leather; here Jonathan Bush, the wheelwright, at work on a broken cart; there John Allyn, his lathe whirring while he displayed his skill in fashioning wooden plates and dishes.

In New England the social, as well as religious and political unit was the village. The people of the little community knew each other's virtues, weaknesses, habits. Every woman in town could tell just how many gowns Goodwife Collins had in her chest, just how many dishes in her kitchen, how many feather beds she inherited from her father, shook her head when word went around that she had lost her temper when the cow kicked over the milk. And when she became ill it was the neighbors who sat beside her bed or did her chores for her. For the minister and the congregation to admit one to the communion was an event of first importance to the villagers. The people passed each other on the street every day, they met several times a week for religious services, they stopped at the town pump to gossip or to pass the time of day, they saw each other at the mill or the smithy or at the shoemaker's shop. As in tidewater and piedmont Virginia and Maryland the key to social life was isolation, so in early New England it was concentration, but concentration chiefly in little units which themselves were isolated.

When the home lots had been put under cultivation, the town proprietors set about the pleasant task of dividing up the arable and meadow. It was usual to begin by marking off two or more fields of several thousand acres each in as close proximity as possible to the village. In Enfield there were "three general fields . . . two of these cornfields to lie downward or southerly from the town, it may be one of them easterly, and the other general cornfield to lie upward or northerly from the town." [19] In time they came to be known as the North Field, the East Field and the South Field.

In dividing the fields care was taken that every town proprietor

[19] *History of Enfield, Conn.*, I, p. 62.

should have a lot in each unless "otherwise suited and provided for." The Enfield Committee ruled that in the South Field each man should have his land "not all in one, but half or thereabouts" in one part of the field and the other in another. The lots were to be of thirty acres, forty acres, fifty acres and sixty acres, granted according to the rule of persons and estates.[20] In Woodbury the home lots and first field lots together varied from twenty-five acres for persons of the first rank to ten acres for those of the lowest rank. The Guilford Committee ruled that land be allotted to the planters "according to his or their estates put in and according to the number of heads in each family, viz. for every £100 estate five acres of upland and six acres of meadow, and for every head three acres of upland and half an acre of meadow, and so proportionately for £50 estates." [21]

Although it was quite contrary to the plans of the founders of New England to grant land in farms, since this would have entailed the dispersal of the people to the discouragement of Church and minister, in some cases when parts of the town were inaccessible to the village, it became necessary to do so. In Cambridge, whereas the land north of the Charles River was laid out in the West Field, Menotomy Field, Pine Swamp Field, etc., with the usual divisions into lots, that south of the river was cut into farms so that the owners would not have to ferry every day from and to the village.[22] In the town of Boston, the narrow confines of the peninsula upon which the first colonists settled, made it necessary to make grants at Mount Wollaston and Muddy River which were at such a distance from the village that the owners were forced to reside upon them. Among the farms laid out at Mount Wollaston were those of William Coddington and Edmund Quincy; at Muddy River, of John Cotton and William Colburne.[23]

The case of Salem was exceptional. Since it was founded before the great exodus, it lacked originally the usual organization with home lots and field divisions, and the first settlers seem to have squatted on the land, with the hope of securing legal titles later. When at last the General Court gave legality to the town and each

---

[20] *Ibid.*, p. 61.
[21] Lewis Henry Steiner, *The History of Guilford, Conn.*, p. 49.
[22] *Records of Newton and Cambridge*, I, pp. 21, 127.
[23] *Second Report*, Record Commissioners of City of Boston, 1634–60, p. 6.

head of a family received a home lot and ten acres of arable, it was a matter of great difficulty to find fertile fields near at hand, for like Boston the village was situated upon a promontory. The Committee at last was forced to select a site across the North River for the North Field which could be reached by a long detour, while they located the South Field south of the river and Gardner's Brook. Although both locations were inconvenient, it was possible for the owners to cultivate their lots and still reside in the village. But when it was discovered that the most fertile lands were to be found at a distance of several miles up the Bass River to the north and to the west in the locality of the present Danvers, it was decided to make grants, not in lots, but in farms, so that the proprietors could dwell upon them. "Although their land be none of the best, yet beyond those rivers is very good soil where they have taken farms, and get their hay and plant their corn," wrote William Wood. "There they cross these rivers with small canoes which are made of whole pine trees, being about two foot and a half over and twenty foot long." [24] Thus at a very early date economic necessity forced this town to relinquish the ideal of social unity and submit to the "scattered seating" which the ministers so greatly dreaded.[25]

A second cause for distintegration at Salem was the opportunity held out to the people to participate in fishing. "Marvill Head is a place which lyeth four miles full south of Salem and is a very convenient place for a plantation, especially for such as will set upon the trade of fishing," wrote William Wood, in *New England's Prospect*. "There was made here a ship's loading of fish last year, where still stand the stages and drying scaffolds; here be good harbor for boats and safe riding for ships." Like the Salem farmers, the Marblehead fishermen found it necessary to live where they did their work and not in the distant village. It would have been hard indeed for them, after bringing their catch safely into harbor and spreading their nets to dry, to trudge or even row in small boats all the way to Salem before reaching the comforts of warmth and food.

[24] William Wood, *New England's Prospect*, p. 48.
[25] *Essex Institute Historical Collections*, XLI, pp. 133, 307; James D. Phillips, *Salem*, p. 71.

The satisfaction which came with the ownership of land was tempered for the Puritans by the costliness of fencing it in. It was the custom to make the owner of every home lot responsible for the fence,[26] and many were the regulations requiring it to be "good and sufficient" with five rails or "double rail and poles," etc. Yet it was frequently a strain upon "brotherly sweetness," when Deacon Smith's cows got into Master Jones' lot and trampled his wheat. Such a serious case might even come before the Selectmen. So it was a saving in labor as well as in tempers when it was ordered that for the common fields the whole, and not the lots of which it was composed, should be fenced. Of the common fence each man took his share both in its construction and maintenance. At Enfield the proprietors of each field met to "appoint men amongst themselves to see that each man's proportion of fence be done and made according to order." [27] Should one dispute their decision or plead that they had assigned him a greater part than his just share, he could bring the matter before the Selectmen. It was a temptation to allow the fence to fall into disrepair at times, but once a rail was broken or a post began to rot, the negligent owner was certain to be called to account by the town fence viewers.

In adopting the manorial field system, the New Englanders were concerned with its social rather than its agricultural bearings. So far as one can judge from the records they did not require each lot holder in a given field to plant in any one season the same crop.[28] Thus the Enfield South Field, or the North Field, may well have presented a variegated appearance, with strips of Indian corn alternating with strips of rye or strips of wheat. Nor is there any evidence to show that each lot was devoted exclusively to one crop in any season. It is possible that Master Grubb preferred to raise wheat in part of his lot, corn in another and barley or rye in a third. Had the strip holder been subject to a common regulation it would have received frequent notice in the town records, either in specific rules or in orders to meet especial needs, or in the protests of dissatisfied proprietors. Yet the records are almost universally silent in this matter. Even had it been left to the group

[26] *Second Report*, Record Commissioners of City of Boston, 1634–60, p. 4.
[27] *History of Enfield, Conn.*, I, p. 100.
[28] James D. Phillips, *Salem in the Seventeenth Century*, p. 93.

of owners of a field to decide upon one crop for all, some record of their meetings would almost certainly have been preserved.

The settlers were delighted to find that many of the fruits and vegetables, the seed of which they had brought with them, throve in the New England soil, and that they could make good use of others indigenous to the country. "Our turnips, parsnips and carrots are here both bigger and sweeter than is ordinary to be found in England," wrote Francis Higginson. "Here are stores of pumpions,* cucumbers and other things of that nature I know not. Plenty of strawberries in their time, and penny-royal, winter savory, carvell and water-cresses, also leeks and onions." So every man laid out his garden in his home lot, perhaps back of his residence, and planted it with the pumpkins, beans, squashes, cabbages, turnips, onions, radishes, beets, spinach, and other vegetables which contributed so greatly to the health and enjoyment of his family.

Nearby was the orchard. "Our fruit trees prosper abundantly," John Josselyn reported. "Apple trees, pear trees, quince trees, cherry trees, plum trees, barberry trees. I have observed with admiration that the kernels on suckers planted produce as fair and good fruit, without grafting, as the tree from whence they were taken. The country is replenished with fair and large orchards." [29] The apple tree especially prospered so greatly in New England soil that it became very important in the economy of the people, and was a source not only of food, but of drink as well. Especial inducements were held out for the erection of cider mills, and in Woodbury the town fathers went so far as to give permission to a certain Matthew Minor to set up one in the highway.[30]

The English were prompt in making Indian corn their most important crop. No doubt they deemed it prudent to trust to a grain which had proved itself by experience, yielded more per acre than the European grains, gave a more uniform return, ripened early and was more hardy in resisting sudden changes of weather. A glimpse in the barn or perhaps in the loft of the typical settler would have revealed, side by side with a few bushels of oats or rye or wheat, a bountiful supply of maize, while a visit to his lots in the

* Pumpkins.
[29] Massachusetts Historical Society *Collections*, 3rd Series, III, p. 337.
[30] William Cothren, *History of Ancient Woodbury, Conn.*, p. 148.

common fields would have shown acre after acre devoted to this staple.[31] Yet the settlers were by no means negligent of the grain to which they and their fathers before them had been accustomed, bringing with them wheat, rye, oats and barley for a trial in the New England soil. When the first wheat crop proved a failure in the sandy soil of Plymouth, the Pilgrims were dismayed at the prospect of doing without English bread. But trials elsewhere proved more successful, so wheat soon attained an importance in the farm economy second only to that of Indian corn.[32] Even when the blast visited New England to destroy whole fields of wheat and force the people to increase their acreage of rye, wheat continued an important part of the food supply. Barley was grown for beer, which was a standard drink, and oats for provender for horses.[33]

Not infrequently the town made individual grants of land to encourage the planting of hops. In 1648 Milford voted Sergeant Camp as much land adjoining the Housatonic river as he needed for this purpose, which explains why this neighborhood for so many years was called the Hop Garden. One suspects that the Sergeant came from Roydon, or some other hop-growing center of Essex, and had only to practice in the New World the art he had learned in the Old.[34] Individual owners also often set aside a tract for flax to supply the village linen-makers, and occasionally hemp for naval stores,[35] while the celebrated Connecticut broad-leaf of today was foreshadowed by the little tobacco plots of the seventeenth century.

The settlers continued to use the agricultural implements which they had brought with them from England until they wore out, and then turned to the village blacksmith to fashion others just like them. Yankee inventiveness had not yet applied itself to producing machinery with which to plow, harrow, harvest and thresh, so that the work was done with infinite toil with the aid of hoes, scythes, sickles, spades and pitchforks. The Pilgrims had

[31] Percy W. Bidwell and John I. Falconer, *History of Agriculture in the Northern United States*, pp. 9, 10.
[32] *Ibid.*, p. 12.
[33] *Ibid.*, p. 14.
[34] Leonard W. Labaree, "Milford, Conn.," Tercentenary Commission, *Historical Publications*, Nos. 1–10, p. 13.
[35] James D. Phillips, *Salem in the Seventeenth Century*, p. 100.

no plow for twelve years after their first landing, while in 1636, so it is stated, there were but thirty plows in all Massachusetts. Not infrequently a town would pay a bounty to a farmer to buy a plow on condition that he use it, not exclusively for his own needs, but for the community as a professional plowman. Crude contrivances these early plows were, whose wooden shares barely scratched the earth despite their four oxen and two drivers.[36]

The settlers brought their cattle with them, for the Indians had none. The ocean voyage, when the animals were penned in a restricted space, where they were bruised and perhaps fatally injured by the tossing of the little vessels, often caused severe losses. If we may believe Captain John Smith, seventy of the two hundred cattle taken on board the Winthrop fleet of 1630 died on the way over. Yet the cattle increased rapidly in New England, so that in a few years all save the poorest family had one or more cows.[37]

Though the arable land was divided among the individual owners, it was the custom to hold the pasture in common. A town meeting in Cambridge in March, 1679, ordered that "all the common land on the south side of the highway leading from Captain Cooke's mill to Watertown . . . be fenced in for a cow common for such as have cow rights recorded in the town book." The fence was to be "done with a stone wall, either a whole wall or a half wall and something of brush upon it and not be less than four foot high."[38] To save the back-breaking labor of erecting walls such as this, the townsmen when possible availed themselves of necks of land, such as Great Neck in Dorchester, or the bend of a river, where the cattle would be confined in part by the water.

The driving of the cattle to and from the common pasture was an important function. Daniel Bosworth, the Ipswich driver, collected his charges "half an hour after sunrise" to start for the field north of the river, and returned with them "a little before sunset." Later Henry Osborn was appointed to aid him and one of the two was to blow a horn at the meeting-house green in the morning as a signal for the assembling of the herd.[39] Enfield employed four

---

[36] Thomas Lechford, "Note Book," *American Antiquarian Society Transactions*, VII, p. 101.

[37] *Records of the Town of Cambridge*, 1630–1703, p. 19.

[38] *Ibid.*, p. 246.

[39] Joseph Barlow Felt, *Ipswich*, p. 44.

field drivers.[40] Salem's driver, Roger Morie, received £40 for eight months' work, out of which he had to pay his two assistants.[41]

The cattle fared well in the summer, but the native wild rye and broom straw, upon which they subsisted in winter during the early years of the settlement, provided poor nourishment. Captain John Smith warned the Puritans that unless they laid by a store of hay, they would lose many of their cows "and hazard the rest," should the weather become exceptionally cold.[42] That this advice was timely is shown by the fact that not infrequently the farmers found it necessary to slaughter part of their cattle to save them from starvation. With the importation of English grasses, especially blue grass and white clover, this danger passed. "Our English clover grass sown thrives well," declared Josselyn.[43]

Though pasture was in common, the meadow was divided, each proprietor receiving his share under the rule of estates and persons. In Enfield the Committee ruled that the meadow should be proportioned to the home lots, four acres to a thirty or forty acre home lot, five acres to a fifty acre lot and six acres to a sixty acre lot. One half of each man's meadow was to adjoin his home lot "where it falls it can be so" and the other half "in the next convenient place."[44] The Enfield meadow lots which adjoined the home lots no doubt were on the bank of the Connecticut River, but there was also "meadowish land or meadow swamp," known as Buckhorn Meadow or Spring Brook Meadow, on the south side of Scantic River. The meadow divisions, like those of the grain fields, were not fenced, but were marked with stones after the custom of the manor. The displacing of these markers from time to time by floods and tides has been the cause of much confusion and many long disputes. Professor Leonard W. Labaree relates that at Milford one family discovered that it had long been gathering its crop of hay five-eighths of a mile from its original holding.[45]

If the village, with its home lots, its gardens and orchards, the

[40] History of Enfield, Conn., I, p. 348.
[41] James D. Phillips, Salem in Seventeenth Century, p. 90.
[42] Massachusetts Historical Society Collections, 3rd Series, III, p. 37.
[43] Percy W. Bidwell and John I. Falconer, History of Agriculture in the Northern United States, p. 20.
[44] History of Enfield, Conn., I, pp. 18, 61.
[45] Leonard W. Labaree, "Milford, Conn.," Tercentenary Commission, Historical Publications, Nos. 1–10, p. 6.

grain fields, the cow commons, the meadows, formed the visible
body of the town, so the congregation constituted its soul. To the
settlers the spiritual side of their community was all-important.
This it was which had led them into the wilderness, which shaped
their characters and their thoughts, which determined the form of
their social and economic life. So one of their first steps upon
reaching the site of their new homes was to form themselves into
a Church. This they did by assembling in some open space, perhaps a long-disused Indian cornfield, to enter into a solemn
covenant with God.

The Pilgrims before them had formed such a covenant when
they reverently repeated the one sentence: "We covenant with the
Lord and with one another and do bind ourselves in the presence
of God to walk together in all His ways, according as He is pleased
to reveal Himself unto us in His blessed word of truth." [46] The
Northampton covenant was more detailed: "Disclaiming all con-
fidence of, or any worthiness in, ourselves either to be in covenant
with God or to partake of the least of His mercies, and also all
strength of our own to help covenant with Him . . . by relying
upon His tender mercy and gracious assistance of the Lord through
Jesus Christ, we do promise and covenant in the presence of the
Lord, the searcher of all hearts, and before the holy angels and
this company, first and chiefly to cleave forever unto God with
our whole hearts as our chief, best, yea and only good, and unto
Jesus Christ as our only Savior, husband and Lord and only high
priest, prophet and king. . . . We promise and engage to observe
and maintain . . . all the holy institutions and ordinances which
he hath appointed for His Church. . . . And as for this particular
company and society of saints, we promise . . . that we will cleave
one unto another in brotherly love and seek the best spiritual good
each of other, by frequent exhortation, seasonable admonition and
constant watchfulness according to the rules of the Gospel." [47]

For the covenant the congregations claimed direct authority
from the Bible and direct precedent in the history of Israel. "The
covenant of grace is the very same now that it was under the

[46] Williston Walker, *A History of the Congregational Churches in the United
States,* p. 104.
[47] James R. Trumbull, *History of Northampton, Mass.,* p. 106.

Mosaical dispensation," stated William Brattle. "The administration differs but the covenant is the same." [48] Urian Oakes in his election sermon of 1673 emphasized God's covenant with the Children of Israel and how they were led into the land of promise.[49] When this question was considered at a general convention of ministers at Boston, on May 26, 1698, all save one agreed that "under the Old Testament the Church was constituted by a covenant." [50] But whatever its origin the covenant gave to each congregation an independence which would have been impossible had it been constituted by any superior human authority. It made of it, in the words of Ames and Cotton and other Puritan leaders, a Church responsible not to bishops or assemblies, or kings, but to God Himself.

The new congregation next proceeded to elect a minister. Had the settlers brought a minister with them it was nonetheless necessary to elect him, since they did not constitute a Church until they had made a covenant. Thus John Davenport, who led a company of Puritans to Quinnipiac to found the New Haven colony, was not elected pastor until his flock constituted themselves into a congregation some months after their arrival.[51] The election at Salem in July, 1629, was preceded by "a solemn day of humiliation," after which the "company of believers . . . joined together in covenant," chose, by the votes of the male members, Endicott to be their minister.[52]

The election of a minister was followed by the ordination. This, according to the *Platform of Church Discipline,* drawn up in 1646, was merely "the solemn putting a man into his place and office in the Church, whereunto he had right before by election; being like the installing of a magistrate in the commonwealth. . . . Ordination doth not constitute an officer, nor give him the essentials of his office." [53] It was, however, a solemn ceremony, marked by prayer, preaching and the laying on of hands by the elders or by neigh-

[48] William Brattle, *MS Sermons,* Harvard College Library.
[49] Urian Oakes, *New England Pleaded With.*
[50] Increase Mather, *The Order of the Gospel,* p. 39.
[51] Benjamin Trumbull, *History of Connecticut.*
[52] Williston Walker, *A History of the Congregational Churches in the United States,* p. 104.
[35] P. 35.

boring ministers. "Reverend Mr. Josiah Sherman was ordained pastor of the First Church for Woburn," Reverend Ebenezer Bridge wrote in his diary, in 1755. "I began with Prayer. Reverend Mr. Dunbar preached of fellowship. It was a very large assembly." [54]

When there was no minister at hand, the company made haste to secure one, offering every inducement in their power, for they considered it a serious peril to their souls to be without a spiritual guide. The town of Enfield, in 1693, promised "for the encouragement and settlement of a minister . . . a house lot containing twelve or thirteen acres of land and fourscore acres of field land . . . and a sufficient quantity of meadow near and convenient," six acres of which was to be fenced in and cleared at the common expense, "some for plowing and some for pasture," and also to erect "a sufficient dwelling" and plant an orchard. All this was to be done "on condition a minister come here and settle five or seven years' time . . . to carry on the work of the ministry." The town also engaged to pay him "fifty and five pounds yearly . . . in good and merchantable currency." [55] These good people had to labor for their salvation in a very practical way, for the clearing, plowing and fencing of the six acres was "done in a general way," each man giving his work when summoned.

It was characteristic of the intimate relationship of State and Church in New England that the congregation elected the minister and the town paid his salary. This was a matter of no great concern when all or almost all the people in a community were among the elect who could participate in the Lord's Supper, but when the number of those excluded became appreciable, murmurings of discontent became widespread. Increase Mather, in *The Order of the Gospel,* printed in 1700, denied that all who were taxed to pay the minister's salary should have the privilege of voting in his election. "It would be simoniacal to affirm that this sacred privilege may be purchased with money," he contended. "If all that contribute have power to vote . . . then many women must have that privilege." Since the choosing of their own pastor was an invaluable privilege for the Churches, "for them to give

---

[54] MSS. *Diary of Ebenezer Bridge,* II, p. 258. Library of Harvard College.
[55] *History of Enfield, Conn.,* I, p. 285.

or rather sell that privilege away to all that will contribute must needs be displeasing with the Lord." [56]

The maintenance of the ministers was all that could have been hoped for. Many of them, in striking contrast to the underpaid clergy of colonial Virginia, not only had comfortable residences, one or more slaves as servants, and collected valuable libraries, but married and reared large families. It was no doubt inconvenient for these good men when they were interrupted in the writing of the next Sabbath Day's sermon to receive the payment of this neighbor or that, perhaps a few bushels of Indian corn, perhaps a calf, perhaps a bit of newly woven cloth, but the scarcity of coin made this necessary. Urian Oakes, in his election sermon of 1673, complained of "the slenderness and shortness of the ministers' maintenance," and commiserated their "family straits and difficulties," [57] but it is obvious that most of them fared excellently when one considers the financial status of their charges.

The ministers wielded a powerful influence, not only moral and intellectual, but political. Many of the original group were graduates of Cambridge, some were distinguished scholars, all were men of piety and religious zeal and several had been acknowledged leaders in the Puritan wing of the Anglican Church. In after years the memory of these men was revered and their praises constantly sung by their successors. "Though the reformed Churches, thus fled into the wilderness, enjoyed not the miraculous pillar, we enjoyed many a person in whom the good spirit of God gave a conduct unto us, and mercifully dispensed those directing, defending, refreshing influences, which were as necessary to us as any that the celebrated pillar of cloud and fire could have afforded," wrote Cotton Mather in his *Magnalia.*[58]

Nor were the ministers of the second and third generation greatly inferior to the "fathers." The founding of Harvard College made it possible for young men to attain the education deemed so essential for spiritual leadership, while the respect in which their calling was held attracted the best talent the colonies afforded. In the words of Urian Oakes it was unthinkable to have "any piece

[56] Increase Mather, *The Order of the Gospel,* p. 68.
[57] Urian Oakes, *New England Pleaded With,* p. 11.
[58] Cotton Mather, *Magnalia* (Hartford, 1820), I, p. 226.

of ignorance . . . dispense the oracles of God and the holy mysteries of religion." [59]

If the responsibilities of the minister were great, so was his authority, and bold indeed was the person who ignored his frowns or his admonitions. Not only might he become a black sheep, suspected and censured by the elders and the congregation, but he might suffer excommunication, with the loss of the privileges, political as well as religious, which were attached to Church membership. But it must not be forgotten that the minister was not only the moral censor and preceptor for his flock, but their loving father as well. It has become too much the custom to regard him as a cold, unrelenting person, who forgot the frailties of the human body in his zeal to save the soul. One has only to become well acquainted with some of these men to discover under the outward cloak of ecclesiastical harshness the devoted husband, the kind father, the sympathetic pastor. But they did not think it kind to condone sin, to temporize with error, or to permit assaults upon what they firmly believed to be God's Church on earth. The men who were instrumental in sending innocent persons to the scaffold as witches or in subjecting the Quakers to cruel persecution acted from a strong sense of duty, were performing a most unpleasant task because they believed with all their hearts that they were carrying out the divine will.

Second to the minister in influence and power were the elders. Under the *Platform of Church Discipline,* the elders were "to open and shut the doors of God's house, by the admission of members approved by the Church, by ordination of officers chosen by the Church and by excommunication of notorious and obstinate offenders"; to call the congregation together, to serve as "guides and leaders," to "prevent and heal such offences in life or in doctrine as might corrupt the Church," to "feed the flock of God with a word of admonition," to "visit and pray over the sick brother."

As the Congregationalists followed the Brownists in Church localism, so they imitated the Presbyterians in discarding democracy for the rule of Church officers. "Church government or rule is placed by Christ in the officers, who are therefore called rulers,"

[59] Urian Oakes, *New England Pleaded With,* p. 30.

stated the *Platform of Church Discipline*. "The Holy Ghost frequently, yea always, where it mentioned Church rule and Church government, ascribeth it to elders, whereas the work and duty of the people is expressed in the phrase of obeying their elders." Thus the Church was to consist of two parts, "some that are governors and some that are governed in the Lord." "The rule and government is appropriated to the elders by the appointment of Jesus Christ," declared Urian Oakes.[60] The New England "fathers" declared that the will of Christ ought to govern the congregations, but, as Henry Martyn Dexter puts it, "they quietly assumed that Christ would reveal His will to the elders, but would not reveal it to the Church members." [61] If any objected to the decisions of the officers, he was stigmatized as "factious" and "obstinate" and his vote "nullified."

Of great importance, also, was the Church teacher. This officer is not to be confused with the schoolmaster, for his duties were concerned entirely with matters of religion. "The office of pastor and teacher appears to be distinct," states the *Platform of Church Discipline*. "The pastor's special work is to attend to exhortation, and therein to administer a word of wisdom; the teacher is to attend to doctrine and therein to administer a word of knowledge." When John Cotton was made teacher of the Boston congregation he was elected by "erection of hands." Then Mr. Wilson, the pastor, demanded of him if "he did accept of that call?" When he had answered in the affirmative "the pastor and the two elders laid their hands upon his head and the pastor prayed. . . . Then the neighboring ministers, which were present, did at the pastor's motion give him the right hand of fellowship." [62]

Of less importance in the congregation than the pastor, the teacher and the elders was the deacon. This officer was to "receive the offerings of the Church, gifts given to the Church and to keep the treasury of the Church and therewith to serve the tables . . . as the Lord's table, the table of the ministers and of such as are in necessity to whom they are to distribute." Although the *Church Discipline* is thus clear as to their duties, it leaves us in doubt as

[60] Urian Oakes, *New England Pleaded With*, p. 53.
[61] H. M. Dexter, *The Congregationalism of the Last Three Hundred Years*, pp. 428, 429.
[62] John Winthrop, *History of New England*, I, p. 136.

to the reasons why certain distinct qualifications were specified, such as their not being "double-tongued, not given to much wine, not given to filthy lucre." [63]

Discipline in the Church was every man's business. If Master Smith broke the Sabbath, it was the duty of his neighbors to reprove him; if Mistress Peters gossiped about her neighbors, it was certain to be reported to the elders. When one member committed an offense against another, the injured brother was to go to him privately to admonish him, and if this did not suffice, to return in the company of one or two others to renew the attempt. In case the offender still remained stubborn, the matter was brought to the attention of the elders, who were to place it before the Church. Should he now make a public penitent confession, he was declared "recovered and gained," otherwise he might be suspended from the fellowship of the Lord's Supper. Excommunication was reserved for exceptionally serious offenses such as heresy or blasphemy, for it was a severe punishment indeed. Not only was the congregation to refrain from communion with the culprit in spiritual matters, "but also from all familiar communion with him in civil things, further than the necessity of natural, domestical or civil relations do require, and are therefore to forbear to eat and drink with him, that he may be ashamed." [64]

It was fundamental to the congregational conception of a true Church that none but saints be admitted. "By saints we understand such as have not only attained the knowledge of the principles of religion and are free from gross and open scandals, but also do, together with the profession of their faith and repentance, walk in blameless obedience to the Word, so that in charitable discretion they may be accounted saints by calling, though perhaps some or more of them be unsound and hypocrites inwardly." But should hypocrisy be discovered the persons concerned were to be cast out, since their example endangered the sanctity of others and "a little leaven leaveneth the whole lump." [65] "Particular Churches ought to consist of saints and true believers on Christ," Increase Mather declared. "Nothing can be more fatal to

[63] *A Platform of Church Discipline*, p. 32.
[64] *Ibid.*, p. 50.
[65] *Ibid.*, p. 22.

the interest of religion than to constitute Churches of unsanctified members." [66]

This high standard was a matter of grave concern to the people, not only because Church membership opened to them the doors to Heaven, but also the doors to political freedom. As early as 1631 the General Court passed a law declaring that "to the end the body of the commons may be preserved of honest and good men . . . no man shall be admitted to the freedom of this body politic but such as are members of some of the Churches." [67]

This drastic restriction upon the franchise has been praised by some historians, severely criticized by others. "Not birth, nor wealth, nor learning, nor skill in war was to confer the power, but personal character, goodness of the highest type," wrote J. G. Palfrey. Others have pointed out that to deny any voice in the government to good citizens merely because they were not in full harmony with the established Church was inconsistent with human rights and English traditions. Yet the Massachusetts leaders clung to the law as the cornerstone of their structure, even though it brought upon them the anger of the King and endangered their charter.

It is well to bear in mind that Congregationalism, because of its emphasis upon localism, would have been hopelessly weak had it not had the full support of the civil authorities. Since the failure of the Puritans to gain such support in England was one of the major reasons for the migration, it follows as a matter of course that in their new commonwealth they would take measures to tie the government with the Church. And having decreed that the voters should be hand-picked by the Churches, they, as usual, turned to the Bible to justify it. It was "a divine ordinance that none should be appointed and chosen by the people of God magistrates over them but men fearing God (Ex. xviii: 21) chosen out of their brethren (Deut. xvii:15) . . . for the liberties of this commonwealth are such, as require men of faithful integrity to God and the State, to preserve the same. . . . In case worldly men should prove the major part, as soon they might do, they would as

[66] Increase Mather, *The Order of the Gospel*, p. 13.
[67] G. H. Haynes, "Representation and Suffrage in Massachusetts," p. 16, *Johns Hopkins University Studies in History and Political Science*, 12th series.

readily set over us magistrates like themselves such as might . . .
turn the edge of all authority and laws against the Church and the
members thereof." [68]

A·similar problem was solved by the Quaker government of
Pennsylvania in a different way. The Friends did not exclude other
sects from their colony, nor would they disfranchise any man
because of his religious views, but they kept their hold on the
government throughout the entire colonial period, by a system of
high property qualifications for voters and a rotten borough
system in the German and the Scotch-Irish districts. In both Massachusetts and in Pennsylvania the injustice done to individuals was
overlooked in the anxiety for legislation designed to safeguard a
distinctive type of religious commonwealth.

Since so much depended upon Church membership, the requirements and the methods of admission were matters of first
importance. "The officers are charged with the keeping of the
doors of the Church and therefore are in a special manner to make
trial of the fitness of such who enter," states the *Platform of
Church Discipline.* "Twelve angels are set at the gates of the
temple, lest such as were ceremonially unclean should enter." [69]
This was corroborated a half century later by Increase Mather:
"Men pretending to be saints . . . for Church fellowship should
be tried. . . . A rigid severity in examination is to be avoided
and such tenderness and charity ought to be used as that the
weakest Christians if sincere may be encouraged and gladly admitted. Yea, it were better to admit divers hypocrites than to keep
out one sincere child of God." [70]

Anyone desiring admission had first to satisfy the minister and
the elders "and other able brethren" that he was duly qualified.
This he must do in a series of conferences, in which he was inter-
rogated upon his beliefs, his understanding of Church doctrines,
his personal conduct and his willingness to join in the covenant.
"I discourse with David Butterfield about coming into full communion," Reverend Ebenezer Bridge wrote in his diary. Thus the
one sure means of enjoying Church fellowship, and also of gaining
the right to vote in civil elections, was for the candidate to con-

[68] Thomas Hutchinson, *History of Massachusetts*, I, p. 26.
[69] *Ibid.*, p. 43.
[70] Increase Mather, *The Order of the Gospel*, pp. 18, 19.

vince this small group of Church leaders that his life had been "subdued to some hope of godly conversation," and that he was in hearty sympathy with the established order.

When the elders recommended a candidate he was fairly certain of admission, even though he might be subjected to additional searching questions by the members of the congregation on the floor of the meeting-house. "No one can be admitted into the Church by the elders without the consent of the brethren," stated Increase Mather. "The community is concerned in who are admitted and therefore should concur therein." [71] One cannot doubt, however, that the real decision was made by the officers and that in this, as in so many other things, it was assumed that it was the duty of the congregation to concur. The machinery of admission was admirably fitted to accomplish the task for which it was devised, the task of keeping the unfit out of Church fellowship and depriving them of the power to undermine the religious and civil order.

The Massachusetts Puritans were severely criticized in England and Scotland for refusing Church membership to so many persons. Thomas Lechford claimed that "here are such confessions and professions required of men and women both in private and public before they are admitted that three parts of the people of the country remain out of the Church." This John Cotton denied. "In the Churches within the Bay we may truly say that for the heads of families those that are admitted are far more in number than the other. . . . Those that are godly they are all admitted to some Church or other." [72] However true this may have been in Cotton's day, the evidence tends to show that before the end of the century the freemen, who alone could vote for governor, deputies and magistrates, had become a minority in every town, while those who were not members of the Churches, but who were in sympathy with the established order, constituted a majority. A third group, consisting at first chiefly of servants and apprentices, but later recruited by newcomers and even the sons and grandsons of ardent Puritans, were hostile to the "theocracy." [73] They it was who protested against their disfranchisement and fomented what

[71] *Ibid.,* p. 23.
[72] John Cotton, *The Way of the Congregational Churches Cleared,* p. 70.
[73] Charles M. Andrews, *The Colonial Period of American History,* I, p. 437.

Urian Oakes called "jealousies and fears in the minds of men concerning magistrates and ministers" and "false alarms of danger that the people may believe that religion and liberties are at stake and in danger to be lost." [74]

The Puritan leaders made an effort to prevent the "unsanctified" groups from increasing in numbers, by restricting immigration. In 1636 the town of Boston ordered "that no townsmen shall entertain any strangers into their houses for above fourteen days, without leave from those that are appointed to order the town's business." Salem was even less hospitable, for there one Thomas Oliver was employed "to go from house to house about the town once a month to inquire what strangers do come to have privily thrust themselves into the town." To quicken his zeal, he was to be rewarded with the fines imposed on those who defied the ordinances against entertaining newcomers. [75] In 1637 the colonial government itself took this matter in hand by enacting a law making it illegal for a town "to receive any stranger resorting thither with intent to reside" without the consent "of some one of the Council or of two other magistrates."

Despite these regulations the influx of strangers continued. He who succeeded in convincing the authorities that he was of good conduct and orthodox in faith might purchase land from an old inhabitant or he might receive a grant of a home lot from the town committee. He must, however, build upon it within a year, or perhaps two years, or forfeit his claim. Gradually the laws became less rigid, the enforcement less severe. The need for labor made it necessary for the town to admit servants, apprentices and journeymen, and common justice made it difficult to eject them after their terms had expired. The port towns attracted many sailors, some of whom were far indeed from being "saints"; English shipwrights came over in response to the demands of the shipyards; when a town was without a physician, or a blacksmith, or a miller, the Selectmen were not apt to be overscrupulous about religious requirements if one presented himself.

In the first days of the settlement, however, there were few inhabitants who were not freeholders and few freeholders who

[74] Urian Oakes, *New England Pleaded With,* p. 41.
[75] *Essex Institute Historical Collections,* XLI. p. 308.

were not members of the Church. This gave a unity to the town which was gradually lost, but which, while it lasted, was the very cornerstone of the social, political and religious fabric. There was a clear distinction at all times between the congregation and the body politic, but this distinction was largely academic so long as the two bodies had an identic personnel. When the freemen assembled in the meeting-house for a town meeting they might, and usually did, concern themselves with religious as well as civic affairs.

It was the town meeting which determined the minister's salary, erected his house, levied tithes, built the meeting-house and allotted the seats in it. It could at one moment be considering the matter of the common fence around a grain field and the next, if it so chose, convert itself into the congregation without leaving the meeting room, and proceed to discipline wayward brothers or sisters, or elect a deacon, or receive a person to communion.

As the individual Church enjoyed a large degree of independence in ecclesiastical affairs, so the town meeting in local civic affairs was supreme. And like the Church, it drew its vigor as an institution in large part from the agricultural village, for the freemen, dwelling as they did in the shadow of the meeting-house, found it possible to constitute themselves a legislative body without the use of representatives. So, when they had been "warned" by the ringing of the bell or the cry of the watchman, they emerged from their houses, made their way down the street to the meeting-house, took their seats and at the order of the moderator proceeded with business. The election of the town officers was always a matter of great concern—the fence viewers, the treasurer, the field drivers, the hog reeves, the sealer of weights and measures, the town clerk, the constable, the tax assessors, the tithemen, the surveyors, the selectmen. Then Master Goodwin might rise and move that the meeting-house be reshingled, or that a bridge over the creek be repaired, or that a road be opened, or that a new division of arable be authorized, or that fifty acres of land be offered any wheelwright who would settle in the town.

In the interludes between town meetings business was carried on by the Selectmen or executive committee. This body enjoyed only delegated authority, usually clearly defined and restricted. "We desire of you and expect from you that you be careful to observe all those things that are enjoined you by the country laws that so the town may not suffer for your neglect therein," the Salem town meeting of January 19, 1678, warned their Selectmen. "You shall neither give, sell or exchange land belonging to the town. You shall raise no money nor town rate without the vote of the town. You shall no ways engage the town so as to bring them into debt except in case of necessity of the poor, etc. wherein we desire God to encourage you." Other towns were not quite so jealous of their committee, and it was not unusual for them to lay out highways, appoint cattle drivers, settle boundary disputes, regulate the cow common, fine persons for cutting trees illegally on the commons, assess tithes for the minister's salary, etc.

The voters in the town, hand picked, as we have seen, for their devotion to the Puritan Church, in the election of governors, assistants and deputies, consistently cast their ballots for godly and orthodox men. "Piety and the fear of God is the prime and principal qualification in those who sit chief in places of authority," insisted Joseph Belcher, in a sermon delivered at Dedham in 1701. "If those who are to govern God's people have not given up themselves to be governed by God, they are not like to devote themselves to the public good." [76] If a candidate for office received the support of the minister, the elders and other leaders in the congregation, he might reasonably count on election; if they threw their influence against him, his defeat was almost certain.

This was all in keeping with the congregational conception of the proper relationship of Church and State. "According to the design of our founders and the frame of things laid by them the interest of righteousness in the commonwealth and holiness in the Churches are inseparable," said Urian Oakes. "To divide what God hath conjoyned . . . is folly in its exaltation. I look upon this as a little model of the glorious kingdom of Christ on earth. Christ reigns among us in the commonwealth as well as in the Church and hath his glorious interest involved and wrapt up in the good of both societies respectively. He that shall be treacherous and false to the civil government, as he is injurious highly to the present

[76] Ebenezer Burgess, *Dedham Pulpit*, p. 127.

and succeeding generations, so he is guilty of high treason against the Lord Jesus." [77]

The words of Oakes were echoed from many pulpits. Samuel Torrey and Josiah Flint declared that "the godly and religious magistracy was "the highest and most saving good and end of government unto a religious people," since it could improve "civil authority in a way of full and direct subserviency unto the work of Christ." When the Quaker missionaries to New England denied the right of civil officers to interfere in matters of religion, the Puritan ministers declared that they were trying to undermine the very foundations of the Church. [78]

The relationship of Church and State is set forth in some detail in the *Platform of Church Discipline*. "It is the duty of the magistrate to take care of matters of religion. . . . The end of the magistrate's office is not only the quiet and peaceable life of the subject in matters of righteousness and honesty, but also in matters of godliness, yea, of all godliness. Moses, Joshua, David, Soloman, Asa, Jehoshaphat, Hezekiah, Josiah are much commended by the Holy Ghost for the putting forth their authority in matters of religion. On the contrary such kings as have been failing this way are frequently taxed and reproved by the Lord."

It was the duty of the magistrate to restrain and punish "idolatry, blasphemy, heresy, venting corrupt and pernicious opinions that destroy the foundation, open contempt of the word preached, profanation of the Lord's Day, disturbing the peaceable administration and exercise of the worship and holy things of God and the like." If any congregation should "grow schismatical, rending itself from the communion of other Churches" or "walk incorrigibly or obstinately in any corrupt way of their own," the magistrate was to "put forth his coercive power."

"Church government stands in no opposition to civil government of commonwealths, nor any way intrencheth upon the authority of civil magistrates in their jurisdiction, nor any whit weakeneth their hands in governing, but rather strengthening them, furthereth the people in yielding more hearty . . . obedience unto them, whatsoever some ill affected persons to the ways

[77] Urian Oakes, *New England Pleaded With*, p. 49.
[78] John Norton, *The Heart of New England Rent*, p. 29.

of Christ have suggested to alienate the affection of kings and
princes from the ordinances of Christ, as if the kingdom of Christ
in his Church could not rise and stand without the falling and
weakening of their government, which is also of Christ; whereas
the contrary is most true that they may both stand together and
flourish, the one being helpful unto the other in their distinct
and due administrations." [79]

That the New Englanders were correct in emphasizing the
importance of State support for congregationalism is shown by the
history of those groups who migrated to New Jersey, where the
provincial government regarded them with suspicion if not open
hostility. It was found impossible to enforce Scriptural law, to
exclude Anglicans, Quakers and other "heretics," to control education, to enforce the Sabbath law. The congregations at Newark,
Elizabeth, Woodbridge and elsewhere became isolated groups
tied together by no more substantial bond than fellowship and
the need for mutual support. In the end they went over to Presbyterianism, seeking in its centralized form of Church organization
the strength which in New England was had from the State. [80]

Nonetheless, in New England as in the mother country, a
degree of unity among the Churches was maintained by what
John Cotton called "brotherly counsel and help." Following
closely the precepts of Ames as set forth in *The First Book of
Divinity,* the *Platform of Church Discipline* declared: "Although
Churches be distinct and therefore may not be confounded one
with another, yet all the Churches ought to preserve Church
communion one with another, because they are all united in
Christ, not only as a mystical but as a political head. The communion of Churches is exercised in sundry ways: By way of
mutual care by taking thought for one another's welfare. By way
of consultation one with another . . . as the Church at Antioch
consulted with apostles and elders of the Church at Jerusalem.
. . . When any Church wanteth light or peace amongst themselves it is a way of communion of Churches according to the
word to meet together by their elders and other messengers in a

[79] *A Platform of Church Discipline,* pp. 60–63.
[80] T. J. Wertenbaker, *The Founding of American Civilization—The Middle
Colonies,* pp. 120–135; 172–5.

synod, to consider and argue the points in doubt or difference, and having found out the way of truth or peace to commend the same. . . . But if a Church is rent with divisions among themselves or lie under any open scandal and yet refuse to consult with other Churches . . . the state of such a Church calleth aloud upon other Churches to exercise a fuller act of brotherly communion, to wit, by way of admonition."

"Synods orderly assembled and rightly proceeding to the pattern we acknowledge as the ordinance of Christ, though not absolutely necessary to the being, yet many times through the iniquity of men and perverseness of times necessary to the well-being of Churches." The synod was "to debate and determine controversies of faith and causes of conscience, to clear from the word holy directions for the holy worship of God and good government of the Church, to bear witness against maladministration and corruption in doctrine or manners in any particular Church and to give directions for the reformation thereof."

Since it was impossible for entire congregations of all the Churches to meet "universally" in one place, they were to send delegates or messengers to represent them, preferably the ministers and elders. Yet any participant in the Lord's Supper was eligible. "The first synod . . . i.e. the synod at Jerusalem . . . did consist not only of elders but of brethren." In the synod which met at Boston in 1679, when some Churches sent only their pastors and elders, the synod would not seat their delegates until they had joined with them some of the brethren.[81]

The weakness of the Congregational synod grew out of the fact that final authority did not reside in it, as it did in the Presbyterian Assembly, but in the individual Churches. Perhaps it would not be inaccurate to compare the synod with the Congress of the Confederation, in that it was fundamentally an assemblage of delegates from independent or semi-independent bodies. Increase Mather, following in the steps of Ames and Parker, declared that the synod was not designed "to infringe the liberty of particular Churches, but from the Word of God to direct and strengthen them in the regular exercise thereof." [82]

[81] *The Necessity of Reformation*, Epistle Dedicatory.
[82] Increase Mather, *The Order of the Gospel*, p. 83.

Thus did the English who came to New England found their Wilderness Zion. Although it was a unique experiment, for nothing like it existed in England, the blueprints had been made long before the exodus began. As Winthrop and Cotton and others were the builders, so Ames, Parker, Baynes and before them Cartwright and Barrow and Browne were the architects. The semi-independence of congregations, the Church covenant, the fellowship of Churches, the synod, the close relationship of Church and State were not put into operation as afterthoughts; the Puritans came to America for the purpose of putting them into operation.

New England was not the extension of old England across the Atlantic, but rather an English conception which for the first time found its practical application. Even though the settlers brought with them the English language, English institutions, English architecture, continued to read English books, wear English clothes, use English implements, the structure of their society was essentially different from that of England. Nor did they constitute a cross section of the English people, since they came in large part from one part of the kingdom and from one religious group in that part.

They were separated from England, also, by the belief that they were God's chosen people, the especial object of His care and guidance, and that they had come to America in obedience to His direct command. "Hath God brought us into a wilderness and caused us to dwell alone and separated us for a peculiar people to Himself, that we should imitate the nations in their vanities?" asked Urian Oakes in rebuking the people for their "garish attire." "The ministers and Christians, by whom New England was first planted, were a chosen company of men," said Cotton Mather, "picked out of, perhaps, all the counties in England, and this by no human contrivance, but by a strange work of God upon the spirits of men that were, no ways, acquainted with one another—inspiring them as one man to secede into a wilderness, they knew not where." [83] The synod of 1679 declared that "the ways of God towards this His people are in many respects like unto his dealings with Israel of old. It was a great and high undertaking

[83] Cotton Mather, *Magnalia* (Hartford. 1820), I, p. 219.

of our fathers when they ventured themselves and their little ones upon the rude waves of the vast ocean, that so they might follow the Lord into this land." [84]

This belief that God had set them apart for His special guidance and blessing pervaded every phase of New England religious and political life and gave to it a purpose and strength lacking in many societies. "In the wilderness we have dwelt in safety alone, being made the subjects of most peculiar mercies and privileges. . . . The Lord hath planted a vine, having cast out the heathen, prepared room for it and caused it to take deep root. . . . We must ascribe all these things, as unto the grace and abundant goodness of the Lord our God, so to His owning a religious design and interest." [85]

And since the established order was the direct work of God, planned especially for His elect, to attempt to overthrow it, even to criticize it, was the most hideous of crimes. "When God hath so graciously settled us upon so good foundation, now to kick and spurn at our cornerstones, to be given to change and ready for innovations and alterations is great ingratitude to God," said Urian Oakes. Nor was it less a crime to rebel against the civil authorities than the Church, and he who did so would be proceeded against as a "rebel and traitor to the King of Kings, when He shall hold His great assizes at the end of the world."

As for religious toleration, it had never been a part of the Puritan plan in England or America. "This people bought the truth with realities: country, relations, estates, opportunities, as to the things of this life, realities, should we now sell it for that which is not bread, yea, for fanatic, erratic, worse than sick imaginations?" asked John Norton in explaining the persecution of the Quakers. The New England minister persecuted in self-defense, in defense of all that was dear in this world and the next.

Their Zion, the leaders hoped, would last for all time. In the remote part of the world where they had founded it the people would be comparatively safe from the errors which had surrounded them in England. And if Satan, in his malice against the elect of God, should plant false doctrines among them or send

---

[84] *Necessity of Reformation*, Epistle Dedicatory.
[85] *Ibid.*

false prophets from other lands to delude them, they had the means at hand to defend themselves. If doubts arose concerning God's wishes in any matter, they had the Bible, interpreted by learned ministers to guide them. They had the hearty support of a body of pious civil officers who were ever ready to put into effect the decisions of the clergy upon all matters of religion. The voters, in whom resided the final authority in civil affairs, were selected in large part because of their devotion to the established order in Church and State. Education, primary, secondary and advanced, was entrusted to safe hands, so that succeeding generations would be taught to follow in the paths they had marked out for them. With the Massachusetts Bay charter safely stored in the colony there was no immediate danger of interference by the King or the bishops. With the mass of the people residing in villages in the shadow of the meeting-house and under the eye of the pastors, they were protected against indifference to religion, moral lapses and false doctrines.

As Winthrop, Cotton, Norton, Shepard and the others viewed their Bible commonwealth, it must have seemed to them almost impregnable. Yet its disintegration began almost at once and within half a century after the settlement of the Bay, ministers were bewailing the degeneracy of the times, the laxity of the new generation, and the decay of religion. "He that remembers the good old spirit of those who followed God into this wilderness . . . cannot but easily discern a sad alteration," complained Urian Oakes in 1673. Among the many things of "solemn significance and awful import," in "the decaying and almost dying state of this poor country," only a few held open the door of hope.[86]

Although Oakes and other ministers exaggerated the situation in their efforts to stay the forces of change, they were quite correct in pointing out that the old order was giving way to the new. The religious zeal of the first settlers was less apparent in the second and third generation; the ministers commanded less respect and love; the charter upon which such hopes had been based had been annulled; the unity of Church and State in the towns had been disrupted, despite all the efforts to exclude them, strangers had come in who were out of sympathy with the Church and the

[86] Urian Oakes, *New England Pleaded With*, p. 27.

government; there were loud demands for the extension of the franchise; in Boston the organization of the Anglican congregation of King's Chapel bore testimony to the break which had been made in the wall of orthodoxy. Before the end of the seventeenth century, although the ideals of the founders still exercised a powerful influence upon the minds and hearts of the people, the experiment of a Bible commonwealth had definitely failed.

Chapter *III*

THE PURITAN SPIRIT IN LITERATURE

IT IS UNFORTUNATE that the spirit of American Puritanism found few media for its expression. There are no paintings which show the fears, the hopes, the temptations and moral victories of the Puritans, as the medieval paintings show the fears and hopes and triumphs of the medieval Christian. There is no great religious music to reveal the Puritan's soul, no ecclesiastical architecture to express in wood or stone his love of God and his hopes for happiness in an after life, no stained glass, no sculpture. But he did produce a literature which expresses accurately the spirit of seventeenth-century New England Puritanism.

It is true that the earlier writers, John Cotton, Thomas Hooker, Roger Williams, William Bradford, Nathaniel Ward, Thomas Shepard and many others were the products of England rather than of America. They had been educated in England, had formed their religious views there, had written or preached there, had taken part in the religious controversies there. The sermons or disputations or letters which they penned in their new homes in the forests of New England show no sharp line of demarcation from those written in England. Nonetheless, they belong to New England, since they express the spirit of the Puritan exodus and reflect the minds and the hearts of the men who founded the American Bible commonwealths. We can no more neglect their writings on the grounds that they are English than we can ignore the political services of John Winthrop or of John Endicott because they were Englishmen.

The theme of New England colonial literature is religion, especially the reformed religion of "God's people" in America. Most of the early histories were designed to prove that the movement across the Atlantic and the founding of the Puritan States were under the direct guidance of God; the poets, usually scorn-

78

ing such "earthly" subjects as love or the beauties of nature, dwelt upon the sinfulness of man and the horrors of Hell; the ministers in their sermons, pamphlets, letters and books not only pleaded for piety and orthodoxy, but, using the Scriptures as a guide, advised Governors, Magistrates and Deputies in vital decisions concerning civil and foreign affairs.

. So much has been said about the dryness and sterility of the outpourings of the New England divines that we are apt to overlook the fact that some of these men were trained orators whose sermons often moved their listeners to contrition, or fear, or hope, or indignation at the speaker's will. No doubt when some preachers entered the pulpit the congregations watched the sexton turn the hourglass with suffering resignation, but when certain others preached they hung upon their words as they painted the tortures of the damned, or dwelt on the infinite love of God for mankind, or lauded the founders or reproved their descendants for their lukewarmness in religion.

We are fairly well acquainted with these sermons. Some of the most important, especially the election sermons, were published; many more have come down to us in manuscript form.[1] As we read them we are surprised at the unevenness of their quality. Many are technical, dull, uninspiring; while others are excellent examples of Puritan pulpit oratory. And we must remember that words which seem lifeless on the printed or the manuscript page become alive in the mouth of a talented speaker. Nothing which John Cotton wrote explains the great influence of this leader among leaders; but could we have listened to one of his sermons, or follow his gestures, or see the earnestness and enthusiasm expressed in his ruddy countenance, or catch the charm of his voice, no doubt we would understand.

When he was a Fellow of Emmanuel College at Cambridge, Cotton had enjoyed a great reputation as a pulpit orator. Several times he preached before the whole university the kind of sermons then popular—pompous, learned, ornate, set off with epigrams and conceits. But when he went over to Puritanism, he became convinced that not only should there be reform in worship, but in the manner of delivering sermons as well. So one

---

[1] There are hundreds in the Pennsylvania Historical Society.

day, when Fellows and undergraduates crowded into ancient
St. Mary's to hear him, he surprised them with a plain Gospel
sermon, free of all false ornament and dramatic postures. The
hearers sat in silent disapproval, regretful that John Cotton had
grown Puritanical.[2]

We wonder, however, whether a modern audience, could they
have listened to his sermons, would not have considered the new
style more powerful than the old. If we may judge Cotton's Puritan delivery by its effect, it must have been effective indeed. "Mr.
Cotton had such an insinuating and melting way in his preaching
that he would usually carry his very adversary captive after the
triumphant chariot of his rhetoric," says William Hubbard.[3]
Another contemporary considered Cotton:

> "A man of might at heavenly eloquence,
>   To fix the ear and charm the conscience." [4]

We catch a bit of this charm in his farewell sermon delivered
at Southampton to a group of Lincolnshire Puritans who were
about to embark for Massachusetts. Choosing as his text "I will
appoint a place for my people Israel, and will plant them, that
they may dwell in a place of their own and move no more, neither
shall the children of wickedness afflict them any more, as before-
time," [5] he bade them be of good cheer as God was their leader.
"What He hath planted he will maintain. . . . When He pro-
miseth peace and safety, what enemies shall be able to make the
promise of God of no effect? Neglect not walls and bulwarks and
fortifications for your own defence; but ever let the name of the
Lord be your refuge. His word that made heaven and earth will
not fail till heaven and earth be no more."

The New England ministers of the second and third generation, in their efforts to preserve the structure of Church and State
established by the leaders of the great exodus, held up the image
of those leaders as the ultimate of human perfection. They were
intellectual giants, they were the most profound of scholars, they

[2] Cotton Mather, *Magnalia* (Hartford, 1820), I, pp. 234, 235.
[3] William Hubbard, *General History of New England*, p. 182.
[4] Nathaniel Morton, *New England's Memorial*, p. 254.
[5] II Samuel 7:10.

led saintly lives, they were the most eloquent of preachers. But even when allowance is made for this exaggeration, there can be no doubt that John Cotton, Thomas Shepard, Thomas Hooker and others were able men and moving public orators. They were so considered even before they left England.

Hooker was an intimate friend of John Rogers, of Dedham, and his preaching was obviously influenced by the vigorous style of the "roaring" lecturer. When he spoke his entire person was fired with enthusiasm, his eyes shone, his gestures were animated. He seemed to be inspired by the "divine relish" he had of his subject, "the sacred panting of his holy soul after the glorious objects of the invisible world." "The distinct images of things would come so nimbly, and so fitly into his mind, that he could utter them with fluent expressions." [6] Upon his listeners the effect was often overwhelming.

One day while he was lecturing at Chelmsford, "a profane person," who happened to be near, said to his companion, "Come, let us go hear what that bawling Hooker will say to us." So the group filed into church and took seats. But the man who had come to scoff remained to pray. Hooker's powerful preaching broke down his defenses and entered his heart. "He came out an awakened and distressed soul" and in the end arrived at a "true conversion."

On another occasion, when Hooker was preaching in the church at Leicester, one of the chief burgesses, who was hostile to his views, hired a group of fiddlers to play just outside in order to drown out his words. But he did not reckon with the determination of the minister and the lustiness of his voice. As the sound of his pleadings and warnings floated out of the door above the scrapings of the fiddlers, the burgess leaned forward to listen. What he heard filled him with such sincere penitence that he later called on Hooker who transformed him from persecutor into sincere follower.[7]

Like many other Puritan preachers, Hooker drew a vivid picture of the horrors of Hell. In his mind the lower regions was a place of brimstone and writhing sufferers, an everlasting Belsen.

[6] Cotton Mather, *Magnalia* (Hartford, 1820), I, p. 306.
[7] *Ibid.*, p. 307.

"Judge the torments of Hell by some little beginnings of it. . . . When God lays the flashes of hell-fire upon thy soul, thou canst not endure it. . . . When the Lord hath let in a little horror of heart into the soul of a poor sinful creature, how he is transported . . . roaring and yelling as if he were in Hell already. . . . If the drops be so heavy, what will the whole sea of God's vengeance be?"

Having thus warned his hearers of the Lord's wrath, he could strike an entirely different note by dwelling on the tenderness of His love. "As a wife deals with the letters of her husband that is in a far country, she finds many sweet inklings of his love and she will read these letters often . . . because she would be with her husband a little, and have a little parley with him in his pen, though not in his presence; so these ordinances are but the Lord's love letters."

But man, in his natural state as a partaker of Adam's sin, was completely lost in evil. "A man is wholly possessed with a body of corruption, and the spawn of all abomination hath overspread the whole man. . . . All noisome lusts abound in the soul and take possession of it and rule it and are fed there." As carrion crows feed upon the body of a dead sheep, "so it is with every poor, natural, carnal creature under heaven—a company of devils . . . prey upon the heart . . . and all base lusts crawl and feed." [8]

Preaching in the early years of New England may be termed the preaching of intense zeal. The ministers thundered out their warning with blazing eyes, they depicted Hell as a fiery furnace, they dwelt on the eternal joys of Heaven, they insisted upon the depravity of man. God was loving and forgiving, but His wrath was terrible. The listeners must have been elated at one moment, perhaps thrown into despair at the next. As we read one sermon after another, we imagine that we can hear Hooker or Shepard or Cotton pour out the burning words as the rough-hewn beams of the meeting-houses echoed to their pleadings and their warnings.

A century later New Englanders were to hear again the same type of preaching, when the Churches were shaken to their foundations by the Great Awakening. Had there been among the

[8] Moses Coit Tyler, *A History of American Literature,* I, pp. 193–204.

throngs who listened to George Whitefield, Gilbert Tennent or
Jonathan Edwards, a centenarian, he might have thought that
John Wilson or Thomas Hooker had returned to this life. The
New Lights, as they were called, like their Puritan predecessors,
preached "after the primitive manner," with exhortations, plead-
ings and threatenings.

If the first generation of New England preachers were constantly on the offensive, those of the second and third generations
took the defensive. They grieved that God's people, whom He had
singled out from the rest of mankind to lead into the new Israel,
should be yielding to the lusts of the world, should become cold
Christians. The prevailing note in the sermons of Urian Oakes,
John Higginson, Increase Mather and others was the decline of
religious life from the heights attained by the founders.

One of the ablest ministers of the second generation was John
Higginson, who came to Salem in 1629 with his father, the
Reverend Francis Higginson. This good man was possessed of the
piety, wisdom and charity which typified the Puritan at his best,
without the sternness and fanaticism which showed him at his
worst. "All men look on him as a common father," and on "old
age for his sake as a reverend thing," wrote John Dunton. "His
very presence and face puts vice out of countenance. . . . His conversation is a glimpse of heaven." [9] Higginson took charge of the
Church at Salem in 1659, and remained there for the rest of his
life, beloved and respected by all.

In 1663 he was chosen to give the Election Day sermon at
Boston. "The Cause of God and His People in New England" is
an earnest and at times eloquent appeal for a return to the piety
and zeal of the founders. God had been very good to his people, he
argued; it would be gross ingratitude and folly should they forsake Him. "The Lord may call this whole generation to witness
and say: 'O generation, see! Look upon your towns and fields, look
upon your habitations and great increase in the blessings of the
land and sea.' If the Lord should ask, 'Have I failed you?' you
needs must answer, 'No, Lord, Thou hast been a gracious God,
and exceedingly good unto thy servants, ever since we came
into this wilderness.'

[9] *Life and Errors of John Dunton*, I, pp. 127, 128.

"When the cause of religion seems ready to be spoiled by the professors of it . . . yet there is one in heaven that is able, and faithful, and watchful and skilful for the preservation of it. . . . Give unto the Lord the glory due unto His name, that He will not forget His people; He may afflict His people, and there may be need of it and cause for it, but He will not forsake His people." [10]

Not less distinguished than Higginson was Urian Oakes. This fiery little man, after graduating from Harvard, went to England in response to a call from the Church at Titchfield, in Hampshire. Though ousted from this charge in 1662 as a result of the Restoration, he remained in England until 1671, when he returned to Massachusetts as minister of the Cambridge Church. So great was the prestige which his work in the mother country won for him that he was accepted at once as one of the leading divines of the colony.

"Welcome, great prophet, to New England shore,
The fam'd Utopia of more famous More."

If we may believe Cotton Mather, Oakes was a pulpit orator of exceptional ability. "He was an Orpheus, that would have drawn the very stones to discipline; had Austin been here, he might now have seen Paul in the pulpit; indeed, he was, as one said, an uncomfortable preacher; why? he drove us to despair, namely, of seeing such another." [11] This opinion must have been shared by others, for within two years of his return he was asked to deliver two important sermons, one in 1672 before the artillery company of Boston, the other the next year before the governor and General Court.

Perhaps it was what Oakes saw in England which made him so ardent a defender of the old order in New England. "I profess I look upon the discovery and settlement of the Congregational way as the boon, the gratuity, the largess of divine bounty, which the Lord graciously bestowed upon his people that followed him into this wilderness." Although only four decades had passed since the founders set foot on Massachusetts soil, the tradition of perfection had already grown around them. In Oakes's

[10] John Higginson, *The Cause of God and His People*, pp. 10, 11, 24.
[11] Cotton Mather, *Magnalia* (Hartford, 1820), II, p. 98.

eyes they were the model of all that was good and saintly. "Those good people that came over showed more love and zeal and affectionate desire of communion with God . . . and the Lord did more for them than for any other people in the world, in showing them the pattern of His house and the true spiritual way of Church government. . . . God was certainly in a more than ordinary way of favor present with his servants in the laying of our foundations." [12]

If in his election sermon the "little giant" struck the note of conservatism, in his artillery company sermon, "The Unconquerable, All-conquering, and more-then Conquering Souldier," he was all belligerency. The view emphasized by the Quakers, that Christianity should be a religion of gentleness, meekness and peace, was not for him. The Christian, like the Israelite of old, must be a soldier in God's army. "He is a man of war from his birth. . . . He comes into the New World in his suit of armor, being vested with the graces of the spirit of Christ. . . . He hath his arms and weapons, offensive and defensive, to fight withal. He hath his soldierly qualifications and military accomplishments —courage, skill, patience, hope of victory . . . a soldier well appointed . . . to dispute it out with any adversary." [13]

When John Dunton visited Ipswich in 1686, he found there as minister of the First Church the able and beloved William Hubbard. "The benefit of nature and the fatigue of study have equally contributed to his eminence," Dunton wrote, "neither are we less obliged to both than himself, for he fully communicates of his learning to all who have the happiness to share in his converse. In a word, he is learned without ostentation and vanity and gives all his productions . . . a delicate turn and grace." This opinion of Hubbard's style has been shared by several modern critics, one of whom goes so far as to say that Hubbard's election sermon of 1676 was not surpassed by any work of the next two generations.[14]

After reading the sixty-three printed pages of this sermon we find it difficult to agree with this judgment. The style is clear and forceful but, save for an occasional burst of eloquence, is unin-

[12] Urian Oakes, *New England Pleaded With*, p. 44.
[13] Urian Oakes, *The Unconquerable, All-conquering, and more-then Conquering Souldier.*
[14] James Savage, *North American Review*, II, pp. 221–230.

spiring. Hubbard is at his best when he describes the suffering caused by King Philip's war, of which he later became the historian, or when he searches the soul of New England to find the reason for God's anger with his chosen people.

"May we not expostulate further with the Psalmist, the heathen are come into thine inheritance, O God, the dead bodies of thy servants, some of them have been given to be meat to the fowls of heaven, the flesh of thy servants to the beasts of the earth, their blood they have shed like water and there is none to bury them. How long, Lord, wilt thou be angry forever, shall thy jealousy burn like fire before thou pour thy wrath upon the heathen that have not and will not know thee nor call thy name? How hath the Lord covered our Sion with a cloud of his anger; how many men and women here present may say, 'We are the men and the women, the persons that have seen affliction by the rod of his wrath.' Here is one like old Jacob ready to say, his gray hairs will be brought down with sorrow to the grave, and that he shall go mourning thither after the children of his old age. There is another with Rachel, weeping and will not be comforted, because her children are not: they are gone into captivity never to return, or removed into the other world by the sword of the enemy. Doth not many an one sit solitary in widowhood, that before might take much content in the husband of her youth, that now, of the children which they brought into the world, have none to take them by the hand." [15]

Hubbard's compassion was not confined to God's elect but was large enough to embrace those who dissented from the established religion. "Doubtless as much tenderness as may should be used out of pity to the infirmities of men's understandings, seeing in many things we sin or offend all. The golden rule laid down by our Savior is of excellent use if it were attended. . . . And indeed it may seem not only unchristian, but very unreasonable, to deny that to others which our friends and ourselves have."

But the gentle Hubbard could be stern and unpitying on occasion. "Such opinions in doctrine . . . as are attended with any foul practical evils as most heresies have been, ought to be prohibited by public authority, and the broachers or fomenters of

[15] William Hubbard, *The Happiness of a People*, p. 50.

them punished by penal law, according to the nature of the offence, like other fruits of the flesh. God never appointed a sanctuary for Satan, nor city of refuge for presumptuous offenders. As Joab was taken from the horns of the Altar, whither he was fled, so let all such heretical transgressors, that fly for refuge to the altar of their consciences, seeing their practices and opinions argue rather fearedness than tenderness of conscience, and therefore such weeds justly deserve the exercise of his power to root them up."

In the galaxy of the Mather family one "lesser light" has been largely ignored. Perhaps it was because death overtook him at a comparatively early age, perhaps because he was overshadowed by Richard, Increase and Cotton, that we hear so little of Eleazer Mather. Yet, if we may judge from his sermons, he was one of the most appealing preachers in New England.

"Men, brethren and fathers, you had once another spirit," he said in a sermon delivered in 1678. "Oh! should I knock at your breast and ask, is the old zeal, love, heavenly-mindedness that was in his heart twenty, thirty years ago, is it there still? Are you the same men you were? Are you not strangely changed? Have you as much of God as you had? Hath not the world got something? Wife and children something? Trials and temptations of a new place, or hard beginnings got something? Oh! have you not lived to see much of your former life and godliness laid in the grave? Have you the same hearts you had? . . . Oh! recover, recover strength for your own souls' sakes, and for the sake of the generation that is to come after you." [16]

The Puritan spirit, so vividly reflected in sermons, found expression also in historical writings. It is remarkable that chronicles of the founding and early history of both Plymouth and Massachusetts Bay colonies have come down to us, each written by a prime actor in the events described. It was William Bradford, many times elected Governor of Plymouth, who wrote *The History of Plymouth Plantation,* and John Winthrop, father of Massachusetts, who wrote Winthrop's *Journal* or *History of New England.* One could wish that the redoubtable Captain John Smith, when he penned the story of the founding of Virginia, had

---

[16] Eleazer Mather, *A Serious Exhortation.*

been as modest, as accurate, as fair as the two Puritan historians. Bradford and Winthrop, even when describing controversies in which they themselves were involved, obviously though not always entirely successfully, attempt to be impartial. It would be too much to expect that Winthrop should present Anne Hutchinson's case against the colony in just its true light, or be quite fair to the Deputies when they were trying to curtail the power of the Assistants, yet he did his best.

And as truth makes their journals good history, so it makes them good literature. When Bradford describes the landing of the Pilgrims, simplicity makes his language eloquent. "Being arrived in a good harbor and brought safe to land, they fell upon their knees and blessed the God of heaven, who had brought them over the vast and furious ocean and delivered them from all the perils and miseries thereof. . . . Being thus passed the vast ocean and a sea of troubles . . . they had now no friends to welcome them, nor inns to entertain or refresh their weather-beaten bodies, no houses or much less towns to repair to, to seek for succor. It is recorded in Scripture as a mercy to the apostle and his shipwrecked company, that the barbarians showed them no small kindness in refreshing them; but these savage barbarians . . . were readier to fill their sides full of arrows than otherwise. . . . Besides, what could they see but a hideous and desolate wilderness full of wild beasts and wild men?"

Winthrop, too, was at his best when describing the perils and the sufferings of the transit of the Puritans to America. It was on April 9, 1630, that the lookout on the *Arbella,* which was off The Needles on its voyage to New England, spied eight sail astern. When word went from mouth to mouth that these vessels might be Spanish warships from Dunkirk, the little band made ready for battle. "Our captain caused the gunroom and gundeck to be cleared; all the hammocks were taken down, our ordnance loaded and our powder-chests and fireworks made ready for our landmen quartered with the seamen and twenty-five of them appointed for muskets. . . . The Lady Arbella and the other women and children were removed into the lower deck that they might be out of danger. All things being thus fitted we went to prayer upon the upper deck. It was much to see how cheerful and comfortable all the company appeared; not a woman or a child that showed fear . . . our trust was in the Lord of Hosts." Fortunately, the eight vessels proved to be friends, so that "fear and danger was turned into mirth and friendly entertainment." [17]

Though one of the chief merits of the works of Bradford and Winthrop is the absence of special pleading, the same cannot be said of Edward Johnson's *Wonder-Working Providence of Zion's Saviour in New England*. As the title indicates, this book was written with the purpose of proving that the migration of the Puritans to America and the founding there of the Bible Commonwealth not only had God's approval but was carried out under his special guidance and protection. A ship-carpenter, farmer, town official, pioneer, Johnson took up the pen to tell the world what to his mind was obvious: that the course of history in New England showed that God's hand was in every event. God it had been who had directed his servants to come to the New World, who had stilled the tempests so that they could cross the vast Atlantic in safety, who had prepared a place for them by sending a devastating epidemic to "remove" the Indians of eastern Massachusetts, who had brought prosperity to the infant colony, who had protected it from heresy.

It was in 1628, Johnson tells us, that God stirred up his servants "as the heralds of a king" to make this proclamation: "All you the people of Christ that are here oppressed, imprisoned and scurrilously derided, gather yourselves together, your wives and little ones, and answer to your several names as you shall be shipped for his service in the western world, and more especially for planting the united colonies of New England, where you are to attend the service of the King of Kings."

Johnson's interpretation of the Anne Hutchinson heresy was simple. It was merely the effect of "the cunning policy of Satan in that machiavellian principle, divide and overcome." So, "in the year 1636 the angels of the several Churches of Christ in New England, sounding forth their silver trumpets, heard ever and anon the jarring sound of rattling drums in their ears striking up an alarm to the battle, it being a frequent thing publicly to oppose

---

[17] J. K. Hosmer, ed., *Winthrop's Journal*, "History of New England," I, pp. 27, 28.

the pure and perfect truths of Christ (delivered by the mouth of his ministers) and that by way of question as the Pharisees, Sadducees and Herodians did Christ." [18] But God intervened to thwart Satan. "And here, Christian reader, the author . . . must mind thee of the admirable providence of Christ toward his New England Churches in preserving them from these erroneous spirits." [19]

If the *Wonder-Working Providence* interpreted history from the point of view of the New England Puritan in the age of triumph when God was still his father and protector, Cotton Mather's *Magnalia Christi Americana* gives us the outlook of the third generation, the generation which had grown cold to religion and which had felt the heavy hand of God's displeasure. And as the *Wonder-Working Providence* was the counterpart in historical writing of the sermons of Cotton, Shepard and Hooker, the *Magnalia* was the counterpart of those of Oakes and Hubbard. Mather's purpose in writing this hodge-podge of history and biography obviously was to glorify the founders of New England in order to bolster the order in Churches and State which they had established.

The preface, or attestation, written by John Higginson, gives the cue. "It hath been deservedly esteemed one of the great and wonderful works of God in this last age that the Lord stirred up the spirits of so many thousands of his servants to leave the pleasant land of England. . . . And that the Lord was pleased to grant such a gracious presence of his with them and such a blessing upon this undertaking that within a few years a wilderness was subdued before them and so many colonies planted, towns erected and Churches settled."

The *Magnalia* is divided into seven books. The first recites in outline the early history of New England, the second and third are devoted to short biographies of the founders, the fourth gives "an account of the university from whence the Churches of New England have been illuminated," the fifth sets forth the order of the Churches, the sixth gives "very many illustrious discoveries

[18] J. Franklin Jameson, ed., *Johnson's Wonder-Working Providence*, pp. 121, 124. [19] *Ibid.*, p. 136.

and demonstrations of the divine providence in remarkable mercies and judgments," the seventh tells of the "wonderful methods and mercies whereby the Churches have been delivered out of their difficulties."

On the pages of the *Magnalia* the early New England leaders become paragons of piety, learning, wisdom, heroism, eloquence. The opening paragraph of the biography of John Winthrop is typical. "Let Greece boast of her patient Lycurgus the lawgiver, by whom diligence, temperance, fortitude and wit were made the fashions of a therefore long-lasting and renowned common-wealth; let Rome tell of her devout Numa, the lawgiver, by whom the most famous commonwealth saw peace triumphing over extinguished war and cruel plunders, and murders giving place to the more mollifying exercises of his religion. Our New England shall tell and boast of her Winthrop, a lawgiver as patient as Lycurgus, but not admitting any of his criminal dis-orders, as devout as Numa, but not liable to any of his heathenish madnesses; a governor in whom the excellencies of Christianity made a most improving addition unto the virtues, wherein even without those he would have made a parallel for the great men of Greece or of Rome, which the pen of a Plutarch has eternized." [20]

And so it goes through the long list of New England notables —the courageous Bradford, the generous Winslow, the wise Bradstreet, the incomparable Cotton, the learned Norton, the eloquent Shepard, the pious Davenport.

Even more clearly than in these histories the Puritan spirit is revealed in three diaries—of John Hull, Samuel Sewall and Cotton Mather.

A zealous Christian, a successful merchant, an officer of militia, a skilled goldsmith, coiner of the famous pine-tree shillings, treasurer of Boston, Deputy in the General Court, the owner of large tracts of land, John Hull was one of the most prominent men in Massachusetts. None was better qualified than he to depict the life of the colony during the first half century of its history, and his *Diary* describes faithfully, though often more briefly than the reader would wish, the course of events—the departure of a ship for the West Indies, the illness of a neighbor, the death of a

[20] Cotton Mather, *Magnalia* (Hartford, 1820), I, pp. 108, 109.

minister, the keeping of a fast, the printing of Eliot's Indian Bible, the ruining of the wheat crop by the blast, the appearance of a comet in the sky, the hanging of a Quaker, the spread of epidemics.

In 1666 Hull wrote: "The Lord tried me by calling for my honored father, Robert Hull, home to himself. . . . Our private meeting kept at our house a day of humiliation to show their sympathy for me and to implore the Lord for his poor people here, to direct us and our rulers, etc. and for his poor, suffering saints in England. . . . I sent to England a considerable adventure in sundry ships, Master Clark, Master Pierce, etc. And it pleased the Lord all that I sent arrived safe and came to a good market. The Lord make me thankful." [21]

More interesting than Hull's *Diary*, more revealing of the spirit of American Puritanism, is the *Diary* of Samuel Sewall, the Pepys of Boston. Like Hull, Sewall was a combination of the hardfisted businessman, civic leader and religious zealot. At a time when the "oligarchy of saints" was beginning to weaken, he remained one of its most uncompromising and ardent defenders. A graduate of Harvard, a man of wealth, a successful merchant, deputy in the General Court, councillor, jurist, captain of the Ancient and Honorable Artillery Company, Sewall was eminently fitted to throw an intimate light upon the principal events of the town of Boston and of Massachusetts in the last quarter of the seventeenth century and the first quarter of the eighteenth.

One day we find Sewall arguing against the trade in slaves, the next relating the quarrels of Deputies and Magistrates, the next making entry of the hanging of Quakers. "Carried my wife to Dorchester to eat cherries, raspberries, chiefly ride and take the air; the time my wife and Mrs. Flint spent in the orchard, I spent in Mr. Flint's study reading Calvin on the Psalms." [22] The great fire of 1676 he ascribed to the carelessness of a tailor boy. Although fifty houses went up in flames, "God mingled mercy and sent a considerable rain, which gave check in great measure to the

---

[21] "Diary of John Hull," American Antiquarian Society *Transactions and Collections*, III, p. 156.
[22] "Diary of Samuel Sewall," Massachusetts Historical Society *Collections*, Fifth Series, V, p. 83.

otherwise masterless flames." [23] On May 13, 1685, he states that Cotton Mather was "ordained pastor by his father,[24] who . . . in his sermon spake of Aaron's garments being put on Eleazer." [25] He tells us that John Holyday was placed in the pillory for counterfeiting, that the General Court had named a day of fasting and humiliation because of the "afflictive sickness in many places," that the people of Boston ignored Christmas despite all that Governor Andros could do, that he read the eleventh chapter of Revelation during an eclipse.

Mather's *Diary,* though less important than Sewall's as a historical document, is an interesting revelation of Mather himself— his ambitions, frustrations, superstitions, self-deception, interest in science. "This day I likewise obtained of God that he would make use of me as of a John to be a herald of the Lord's kingdom now approaching, a voice crying in the wilderness for preparation thereunto." [26] On May 14, 1692, Mather shows himself in one respect far in advance of the group of which he was a leader, by preaching against the persecution of heretics. "A great and general assembly was now called. . . . By the providence of God it then fell unto me to preach. . . . I ran the hazard of much reproach by testifying in that sermon against the persecution of erroneous and conscientious dissenters by the civil magistrate." Yet the man who could write this jotted down a page further on: "The summer was a very doleful time unto the whole country. The devils, after a praeternatural manner, by the dreadful judgment of Heaven, took a bodily possession of many people in Salem and the adjacent places, and the houses of the poor people began to be filled with the horrid cries of persons tormented by evil spirits."

Despite the fact that frontier life is not favorable to the writing of verse, seventeenth-century New England produced a surprisingly large body of poetry. It was not to be expected that we should find a Milton or a Pope or a Spenser among the pioneers of the New World. Their task was to subdue, not to glorify, the

[23] *Ibid.,* p. 29.
[24] Increase Mather.
[25] "Diary of Samuel Sewall," Massachusetts Historical Society *Collections,* Fifth Series, V, p. 76.
[26] "Diary of Cotton Mather," Massachusetts Historical Society *Collections,* Seventh Series, V, p. 147.

vast wilderness; they were too busy clearing away trees, planting crops, building residences and churches, founding schools, to give expression to their thoughts and sentiments in verse. It was inevitable, then, as Cadwallader Colden wrote, that "no thing new and extraordinary in literature" from that part of the world was to be expected. Nonetheless, the New England poets, quite as accurately as the historians and the diarists, succeeded in reflecting the spirit of American Puritanism. Whatever may be the judgment of the literary critic as to the merits of the works of Michael Wigglesworth, Anne Bradford and others, to the historian they are invaluable documents.

But the first attempt at verse making was a complete failure. When the ministers decided to print a metrical version of some of the Psalms so that they could be set to music, it would have been well had they turned the task over to a real poet, even had it been necessary to send to England for him. Instead they divided the work among themselves. "It hath been one part of our religious care and faithful endeavor to keep close to the text," Richard Mather explains in the preface. "If, therefore, the verses are not always so smooth and elegant as some may desire or expect, let them consider that God's altar needs not our polishings." As a consequence, the creators of the *Bay Psalm Book,* in thus adhering so closely to the original Hebrew words, destroyed most of the beauty of the King James version.

It is hard to forgive these reverend gentlemen for what they did to the immortal Twenty-third Psalm:

> "The Lord is my shepherd; I shall not want.
> "He maketh me to lie down in green pastures: he leadeth me beside the still waters.
> "He restoreth my soul: he leadeth me in the paths of righteousness for his name's sake."

This the *Bay Psalm Book* turns into:

> "The Lord to me a shepheard is,
> want therefore shall not I.
> Hee in the folds of tender-grasse
> doth cause me down to lie:

To waters calm me gently leads
Restore my soul doth hee:
he doth in paths of righteousness:
for his names sake leade mee."

The ministers themselves realized that there was room for improvement and the employment of more "art." So the Psalms "were committed unto Mr. Dunster, who revised and refined this translation . . . with some assistance from Mr. Richard Lyon." [27] Fortunately, President Dunster proved a better poet than his predecessors, and *The Psalms, Hymns and Spiritual Songs of the Old and New* proved to be a decided improvement on the *Bay Psalm Book*.

It is regrettable that the period of triumph of New England Puritanism found little expression in verse. But the opportunity was lost for an epic poem on the theme of *Wonder-Working Providence*—the assembling of the saintly in England at God's summons, the stilling of the waves so that they might cross the ocean in safety, the conquest of the wilderness, the growth of prosperity, the victory over heresy.

The poet laureate of Puritanism in America, Michael Wigglesworth, though his most important works were written only three decades after the *Arbella* cast anchor in Boston harbor, belongs to the second period, the period of doubt and fear in which the old zeal was cooling and God's anger only too apparent. There is no note of elation in *The Day of Doom* or in *God's Controversy with New England*, but merely grim warnings that man is a lost being whom God alone can save from a fate terrible beyond imagination.

Yet Wigglesworth, himself, was no sadist, but "a little, feeble shadow of a man," an affectionate father, kindly teacher and dutiful pastor. His sole object in holding before his readers such macabre pictures of the after life was to warn them, and perhaps save some of them from eternal torture. No doubt, also, the fact that he was throughout life the victim of grief and pain added a touch of vividness to his pen.

[27] Cotton Mather, *Magnalia* (London, 1702), III, p. 100.

In *God's Controversy with New England* the poet begins with a description of primeval America:

> "A waste and howling wilderness,
>   Where none inhabited
> But hellish fiends, and brutish men
>   That Devils worshiped."

But with the coming of the Puritans:

> "Where Sathan had his scepter sway'd
>   For many generations,
> The King of Kings set up his throne
>   To rule among the nations."

When the Indians resisted, God broke them like vessels of clay:

> "Those curst Amalekites, that first
>   Lift up their hand on high
> To fight against God's Israel,
>   Were ruined fearfully."

With God's servants in control, with temporal blessings showered upon them, with the woods resounding to the praises of the King of Kings:

> "Our morning starrs shone all day long:
>   Their beams gave forth such light,
> As did the noon-day sun abash,
>   And's glory dazle quite."

But then came a dismal change:

> "The air became tempestuous;
>   The wilderness gan quake:
> And from above with awfull voice
>   Th' Almighty thundering spake.
> Are these the men that erst at my command
>   Forsook their ancient seats and native soile?

Whence cometh it, that Pride and Luxurie
  Debate, Deceit, Contention and strife,
False dealing, Covetousness, Hypocrisie
  (With such like crimes) amongst them are so rife
That one of them doth over-reach another?
  And that an honest man can hardly trust his Brother?"

After he had continued the recital of the sins of the New Englanders through a score or more stanzas, the poet has the Lord proceed from accusation to chastisement:

"Thus ceast his Dreadful-threatening voice
  The High & lofty-One.
The Heavens stood still Appal'd thereat:
  The Earth beneath did groane:
Soon after I beheld and saw
  A mortall dart come flying:
I lookt again, & quickly saw
  Some fainting, others dying." [28]

As *God's Controversy with New England* describes the terrors of the Lord's anger against living men, so *The Day of Doom* depicts the infinitely more horrible torments inflicted on the dead. It seems that Wigglesworth one night dreamed of the "dreadful day of judgement" and was thereby so "exceedingly awakened in spirit" that he decided to write a poem on the subject. Nine years later, when his work appeared in two hundred and twenty-four stanzas, it immediately became a best seller. "It pleased the Lord to give vent for my books and greater acceptance than I could have expected: so that of eighteen hundred there were scarce any unsold (or but a few) at the year's end," Wigglesworth tells us. About one of every twenty persons in New England purchased a copy of *The Day of Doom* and probably more than half the adult population read it. For those who missed the first edition there were more to come, six before 1701, one in 1701, one in 1711, one in 1715 and one in 1774.

It is impossible to exaggerate the immensity of the sufferings

[28] Massachusetts Historical Society *Proceedings*, 1871–73, pp. 83–93.

which the gentle little Wigglesworth, with the best of intentions, inflicted upon his fellows. The people who pored over the pages of *The Day of Doom,* so far from regarding the horrors it depicted as figments of the imagination, accepted them as only too real. These were not detached horrors at which they might shudder, but which they could never experience. There were few indeed in New England, even among the clergy themselves, who were without their moments of fear of hellfire. It was as though an audience today, while witnessing on the screen the torments of the victims of the German concentration camps, believed that the day might come when they themselves might become the victims. Of the thousands who read this book there must have been many who suffered with the damned, who in imagination felt the heat of the flames, received in their hearts the poisoned arrows, who raised despairing cries for relief to Heaven. So for a century Wigglesworth's nightmare continued to multiply itself.

The poem begins with a picture of the wickedness and indifference of the world before the day of judgment:

> "Wallowing in all kind of sin
>   vile wretches lay secure:
> The best of men had scarcely then
>   their Lamps kept in good ure."

Then, suddenly, men are awakened from their security by the day of doom, when the world is rent asunder:

> "They rush from bed with giddy heads,
>   and to their windows run,
> Viewing this light, which shines more bright
>   than doth the Noon-day Sun.
> Straightway appears (they see't with tears)
>   the Son of God most dread;
> Who with his train comes on amain
>   To Judge both Quick and dead."

Now that it is too late, despairing sinners repent and tremble before the avenging deity:

"Mean men lament, great men do rent
  their Robes, and tear their hair:
They do not spare their flesh to tear
  through horrible despair.

.   .   .   .   .   .

"Some hide themselves in Caves and Delves,
  in places under ground:
Some rashly leap into the Deep,
  to scape by being drown'd:
Some to the Rocks (O senseless blocks!)
  and woody Mountains run,
That there they might this fearful sight
  and dreaded Presence shun."

But flight and suicide alike avail nothing.

"Before his Throne a Trump is blown,
  Proclaiming th' Day of Doom:
Forthwith he cries, Ye Dead arise,
  and unto Judgement come.
No sooner said, but 'tis obey'd;
  Sepulchers open'd are:
Dead bodies all rise at his call,
  and 's mighty power declare."

When the hosts are assembled before the judgment seat, the
good are separated from the bad.

"At Christ's right hand the Sheep do stand,
  his holy Martyrs, who
For his dear Name suffering shame,
  calamity and woe.

.   .   .   .   .   .

"At Christ's left hand the Goates do stand,
  all whining hypocrites,
Who for self-ends did seem Christ's friends,
  but foster'd guileful sprites.

.   .   .   .   .   .

> "These numerous bands, with wringing hands,
>   And weeping all stand there,
> Filled with anguish, whose hearts do languish,
>   Through self-tormenting fear.
> Fast by them stand, at Christ's left hand,
>   The lion fierce and fell,
> The dragon bold, that serpent old,
>   That hurried souls to Hell."

Now follow the proceedings of the court. After the saints have their reward, judgment is passed on the wicked.

> "There Christ demands at all their hands
>   a strict and strait account.
>
>   .   .   .   .   .   .
>
> "All filthy facts, and secret acts,
>   however closely done,
> And long conceal'd, are there reveal'd
>   before the mid-day Sun.
>
>   .   .   .   .   .   .
>
> "They all draw near, and seek to clear
>   themselves by making pleas. . . ."

But all in vain. Their arguments are answered, their piety shown to be a sham. Some plead lack of opportunity to repent, some that they were misled by the example of godly men, some that they misinterpreted the Scriptures, others that they feared persecution. But all to no avail. Not even newborn babes are excused.

> "Then to the Bar, all they drew near
>   Who dy'd in Infancy,
> And never had or good or bad
>   Effected pers'nally."

They are told that Adam's sin was their sin.

> "He was design'd of all Mankind
>   to be a publick Head,
> A common Root, whence all should shoot,
>   and stood in all their stead.

He stood and fell, did ill or well
    not for himself alone,
But for you all, who now his Fall,
    and trespass would disown."

And so the despairing host was hurried away to the lake of brimstone.

"With iron bands they bind their hands,
    and cursed feet together,
And cast them all, both great and small,
    into that Lake for ever
Where day and night, without respite,
    they wail, and cry, and howl
For tort'ring pain, which they sustain
    in Body and in Soul.

"For day and night, in their despite,
    their torments smoak ascendeth.
Their pain and grief have no relief,
    their anguish never endeth.
There must they ly, and never dy,
    though dying every day:
There must they dying ever ly,
    and not consume away."

It is with relief that we turn from *The Day of Doom* to the verse of Anne Bradstreet. Mistress Bradstreet was the daughter of Thomas Dudley, steward for the Earl of Lincoln, so that 'she was brought up amid the refinements of a great English estate. At the age of sixteen she married Simon Bradstreet, and two years later, in 1630, accompanied him to New England, probably aboard the *Arbella*. There the young wife endured all the hardships and dangers of frontier life, made worse by constant moves —from Charlestown to Cambridge, from Cambridge to Ipswich, from Ipswich to North Andover. Thus the aristocratic Anne carried out her duties as the mother of eight children, within sight of the great forest and to the nightly howling of wild beasts. Fortunately, she loved the beauty of the woods, for she saw in it not only an evidence of God's handiwork but of His tender love and care.

We could wish that Mistress Bradstreet had left us more poems of the stamp of her *Contemplations*. This work, so expressive of the best in the religious life of New England, remains a lone star in an otherwise somber sky. That at least one of the leaders of the Churches was not entirely blind to the glories of creation we know from Cotton Mather's *Christian Philosopher.* "I hear a great voice from the starry Heavens ascribe the greatness to our God. Great God, what a variety of worlds thou created! How stupendous are the displays of thy greatness, and of thy glory in the creatures with which thou hast replenished the world." A passage such as this reveals what the New England poets might have accomplished had their eyes been turned upward rather than downward to the region of lost souls.

But Anne Bradstreet was more discerning. For her the cricket's song, the autumn woods, the rippling streams were but manifestations of God. Her *Contemplations* begin:

> "Some time now past in the Autumnal Tide,
> When Phoebus wanted but one hour to bed,
> The trees all richly clad, yet void of pride,
> Were gilded o're by his rich golden head.
> ·Their leaves & fruits seem'd painted, but was true
> Of green, of red, of yellow, mixed hew,
> Rapt were my sences at this delectable view.

> "I wist not what to wish, yet sure thought I,
> If so much excellence abide below;
> How excellent is he that dwells on high?
> Whose power and beauty by his works we know.
> Sure he is goodness, wisdom, glory, light,
> That hath this under world so richly dight:
> More Heaven than Earth was here no winter & no night."

It is difficult to believe that this God, the God of gentle Anne Bradstreet, is also the God of *The Day of Doom*. It would seem impossible to reconcile the "goodness, wisdom, glory, light" of

the one, with the action of the other in condemning new-born
babes to eternal torment.

The *Contemplations* continue:

> "Then higher on the glistering Sun I gaz'd,
> Whose beams was shaded by the leavie Tree,
> The more I look'd, the more I grew amaz'd,
> And softly said, what glory's like to thee?
> Soul of this world, this Universes Eye,
> No wonder, some made thee a Deity:
> Had I not better known, (alas) the same had I.

.   .   .   .   .   .   :

> "I heard the merry grashopper then sing,
> The black clad cricket, bear a second part,
> They kept one time, and plaid on the same string,
> Seeming to glory in their little Art.
> Shall Creatures abject, thus their voices raise?
> And in their kind resound their makers praise:
> Whilst I as mute, can warble forth no higher layes." [29]

Unfortunately, Mrs. Bradstreet's most ambitious work was
inferior in every respect to the *Contemplations,* for it was less
original, less sincere, less charming. Its title, which is a table of
contents and a publisher's "blurb" combined, will suffice to reveal
its character: "The Tenth Muse lately sprung up in America;
or, Several Poems, compiled with great variety of Wit and Learning, full of delight; Wherein especially is contained a compleat
discourse and description of the Four Elements, Constitutions,
Ages of Man, Seasons of the Year; together with an exact Epito-
mie of the Four Monarchies, viz. the Assyrian, Persian, Grecian,
Roman; Also a Dialogue between Old England and New, concerning the late troubles." Since in this ambitious work Anne
strays far away from the spirit of Puritanism and of America, we
need not concern ourselves with it further.[30]

All in all the literary effort of New England in the seventeenth
century was remarkable. Remarkable not for its quality, but for its

---

[29] John H. Ellis, ed., *The Works of Anne Bradstreet,* pp. 370–381.
[30] *Ibid.,* pp. 77–343.

volume, its vigor, its accurate reflection of the minds of the people. The intellectual life of Puritan America was unique in that it was creative. The tobacco planters of the James and the Potomac took keen pleasure in cultural things, in poetry, history, the classics, philosophy, but they wrote very little themselves; their interest was receptive rather than productive. But the Puritan mind was not content to receive only, it wished to share its thoughts, fears, beliefs with others. So New England gave us a Bradford, a Winthrop, a Cotton, a Hooker, a Wigglesworth, a Bradstreet. And without them our knowledge and understanding of the men and women who planted the banner of Calvin in the New World would be meager indeed.

Chapter IV

THE PURITAN SPIRIT IN ARCHITECTURE
AND MUSIC

ART, architecture, music, literature are windows to the soul of a people through which we may view what is going on within. To the historian it is not a matter of great concern whether the art is beautiful, or the music inspiring, or the literature profound, so long as they reveal the thoughts, aspirations, fears, joys, heartburnings of those who create them. How imperfect would be our understanding of Puritanism if we confined our attention to the writings of Baxter, Bayne, Ames and other theologians, while neglecting Milton and Bunyan; or if we pored over the sermons of John Cotton without knowing the character of the building in which they were delivered, or of the music which accompanied them!

The Puritan's insensibility to human beauty, both of form and character, his distrust of the charm of music or the loveliness of nature—a blue sky, a cloud bank, a shady grove, a quaint village —have been overemphasized. We are told that since his religion taught that man is vile and given over to evil and that all that seems pure and beautiful here on earth is but a snare to divert him from the supremely important task of preparing his soul for the next world, he had no conception of the nobleness of God's creation. Yet the Puritan was not fundamentally different from other Englishmen. He spoke the same language, lived in the same kind of house, ate the same food served on the same wooden or pewter plates, sat in the same kind of chairs, often read the same books, drove his cart down the same hedge-lined lanes, loved the same quiet villages, the same green fields. And after he had come to America it was with an aching heart that he paused in his work of clearing the forest, or building his crude house, or laying out his crop, to think of his far-off home in lovely England.

It is true, however, that the habit, inculcated by sermons, lectures and religious books, of constant contemplation of Heaven and Hell, tended to distract attention from things of this world. It is seldom indeed that we find in the sermons of the migrating ministers or in the writings of Bradford, Winthrop, Johnson and others any appreciation of the wild beauty of aboriginal New England. They tell us little of the misty marshes and sand cliffs of Cape Cod, of the vast green forests, of the song of the birds, the color of the wild flowers. To them the country was dark and forbidding, "the most hideous, boundless and unknown wilderness in the world." [1]

Though they based their society in large part upon the Old Testament and were so familiar with it that even the children could quote entire chapters, they failed to catch the poetic beauty, the love of life, the appreciation of nature so lavishly displayed in the Book of Psalms and elsewhere. One seldom finds in New England colonial literature an answer to the call of nature such as is made in the 104th Psalm: "The trees of the Lord are full of sap; the cedars of Lebanon, which he hath planted; where the birds make their nests: as for the stork, the fir trees are her house. The high hills are a refuge for the wild goats; and the rocks for the conies."

Whatever appreciation of art, architecture, music and literature the Puritan possessed was deeply affected only in those aspects which touched his religion. He had no objection to secular music, but he banned from religious services all instrumental music and with it the masterpieces of the medieval Church; his residence was not different from those of his neighbors, but he preferred to worship in a plain, barnlike building as unlike the time-honored Norman and Gothic churches of England as possible. As for the drama, he would have none of it.

To the Englishman of pre-Reformation times, his church building, whether a great cathedral or a village chapel, was almost as much a part of his religion as the Sacraments or the creed. The tower, perhaps built in the days of Edward III, perhaps of the Conqueror, typified his aspirations for an after life above the world; the stained-glass windows portrayed for him more vividly

[1] J. Franklin Jameson, ed., *Johnson's Wonder-Working Providence,* p. 248.

than could the written word the holy personages of the Christian religion—Christ, the Virgin Mary, St. Peter, St. Paul, and many others; the gargoyles which projected from the outer walls symbolized the ugliness of Satan and his imps; the representation of the cross by the conjunction of nave and transepts was a constant reminder of the sacrifice of the Savior; the carved marble of the capitals or the ceiling and the equally delicate carving of wooden altars or screens reflected the beauty of religion.

But with the advent of Calvinism much that had so long been venerated became abhorrent. The cruciform building typified no longer the cross, but "Popery"; the carved images of Christ and the saints savored of idolatry; the stained-glass windows, the ornate altars, the reredos, the screens, the vaulted ceilings, the tower with its pinnacles and its spire became for the Puritan mere devices to divert his mind from the sermon or God's ordinances. The change cost England dear in the loss of many priceless works of art, for during the period of Puritan supremacy iconoclasts shattered hundreds of images, altars, windows and screens. And though the Puritans continued, when they had the power, to worship in the church buildings erected by their ancestors, these buildings lost for them their consecrated character, became merely convenient shelters against wind and cold and rain. "In times of persecution the Godly did often meet in barns and such obscure places," wrote James Ussher, "which were indeed public because of the Church of God there; as wherever the prince is, there is the court, tho' it were in a poor cottage." [2]

"There is now no place which renders the worship of God more acceptable for its being performed there," declared Cotton Mather. "To prepare and repair places for the public worship . . . is but an act of obedience to him who requires worship from us . . . but the setting of these places off with a theatrical gaudiness does not savor of the spirit of a true Christian society. While the duties of divine worship are performing in any places, an agreeable reverence is to be maintained in those places, not so much out of respect for the places, as to the duties therein performed." [3]

When the Puritans who came to New England built their

[2] Quoted by Cotton Mather, *Magnalia* (London, 1702), Book V, p. 54.
[3] *Ibid.*

houses of worship, they refused to call them churches. "There is
no just ground from the Scriptures to apply such a trope as church
to a house for a public assembly," argued Richard Mather.[4] "A
house for the town" is what the people of Northampton called
their first meeting-house, a term which exactly describes its character and purpose. It was not invested with religious sanctity, was
never referred to as a "house of God," and was used not only for
public worship but for town meetings and other secular gatherings.[5] "Places intended for the sacred worship of God may law-
fully be put into any civil service for which they may be
accommodated at the times when the sacred worship is not there
to be attended," explained Cotton Mather.[6]

The European immigrant groups to North America almost
invariably built their houses as nearly like those to which they
had been accustomed in their native lands as pioneer conditions,
climate and materials permitted. The seventeenth-century Virginia cottage, the Pennsylvania German log house, the combination store and residence of New Amsterdam with its distinctive
gable end, all were importations. Even the so-called Dutch
colonial cottages of the lower Hudson region, which some writers
long thought a distinctive product of America, we now know to
be the Flemish peasant house. But the first settlers in New England had no precedent to guide them in the erection of their
meeting-houses. In England, when driven out of their ancient
church buildings, they had worshiped in private houses, or barns,
or in any available hall. There had been no opportunity for them
to develop a distinctive type of meeting-house.

Upon their arrival in America, they could hardly have had any
model before them, any preconceived ideas of what their houses
of worship should be like. So they erected a simple type of rectangular building, using for it wood hewn from the trees of the
forests which surrounded it. The first meeting-house in Billerica,
in Middlesex County, Massachusetts, was typical. In 1659 the
inhabitants agreed "that there shall be a meeting-house built this
winter following, thirty foot long and twenty-four foot wide and

[4] Noah Porter, *The New England Meeting House*, p. 5.
[5] James R. Trumbull, *History of Northampton, Mass.*, I, p. 25.
[6] Cotton Mather, *Magnalia* (London, 1702), Book V, p. 54.

twelve foot high, and the studs to be three foot asunder; the sides and ends shall be covered with boards and the roof with thatch." [7] The Medford meeting-house was similar. This little building, which was placed "on a rock on the north side of Woburn road," was "seven and twenty feet long, four and twenty wide and fifteen feet between joints." [8]

In time there evolved from these crude structures a new and interesting type of building. The size was increased, the body of the meeting-house became square or nearly so, the gable ends disappeared and the roof receded on all four sides to a central platform which was protected by a balustrade and surmounted by a cupola where hung the bell. The building was framed with heavy hand-hewn oak beams, the walls covered with shingles or weatherboarding and pierced by casement windows, the interior was plain, the exposed timbers and lack of ornamentation giving a barnlike impression. The pulpit, or perhaps the table behind which the ministers stood while preaching, was opposite the door and facing the bell rope which hung down from the cupola to the central aisle. Distributed over the main floor and in the galleries were the benches for the congregation, those reserved for the men on one side, for the women on the other.

Typical was the Woburn meeting-house erected in 1672. The building, which was forty feet square, framed with massive oak beams, lighted by casement windows with iron hinges and tiny leaded panes, and surmounted by a belfry, must have seemed more like a schoolhouse than a church. [9] Similar was the meeting-house of Lynn, save that the monotony of the roof lines was broken by the insertion of a gable on each of the four sides. The meeting-house at Hatfield also had "gable windows upon each square of the roof." This building was forty-five feet square, that at New London forty feet square, at West Springfield forty-two feet square. The town of Salem, in 1670, ordered "that there shall be a new meeting-house built . . . and that it be about 60 foot long, 50 foot wide and about 20 foot in the stud." [10] In some cases

[7] Samuel A. Drake, *History of Middlesex County*, I, p. 256.
[8] Charles Brooks, *History of the Town of Medford*, p. 325.
[9] Samuel Sewall, *The History of Woburn*, pp. 80–84.
[10] *Essex Institute Historical Collections*, XLI, p. 307.

when pioneer conditions made it difficult to secure a bell, it was customary to call the villagers together for religious or other meetings by beating a drum or sounding a trumpet.[11]

Most of these interesting old buildings, which two and a half centuries ago echoed to the sermons and prayers of the ministers, have long since fallen victims to decay or fire or have been pulled down to make room for more modern structures. Fortunately one of the most interesting, the "Old Ship" at Hingham, remains, a lonely survivor of a unique and almost forgotten architecture. As we stand before it, to view the simple proportions, the flaring eaves of the four-sided roof, the railed platform and the cupola, it seems to breathe the very spirit of early New England Puritanism. It requires no great stretch of the imagination to hear the little bell summon the people to worship, to see the sober men and modestly clad women pass in through the door, to listen to the preacher's warnings against the snares of Satan.

Since the four-square meeting-house made its first appearance years after the great exodus, it certainly was not brought over by the early settlers. Nor does it seem to have been an importation of later times. It is true that Edward Ward, a native Londoner, tells us that when he visited Boston in 1699 he found there "four churches, built with clap-boards and shingles, after the fashion of our meeting-houses." But it seems certain that when Increase Mather and Joseph Dudley and John Richards went to London they found there no counterpart to the "Old Ship" or the West Springfield meeting-house, or the "Old Tunnel" at Lynn. In fact, the London Congregationalists usually held services, not in buildings erected for the purpose, but in any house or hall they could purchase or rent. One group met over a tavern in the Founders' Hall, another occupied the Girdlers' Hall, a third the Brewers' Hall, a fourth the Plasterers' Hall. And when they did build, their meeting-houses, if we may judge from the records left us, did not tally with those of New England.[12]

The New England four-square meeting-house persisted well into the eighteenth century. In 1713, after the burning of the

[11] James R. Trumbull, *History of Northampton, Mass.*, pp. 120, 121.
[12] Walter Wilson, *The History and Antiquities of Dissenting Churches*, I, p. 462; II, pp. 294, 514, 525; III, p. 308.

meeting-house of the First Church of Boston, the congregation replaced it by another which conformed exactly to the traditional type save that its walls were of brick rather than of timbers covered with clapboards, its dimensions were larger, there were three tiers of windows instead of two, while sashes had taken the place of the old casements. But we recognize at once the square form, the roof, the platform, the cupola.

Nonetheless, decades before the cornerstone of the Old Brick was laid, forces were at work which were to bring about a changed conception of the character and function of the meeting-house and the introduction of a new type of church architecture. So long as the congregation and the town remained one and the same and the meeting-house served as a town hall as well as a place of worship, the people regarded the building with no espe-cial reverence. But when a second religious society split off from the first and the town erected a hall of its own, thus reserving the meeting-houses entirely for divine worship, they assumed a char-acter of sanctity. The ministers might combat this change, but in the minds of the people the meeting-house became not only a place in which to worship God, but a house of God.

Not infrequently when the congregation built a new meeting-house, the old one was abandoned or pulled down, but in many cases it continued to serve as a town-house or a school. It might be necessary to move it, or perhaps to take it down and use the solid oak beams in the construction of a new building, but it retained its original form. In this way the four-square type of achitecture in time became identified with the town-house and the school, and when the old building fell into decay, or burned, the structure which replaced it frequently was planned in a similar mold. The old town-house at Lenox, shown in Barker's *Historical Collec-tions,* published in 1839, with its roof receding on four sides to the balustraded platform and cupola, is clearly a descendant of the seventeenth-century meeting-house. Similarly the original acade-mies at Andover, Groton, Westfield, and elsewhere were cast in the old four-square model.[13]

At the same time, as sanctity gradually attached itself to the house of worship, it was called a church with increasing fre-

[13] John N. Barker, *Historical Collections,* pp. 80, 162, 285, 301, 391.

quency. We can follow the change in the *Diary* of Samuel Sewall. In the first years of this interesting document he referred to the place of worship almost invariably as the "meeting-house," but as the years passed the term "church" begins to appear. A friend made a request for "land to set a church on"; he fasted in the "new church"; he was indignant when Governor Andros demanded contributions for an Anglican "church" and retorted that the bishops would have been astonished had they been asked to assist in erecting "churches" in America. As early as 1676 Sewall spoke of the meeting-house as God's house,[14] a term which was echoed by a group of prominent ministers when they reproved members of the congregations for resorting "from the House of God into the tavern." [15]

It was inevitable that with the increasing tendency to regard the meeting-house as a church, sentiment would develop in favor of making it resemble a church. It was not to be expected that all the old prejudices would be discarded at once and the four-square meeting-house supplanted by Gothic structures with stained-glass windows, buttresses, ornate spires, carved woodwork and altars. Such a reversion to the things against which their fathers had revolted would have outraged all who nourished the old traditions. But should a new style of ecclesiastical architecture present itself, a style unostentatious and simple, yet making the church look like a church, the time was ripe for its adoption.

This style the New Englanders found in the churches with which Sir Christopher Wren had enriched London after the fire of 1666. Builders who came to Boston or Newport or New Haven to hang out their signs were well acquainted with St. James, Westminster; Christ Church, Newgate; St. Bride's, Fleet Street; St. Magnus, London Bridge; and undoubtedly tried to persuade the congregations to imitate these masterpieces. They could point out that the Wren churches were beautiful without being over ornate and were entirely unrelated to the Gothic which in the Puritan mind was associated with Catholicism and the Anglican bishops. These arguments were the more acceptable as they fitted in with

[14] "Diary of Samuel Sewall," Massachusetts Historical Society *Collections,* Fifth Series, V, pp. 29, 207.
[15] *A Testimony Against Evil Customs,* p. 2.

"OLD SHIP" MEETING HOUSE, HINGHAM, MASSACHUSETTS

OLD SOUTH CHURCH, BOSTON,
MASSACHUSETTS

FIRST PARISH MEETING HOUSE, COHASSET,
MASSACHUSETTS, BUILT 1747

the mood of the New England churchmen, who did not stop to consider the inconsistency of rejecting the ancient church architecture of Christian Europe while accepting a new style based on the architecture of pagan Greece and Rome.

So, turning their backs on the four-square meeting-house, of which Old Brick was the last conspicuous example, one congregation after another, as the need for a new building arose, went over to the "modern style." One of the first of the Wren churches was the New Brick Church on Hanover Street, which was erected in 1721, after plans drawn by a member of the congregation, Edward Pell. Unfortunately, Pell proved to be an architect of very limited ability and the building lacked the grace and the delicacy of St. Mary-le-Bow or St. Clement Danes. Yet the heavy tower, rising from the ground and abutting one gable end, with a smaller rectangular clock section at the top which in turn was surmounted by a cupola and small spire; the oblong form of the main body of the church; the three tiers of windows; the side porches; the classical ornamentation clearly mark it as belonging to the Renaissance school of architecture.

But it was Christ Church, erected by the Second Episcopalian congregation in 1723, rather than New Brick, which fixed New England ecclesiastical architecture for the next half century. Its distinguishing feature was the graceful square tower rising from the ground at the front of the building, which from its elevated position on Salem Street dominated all north Boston. To the people of the town, accustomed as they were to the plainness of the traditional meeting-houses, the arched windows, the ornate cornices, the quoins, the pilasters, the urns, the balustrades, the pinnacles must have seemed elegant indeed. It was from this tower that the flicker of lanterns gave warning to the patriots in 1775 that British troops were on their way to Lexington and Concord.

When the Third Church of Boston in 1729 decided to erect a new structure, the congregation followed closely the model of Christ Church. The South Church is by no means a replica of its Anglican sister, has its own individuality, but there is the same oblong form, the same arched windows, the same type of tower rising from the ground and cut by bands and pierced by windows, some round, some arched; a similar tower platform, a similar cupola, a similar spire. Old South is even richer in history than Christ Church. Here Joseph Warren, after climbing in through a window, harangued the people on the anniversary of the Boston Massacre; here assembled the throng which planned the Tea Party; here General Burgoyne's cavalry had their riding school.[16]

It must have been with admiration that ministers or elders from the smaller Massachusetts towns viewed Christ Church and Old South when religious or business affairs brought them to Boston. They, too, would like to replace their old four-square meeting-houses with a more ornate building, with a real church. In a few decades New England was dotted with little Wren churches, their white spires rising over the clustered roofs of the villages like fingers pointing to Heaven. But the country churches differed from Old North and Old South in that they were usually constructed of wood, not brick. In Boston it was possible to import the lime necessary for mortar, but the cost of transportation in wagons over the colonial roads was so great that for the inland town the use of brick was seldom possible. Perhaps this was fortunate, for wood lent itself well to the new architecture. Sir Christopher Wren himself would have been charmed had he visited New England to view these simple village churches with their white towers set off with arched windows, pilasters, pediments, cornices, balustrades, belfries and spires.

The Medford church, erected in 1770, was typical. It was sixty-six feet by forty-six, with two tiers of windows fitted with sashes, gabled roof, a rectangular tower at one end rising from the ground with the faces of a clock showing one on each side; at the top a balustraded belfry surmounted by a slender spire. On entering through one of the side porches, one found oneself facing the pulpit, which was raised about eight feet above the floor and fitted with a sounding board to make sure that no word of the interminable sermons was missed even by those who were "hard of hearing." In the gallery, which extended across three of the four walls, sat the choir and on the floor beneath were seats for the congregation, with the deacon's pew in front of the pulpit and a

[16] Justin Winsor, *The Memorial History of Boston,* II, pp. 516, 517.

row of pews higher than the rest lining each wall. The sexton sat near the preacher to attend his needs and turn the hour-glass.[17]

Religious thought, which in the seventeenth century thus developed one distinctive form of New England church architecture and in the eighteenth century converted the Wren church into another, had no such profound influence upon domestic architecture. The ministers and elders, of course, decried ostentation in building as they condemned extravagance in dress or drinking or even eating. To give too much thought to ornate doorways, or carved mantels, or fine cornices, or inlaid floors was wrong only in so far as it diverted one from religion. But what plainness there was was more the result of pioneer conditions than of Puritan austerity. The minister usually had the best house in town, a house which would have done credit to England itself. Later, when many families, having acquired wealth through trade, built fine mansions and furnished them handsomely, there seems to have been little objection from the clergy. So the Puritans, when they came to New England, while discarding the Gothic church architecture of their fathers, built their residences as nearly like those of East Anglia as local conditions permitted.

There is no evidence that the Pilgrims at Plymouth or the Massachusetts Bay settlers constructed log houses. The English, unlike the Swedes and Germans who came to the lower Delaware, the Lehigh and the Susquehanna regions, were unacquainted with this type of building, and it is unreasonable to assume that they hit upon it by chance or by invention the moment they set foot on American soil. The log cabin myth in New England, as in Virginia, persisted for decades, and many historians, without giving the matter sufficient thought, committed themselves to it. But in 1928 George Francis Dow pointed out that the belief that the early settlers built log cabins was entirely without historical proof, and eleven years later Harold R. Shurtleff and Samuel Eliot Morison, in *The Log Cabin Myth*, substantiated his findings.[18]

Like other Europeans, when they first established a beachhead

[17] Charles Brooks, *History of the Town of Medford*, pp. 336–338.
[18] The discovery of an old log house at Easton, Connecticut, which is thought to have been built in the fourth quarter of the seventeenth century, by no means alters these conclusions.

in the American wilderness, the Puritans threw up rude huts, or wigwams, to provide temporary shelter. But when the initial difficulties of settlement had been overcome, they began the construction of more substantial houses. And these houses were framed after the manner to which the housewrights had been accustomed in England. When Winthrop decided to move from Charlestown to Boston in 1630, "the frame of the governor's house," was taken to the latter place and set up there.[19] That the humbler type of house was also framed we may infer from a builder's contract drawn up in 1640, which specified that John Davys, joiner, was to construct for William Rix "one framed house" sixteen feet by fourteen.[20] At Plymouth Bradford tells us that the Pilgrims built a fort "with good timber," which seven years later a visitor described as a large square house, "made of thick sawn planks, stayed with oak beams."

Some of the first houses in New England were half-timbered. Since the Puritans had been accustomed to this method of construction, it was inevitable that they should attempt it in their new homeland. At Plymouth at least one building was wattled up with boughs, which undoubtedly were daubed over with clay. To this day an original outer wall of the famous old Fairbanks house at Dedham retains the "wattle and daub" with which it was constructed three centuries ago.[21] But the colonial carpenters were not long in discovering that half-timbering was impractical in a country where lime was difficult to procure, for without lime the daubing would not withstand the weather—the heavy rains, the bitter cold, the extreme heat of summer. From *Mount's Relation* we learn that a severe storm which swept New England in February, 1621, "caused much daubing of our houses to fall down." [22] The obvious remedy was to cover the walls, both timbers and daub, with clapboards, which were plentiful and cheap; a step which did not alter the form and proportions of the building, but transformed its outward appearance.

We have seen in the first chapter that the people of East Anglia were accustomed to two distinct types of houses—the one-and-a-

---

[19] *Charlestown Records*, p. 381.
[20] Thomas Lechford, *Notebook*, pp. 302, 303.
[21] *Historical Collections of the Topsfield Historical Society*, XXIX, p. 4.
[22] *Mount's Relation* (ed. H. M. Dexter, 1865), p. 79.

half story Flemish cottage and the two-story medieval house. Both were brought to New England. Of the former type was the house of Deputy Governor Symonds, built in 1638. "I am indifferent whether it be 30 foot or 35 foot long, 16 or 18 foot broad," wrote Mr. Symonds. "I would have wood chimneys at each end, the frames of the chimneys to be stronger than ordinary to bear good heavy load of clay for security against fire. You may let the chimneys be all the breadth of the house if you think good." [23] Build such a house of brick instead of wood and it would be quite as much at home in the English villages of Cottenham, or Grantham, or Braintree as in early Massachusetts; it would almost duplicate John Bunyan's cottage at Elstow.

An unfortunate incident at Topsfield in 1668 shows that the house of Jacob Perkins was also in the style of the East Anglian cottage. Perkins and his wife had gone to town, leaving their place in charge of the sixteen-year-old maid, Mehitable Brabrooke. Mehitable "went out of the house with her pipe and got upon the oven on the outside and backside of the house to look if there were any hogs in the corn, and she laid her right hand upon the thatch of the house to stay herself, and with her left hand knocked out her pipe over her right arm upon the thatch, on the eaves of the house, not thinking there had been any fire in the pipe." When smoke was seen curling up from the roof the wife of a neighbor came running, and looking in both fireplaces saw only a few embers under the great chimney. She also looked up into the loft chamber through the floor boards.[24] The old cottage could hardly be more vividly portrayed had we stood before it as this scene was enacted—the two rooms on the ground floor, the two fireplaces, the loft, the thatched roof, the wide cracks in the floor, the oven built partly outside the house.

However humble the Symonds house and the Perkins house may seem, they were too costly for the average early New England settler. So he built an East Anglian cottage with one instead of two rooms on the main floor, a small loft chamber and one chimney. Thomas Lechford in his *Notebook* records a contract for such a house to be built for William Rix in 1640. It was to be

---

[23] *Essex Institute Historical Collections*, XXXIII, p. 57.
[24] *Historical Collections of the Topsfield Historical Society*, XXIX, pp. 13, 14.

"16 foot long and 14 foot wide, with a chamber floor finished, . . . a cellar floor with joists finished, the roof and walls clap-boarded on the outside." The Joseph Goodhue house was eighteen feet square, the Ephraim Fellows house sixteen feet square, the Thomas Burnam house twenty feet square, the Obadiah Bridges house eighteen feet square, the Deacon Goodhue house sixteen feet square. One wonders how it was possible for the large New England families to find living space in these tiny houses in which the one lower room did service as kitchen, dining room and bed-chamber.

As time passed and the first difficulties of pioneer life had been overcome, the settler doubled the size of his house by adding another room and loft. In the original East Anglian Flemish cot-tage the chimneys were often, though not invariably, at the gable ends; but the New Englander, when he made the addition to his one-room house, built against the existing chimney, so as to make it serve all the rooms and also to conserve heat. Thus, unlike the Virginia cottage, which had chimneys at the gable ends, the Massachusetts cottage had but one chimney and that was located in the center. Also unlike the Virginia cottage, in which a hallway with front and back doors gave a cooling draft in the heat of summer, it had but a small entry in front of the chimney with a ladderlike stairway to the loft. Later still, when a large living room was added in the rear, thus making the house two rooms in depth, it so altered the proportions as to render it quite unlike its parent cottage of England or its sister cottage of Virginia. With its large expanse of roof, unbroken by dormers, its one, low, central chimney, its small casement windows, its battened door, it was as unique as it was charming.

Many of the houses were thatched. *Mount's Relation* states that in constructing the storehouse at Plymouth in 1621, "some gather thatch, so that in four days half of it was thatched." [25] As we have seen, the Jacob Perkins house was thatched. When the minister's house at Springfield was constructed in 1639, one John Alline contracted for the thatching, "he to undertake the getting of the thatch and all other things belonging to it, with lathing and nails,

[25] *Mount's Relation* (ed. H. M. Dexter, 1865), p. 72.

only the carriage of thatch excepted." [26] In fulfilling this contract Alline undoubtedly followed exactly the practice in England, gathering the rushes or straw into bundles about six inches in diameter, placing them in even rows upon the framework of the roof, one row overlapping the other, and fastening them securely with willow sticks.

The settlers were not long in discovering, however, that in America thatch was a great fire hazard. In England, where a week seldom passes without rain, the thatch remained permanently damp and so was not especially combustible; but under the New England sun it became tinder. Bradford tells us that in the winter of 1620–21, the storehouse at Plymouth, which had cost the Pilgrims so much hard labor, was set on fire "by a spark that flew into the thatch, which instantly burnt it all up." In 1630 Mr. Sharp's house in Boston caught fire which, "taking the thatch burnt it down." [27] The next year Thomas Dudley wrote that an order had been made that no man should cover his house with thatch, since thatch had been responsible for the burning of "divers houses." [28] Thus did the New Englanders learn in the hard school of experience that they must modify their architecture to suit conditions in America, that they could not use the thatch to which they and their fathers had been accustomed in England, just as they could not continue the time-honored half-timber construction. It was New England itself, its climate, the abundance of certain building materials and the scarcity or absence of others, which created colonial Massachusetts architecture.

Of this we have an interesting illustration in the early New England windows. It was the severity of the winters which dictated that they be small, for many were provided only with sliding shutters, which left the inmates the alternative of being cold or in the dark. "For windows let them not be over large in any rooms and as few as conveniently may be," Deputy Governor Symonds specified for his house, "let all have current shutting draw windows." [29] Even when casement windows were used, they

[26] Harold R. Shurtleff, *The Log Cabin Myth*, p. 98.
[27] *Essex Institute Historical Collections*, XXXIII, p. 50.
[28] *Historical Collections of the Topsfield Historical Society*, XXIX, p. 4.
[29] *Essex Institute Historical Collections*, XXXIII, p. 57.

too were small, for the hinged sashes, with diamond-shaped or oblong panes set in lead, were very expensive. In contracting for their meeting-house in 1645 the people of Springfield required the builder to "provide glass for the windows, if the pay he hath of the plantation will procure it." [30]

In its transit to New England the medieval two-story house of East Anglia was less altered than the Flemish cottage, those first constructed in the Massachusetts Bay region being as nearly like those of Ipswich or Ely or Harwich as the builders could make them. There was the same heavy timbering of hewn oak; the same wattle and daub; the same casement windows; the same entrance in the center of the front wall, in some cases through a small porch; the same gable ends superimposed on the long side of the roof; the same overhang of the second story in front and not infrequently of both second story and attic at the gable ends. The overhang, which was a device to give protection from the weather to the wall below, was even more necessary in New England than in the mother country in the early days when the settlers continued to experiment with half-timbering, for the rains were heavier and the daub easier to wash away. Later, when the builders began to protect the wattle and daub with clapboards, though the overhang was no longer necessary, it was continued merely as a matter of tradition. In some cases the overhang was set off at the corners with pendants or dewdrops, in others with ornate brackets. The tradition that the second story was made to project over the walls of the first for purposes of defense against the Indians is entirely without foundation. In fact, the overhang would have been a protection to a group of attackers when they closed in on the house and were trying to batter down the door or get in at the windows below.

Typical of the medieval East Anglian house were the Deacon Bridgham house, Boston; the Roger Conant house, Gloucester; the Ironworks house, Saugus; the John Ward house, Salem; the Peter Aspinwall house, Brookline; the Leonard house, Raynham, and the John Turner house, which was the nucleus of the famous House of the Seven Gables at Salem. Turner, who was a prosperous merchant, could afford a fairly pretentious house, so his plans

[30] Harold R. Shurtleff, *The Log Cabin Myth*, p. 99.

JABEZ WILDER HOUSE, HINGHAM, MASSACHUSETTS

MORTON–CORBETT HOUSE, IPSWICH, MASSACHUSETTS

KITCHEN OF THE CAPEN HOUSE, TOPSFIELD, MASSACHUSETTS

WHIPPLE HOUSE, IPSWICH, MASSACHUSETTS

MAJOR JOHN BRADFORD HOUSE, KINGSTON, MASSACHUSETTS

JOHN WARD HOUSE, SALEM, MASSACHUSETTS, SHOWING OVERHANG,
CASEMENT WINDOWS AND FRONT GABLES

called for a large hall or living room to the left of a central chimney, a kitchen to the right, two bedrooms on the second floor and an attic running the length of the building. The front door opened into a small entry, where the stairs, which began with a few steps, winding around the newel post, continued with a straight run and ended with another turn at the top. There were gables at each end of the house and two more springing from the front slope of the roof.

As Turner's ventures prospered, ventures which no doubt involved him in the molasses and sugar trade with the West Indies and the fish trade with southern Europe, he found need for a store where he could display for sale the cloth, clothing, kitchen utensils and other articles imported from England. So he built a lean-to in the rear, to which he transferred the kitchen, and converted the old kitchen into the store. Later, he made an addition in front of the hall, which contained a large parlor, the great chamber over it and the great chamber garret. This wing had double casement windows, overhang with dewdrops, and three gables. The secret staircase in the rear of the central chimney is supposed to have been built as a hiding place for any member of the family so unlucky as to be accused of witchcraft.[31]

The Bridgham house was quite similar to the original Turner house; its two stories with overhang and brackets, its four gables, one at each end and two in front, its massive central chimney stack clearly marking it as the East Anglian medieval house. But unlike the Turner house it had a front porch approached by several steps, with a small chamber above. The porch, though less common than in the early Virginia cottages, was by no means a rarity, as evidenced by the Springfield parsonage; the Beverly parsonage;[32] the William Curtis house, Roxbury; the Floyd House, Revere, and many others. In time, however, it disappeared, no doubt because the small front entry in front of the central chimney made it unnecessary as a protection against the New England cold and rains.

Typical, also, is the John Ward house, Salem. For over two centuries this quaint building stood at 38 St. Peter Street, when

[31] Caroline C. Emmeston, *The Chronicles of Three Old Houses*, pp. 7–17.
[32] *Essex Institute Historical Collections*, XXXIII, p. 52.

it was taken down and rebuilt in the grounds of the Essex Institute. A study of the framing and of old records made it possible to restore the house as it stood at the time of Ward's death in 1732, with the old staircase, the old chimney, the interior boarding, casement windows and the two front gables. When we view this fascinating old house, we people it with the pious men and the simply clad women of seventeenth-century Massachusetts, people of the stamp of the unfortunate Rebecca Nourse; the shipbuilder Daniel Bacon; Colonel John Hathorne, the leading citizen of Salem; the Reverend Samuel Parris. But if we in imagination strip the house of its coating of boards so that the frame is visible, our fancy takes us back another century or two to the houses of Cambridge or Lavenham or Lacock, from which it was descended.

There stood in Dock Square, Boston, from 1680 to 1860, a quaint building known as the Old Feather Store. The frame was of hewn oak and the walls covered with rough-cast cement mixed with broken glass. At one time the store was so close to the water that the prows of the vessels moored in the dock almost touched it. If this relic was typical of the seventeenth-century stores, the business section of Boston must have reproduced almost exactly those of the eastern English towns. If one, even today, strolls through some of the old streets of north Cambridge one will find houses so much like the Old Feather Store that they would have been quite at home in the Boston of two and a half centuries ago. The central chimney stack, the overhang for both second and third floors, the casement windows, the multiple gable ends, the hewn timber frames are almost identic.

The multiple gable is an architectural feature by no means unattractive in appearance and has the additional merit of providing for the attic floor greater space and more air, but it was not well suited to the New England climate. The settlers soon discovered that a large, unbroken expanse of roof afforded little opportunity for ingress to the bitter winds and shunted it upwards. The consequent discarding of dormers and front and rear gables made the attic rooms dark and gloomy, but this was more than compensated for by the protection it gave against drafts. When lean-tos were added, the back roof often extended from the ridge forty or fifty feet down to within a few feet of the ground.

Typical are the Fairbanks house at Dedham, the Whipple house and the Emerson house, Ipswich.

Upon entering one of these houses we find that Puritan plainness and pioneer conditions have not robbed the interior of charm. In the kitchen the huge fireplace spanned by a massive lintel and large enough for a six-foot log occupies half the wall. Here, suspended by pothooks and trammels, are kettles and pots, while on either side hang bellows, pans, skimmers, ladles and tongs. Unfailing, also, is the warming pan, the predecessor of the hot-water bottle, so indispensable for New England beds in the cold of the northern winter. The sunlight filtering in through the greenish little panes gives a subdued tone to the hewn oak ceiling beams, the vertical sheathing of the walls, the wide floor boards, the tableboard and benches, the mortar and pestle, the pewter candlesticks, spoons, flagons, saltcellars, cups and porringers, the wooden dishes and platters, the clay bottles and jugs.

In the hall or parlor, which often did duty not only as a reception room but a chamber, linen closet and armory as well, we find a table, stools, chairs, a feather bed, a spinning wheel, and a great chest for sheets, pillowcases, napkins and tablecloths. Hanging on the walls or resting in the corners are swords, muskets, rapiers, halberds, corselets and helmets. The chamber, especially if there is but one, is often so crowded with beds that there is little room for anything else save perhaps a chest or two.[33]

The loft, when not finished as an additional chamber, we find to be a storeroom, with barrels of Indian corn, bags of malt, packages of shot and powder, spinning wheels, a churn, a saw, a rake, an axe, an old trunk or two piled up in confusion.

Before the end of the seventeenth century Massachusetts had developed an architecture of its own. The Flemish cottage and the medieval East Anglian two-story house had both been so modified by local conditions as to make them distinctly American. The concealing of the wattle and daub by clapboards, the concentrating of all flues in one centrally located chimney, the lowering of ceilings, the discarding of dormers and front and rear gables, the substitution of roof shingles for thatch combined to give the houses of the farms and villages, as well as of Boston and

[33] *Essex Institute Historical Collections,* LI, p. 159.

Salem, individuality and charm. Had the region been cut off from the rest of the world, as the founders had desired, this type of architecture might have become in time more and more distinctive, more the product of New England.

But isolation had proved impossible. When Samuel Sewall or Increase Mather or Joseph Dudley went to England, whenever a New England ship's master put in at Bristol or London, they must have been interested in the latest changes in architecture. Some, at least, determined that they, too, when they built their own residences, would adopt the Renaissance style of Wren or Harksmoor. If the local builders of Boston or Salem had not kept pace with changes in England, it was not difficult to find some recent arrival who could boast that he was prepared to build "in the modern taste." In time every "carpenter" had to become acquainted with the architectural designs shown in the books of James Gibbs, Isaac Ware, Abraham Swan and Batty Langley, or go out of business.

The change was the easier in that the Renaissance architecture was in keeping with the spirit of the times. The New England of the early eighteenth century was quite different from the New England of John Winthrop and John Cotton. The pioneer days were past, wealth had been accumulated, there was a demand for more spacious, more dignified, more ornate houses. And this demand coincided with the loosening of religious austerity and less insistence upon plain living. It was not only the wealthy merchants who built stately residences after the Georgian mode, but some of the prominent clergymen as well. The three-story house of Cotton Mather, on Hanover Street, Boston, with its classic pilasters, its roof balcony, its elaborate front doorway set off by an ornate flat arch and transom, rivals those of Peter Faneuil, or Edward Bromfield, or John Mico.

In the New England Georgian house consideration of comfort yielded to dignity and elegance. The huge fireplace of the seventeenth century was replaced by one far smaller but set off by carved mantels; the ceiling, which formerly had been pitched low to conserve heat, was now raised to ten or twelve feet; the insertion of a hallway running through the house led to the substitution for the massive central chimney of end chimneys or chimneys between the front and rear rooms; in some instances the dormers reappeared.

Outwardly the new houses were models of correct proportion and balance. The old irregularities, inherited from the Middle Ages, in which dormers or gable ends or windows were inserted wherever utility demanded, were carefully avoided. If there were three windows to the right of the front door, there must be three to the left. The rooms on one side of the hallway had to balance those on the other. With this careful attention to form was coupled a restrained ornamentation borrowed from classical architecture—a Doric door, a Palladian window, flat arches over the windows, ornate cornices, often a roof balustrade to enclose what became known as the captain's walk, perhaps quoins at the house corners, perhaps pilasters.

In the larger ports, such as Boston, Salem, Portsmouth and Newport, where lime for mortar could be imported, the Georgian house was usually built of brick, but in the country villages and on the farms it was necessary to adhere to the old timber construction. Had anyone suggested to Sir James Gibbs or Batty Langley that their designs could be executed in wood, they would have been incredulous, yet the white wainscoted Georgian houses of rural New England have a charm which has made them famous.

Typical of the Boston Georgian houses was the Mico mansion. Sixty feet in length, three stories high, with two chimneys at each gable end, the windows set off with flat arches, it was one of the most imposing residences in the city. On the first floor were the hall or living room, a small library, the dining room and kitchen; on the second floor, the master's bedroom, two other bedrooms and a sitting room; on the third floor four "upper chambers."[34] John Adams, who dined in this house in 1766, thus describes it: "A seat it is for a nobleman, a prince. The Turkey carpets, the painted hangings, the marble tables, the rich beds with crimson damask curtains and counterpanes, the beautiful chimney clock, the spacious garden are the most magnificent of anything I have ever seen."

Pretentious though the Mico mansion was, it was surpassed in size and elegance by the Frankland house on Garden-Court Street

[34] James W. Spring, *Boston and the Parker House*, p. 65.

in the northern part of Boston. Three and a half stories high, its front door ornate with pilasters and pediment, the severity of its brick walls relieved by stone bands, the roof pierced by dormers, the two chimneys set at the gable ends, its fame spread to all parts of New England. "The parlors were ornamented with fluted columns, elaborately carved, and richly gilded pilasters and cornices; the walls were wainscoted and the panels embellished with beautiful landscape scenery; the mantel-pieces were of Italian marble, the fire-places of the finest porcelain. . . . The floor of the eastern parlor was laid in diamond-shaped figures and had in the centre a unique and curious tessellated design, consisting, it is said, of more than three hundred different kinds of wood." [35]

Less pretentious than the parlors of the Frankland house, but more representative of the typical interior of the early eighteenth-century New England residence, is the Newington room, shown in the American Wing of the Metropolitan Museum of Art in New York. The arched panels in the Queen Anne style, with crossed stiles beneath, the grooved pilasters which flank the fire-place, the shell cupboard, the beveled summer beam, the heavy though simple cornice, the sliding shutters, combine to make a delightful hall far more ornate than those of the seventeenth century.[36]

If we ignore the initial stage of the settlement, embracing the first few months or at most a year or two, when most of the people lived in dugouts or in wigwams, the history of New England domestic architecture in the colonial period falls into three distinct periods. The first was the period of transit, in which the carpenters and other workmen tried to build houses exactly like those to which they had long been accustomed, in exactly the same way, with the same tools and, so far as possible, with the same materials. It was the period of the Flemish cottage and the medieval two-story house, of half-timbering and wattle and daub, of multiple gables, of thatched roofs.

The second period was marked by the development of a distinct New England architecture under the influence of local

[35] Nason's *Life of Sir Charles Henry Frankland,* quoted by Justin Winsor, *The Memorial History of Boston,* II, pp. 519, 520.
[36] R. T. H. Halsey and Elizabeth Tower, *The Homes of Our Ancestors,* pp. 41–46.

conditions. The covering over of wattle and daub with clapboards, the substitution of shingles for thatch, the elimination of all unnecessary gables, the adding of the lean-to, the clustering of the rooms around one massive central chimney combined to transform the East Anglian house into a New England house. Had a builder of Ipswich, England, visited Ipswich, Massachusetts, in the second half of the seventeenth century, he would have found the architecture of the Whipple house and the Emerson house quite unfamiliar. He would probably have remained unconvinced had one explained to him that both were basically English and East Anglian, with no more than an American veneer.

The third period witnessed the gradual supplanting of seventeenth-century New England architecture by English Renaissance or Georgian architecture. The colonies, which were even more subject to the mother country in cultural matters than in government, could not resist the influence of a Wren or a Gibbs. From Maine to Georgia all former architectural concepts became out of date, and the medieval inheritance was discarded for the formality and the classic beauty of the new style. Yet the Georgian, like its predecessor, had to make concessions to local conditions—to the heat of South Carolina, the abundance of stone in Pennsylvania, the scarcity of lime in New England. So there developed several regional types—the Charleston Georgian, the Annapolis Georgian, the Virginia Georgian, the Philadelphia Georgian, the New England Georgian. The last named, whether expressed in the brick mansions of Boston or the white wood houses of village and farm, is quite as distinctive as the rambling old houses of the seventeenth century.

But in these developments religion seems to have had little influence. If in the early years of New England the houses were plain, it was because of pioneer conditions; if later they developed an individuality which made them distinctive of New England, it was climate and building materials which were responsible, not the principles of Puritanism; if in the eighteenth century the New England Georgian added a touch of dignity and stateliness to the cities and villages, it was the growth of wealth and the cultural influence of the mother country which were responsible, not the sermons of the clergy.

On music, as on architecture, Puritanism made an appreciable imprint only in so far as it affected religion. Unlike the Quakers, who regarded music with suspicion as a sensuous enjoyment which beclouded the realities of life, the Puritan had no serious objection to secular music. Oliver Cromwell kept an orchestra at his court, while during his Protectorate John Playford published no less than seventeen secular musical works.[37] In New England, though there is no evidence of an orchestra in the seventeenth century, we must ascribe the fact to pioneer conditions rather than to prejudice. A search through old inventories and wills shows that at least a few violincellos, guitars and virginals found their way across the Atlantic to add a bit of innocent pleasure to the homes of the New Englanders, and even so staunch a Puritan as Samuel Sewall could write: "I am a lover of music to a fault." [38]

Very different was it with sacred music. Long before the great exodus to New England the Puritans became convinced that instruments should have no part in church services. You could search the New Testament from cover to cover, they argued, without finding any mention of musical instruments in the services of the early Christians. It would not do to argue that because organs and viols and trumpets were not expressly forbidden their use was legitimate. Had God wanted them in His worship He would have said so.[39] It would be far better to leave instrumental music to the heathen who had originated it, for it had been Nebuchadnezzar, not St. Paul or Timothy, who worshiped to "the sound of the cornet, flute, harp, sackbut, psaltry, dulcimer and all kinds of music." [40]

It was in 1711 that Thomas Brattle, the well-known merchant and scientist, imported an organ for his own enjoyment and the entertainment of his friends. Two years later, after his death, it was found that he had left to the Brattle Street Church "a pair of organs, which he dedicated and devoted to the praise and glory of God." But in this, as in so many other things, Brattle was many decades ahead of his fellow Congregationalists, even those of the

[37] Percy A. Scholes, *The Puritans and Music in England and New England*, pp. 133, 144.
[38] Henry W. Foote, *Three Centuries of American Hymnody*, p. 79.
[39] Cotton Mather, *Magnalia* (London, 1702), Book V, p. 55.
[40] Daniel 3:5.

ROPES MEMORIAL, SALEM, MASSACHUSETTS

ROYALL HOUSE, MEDFORD, MASSACHUSETTS

liberal congregation to which he had been a benefactor. The Church resolved, with due respect to their "devoted friend," that they did not "think it proper to use the same in the public worship of God." Brattle had no doubt foreseen this result for he had stipulated in his will that should the Brattle Street Church refuse the organ it was to go to the Anglican congregation of King's Chapel.[41]

The prejudice against the use of organs in worship was slow to die. In July, 1770, when President Ezra Stiles of Yale visited Princeton and found that an organ had been installed in Nassau Hall "for the use of the students at Public prayers," he "thought it an innovation of ill consequence." The college trustees were "a little sick of it," he said, and it had been "disused for sundry years and never was used much." But the spirit of change was in the air, so that before the end of the century many pious Congregationalists had been won over to the more liberal point of view. Even the conservative congregation of the First Church of Boston, despite the bitter opposition of their minister, the venerable Charles Chauncy, made up their minds to have an organ. After Mr. Chauncy had preached his farewell sermon he told the committee who called to consult him in the matter that they could do as they pleased, as "it would not be long before he was in his grave" and then "before his head was cold they would have an organ." [42]

But during the long years when the congregations were without the assistance of any musical instrument, singing had become a painful performance. Metrical psalmody, typified by "Old Hundred," is in itself capable of much beauty, much grandeur, if properly rendered. But the *Bay Psalm Book* gave only the words, not the music, so that it became the practice for the deacon to sing the first line, in order to set the pitch and the tune, and then pause while the congregation joined in. The effect was often dismal, even when the leader happened to have a good voice and a knowledge of music, and when he had neither, as was often the case, the result was chaos. Judge Sewall, who was one of the precentors

[41] Justin Winsor, *The Memorial History of Boston*, II, pp. 210, 211.
[42] T. B. Dexter, ed., *The Literary Diary of Ezra Stiles*, I, pp. 58 (May 16, 1685).

for the South Meeting, details his troubles in his *Diary*: "Mr. Willard . . . spoke to me to set the tune; I intended Windsor and fell into High Dutch, and then essaying to set another tune went into a key much too high." On another occasion he "set York" but did it so badly that the people in the gallery failed to recognize the tune and "carried it irresistibly to St. Davids," which discouraged the good judge very much.[43]

That Sewall was by no means the only one who was discouraged we gather from a description of congregational singing in a pamphlet entitled: *Cases of Conscience about Singing of Psalms*. "In our late customary way of singing we have degenerated from the right and established rules of musical singing; and many congregations have sung near one-third too long, and some syllables have been quavering, as in the singing of mass; and in their singing have borrowed and taken, some half a line, some a whole line, out of one tune and put it into another. And the singing of the same pretended tunes in one congregation hath not been alike to the singing of them in another. And several singers in the same congregation have differed one from another in the tunes and flourishes of the tune they have sung and have been too discordant. And sometimes he that hath set the tune has been forced to sing two or three lines before the generality of the congregation could know what tune was set, so as to fall in with it."[44]

It is not difficult to understand how one listener in a Salem church gave expression to his disgust by writing the following lines on a panel of his pew:

> "Could poor David but for once
> To Salem church repair,
> And hear his Psalms thus warbled out,
> Good Lord, how he would swear."[45]

That Cotton Mather agreed with this view we gather from several entries in his *Diary*. "The Psalmody is but poorly carried on in my

[43] "Diary of Samuel Sewall," Massachusetts Historical Society *Collections*, Fifth Series, VII, p. 164; VI, p. 151.
[44] "An Essay Concerning the Singing of Psalms," in S. H. Emerys, *The Ministry of Taunton*, pp. 274, 275.
[45] Quoted by W. A. Fisher, *Notes on Music in Old Boston*, p. 17.

flock, and in a variety and regularity inferior to some others."
Again he writes: "I must of necessity do something that the exercise of singing the sacred Psalms in the flock may be made more
beautiful and especially have the beauties of holiness more upon
it." [46]

Had someone suggested to Mather that the beauties of holiness,
as well as other beauties of religion, might have been better expressed by a choir of chosen voices assisted by musical instruments, he would no doubt have been unconvinced. "If we admit
the instrumental music in the worship of God, how can we resist
the imposition of all the instruments used among the ancient
Jews?" he argued. "Or how can we decline a whole rabble of
Church officers necessary to be introduced for instrumental music,
whereof our Lord Jesus hath left us no manner of direction?" [47]

Thus did Puritanism impoverish itself in the expression of its
spirit in music. The congregations who met in the little wooden
meeting-houses must have experienced varying emotions as the
minister told them of Christ's great sacrifice, of His love for mankind, His solicitude for his people, or of the marvels of God's
creation, or of the mighty power of the heavenly hosts, or the
terrors of the Lord's anger. But there was little of love, or trust,
or devotion, or piety, or fear, or grandeur in their inharmonious
rendering of "Old Hundred" or "Litchfield" or "Martyrs" or
"Oxford," or the "One Hundred and Fifteenth Psalm Tune."

The poverty of early New England sacred music was a matter
of choice, not a consequence of pioneer life. The Moravian
Brothers, when they made their settlements in the forests of
Pennsylvania, Maryland and North Carolina, brought with them
hundreds of hymns from Germany, added scores of their own and
made music, instrumental and vocal, an integral part of their
worship. The founders of Bethabara carved their first trumpets
from the hollow limbs of trees, and with these crude implements
welcomed the Easter's dawn, or celebrated the laying of a cornerstone, or signalized with joyous note the "home-going" of some
departed brother or sister.[48] The immortal music of Bach, Mozart

---

[46] "Diary of Cotton Mather," Massachusetts Historical Society *Collections*,
Seventh Series, VII, pp. 560, 624.
[47] Cotton Mather, *Magnalia* (London, 1702), Book V, p. 55.
[48] T. J. Wertenbaker, *The Old South*, pp. 180, 181.

and Haydn was as familiar to the wilderness homes of the United Brethren as to the cathedrals of Europe.

But this was not for New England. Congregational singing there went from bad to worse. In the early days the settlers were more or less familiar with the music, since they all had heard the psalms sung in England. But the lack of musical notes in the *Bay Psalm Book* made it difficult for the second and third generations to render the songs in their original form. Changes crept in until it was seldom that any two congregations sang the same tune in the same way.

It was the Reverend John Tufts, minister of the Newbury Church, who first attempted to bring something like order out of this dismal chaos. It was about 1712 that he published his *An Introduction to the Singing of Psalm Tunes in a Plain and Easy Method with a Collection of Tunes.* Since the local press possessed no musical type, the notes were indicated by letters on a scale and the length by punctuation marks. So enthusiastic was Mr. Tufts in the cause of good music that he reinforced this work by personal instruction, traveling from place to place to give lectures and organize singing schools.[49] Sewall was among Tufts' listeners at one of his lectures in Boston, with profit, it is to be hoped, to himself and the long-suffering South Meeting congregation.

The movement inaugurated by Tufts was carried on vigorously by the Reverend Thomas Symmes of Bradford. But the battle was a severe one. No sooner had he suggested to his own congregation that singing by note was not only the best but "the most ancient way," than the older members of the congregation, with many shakings of the head and with grave faces, protested against this innovation. The old way of singing had been good enough for their ancestors; it ought to be good enough for them. They argued that the new method was less melodious; it would take too long to learn the tunes; it all smacked of Quakerism and Catholicism; it was an opening wedge for instrumental music.

These arguments Mr. Symmes answered in a discourse which he printed in a pamphlet entitled: *The Reasonableness of Regular Singing, or Singing by Note, in an Essay to revive the true and ancient mode of Singing psalm-tunes.* This he followed by an-

[49] Henry W. Foote, *Three Centuries of American Hymnody,* pp. 97–100.

other publication, *Utile Dulci, or a Joco-Serious Dialogue.* "If the Papists sing a better tune, or a better air, than we do, I'd as soon imitate them and a thousand times sooner, than the honestest man among you that had no skill in singing," he declared. As for the Quakers, there was no question of imitating their music "because the Quakers don't sing at all."

As the new movement gathered strength through New England, the opposition became more bitter. In some of the small country churches the older people denounced the new singing as a wicked innovation, "a worshipping of the Devil." Often, when the singing began they would rise from their seats and rush out of the meeting-house. It was monstrous, they thought, that such an unholy change in the worship of God should be brought about by a group of young upstarts.[50]

At this point Cotton Mather, unpredictable in this as in so many other matters, threw his great influence on the side of Tufts and Symmes. "Those fond of old tunes should not be too stiff and wilful in their own opinion," he wrote. "It is said, those fond of new tunes, are for bringing indifferent things into the worship of God: it may equally be said, those fond of old tunes are for continuing indifferent things. . . . If you say, the most that are for new singing (as it is called) are generally of the younger set of people: what then? If they are willing to take pains and learn, that they may be better able to worship God by singing psalms, would you discourage them from this?"[51]

And so, amid the din of controversy, the old method of singing the psalms went down to defeat. But many a sturdy old Puritan to his dying day rued the change and prayed God to forgive his people for making unsanctioned innovations in his worship.

On the whole the spirit of Puritanism in New England found a far less accurate reflection in architecture and music than in literature. There developed in the seventeenth century a distinctive type of domestic architecture based on the architecture of East Anglia, and in the eighteenth century another based on the English Georgian, but there is little in either which is typically

---

[50] *Ibid.*, pp. 109, 110.
[51] Cotton Mather, *Pacificatory Letter.*

Puritan. Had the region been settled by Englishmen of a different religious faith, there is no reason to suppose that either style would have been different.

On the houses of worship only did Puritanism have a major influence. In the crude little meeting-houses of the first decades, the quaint four-square building of the second half-century and the simple, wooden Wren churches of the eighteenth century, one finds the image of the religious spirit of the men and women who worshiped in them. The hewn beams, the windows devoid of stained glass, the lack of ornamentation, the absence of a steeple of the earlier types, and the restrained and simple beauty of the latter type alike bespeak the belief that religion is a thing of the spirit and so needs no visible manifestation.

Had the Puritans taken a similar view of music and banned it entirely from their worship their position would have been more logical. But to accept church music and then throw around it such restrictions as to rob it of its beauty was to make it meaningless. As an expression of Puritanism—its aspirations, devotion, piety, hopes and fears, the congregational singing of the first century of New England history was totally inadequate.

Chapter V

THE LIBERALS SEIZE THE FERULE

THE LEADERS of the great exodus to Massachusetts, as they held earnest consultations before sailing, or on board their little ships while crossing the Atlantic, or in Governor Winthrop's house in Boston, must have had grave misgivings concerning the educating of their children. Upon the establishing of an efficient educational system in the American wilds depended the success of their great venture. How otherwise could they instill into the next generation the great truths of religion? How protect them from error? How rear a group of learned ministers to take the places of the present "leading lights" when death had deprived the colony of their services? How prevent misinterpretation of the Bible if many of the people were unable to read it?

So Winthrop, Coddington, Dudley, Saltonstall and the others decided that they must erect a system of schools which, like the civil government, would be the handmaid of the Churches. For this they had excellent precedent. "What advantage the reformed Churches have had by their princes and States erecting schools of learning in their several dominions is so well known that there needs no more be said about this argument," stated William Hubbard.[1] Had not the Dutch schools been recast to fit the model of the Dutch Reformed Church? Were not the Scotch schools guided and controlled by the Presbyterian General Assembly? Had not the Huguenots, refusing to permit their children to attend schools which were under the influence of the Roman Catholics, established schools of their own?

At the time few, if any, had dreamed of divorcing education and religion. A century and a half had to elapse before Thomas Jefferson made his revolutionary proposal to the Virginia legislature that they found a system of public schools which would be

[1] William Hubbard, *The Happiness of a People*, p. 37.

under the control of no religious sect. Throughout the Middle
Ages learning was so exclusively in the hands of the Church that
to know how to read was accepted by the courts as evidence that
one was a clergyman. The great centers of learning had been from
their founding also centers of religion. At Oxford one could not
go ten steps in any direction from Carfax without meeting hooded
and gowned churchmen—Dominicans, Carmelites, Augustinians,
Benedictines. Most of the Oxford colleges were founded by clergymen—University College by William, Archdeacon of Durham;
Balliol by the Bishop of Durham; Merton by the Bishop of
Rochester; Exeter by the Bishop of Exeter; Oriel by Adam de
Brome, rector of St. Mary's Church; The Queen's College by
Robert Eglesfield, chaplain to Queen Philippa. For centuries Oxford was the very citadel of the Catholic faith in England. But
when Catholicism was overthrown by the Anglican Revolution
every member of the university was required to subscribe to the
Thirty-nine Articles, so that the institution would serve the needs
of the new faith as it had served the old. At the very time when
the founders of the Massachusetts colony were planning their
Bible commonwealth, Archbishop Laud, who was also Chancellor of Oxford, was promulgating a body of statutes designed
to bind the university irrevocably to the Anglican Church.

The view that education should be made to serve the ends of
religion was accepted almost without question by all the groups of
immigrants who came to America in the seventeenth century.
The Swedish schools on the lower Delaware were strongholds of
the Lutheran Church; it was the learned clergymen of the Dutch
Reformed Church who established schools in New Amsterdam
and on the banks of the Raritan and the Passaic and later founded
Rutgers College;[2] the Anglican Church gave us William and
Mary College; the Presbyterians, Princeton; the Baptists, Brown.
In the present day, when it is a cardinal principle of our vast
public school system that it should not further the distinctive
tenets of any one religious group, it is well to remember that
American education was founded by the Churches and for two
centuries in large measure was controlled by them.

It was inevitable, then, that in a colony such as Massachusetts,

[2] Nelson R. Burr, *Education in New Jersey*, Chapters I, II and III.

founded by religious zealots, the schools should be enlisted for the service of the Churches. If its school system was better than those of other colonies, it was partly because the Puritans were so deeply concerned with having their children under orthodox guidance. "The interest of religion and good literature have been wont to rise and fall together," declared the Synod of 1679 in a pamphlet entitled *Necessity of Reformation*.[3] "We read in the Scriptures of masters and scholars, and of schools and of colleges. And the most eminent reformers amongst the Lord's People of old, thought it their concern to erect and uphold them. Was not Samuel, that great reformer, president of the college at Najoth and is thought to be one of the first founders of colleges? Did not Elijah and Elisha restore the schools erected in the land of Israel? . . . Ecclesiastical story informs that great care was taken by the Apostles and their immediate successors for the settling of schools in all places, where the gospel had been preached, that so the interest of religion might be preserved and the truth propagated to succeeding generations. And we have all cause to bless God that put it into the hearts of our fathers to take care concerning this matter."

"After God had carried us safe to New England," states an early account of the founding of Massachusetts, "and we had builded our houses, provided necessaries for our livelihood, reared convenient places for God's worship and settled the civil government; one of the next things we longed for and looked after was to advance learning, and perpetuate it to posterity, dreading to leave an illiterate ministry to the Churches when our present ministers shall lie in the dust."[4]

In this mission the schools and the college were remarkably successful. Cotton Mather could boast: "Europe, as well as America, has from this learned seminary been enriched with some worthy men." In fact, old England had had more ministers from New than New England from old.[5] Similarly, the author of the pamphlet entitled *A Vindication of New England* stated that the college had "sent forth able and faithful pastors to more than

[3] Pp. 14, 15.
[4] *New England's First Fruits,* Sabin's Reprints, Quarto Series, VII (1865).
[5] Cotton Mather, *Magnalia* (Hartford, 1820), II, p. 20.

a hundred Christian congregations" in America, besides the help "afforded to some other parts of the world." So, early in 1664 the General Court reported to the King's Commissioners that "at least one hundred able preachers, physicians and surgeons and other useful persons" had "issued" from the college.[6]

It was obvious to the New England founders that they must make their educational system so far as possible independent of that of the mother country. It would be like administering poison to their children to place them under masters brought over from England who might have fallen under the influence of the high church Anglicans. Even though care should be taken to select good dissenters, the time might come, and quickly, when the American Puritans no longer would see eye to eye with the English Puritans. The only safe course was to found a college in America which could train teachers for the grammar schools under the eyes of their own clergy. Then the grammar schools could be trusted to send up to the college the most promising youths to prepare for the ministry. The college would thus become the fountain of youth for the Churches, pouring out an unending stream of young ministers to take the places of those incapacitated by old age or removed by death.

The importance to the Churches of educational independence was emphasized by William Hubbard. "It is not meet that the Israelites should always go down to the Philistines to sharpen their weapons, which they are to use in fighting against the enemies of God's Church, or for whetting their tools they must use in tilling God's field . . . Julian complains that the Christians beat the heathen philosophers with their own weapons, therefore did he subtly contrive to deprive the Christians of the benefit of schools and other means of humane learning, thinking that to be the likeliest means whereby to overthrow the Christian religion. . . . While Israel was without a teaching priest and without a law, they were also without the true God. While the Scriptures are locked up in an unknown language, how can they be opened without the key of humane learning? . . . What considerable benefit this place hath already reaped, and 'tis hoped may further receive by

[6] *Clarendon State Papers* (Bodleian Library, Oxford), p. 49.

this one college in the country,[7] founded and hitherto carried on by the pious care and religious endeavors of our former worthy leaders and other liberal benefactors, is sufficiently demonstrable to the view of the world."[8]

Hubbard's words were echoed by Increase Mather in a sermon preached in 1677. The colony must nourish the schools and the college, he pointed out, "that so there might be able instruments raised up for the propagating of truth in succeeding generations." The General Court also placed itself on record in this matter by declaring "skill in the tongues and liberal arts" not only laudable but necessary for the being of the commonwealth and the Churches.

The young Harvard graduate who accepted a position as master of a grammar school, or the goodwife who taught small children in the dame school, alike understood that they were expected to give instruction in the religion of the reformed Churches. But if they had any doubts of their duty in this matter, the ministers were not backward in instructing them. "We earnestly move and urge that such as are employed in the reading, the writing and the grammar schools may do their utmost that the children under their care may be furthered as much as it is possible in the knowledge and practice of Christianity," declared a group of Boston ministers headed by Cotton Mather. "We are thankful for what is done this way."[9] This statement Mather followed up with a query in his *Magnalia*: "May not school-masters do much to instil principles of religion and civility, as well as other points of good education, into the children of the town? Only let the town well encourage its well deserving school-masters."

The insistence of the New England leaders that education should be the handmaid of religion by no means implies that they were not interested in education for its own sake. As university graduates, many of them, they would have been deeply distressed had they thought that by migrating to America they had doomed their children to ignorance. Thomas Jefferson said that of all the

[7] Harvard.
[8] William Hubbard, *The Happiness of a People*, p. 36.
[9] *A Testimony Against Evil Customs*, p. 3.

blessings the loving care of his father had bestowed on him, the greatest was the ability to read the classical authors in the original Greek and Latin. The Puritans, though not so emphatic as the great Virginian, appreciated fully the vistas of beauty and thought which a knowledge of the classics opened to them, and wished their sons to enjoy them also.

A contribution which was expected of the educational system, hardly less important for the future of the Bible commonwealth than the training of ministers, was the turning out of a group of educated men from whom the people could choose their magistrates, deputies and other civil officers. The founders were fully conscious that knowledge is power and that power was as essential in the State as in the Churches. The leading ministers, when they were called to deliver the election sermons, repeatedly asserted that without a well-educated, able, enlightened, godly group of magistrates who were devoted to the reformed Churches, all would fall in ruins.

William Hubbard gave an excellent illustration of the current point of view in the election sermon of 1676: "It was well replied by an officer of the state to a nobleman that made small account of learning in the education of his son, aiming at no higher learning than to be able to ride a horse or fly a hawk, that if it were so, then noblemen's sons must be content that mean men's children should govern the kingdom." New England needed men of "experience, education and study," Hubbard declared, who had the "advantage above others to be acquainted with the affairs of the world abroad, as well as with the laws and customs of their own people." Persons "of that alloy" generally had the "managing of affairs in other nations" and were equally necessary for the New England Israel.[10] Urian Oakes was even more emphatic. "The fall of schools and contempt of learning," he warned, "will make way for rudeness, ignorance, want of able instruments to manage church and state affairs, irreligion and ruin to this poor country. . . . Think not that the commonwealth of learning may languish, and yet our civil and ecclesiastical state be maintained in good plight and condition." [11]

[10] William Hubbard, *The Happiness of a People*, p. 28.
[11] Urian Oakes, *New England Pleaded With*, pp. 57, 60.

In establishing their educational system the colonists quite logically began with a college. They realized, of course, that the college would soon wither and die unless schools were set up to supply it with properly prepared students, but the chief requisite for schools was trained teachers; in the case of the grammar schools, teachers who had earned their Bachelor's degree. No doubt a few young men suited for the task were found among the early settlers, but without a college there would be no one to take their places. When the Reverend Jonathan Mitchell, Senior Fellow, made an appeal for funds for the college, he emphasized the need for training "choice and able schoolmasters."

Several years after the *Arbella* nosed into Boston harbor to herald the coming of the Puritan host, the General Court appropriated £400 "towards a school or college." The project hung fire for some months while the ministers and magistrates battled furiously to cast out the Hutchinson heresy and the intractable Anne with it, but in 1636 a Board of Overseers was appointed, a house purchased in Cambridge, and a professor engaged. The next year, when John Harvard died, leaving his library and half of his estate to the infant institution, it was named Harvard College.

Nathaniel Eaton, the first head of the college, was not the godly man the ministers and magistrates who made up the Overseers had hoped for. After he had flogged many of his students unmercifully, had fed them tainted beef and beer and moldy bread and had attacked his assistant with a cudgel "big enough to have killed a horse," he was dismissed.[12] Later it was discovered that he was a thief as well as a ruffian, for when he left the country he made off with a goodly share of the college funds.

The next choice was far happier, for Henry Dunster, a recent Cambridge graduate, proved an able administrator, an educational leader, a teacher who had better means of inspiring his students than the rod. Dunster brought in two able tutors, lengthened the course for the Bachelor's degree to four years, secured an act of incorporation from the General Court, erected a new

---

[12] Cotton Mather, *Magnalia* (Hartford, 1820), II, p. 7.

building and instituted a curriculum based on those of the English universities.[13]

The requirements for admission were such that few graduates of the preparatory schools today, when the classics are so often neglected, could satisfy them. "When any scholar is able to understand Tully, or such like classical Latin author extempore, and make and speak Latin in verse and prose . . . and decline . . . the paradigms of noun and verbs in the Greek tongue, let him then . . . be capable of admission." Once safely past this formidable barrier and housed in the college building, the student entered upon a prescribed course in grammar, logic, rhetoric, arithmetic, geometry and astronomy, metaphysics, ethics, natural philosophy, Greek, Hebrew and ancient history. It was a curriculum which squared with the rather advanced educational ideals of the Puritans. As a foundation for divinity, undergraduates studied the Bible in the original tongues and William Ames's *Medulla* or Wolleb's *Abridgement of Christian Divinity*. Having completed his work, the student received his diploma at the commencement exercises in July in the presence of the great men of the colony. If he then wished to prepare himself for the ministry, he usually remained in residence for an additional three years to read theology and philosophy. At last, when he had received the Master of Arts degree, he went forth to assume his clerical duties and with them his position of power and prestige.

It was no easy matter for the New Englanders to support the college, and the contributions from the farmers of New Haven and Connecticut, as well as those of Massachusetts, of wheat, wampum, malt, corn, apples, etc., gave evidence of their interest. It was justly pleaded in behalf of the New Englanders that: "Though they have had no royal founders, no Alfreds, no Balliols, no Henry VI or VIII, no Queen Eleanors, etc., no great prelates, such as Chicheley, Fox, Wycliffe, Woolsey, etc., to promote so glorious a work, no extraordinary benefactors, . . . they have erected a considerable college amongst them for the education of their youth in piety and good literature." [14] From 1662 to 1669 the good people of Portsmouth, New Hampshire, contributed

---

[13] Samuel Eliot Morison, *The Puritan Pronaos*, pp. 27–29.
[14] *A Vindication of New England.*

£60 a year to the college. When the old building had to be replaced by a new one the cost was defrayed by circulating a sub-
scription list.

More important than contributions of money or in kind were
the contributions of the most promising youths in New England.
Without this the college would have been helpless. Every town
of a hundred families was required to have a grammar school
under the care of a master capable of giving instruction in Latin
and Greek, so that boys could be prepared for college. So, from
Connecticut, Plymouth and New Haven, as well as from all parts
of Massachusetts, the youth who had been picked as future leaders
in the Churches or in the State came to Cambridge to present
themselves for admission.

The grammar schools were supported in part by endowment,
in part by tuition fees, and in part by the towns. This, it has been
contended, made them entirely secular, and in no sense Church
schools. But in a community where only Church members could
vote and where, often for decades, the town and the congregation
had identic personnel, the distinction loses its point. The same
body—i.e., the town meeting—which voted the minister's salary
voted the master's salary, and it would seem a matter of slight
importance whether they did so as congregation or town meeting.

What did matter was the choice of a master, and the selectmen
or the special committee which was entrusted with this responsibility were careful to consider none but orthodox Congregationalists. To do otherwise would have incurred the risk that
religious error might slip in between the lines of Tully or Virgil
or Homer. It also would have been illegal, for an act of Massachusetts of 1654 required selectmen "not to admit or suffer any such
to be continued in office or place of teaching . . . that have manifested themselves unsound in the faith or scandalous in their
lives." [15]

To make doubly sure, the local minister, often with the assistance of neighboring ministers, inquired into the orthodoxy,
preparation and character of the new master. If they found all
satisfactory, they certified him to the town and selectmen. "These
are to certify that Mr. William Goddard, of Watertown, whom

[15] *Massachusetts Bay Records*, IV, part I, pp. 182, 183.

the . . . town by covenanting engaged to teach such children as
should be sent to him to learn the rules of the Latin tongue, hath
those accomplishments which render him capable to discharge the
trust," wrote the Reverend John Sherman to the town of Watertown in 1680.[16]

It by no means follows, then, that because *officially* the
Churches and ministers had nothing to do with the selection of
teachers, the payment of salaries, the choice of books, or the supervision of schools, their influence was not great, if not decisive, in
all these matters. Princeton has never had any official connection
with the Presbyterian Church, but that Church controlled its
Faculty and its policies for many decades. Who can doubt that the
minister of any Massachusetts congregation in the seventeenth
century who discovered that the master of the local grammar
school was using an unorthodox text, or had defended some
theological "error," could and would see to it that he was not
reengaged? A mere hint to the selectmen that the Act of 1654
was being violated would have been enough.

But there was little need to watch the pious professional master
or the youthful student of divinity who accepted a temporary
teaching post before completing the work for his Master's degree
or, having graduated, before entering the ministry. Some of the
schools were supplied almost entirely from the latter source. At
Hadley, for instance, Caleb Watson, who served from about 1666
to 1673, acted also as assistant to the local minister; John Young-
love, who was at Hadley from about 1674 to 1680, became the
minister at Suffield; Samuel Russell, son of the Reverend John
Russell, later was the minister for Branford; John Morse, master
in 1693-1694, went to the Church at Newtown, Long Island;
Salmon Treat, master in 1694-1695, to the Preston Church; Joseph
Smith, master in 1695-1696, to the Upper Middletown Church;
John Hubbard, 1696-1697, to the Jamaica Church; Samuel
Melyen, 1700-1701, to the Elizabeth Church; Nathaniel Chauncey,
1702-1703, to the Durham Church; Samuel Ruggles, 1703-1704,
to the Billerica Church; Jonathan Marsh, 1706-1707, to the Wind-
sor Church; Aaron Porter, 1708-1709, to the Medford Church;
Daniel Broadman, 1709-1710, to the Church at New Milford.

[16] Walter Herbert Small, *Early New England Schools*, pp. 91, 92.

Interspersed among this procession of young divines was an occasional master destined for some lay occupation, but he invariably came of a religious family. Warham Mather, who became Judge of Probate at New Haven, was the son of the Reverend Eleazer Mather; Samuel Migill, who became a professional schoolmaster, was the son of Reverend Thomas Migill of Scituate.[17] It would seem that Satan himself would find it well-nigh impossible to break through this solid array to inculcate erroneous ideas into the Hadley schoolboys.

The situation at Woburn was similar. Of the masters who held sway in this town from 1712 to 1736 no less than twelve became ministers: John Tufts at Newbury; Peter Clark at Danvers; John Gardner at Stow; Mr. Cotton (presumably Nathaniel Cotton) at Bristol; John Hancock, father of Governor Hancock, at Braintree; Ebenezer Flagg, Jr., at Chester, New Hampshire; Timothy Walker at Concord, New Hampshire; Habijah Weld at Attleborough; Thomas Balch at Dedham; Ebenezer Wyman at Union; the Reverend Nathaniel Hancock and the Reverend Samuel Jennison.[18] At Woburn almost all the grammar school masters were Harvard graduates; at Hadley, graduates of either Harvard or Yale.

By far the best known of the professional masters was Ezekiel Cheever, who held the rod in New England schools for seventy years and died in harness at the age of ninety-four. Samuel Sewall tells us that he labored "skilfully, diligently, constantly, religiously . . . a rare instance of piety, health, strength, serviceableness." Teaching at New Haven twelve years, at Ipswich twelve years, at Charlestown twelve years and at Boston thirty-eight years, he prepared for college many of the leading men of New England. He was a believer in the rod as an aid to learning, and when he began to stroke his long, white beard the boys knew trouble was at hand. When John Barnard entered school his mischievousness so diverted his classmates from their work that Cheever announced that he would be punished whenever any one of them failed. This proved effective until one youngster, who disliked Barnard, failed several times in order to get him a beating.

[17] Sylvester Judd, *History of Hadley,* pp. 66, 67.
[18] Samuel Sewall, *The History of Woburn,* pp. 586, 587.

Cheever was a writer as well as a teacher, and his *Latin Accidence* was in use in New England schools for two centuries.[19]

The liberality of the people of New England to Harvard was matched by their bequests to the schools. Edward Hopkins of Hartford, who died in England in 1657, left part of his estate "to give encouragement in those foreign plantations for the breeding up of hopeful youths in a way of learning, both at the grammar school and college, for the public service of the country in future times." Of this bequest the grammar school at New Haven received £412, the Hartford school £400, the Hadley school £308 and Harvard £100.[20]

At Roxbury, Samuel Hagburne in 1642 bequeathed £20 a year to a free school whenever the town should found one. Inspired by this good example, three years later sixty persons "out of their religious care of posterity" and the necessity of educating "their children in literature" to "fit them for public service," subscribed liberally, even pledging their houses, barns and orchards. One of the most liberal was Mr. John Prudden, who in 1668 promised to give £25 annually to assist in the instructing of the children "in all scholastical, moral and theological discipline." [21]

As the grammar schools were feeders for Harvard, so the primary schools were feeders for the grammar schools. An act of Massachusetts in 1642 required the selectmen of every town to see that none suffered "so much barbarism in any of their families as not to endeavor to teach by themselves or others their children and apprentices perfectly to read the English tongue." Three years later this law was buttressed by another requiring each town of fifty families to provide a schoolmaster to teach reading and writing, "it being one chief project of that old deluder Satan, to keep men from the knowledge of the Scriptures." [22]

To some of the poorer people this law seemed hard. They needed the help of their sons in clearing away the forest trees, planting crops, building barns, putting up fences, and in the other arduous tasks of life in a frontier community. If the youths

[19] Samuel Eliot Morison, *Builders of the Bay Colony*, pp. 184, 185; *The Puritan Pronaos*, pp. 98, 100.
[20] Sylvester Judd, *History of Hadley*, p. 56.
[21] Justin Winsor, *The Memorial History of Boston*, I, p. 419.
[22] *Laws and Liberties of Massachusetts* (1929), p. 47.

spent much of their time conning over the hornbook or the primer, their fathers must do double work. Where the town was too small to support a school and the parents themselves must teach their own children the burden was especially heavy. Yet it was not uncommon for the courts to warn or even fine a father for negligence in this matter. Nor did they hesitate to punish the town itself if it failed to comply with the law of 1642.

John Locke tells us that in England the primary schools used "the hornbook, primer, psalter, Testament and Bible," and the New Englanders followed the same path in an effort to "engage the liking of children and tempt them to read." [23] The hornbook, or leaf of paper fixed to a wooden frame with a handle, contained the alphabet, the nine digits and the Lord's Prayer. Perhaps it was by chance that this device, used to introduce the youthful mind to the world of learning, was in the shape of a paddle, but many a lad had reason to catch the significance. Religious precepts were inculcated, not only by the catechism, psalter and Testament, but by the primers as well, which were full of religious allusions.

> "Zaccheus he
> Did climb a tree
> His Lord to see."

Norris's *Catechism,* used in the early schools, was replaced later by John Cotton's *Spiritual Milk for Babes.* Although among the first books printed in New England was a speller, that instrument of youthful torture was uncommon in many schools until the eighteenth century.

The New England educational system, with its primary schools, its grammar schools and its college, was the most efficient of any in the American colonies. For this there were several reasons. Of first importance was the fact that among the ministers and Puritan gentlemen who led the migration to Massachusetts and were so instrumental in shaping the Bible Commonwealth was a high percentage of university graduates. This in itself gave education great prestige. Not only would a Cotton or a Winthrop want his sons to go through the schools and college, but the artisan

[23] Sylvester Judd, *History of Hadley,* p. 69.

and the farmer who had for these leaders such deep admiration would hope that they, too, might have an offspring who could drink at the fountain of learning.

The New Englanders, because of the agricultural village, were less hampered by pioneer conditions in establishing their schools than were the people of other colonies. Where all the children of a community were within walking distance of the schoolhouse it was far easier to have an efficient school than amid the scattered plantations of the South, or even in the farm districts of the Middle Colonies. As we have seen, this was not a matter of chance. The New England village was planned, not because it was convenient or necessary for agriculture, but because the founders realized how favorable it would be for Church and school.

Favorable, also, was the fact that in New England there was but one language, and that all save a small minority of the people adhered to one creed. Had a Mather or a Sewall visited New Jersey or Pennsylvania to witness the confusion and inefficiency resulting from the multiple educational systems—schools founded by the Dutch Reformed ministers in which Dutch was the language of instruction; Congregationalist schools, where the language was English; Swedish schools which fostered the Swedish tongue and the Lutheran faith; German schools, Quaker schools, Presbyterian schools—he would have returned to Boston thanking God that in New England things were different.

Success was achieved also because the college and the schools had the enthusiastic support of the Churches in a region where the power of religion was very great. How important this factor was is shown by the zeal with which the clergy came to the support of the educational system when, in the eighth decade of the seventeenth century, it began to show signs of weakening. This was the period when the college was threatened with extinction, when the grammar schools lapsed in New Haven and Hartford and when there were frequent warnings of educational decay.

Samuel Torrey declared in 1674 that if things did not change for the better it would bring ruin to the Churches. "If we do consider how much both civil and religious education is neglected, and if we look upon the sad face of the rising generation and see how much of ignorance . . . doth already appear in the countenance of it; what an ungracious, irreligious generation there is likely to arise among us unless God in infinite mercy work a great and wonderful change, our hearts may well tremble to think what will become of the worship and ordinances of God in the next age." [24]

The Synod of 1674 gave it as their opinion that it was the proneness of most men to seek their own ends rather than Christ's which explained why "schools of learning and other public concerns" were "in a languishing state." [25] As early as 1672 the Reverend Thomas Shepard, Jr., of Charlestown, declared: "There is a great decay in inferior schools, it would be well if that . . . were examined and the cause thereof removed." [26] The following year Urian Oakes, in his election sermon, again sounded the alarm: "It is the observation of wise men, and indeed a general sad complaint, that the schools languish and are in a low condition in the country. And what the end of this will be, who cannot apprehend?"

Oakes then proceeded to give what he considered the chief cause of "decay": "Though there are doubtless many reasons of the languishing of schools, yet I am very apt to think that the bottom of all is the want of due encouragement to scholars when they come to maturity and [are] fitted for service in the Churches. . . . Parents will have no heart to breed their children to learning. Rich men . . . have better ways before them to provide for the comfortable subsistence of their children, and persons of meaner condition cannot, or at least are discouraged from expending all they can upon their children's education, because when that is done and they are ready for service, there is no encouragement through the slenderness and shortness of the ministers' maintenance in most places. . . . It is a matter of sorrowful and sad resentment with me that the nurseries of piety and learning and liberal education should languish and die away, as they do in my apprehension, on this account." [27] Oakes here not only touches on a reason for the temporary decline of education, but makes it clear

[24] Samuel Torrey, *An Exhortation unto Reformation*, p. 16.
[25] *Necessity of Reformation*, p. 8.
[26] Election Sermon of 1672, quoted by John L. Sibley, *Harvard Graduates*, I. pp. 330–331.
[27] Urian Oakes, *New England Pleaded With*.

that in his opinion the preparation of youths for the ministry was the vitalizing force for the entire school system.

But Mr. Oakes no doubt would have agreed readily that the drift from the agricultural village to the farm, a movement which assumed large proportions in the second half of the seventeenth century and caused the Puritan leaders grave concern, was a contributing factor to the troubles of the schools.[28] With a large part of the population living at a distance from the village so that it became difficult to bring the children in to school, especially during the winter months, the total of absences mounted. And when new schools were established in the farm districts, they were often small and inefficient.

On Cape Cod the people found it necessary to adopt the unsatisfactory "squadron system," in which the master, in the manner of the circuit-riding parsons of a later day, moved from community to community. In Harwich at one period it took the master three and a half years, and no less than six moves, to make the circuit. Since he remained only six months in any one place, some of the children had to go without schooling for many months at a time.[29]

Still another reason for the decline of the schools was the low state into which Harvard had fallen. With the average graduating class numbering only seven in the years from 1661 to 1670, the supply of young men fitted to be masters in the grammar schools became woefully inadequate. Even the "great and civil" class of 1671, eleven strong, must have fallen far short of the demand.[30]

The weakness of the college in the later decades of the seventeenth century was the result in large part of the localism inherent in Congregationalism. When we consider the vital role which Harvard played in the life of the Churches and the State, we might conclude that its president would be the unofficial "bishop" of all New England, with an influence hardly less than that of the Governor, in like manner as the president of Princeton in the eighteenth century was the acknowledged though unofficial head of the Presbyterian Church. But in New England there was no

[28] See pp. 184–189.
[29] Henry C. Kittredge, *Cape Cod*, pp. 109, 110.
[30] Samuel Eliot Morison, *Three Centuries of Harvard*, pp. 39, 40.

collective Church, of which one could be the head, but merely a
federation of autonomous congregations. So it was the congregation and not the federation which played the vital role in the
religious life of the region. The minister of one of the larger
Churches was a man of such influence and power and received
such a satisfactory salary that he was reluctant to relinquish them
for the somewhat threadbare honor of being president of Harvard.

This proved a blessing in disguise, for it weakened the grip of
the conservative group of clergymen who wished to make the
college a mere feeder for the Churches and a bulwark of the old
order rather than a liberal arts college. Had Harvard, in the years
from 1660 to 1724, been presided over by a series of such commanding clergymen as Increase Mather and Cotton Mather, and
had these men given to it all their time and energy, it would not
so soon have become a center of liberal thought. It was a matter
of bitter resentment to those who still cherished the stern, intolerant ideals of the first settlers that the college founded to
uphold and perpetuate them was yielding to, or even taking the
lead in, the pattern of thought known as the Enlightenment. But
New England was the gainer.

When President Dunster resigned in 1654 because he would
not recant his belief that infant baptism is "unscriptural," the
Overseers replaced him with another able scholar whose religious
views made a career as a Puritan minister out of the question. But
Charles Chauncy, more compliant in matters of conscience than
his predecessor, promised to keep his belief on immersion of
infants to himself. Chauncy made a good president, despite the
rigid regimen of prayer, catechism and sermons which he inflicted
upon the undergraduates, but this could not conceal the fact that
the college, that fountain of youth for the Churches, was under
the direction of one who could not be ranked among the religious
leaders of New England.

Upon Chauncy's death in 1672 the Overseers made an unhappy
choice in selecting his successor. Leonard Hoar, a Harvard graduate who had taken an ecclesiastical living in England under
Cromwell only to return to America after the Restoration, proved
to be quite unsuited for the presidency. Cotton Mather, who was

in college at the time, tells us that the students "set themselves to travesty whatever he did and said . . . with a design to make him odious." [31] In 1675 Hoar threw up the sponge and resigned.

Urian Oakes, who succeeded Hoar, would have brought considerable prestige to the office of president, for this learned, pugnacious little man was a recognized leader among the ministers, had he consented to give to it his entire time and thought. But he accepted only temporarily and on condition that he might continue to fill his pulpit at Cambridge. And when, after five years of futile president-hunting, the Overseers persuaded him to make the arrangement permanent, he served but a few months before death overtook him.

The choice now fell upon the Reverend John Rogers of Ipswich, who, after a year's delay, came to Cambridge, only to die a few months later. So once more the search began, with the presidency losing in prestige as one minister after another declined to accept it. At last, in 1685, Increase Mather came to the rescue by consenting to assume the place temporarily, giving to it such time as he could spare from his duties as minister of the Second Church of Boston. Once more Harvard had one of the ablest men in the colony at its head, but once more the college was with the president only a secondary interest.

In these days when the subway trains whisk one from Boston to Harvard Yard in a few minutes, it is no hardship to commute to Cambridge, but in Mather's day the long horseback ride and the ferry crossing must have consumed several hours. It is not surprising that he went no oftener than was absolutely necessary. And when he did go he hastened back to his comfortable Boston residence, his Church and the political intrigues of the little capital the moment he had completed the task immediately in hand. From 1688 to 1692 he was absent in England, where he was pleading for the restoration of the Massachusetts charter.

This was wholesome neglect, for it left the running of the college in the hands of the two tutors, John Leverett and William Brattle, both of them able, liberal and broad-minded men. Excellent teachers, sharing their enthusiasms for science with their students, they labored to make Harvard a liberal arts college

[31] Cotton Mather, *Magnalia* (Hartford, 1820), II, p. 11.

abreast of the best English standards.[32] As Professor Samuel Eliot Morison points out: "It is largely owing to Brattle as tutor and to Leverett both as tutor and President that Harvard was saved from becoming a sectarian institution at a time when the tendency of most pious New Englanders was to tighten up and insist on hundred-per-cent puritanism in the face of infiltrating ideas that heralded the Century of Enlightenment." [33]

Had Mather been more observant of what was going on under his very nose and less concerned with buttressing the control of the orthodox group over the college by means of a new charter, he might have checked this liberal drift. The charter of 1650 had gone down in 1686 with the colonial government which had granted it, and for six years the college operated without a charter. In 1692 Mather returned from England with the new Massachusetts charter which, though it did not reinstate in power the Puritan elect, gave the people a large degree of self-government. Under its authority the General Court, at Mather's suggestion, placed the control of the college in a president and a Corporation, of whom two were resident tutors and the rest Congregational ministers. But this plan fell through in 1697 when the King in Council disallowed it on the ground that it excluded the royal Governor from any share in the government of the college.

By no means discouraged, Mather drew up another charter in which the Governor and Council were to have the power of visitation, but this, too, proved unsatisfactory. Still another plan, which was accepted by the General Court in 1699, was vetoed by the royal Governor because Mather insisted upon inserting a clause that none but orthodox Congregationalists could be president or Fellow. The General Court next tried the old political trick of passing a bill for a charter which was to be in force until the King vetoed it, perhaps several years later.

But opposition now developed in the General Court itself. Leverett and Brattle had been excluded from the Corporation and this outraged some of the Deputies. Others, among them so staunch a conservative as Samuel Sewall, had become wearied of Mather's refusal to reside in Cambridge. When a resolution was

---

[32] Perry Miller and Thomas H. Johnson, *The Puritans*, p. 734.
[33] Samuel Eliot Morison, *Three Centuries of Harvard*, p. 46.

passed requiring him to do so, Mather protested to Governor
Stoughton: "Should I leave off preaching to 1500 souls, for I suppose that so many use ordinarily to attend in our congregation,
only to expound to 40 or 50 children, few of them capable of
edification by such exercises?" [34] Yet when he was given the
option of complying or resigning, with a wry face he moved to
Cambridge. A few months was all he could stand, however, and
by the last of October, 1700, we find him back in town. Cambridge did not suit his health, he said. Perhaps it would be best
for the General Court to find another president.

This threat the General Court answered with one of its own,
resolving: "For as much as the constitution requires that the president reside at Cambridge, in case of Mr. Mather's refusal, absence,
sickness or death, that Mr. Samuel Willard be vice-president." Not
wanting to relinquish the presidential salary of £220 and anxious
to guard the college against religious error, Mather managed to
endure life north of the Charles for three months more. Then he
wrote Governor Stoughton that he was determined "no more to
reside in Cambridge" and therefore desired the General Court to
"think of another president." "But it would be fatal to the interest of religion," he warned, "if a person disaffected to the order
of the Gospel, professed and practiced in these Churches, should
preside over this society."

When the General Court took him at his word by declaring
the presidency vacated and inviting Vice-President Willard to
take charge, Mather was deeply chagrined. Willard was an able
and pious minister, but his views on baptism had brought him
into conflict with the other ministers, so that Mather could hardly
have considered him the ideal defender of orthodoxy. Galling,
also, was the apparent discrimination in the permission granted
to Willard to reside in Boston five days and nights a week.

So outraged was Cotton Mather at the rebuff to his father that
he declared that Samuel Sewall, who was a member of the
Council, "had used his father worse than a neger." [35] Sewall tried
to placate the former president by sending him "a good hanch of

[34] Justin Winsor, *The Memorial History of Boston,* II, p. 202.
[35] "Diary of Samuel Sewall," Massachusetts Historical Society *Collections,*
Fifth Series, V, p. 43.

venison." Happening upon Cotton Mather, he asked him whether it was consistent with his book *The Law of Kindness for the Tongue* to revile him in public—"whether correspondent with Christ's rule?" To this Mather replied that he had nothing more to say to him. But that he did say a great deal more we gather from Sewall's statement that he "charged the Council with lying, hypocrisy, tricks and I know not what all." [36]

The concern of the Mathers for the "safety" of the college was all the greater because dissatisfaction with certain features of the old order was leading to concrete action within the Churches themselves. In 1699 a group of Bostonians, influential and wealthy men many of them, founded the Brattle Street Church. When they published a manifesto, endorsing the Half-way Covenant, condemning public confessions as a requisite to admission to membership, discarding the old order of worship—one praying, one singing, one preaching—and giving to noncommunicant members of the congregation a share in Church government, the conservative ministers were alarmed and outraged. Immediately the air was filled with rebukes, expositions of error, advice, threats. Increase Mather and James Allen wrote a letter of admonition to the new Church, the Reverend John Higginson and Nicholas Noyes wrote "a letter of admonition and rebuke" which was "severe without being unkind or disrespectful"; [37] Increase Mather published a tract entitled *The Order of the Gospel,* in which he urged strict adherence to the tenets of the founders. At last a truce was affected in a joint service held on a "close dark day," marked by sermons and blessings and prayers that God would "pardon all the frailties of ministers and people." Yet the breach was by no means healed and the defenders of the old order continued for many years to regard the liberals with suspicion.

What it would mean for the future of religion in New England if the latter got control of the only institution in Massachusetts for training ministers, it was not difficult to see. So when the *de facto* Corporation, taking it upon itself to fill vacancies, admitted to its membership Thomas Brattle, one of the chief movers in organizing the Brattle Street Church, and the donor of

[36] *Ibid.,* p. 44.
[37] Justin Winsor, *The Memorial History of Boston,* II, pp. 206–209.

the land on which it erected its house of worship, together with
William Brattle and John Leverett, the conservatives were thoroughly alarmed. They picked up courage, however, when Vice-
President Willard resigned because of ill health. Surely the
Corporation, in selecting a new president, could not ignore the
claims of one or the other of the Mathers. And with either in control in Harvard Yard, the danger of having the future occupants
of the New England pulpits inoculated with the Brattle Street
errors would be averted.

The Corporation, nonetheless, did pass over both Mathers and
elected John Leverett.[38] Instantly the conservatives were in arms.
Was it right to ignore the claims of the two most distinguished
ministers in New England? It was unheard of for a layman to be
president of the college. The authority of the Corporation to make
the selection was questionable. Despite a petition to the General
Court signed by thirty-nine ministers, many of whom had studied
under Leverett, testifying to his piety and learning, that body
would probably have refused to vote him a competent salary had
not his friend, Governor Dudley, come to his rescue. The Governor promised that if the salary were forthcoming he could declare
the Charter of 1650 in force again. This maneuver succeeded;
Leverett was voted £150 a year, and the control of the liberals
over Harvard was assured.

The inauguration of Leverett in Old Harvard Hall assumed
the aspect of a victory celebration. "The governor prepared a Latin
speech for installment of the president," wrote Sewall. "Then took
the president by the hand and led him down into the hall. . . .
The governor read his speech. . . . Then president made a short
Latin speech, importing the difficulties discouraging and yet he
did accept. . . . Closed with the hymn of the Trinity. Had a very
good dinner upon three or four tables." [39]

But for the Mathers there was no celebration. Enraged at
Dudley for his part in the triumph of the liberals, they each wrote
him a letter accusing him of perfidy, hypocrisy, bribery, cruelty,

[38] Leverett had eight votes, Increase Mather three, Cotton Mather one and
William Brattle one. "Diary of Samuel Sewall," Massachusetts Historical Society
Collections, Fifth Series, VI, p. 196.
[39] "Diary of Samuel Sewall," Massachusetts Historical Society Collections,
Fifth Series, VI, p. 209.

corrupt dealing and other equally hideous crimes. Upon reading
these letters one wonders at the facility with which the two ministers expressed themselves despite the fact that their vocabulary
was restricted by the ban which their calling placed on profanity.[40] The Governor gave himself two weeks in which to cool off
after receiving these violent epistles, but others who had learned
the contents were loud in their disapproval. The Reverend Ebenezer Pemberton of the South Church declared "with great vehe-
mency" that "if he were the governor he would humble him
[Cotton Mather] though it cost him his head."

But Dudley's reply was as restrained as it was telling. "Gentlemen, Yours of the 20th instant received; and the contents, both
as to the matter and manner, astonish me to the last degree. I must
think you have extremely forgot your own station, as well as my
character; otherwise it had been impossible to have made such an
open breach upon all the laws of decency, honor, justice and
Christianity, as you have done in treating me with an air of supe-
riority and contempt. . . . Really, gentlemen, conscience and
religion are things too solemn, venerable or sacred, to be played
with, or made a covering for actions so disagreeable to the Gospel,
as these your endeavors to expose me and my most faithful services to contempt." [41]

The Mathers, though they remained on the Board of Overseers,
now "ceased all official interference in the affairs of the college."
"Though the college be under a very unhappy government,"
Cotton Mather wrote Governor Shute in 1718, "yet for my own
part I earnestly desire that it may go on as easily and as quietly as
possible. . . . I desire to keep at the greatest distance imaginable
from all the affairs of Harvard." On July 3, 1717, we find him
writing in his *Diary*: "This day, being our insipid, ill-contrived
anniversary solemnity, which we call the Commencement, I chose
to spend it at home." [42]

Leverett made an excellent president. A good administrator,
an able scholar, a far-seeing educational leader, respected by the

[40] Justin Winsor, *The Memorial History of Boston,* II, p. 218.
[41] Quoted by M. C. Crawford, *Old Boston in Colonial Days,* pp. 231, 232.
[42] "Diary of Cotton Mather," Massachusetts Historical Society *Collections,*
Seventh Series, VIII, p. 462.

students, he brought new prestige to Harvard, put its finances upon a firm basis, added a new professorship, greatly increased student attendance. But his most valuable service was his defense of the college against the ideals of the Mathers and the conservative group who would have made it little more than a divinity school.

Every graduate of Harvard for the better part of three decades left the Yard with the imprint of Leverett upon him. The broader outlook upon life, the more democratic views of Church government, the desire for more variety and freedom in public worship which they gained at college those who became ministers took with them to the Churches from one end of New England to another. In short, the control of Harvard by the liberal group meant that the future was theirs, that the next generation of clergymen would cast off at least some of the most cherished ideals of John Cotton, Thomas Shepard and John Norton, and also of Increase Mather and Cotton Mather.

If some in the congregations—the older men and women, perhaps—resented the expounding of new ideas from the pulpit, there would be others, who had imbibed the same views in school from masters who had studied under Leverett, to give them hearty support. In public life the situation was similar. The liberal minister—a Benjamin Colman or a William Brattle—could be sure of the support of a group of liberal laymen—Councillors, Deputies, Judges—who had also studied at Harvard.

This liberalism seems mild indeed according to twentieth-century standards. "There was just enough notion of academic freedom to give Harvard a bad name among strict Calvinists." [43] The influence of religion upon the institution was still strong. The Overseers retained the "right to examine into the principles of all those that are employed in the instruction of the students." But the breach with the past was nonetheless real. With the triumph of Leverett and the Brattles and the group they represented, one of the chief props of the old order, the Bible Commonwealth of Winthrop and Cotton, was seriously weakened, if not actually knocked away.

[43] Samuel Eliot Morison, *Three Centuries of Harvard*, p. 83.

Chapter VI

GOD'S CONTROVERSY WITH
NEW ENGLAND

HARDLY less damaging to the old order than the loss of control over education was the gradual decline from the strict code of Puritan morals. To the Puritans this world was little more than a testing ground for the next. God's people were to share in the divine, the eternal pleasures of Heaven; they must not permit themselves to be cheated of this supreme prize by reaching for the temporary, unreal pleasures of human existence. And the danger was great, for Satan was always at hand to tempt them. "Should I tell, in how many forms the Devil has assaulted me," wrote Cotton Mather in his *Diary*, "and with what subtilty and energy his assaults have been carried on, it would strike my friends with horror."[1] If this eminent minister, the champion of the Puritanism of the founders, quailed before the tempter, many lesser souls must have lived in constant dread.

This conception of life found its expression in the Puritan moral code. God in His mercy had plainly marked every one of Satan's booby-traps. He had given to mankind not only the Ten Commandments, but He had pointed out the narrow path to safety by tracing the journey of the saints along it. It was the duty of the State as well as of the Churches to protect the unwary and the weak by adding to God's admonitions man's prohibition of every sinful action, and to anticipate God's punishment by the earthly punishments of fines, imprisonments, the stocks, the whipping post, the branding iron, or the gallows.

To require strict morality of all persons was of great importance to the Churches and the Bible State; not only morality

---

[1] "Diary of Cotton Mather," Massachusetts Historical Society *Collections*, Seventh Series, VII, p. 475.

according to the standards of today, but the stern Calvinist morality. The Puritans believed that no man could enter Heaven
through good works alone, even though his life were entirely
blameless, for salvation came through election by God; but in
determining whom God had elected, the ministers and elders
could not throw out the evidence of good or bad deeds. A saintly
life was the inevitable accompaniment of sainthood.

The upholding of the rigid rule of conduct imposed upon
every man, woman and child was everybody's business. If Goodman Hathaway split wood on the Sabbath, if Master Perkins was
seen bowling at the tavern, if Master Johnson was idling away
God's precious time, the neighbors would be sure to report it to
the minister. Thus the minister was thoroughly acquainted with
the lives of the members of his congregation, and this fact added
to his influence and power. Those who were guilty of infractions
of the moral code knew that they might be excluded from Church
membership, with all that that implied. Even those who had no
hope of admission had good reason to fear the minister's frowns,
for frowns might be the prelude to a summons to appear before
the judge.

The Puritans attached the utmost importance to the Sabbath.
"It has truly and justly been observed that our whole religion fares
according to our Sabbaths," wrote Cotton Mather, "that poor
Sabbaths make poor Christians, and that a strictness in our Sabbaths inspires a vigor into all our other duties." [2] The Lord's Day
must be a day of worship and prayer and meditation. John Cotton
was doubtful of the propriety of preparing a sermon on the
Sabbath, "so far as it might be any wearysome labor to invention
or memory," preferring to devote the time to meditation on what
he was to deliver. To profane this holy day with worldly pleasures, however innocent in themselves, or to do any work, even the
work of preparing food, he considered a serious offense against
Church and State.

Had not the Puritans been fired with the zeal of the prophets
their Sabbath would have been unbearably boring, a kind of self-
imposed penance. And to the lesser lights, to those who were the
hangers-on in the army of the Lord, such it was. But to a John

[2] Cotton Mather, *Magnalia* (London, 1702), Book III, p. 178.

Cotton, to a Thomas Shepard, to a John Eliot the Lord's Day was a day of glory, a day of communion between man and his Maker.

Cotton Mather, who introduces us to so many phases of New England life and so often withdraws the veil from the Puritan mind, describes vividly the Sabbath observances of the sanctified John Eliot. "The sun did not set the evening before the Sabbath till he had begun his preparation for it, and when the Lord's Day came, you might have seen John in the spirit every week. Every day was a sort of Sabbath with him, but the Sabbath day was a kind, a type, a taste of Heaven with him. He labored that he might on that day have no words or thoughts but such as were agreeable thereto; he then allowed himself no actions but those of a raised soul. One should hear nothing dropping from his lips on that day but the milk and honey of the country." But this benign mood would change instantly "if he beheld in any person whatsoever, whether old or young, any profanation of that day," and he would "be sure to bestow rebukes upon it." [3]

Had rebukes from the pious Indian missionary been all the Sabbath breakers had to fear, they might have persisted in their way, but they faced also arrest and fine. There was indignation among the members of the General Court when reports came in that certain persons, both strangers and residents, had been seen "uncivilly walking in the streets and fields" on the Lord's Day, "travelling from town to town, going on ship-board, frequenting common houses and other places to drink, sport or otherwise mis-spend that precious time." All this tended to the "dishonor of God, the reproach of religion," and to "grieving the souls of God's servants."

So a law was enacted to punish these "provokers of the high displeasure of the almighty God." The parents of children over seven years old for the first breach of the Sabbath were to be admonished and for subsequent breaches fined. "Not that we approve younger children in evil," the legislators explained, lest the drawing of the line at seven be misinterpreted. All youths and maids above fourteen and all elder persons who offended by "playing, uncivil walking, drinking, travelling from town to town" on

[3] *Ibid.*

the Sabbath were to be admonished or fined. If they could not pay the fine, they were to be whipped by the constable "not exceeding five stripes for ten shillings fine." [4]

Nor was this an idle threat to be disobeyed at will, as are some of the blue laws which have remained on the statute books in certain States even today. Bennett, who visited Boston nearly eighty years later, was surprised at the strictness of the Sabbath observance. The gates were closed, the ferry guarded, he tells us, so that on that day no man, woman or child was permitted to leave town. Thus confined where their conduct could be scrutinized, they were not permitted to go down to the water front, nor walk in the Common even in the hottest days of summer. If two or three people met by accident on the street and stood talking, the officers warned them to disperse.[5]

It seemed strange to Bennett that the New Englanders began their Sabbath from the setting of the sun on Saturday evening. "All trade and business ceases and every shop in town is shut up, even a barber is finable for shaving after that time." But the observance of the Lord's Day did not end on Sunday evening, for the restrictions upon personal conduct continued until Monday. It seems to have been John Cotton who originated the New England Sabbath, for it is known that he not only adhered to it himself but wrote arguments in its favor.[6]

Levity was frowned upon as unworthy of God's chosen people. In like manner as a courtroom where a man was on trial for his life was not the place for laughter and gaiety, in the world, where man was on trial before his Maker, with eternal punishment hanging in the balance, merry-making was inappropriate and blameworthy. Though there were no written laws prohibiting levity, the ministers condemned it as "inconsistent with the gravity to be always preserved by a serious Christian and especially by those who sustain public station among the people of God." At weddings happiness and even innocent mirth were permissible, but not "riotous or immodest irregularities"; after the midweek

[4] *General Laws of the Massachusetts Colony*, 1658, pp. 69, 70.
[5] Justin Winsor, *The Memorial History of Boston*, II, pp. 467, 468.
[6] *Ibid.*, I, p. 516 n.

lecture it was very wrong to go direct from the meeting-house to the tavern; at huskings the joy of harvest should not be turned into revelry.[7]

For the Maypole the Puritans had an especial aversion. In England they not only refused to join in the Maypole festivities, but condemned them as immoral and pagan, while in New England they banned them completely. The Pilgrim fathers were horrified when they found that the decidedly un-Puritan crew who had begun a settlement at Mt. Wollaston within the present town of Quincy had set up a Maypole. Bradford reports that they danced about it "many days together, inviting the Indian women for their consorts, dancing and frisking together like so many fairies or furies," and so revived "the beastly practices of the mad Bacchanalians." [8] We are not surprised that the stern John Endicott visited the place with an armed force to cut down the pole and admonish the merry band to "look there should be better walking."

Seven decades later, during the Andros regime, New England was once more shocked by the news that a Maypole had been set up, this time in Charlestown, by sailors from the English frigate *Kingfisher*. Thereupon Samuel Phips, one of the Selectmen, ordered the "watch" to cut it down. When the crew defiantly set up another pole with "a garland upon it," Phips and the captain of the frigate "came to blows." At that time few in New England had ever seen a Maypole and many were the inquiries as to just what it was and what were the orgies which accompanied it. When it was explained that the "manner was in England to dance about it with music," there was great apprehension lest this "abomination" should gain a foothold in Massachusetts.[9]

Cards and dice were sternly forbidden. Since the Scriptures revealed that lots were to be used in important cases to discover God's will, to employ them in common sports was a sacrilege. Moreover, as Cotton Mather explains in his *Magnalia,* "these diversions fascinate the minds of those that practice them at such

[7] *A Testimony Against Evil Customs,* p. 2.
[8] William Bradford, *History of Plymouth Plantation,* pp. 237 ff.
[9] "Diary of Samuel Sewall," Massachusetts Historical Society *Collections.* Fifth Series, V, p. 178.

a rate that if ever those persons come to be converted unto God, they bitterly lament the loss of time." [10] Even bowling and shuffle-board, though games of skill rather than of chance, were forbidden by law, if indulged in at houses of common entertainment, because of the time spent unprofitably and the "waste of wine and beer occasioned." [11]

Gambling in any form was strictly forbidden. The law stated: "Nor shall any person at any time play or game for any money or money worth, upon penalty of forfeiting treble the value thereof, one half to the party informing and the other half to the treasury." [12] Cotton Mather was emphatic in declaring that "gains of money or estate by games, be the games what they will, are a sinful violation of the law of honesty and industry which God has given us." But he is less logical when he defends public lotteries. "Great is the difference between a lottery set up by persons acting in a private capacity, and a lottery set up by the government, who have power to lay a tax upon the people but choose to leave unto the more easy determination of a lottery the persons who shall pay the sum." [13]

But Mather was emphatic in condemning the drinking of toasts. "It is too notorious to be denied that it was originally a heathen custom to drink those which were called the cups of health. That which very much adds to the obligation lying upon Christians to abandon this relic of paganism is the idolatrous and diabolical intentions that gave the first rise unto it. We are assured from all the monuments of antiquity that the healths drunk by the pagans were first of all drink offerings to their demons. . . . It becomes Christians to beware of having any fellowship with such unfruitful works of darkness." [14] In 1639 a law was enacted forbidding "that abominable practice" of drinking healths, not only because of its pagan origin but because it led on to other sins, such as "drunkenness, quarreling, bloodshed, uncleanness." But that this law was not always obeyed we learn from the statement

---

[10] Cotton Mather, *Magnalia* (London, 1702), Book V, p. 54.
[11] *General Laws of the Massachusetts Colony,* 1658, p. 33.
[12] *Ibid.*
[13] Cotton Mather, *Magnalia* (London, 1702), Book V, p. 57.
[14] *Ibid.,* p. 55.

of the Synod of 1679 that "that heathenish and idolatrous practice of health-drinking is too frequent." [15]

The Puritans did not condemn drinking in moderation and licenses were frequently granted to sell wine, beer and even "stronger waters"; but drunkenness was abhorred. Since nothing was easier for one accused of intoxication than to claim, as he stood before the judge, that though he had been drinking he had not been drunk, attempts were made to make clear just where the line should be drawn. "By drunkenness is understood a person that either lisps or faulters in his speech by reason of overmuch drink, or that staggers in his going, or that vomits by reason of excessive drinking, or cannot follow his calling," explains the Plymouth law.[16] The Massachusetts law was less precise: "Every person found drunken, viz., so as he be thereby bereaved or disabled in the use of his understanding, appearing in his speech or gesture, . . . shall forfeit ten shillings." [17] We may be sure that if an elder or a selectman or some other prominent Church member detected any of these symptoms in a neighbor or a passer-by, the erring person would soon find himself behind prison bars.

In fact, some of the towns had what today would be called a snooping committee, whose duty it was to pry into the conduct of their neighbors to see that they lived up to the rigid Puritanical standards. Tithing men, they were called, because each one had supervision over the ten families who lived nearest him. If he noted that any one of these families neglected private worship, or failed to observe the Sabbath properly, or were guilty of intemperance, or used profane language, or idled away their time, he was required by law to report it to the nearest magistrate.[18]

Idleness in colonial New England was not just a fault, but a serious misdemeanor. If the constable discovered a group of youths coasting on a winter's day, or in harvest time swimming instead of working in the fields, or if he saw a neighbor taking his ease while enjoying a quiet smoke, he was to report them to the magistrate. Time was God's gift and should be used for His service. At

---

[15] *Necessity of Reformation,* p. 5.
[16] Justin Winsor, *The Memorial History of Boston,* I, p. 495 n.
[17] *General Laws of the Massachusetts Colony,* 1658, p. 44.
[18] Samuel Sewall, *The History of Woburn,* pp. 49, 50.

a meeting of the Selectmen of Woburn, on January 13, 1699, John Carter, Jr., was sent for and reproved for idleness and admonished to improve his time for the future on pain of severe punishment.[19]

For the incorrigible child life in early New England was hard indeed. If the parents could not manage him, any magistrate had the authority to call him into court and upon conviction "sentence him to endure . . . corporal punishment by whipping . . . not exceeding ten stripes for one offence." How frequently the magistrates put this law into effect does not appear, but its very existence must have reinforced greatly the father's authority in his own household. If the disobedient child grew into the delinquent youth, who would not harken to the voice of his parents, they were to lay hold on him and bring him to the magistrates and prove to them that he was rebellious and stubborn. Then, upon conviction, such a son was to be put to death.[20] When the English Attorney-General, John Banks, in examining the laws of Massachusetts in 1677, came upon this order he was greatly shocked and recommended its immediate repeal.[21] But so far as we know the law was never put into effect, for it would have been an unnatural father who would send his own son to the gallows.

The Puritans, believing that woman was one of Satan's chief instruments for gaining control over men's souls, insisted that she hide as much of herself as possible. Though it was permissible for a woman to appear in public with uncovered face and hands, it was wicked to wear gowns with low necks or short sleeves or skirts which fell short of the ankles. In 1656 a law was passed forbidding "short sleeves, whereby the nakedness of the arm may be discovered." Some years later the ministers were deploring the "hainous breaches of the Seventh Commandment," which they attributed to the temptations of "immodest apparel," especially from "naked necks and arms," or, which was even more abominable, "naked breasts." [22]

But even though a woman's sleeves were long and her breast

[19] *Ibid.*, p. 57.
[20] Order of General Court, Nov. 4, 1646.
[21] *Calendar of State Papers, Colonial, America and West Indies, 1677–1680,* p. 140.
[22] *Necessity of Reformation,* p. 6.

and neck covered, she was liable to censure or even punishment if her attire were so costly or showy or above her station as to reveal "pride of raiment." Men, too, might get into trouble through this weakness. In 1634 the General Court, in view of "some new and immodest fashions," prohibited the use of apparel "with any lace on it, silver, gold or thread . . . slashed clothes, other than one slash in each sleeve and another in the back; also, all cutworks, embroidered or needlework caps, bands and rails . . . all gold and silver girdles, hat-bands, belts, ruffs, beaver hats." Five years later they added to the list of prohibitions "immoderate great breeches, knots of ribbon, broad shoulder-bands and rails, silk rases, double ruffs and cuffs," with the warning that such "superfluities" tended "to little use or benefit, but to the nourishment of pride." [23] "There is pride appearing in the garb, in garish attire, in affected trimmings and adornings of the outward man, that body of clay that is going to the dust and the worms," complained Urian Oakes. "Hath God brought us into a wilderness and caused us to dwell alone and separated us for a peculiar people to himself, that we should imitate the nations in these vanities? . . . When persons spend more time in trimming their bodies than their souls . . . you may say of them, as a worthy divine wittily speaks, that they are like the cinnamon tree, nothing good but the bark." [24]

But the colonial legislators found pride a very difficult thing to suppress. The minister might reprove and threaten the members of his congregation who appeared before him in silks and laces, but the desire for personal adornment was too great to be overcome. The authorities were especially outraged when persons of mean position, servants or the wives of day laborers, dared to don fine apparel. "We cannot but . . . declare our utter detestation . . . that men or women of mean condition should take upon them the garb of gentlemen," declared the General Court, "by wearing gold or silk lace, or buttons, or points at their knees, or to walk in great boots, or women of the same rank to wear silk or taffeta hoods, or scarfs, which though allowable to persons of greater estates or more liberal education, yet we cannot but judge

[23] *Massachusetts Colonial Records*, I, p. 126.
[24] Urian Oakes, *New England Pleaded With*, p. 34.

intolerable in persons of such like condition." [25] The Court did not pause to consider that servant girls and others of "mean condition" had probably long envied the silk, or lace, or great boots of their "superiors," and were not to be thwarted if high wages gave them the means of indulging themselves. That human nature has not changed in the three centuries which have elapsed we had ample evidence during both World Wars, when servant girls laid out their incomes in fur coats and silk or nylon stockings.

But whereas extravagance in raiment incurs today nothing more serious than criticism, in colonial New England it was apt to draw a heavy fine, especially if the silks and laces were worn in a "flaunting" manner. In the county of Hampshire in 1673 alone, thirty women were presented to the jury as persons of small estate who wore silk contrary to law. All were let off with a warning save the wife of Joseph Barnard, who was fined ten shillings and costs. The next year, when the wife of Edward Grannis was presented, she also was fined ten shillings because her hood and scarf, though a bit shabby, were of "good silk." In 1676 the men, too, had their inning, no less than thirty being summoned along with thirty-eight women. In Hadley, in 1677, a Mrs. Hannah Westcarr was admonished "for wearing silk in a flaunting garb, to the great offence of several sober persons." [26]

Nathaniel Ward, in his *Simple Cobbler of Agawam,* was unrestrained in his indignation at the foppery of a few women in the Boston of 1645, at a time when God was "shaking the heavens over his head and the earth under his feet." He did not quarrel with good taste in women's dress, he avowed, nor whatever Christianity or civility allowed, but it was beyond his understanding how any woman could have so little wit as to disfigure herself with "exotic garb" and transform herself into a bar-goose, an ill-shapen shell fish. "It is no marvel they wear drails on the hinder parts of their heads; having nothing, it seems, in the forepart but a few squirrel's brains." [27]

From the first the Puritans of New England had trouble in enforcing their moral code. Most of the settlers led pure and godly

[25] *General Laws of the Massachusetts Colony,* 1658, p. 3.
[26] Sylvester Judd, *History of Hadley,* pp. 99, 100.
[27] Pp. 26, 27.

lives, but among them was a sprinkling of servants and laborers whose sinfulness was a source of sorrow to the leaders of the migration. Governor Bradford of Plymouth wondered how it was possible that "so many wicked persons and profane people should so quickly come over." Then he explains that in addition to a number of "untoward servants," certain profligate persons were sent to New England by their friends, some under the hope that the pious atmosphere of the colony would reform them, others that their families should "be kept from shame at home." [28]

But the cases of gross impurity which appear in the records—of adultery, sodomy, even bestiality—cannot obscure the fact that the great majority of the settlers tried to live in conformity with their religion. John Dunton says they were certainly the most pious and religious men in the world, "the lively patterns of primitive zeal and integrity." The ministers of the second and third generation were apt to exaggerate the sanctity of their fathers and grandfathers, but much of the praise which they handed out in such unstinted measure was certainly deserved. "Their hearts were then raised to so eminent a degree of holiness and piety that they could discern the least buildings of sin," said William Hubbard, "and the first rise of any worldly lusts, which made them ready to condemn themselves under those several fiery trials in the furnace of affliction." [29] "Your fathers before you served God in their generation," Eleazer Mather told his congregation, "they lived and died in the faith of the Gospel and the profession thereof." [30] Urian Oakes praised the founders for "the faith, the fervency, the zeal for God, the good affection to his ordinances, the dear love to his messengers, the Heavenly-mindedness, the diligence in working out their own salvation and watching over their hearts and tongues and conversations, that practical piety and power of Godliness" which animated their every action.[31]

But the very rigidity of the Puritan moral code eventually tended to undermine morality. It did harm in not discriminating sufficiently between petty misdemeanors and serious crimes. When

[28] "William Bradford, History of Plymouth Plantation," Massachusetts Historical Society Collections, Series 4, III, pp. 398, 399.
[29] William Hubbard, The Happiness of a People, p. 54.
[30] Eleazer Mather, A Serious Exhortation.
[31] Urian Oakes, New England Pleaded With, p. 27.

the gathering of firewood on the Sabbath was punished with the same severity as adultery or theft, adultery and theft lost some of their flagrancy. When a man or woman had been put into the category of evil-doers by an admonition, or had been fined or exposed to public scorn in the stocks, there must have been a temptation to play the role. Certain it is that before the first half century had passed there was a decided weakening in the moral standards imposed by the founders. John Dunton tells us that many of the second and third generation walked in "the steps of their pious fathers," but that others, while retaining the outward form of godliness were in fact "the most profligate and debauched wretches in the world." [32]

One would be inclined to reject this statement as an exaggeration, were it not substantiated by the ministers in sermon after sermon. "Oh! have you not lived to see much of your former life and godliness laid in the grave?" asked Eleazer Mather. "Truly, the very heart of New England is changed, and exceedingly corrupted with the sins of the times," bemoaned Samuel Torrey in 1674. "There is a spirit of profaneness, a spirit of pride, a spirit of worldliness, a spirit of sensuality, a spirit of gainsaying and rebellion, a spirit of libertinism, a spirit of carnality." [33] In 1692 Cotton Mather declared that some of the rising generation had given themselves up to the "most abominable impieties of uncleanness, drunkenness and a lewd, rude, extravagant sort of behavior." Among them were some "prodigies of wickedness," veritable "children of Belial."

Increase Mather, as early as 1673, in two sermons on the sin of drunkenness, denounced the "dark houses" where wicked persons sold drink and destroyed souls, which were "the very sinks of sin," the corruptors of youth. Four decades later he was still pleading the cause of temperance. "Is not that worse than brutish sin of drunkenness become a prevailing iniquity all over the country? How has wine and cider, but most of all rum, debauched multitudes of people, young and old?" Again and again the min-

[32] John Dunton, *Letters from New England* (Prince Society, *Publications*, IV), p. 66.
[33] Samuel Torrey, *An Exhortation unto Reformation*, p. 8.

isters pleaded and threatened. Was piety and morality to be laid in
the grave with the fathers of New England? Would the rising
generation turn their backs upon the ways of godliness, which
were the foundation stones of New England, and give themselves
over to sin and corruption?

God's people had an especial obligation to holiness, since they
had been favored with greater light. God had been patient with
them, had shown himself loath to give them up. "And therefore,"
said Samuel Torrey, "after all our backslidings, unworthy, sinful,
shameful carriages, evil requitals, high provocations of Him,
whereby we have so much grieved and wearied Him . . . yet
He is after all . . . still calling and crying after us, 'Return, ye
backsliding children.'" But His patience was not inexhaustible.
"That God hath a controversy with His New England people is
undeniable, the Lord having written His displeasure in dismal
characters against us," warned the Synod of 1679. "Would the
Lord have whetted his glittering sword? . . . Would he have
sent such a mortal contagion like a besom of destruction in the
midst of us? Would He have said, 'Sword, go through the land
and cut off man and beast?' Or would He have kindled such
devouring fires and made such fearful desolations in the earth, if
He had not been angry?" [34]

Nor were the ministers hesitant in naming the transgressions
which were so provoking the Maker. Despite Bennett's description of the strictness of Sabbath observance in New England, the
clergy complained as early as 1679 of frequent breaches of the
Lord's Day. The Synod of 1679 bewailed the fact that many persons did not keep a seventh part of the holy time for the Lord as
the Fourth Commandment requires. Others insisted upon "walking abroad" and traveling; others went about their "servile callings and employments" after the Sabbath had begun or before it
had ended; "worldly, unsuitable discourses" were very common
on the Lord's Day, which was "contrary to the Scripture"; many,
failing to prepare in advance for the Sabbath, desecrated the day
under the pretense of necessity. Those who doubted that sin of
this kind would provoke God to anger and bring "fires and other

[34] *Necessity of Reformation,* pp. 1, 2.

judgments" were referred to Nehemiah 13: 17 and Jeremiah 17: 27.[35]

If those who read this warning had forgotten it when the great fire of 1711 swept over Boston, Increase Mather was prompt to remind them of it. "Has not God's holy day been profaned in New England?" he asked. "Has it not been so in Boston this last summer? Have not burdens been carried through the streets on the Sabbath day? Nay, have not bakers, carpenters and other tradesmen been employed in servile works on the Sabbath day? When I saw this, my heart said, 'Will not the Lord for this kindle a fire in Boston?'" [36]

These breaches of the Lord's Day brought forth new prohibitive legislation. A law of October, 1692, required all persons to "apply themselves to duties of religion and piety, publicly and privately" on the Sabbath, and not to do any "work of their ordinary callings," nor to indulge in "any game, sport, play or recreation." Even the dead had to observe the day, for a law of May, 1701, orders that no person should make a coffin or dig a grave on the Sabbath. And should both casket and grave be ready by sunset on Saturday, the interment still would have to wait until Monday, because funerals occasioned profanation of the Lord's Day "by servants and children gathering in the street." Additional acts against Sabbath-breaking were passed in 1716 and 1727. In 1746 a notice appeared in the *News-Letter,* warning the people that the justices would patrol the streets of Boston to apprehend those found "walking, standing in the streets or other ways breaking the laws made for the due observation of the Lord's Day." [37]

There could be no surer sign that the Puritan code of morals was beginning to weaken than the growing use of profanity. We would be inclined to doubt Nathaniel Ward's statement that notwithstanding the "sanctity" of the New Englanders they were "very profane in their common dialect," were it not confirmed by the ministers and other leading Puritans. The Synod of 1679 bemoaned the fact that "the glorious name of God" had been "pol-

---

[35] *Ibid.,* p. 4.
[36] Justin Winsor, *The Memorial History of Boston,* II, p. 470 n.
[37] *Ibid.,* pp. 469, 470.

luted and profaned," and their oaths and imprecations in ordinary discourse were so common that the whole land had good reason to mourn.[38] As early as 1663 John Higginson, in his election-day sermon, declared that many persons were so profane, so free with their oaths and blasphemies that God and His people were no longer in their thoughts.[39]

In September, 1686, staunch Samuel Sewall was greatly shocked by the drunken revels of a coaching party. "Mr. Shrimpton, Captain Lidget and others come in a coach from Roxbury about nine o'clock or past," he wrote in his *Diary,* "singing as they come, being inflamed with drink. At Justice Morgan's they stop and drink healths, curse, swear, talk profanely and baudily to the great disturbance of the town and grief of good people. Such highhanded wickedness has hardly been heard of before in Boston." [40] But that this incident was not entirely exceptional we learn from Sewall himself, when a few months later he tells us that Increase Mather in the midweek lecture had spoken sharply against "health-drinking, card-playing, drunkenness, profane swearing, Sabbath-breaking, etc." [41]

The ministers were deeply concerned at the excessive drinking in taverns. "We cannot but particularly exhort and most pressingly move and urge that all needless frequenting of taverns may be carefully avoided," declared the Boston clergy. Church members should not set an evil example to their own children in this matter for fear of ruining them "in their very infancy." [42] "Oh! that the drinking houses in the town might once come under a laudable regulation," said Cotton Mather. "The town has an enormous number of them; will the haunters of these houses hear the counsels of Heaven? For you that are the town dwellers to be oft or long in your visits to the ordinary, 'twill certainly expose you to mischiefs more than ordinary. I have seen certain taverns where the pictures of horrible devourers were hanged out for signs. . . .

[38] *Necessity of Reformation,* pp. 3, 4.
[39] John Higginson, *The Cause of God and His People in New England,* Preface.
[40] "Diary of Samuel Sewall," Massachusetts Historical Society *Collections,* Fifth Series, V, p. 150.
[41] *Ibid.,* p. 169.
[42] *A Testimony Against Evil Customs,* p. 3.

Don't countenance drunkenness, revelling and misspending of precious time." [43]

The records show that the Selectmen and justices made every effort to put an end to excessive drinking and at least succeeded in making life hard for the toper. At Woburn, a certain William Deane was fined for "excess in drink," and after the third offense was set in the stocks to sober up at leisure. Three Indians who had imbibed too freely of firewater were given the option of paying ten shillings or receiving ten lashes each. John Johnson's spree must have been a mild one, for he was let off with a fine of only ten groats. [44]

It was the aversion of the Puritans to the wearing of long hair by men which caused the Cavaliers in derision to dub them Roundheads. This aversion the emigrants to New England took with them and the General Court as late as 1675 condemned flowing locks as a dangerous vanity. John Gatchell of Marblehead, when he incurred a fine for building on town land, was informed that half the sum would be remitted if he would "cut off the long hair off his head into a civil frame." John Hull thought "pride in long hair" an evil comparable to drinking, gaming or idleness. [45]

On the other hand, we know from the portraits of prominent Puritans both in England and in New England that some allowed their hair to grow. Oliver Cromwell, Sir Harry Vane, Sir Richard Saltonstall, John Winthrop, Simon Bradstreet, John Endicott, all are shown with long hair. Perhaps it was thought that with hair as with fine raiment what was mere "vanity" for the poor and humble was quite appropriate for the great and the wealthy. At all events, before the end of the seventeenth century the fashion of wearing long hair seems to have gained universal acceptance. As early as 1675 the General Court deplored the "manifest pride" which was appearing in New England "in that long hair, like a woman's hair," was worn by some men. [46]

An even more startling innovation was the wearing of wigs, a vogue which gained wide acceptance at the turn of the century.

[43] Cotton Mather, *Magnalia* (Hartford, 1820), I, p. 92.
[44] Samuel Sewall, *The History of Woburn*, p. 60.
[45] "Diary of John Hull," American Antiquarian Society *Transactions and Collections*, III, p. 211.
[46] N. H. Chamberlain, *Samuel Sewall*, p. 209.

Staunch Samuel Sewall to his dying day resisted this "abomination," and any neighbor who was bold enough to appear in public with artificial hair was sure to receive a visit from him. "Having occasion this day to go to Mr. Hayward," he wrote in his *Diary*, "I speak to him about the cutting off his hair and wearing a periwig of contrary color. Mention the words of the Savior, 'Can ye not make one hair white or black?' and Mr. Alsop's sermon. He alleges the doctor advised him to it." [47]

It was in June, 1701, that Sewall heard that Josiah Willard, son of the Reverend Samuel Willard of the Old South Church, had cut off "a very full head of hair" and put on a wig. Losing no time in calling on him, he asked "what extremity had forced him to put off his own hair and put on a wig?" Young Willard, looking at Sewall's clean-shaven face, replied that he saw no more reason for prohibiting the cutting of hair from the top of the head than from the chin. But the judge was not to be so easily repulsed. "Men were men before they had hair on their faces, half of mankind have never any," he answered sternly. "God seems to have ordained our hair as a test to see whether we can bring our minds to be content to be at His finding; or whether we would be our own carvers, lords, and come no more at Him." The judge then reminded Willard that he had been present at a meeting of ministers at Northampton when the wearing of wigs had been condemned. Five months later Sewall, turning his back on the Old South Church for one Sabbath, attended the services at the Brattle Street Church, "partly out of dislike of Mr. Josiah Willard's cutting off his hair and wearing a wig." "He that condemns the law of nature is not fit to be a publisher of the law of grace." [48]

But the Brattle Street Church did not long continue a refuge for the condemners of wigs, for the minister himself, the distinguished Benjamin Colman, succumbed to the prevailing fashion. His portrait shows him looking out from an enveloping mass of curled locks much as though someone had poured a bushel of cotton over his head. Soon it became difficult for Sewall to find

[47] "Diary of Samuel Sewall," Massachusetts Historical Society *Collections*, Fifth Series, V, p. 102.
[48] Quoted by N. H. Chamberlain, *Samuel Sewall*, p. 210.

any place in Boston free from this "vanity." The clergy were frequent visitors to Farnham, the "peruke-king" of the town, and adorned their heads with mops of false hair that would have done credit to the models of fashion in the Court of Queen Anne. Cotton Mather wore a huge wig, the Reverend William Cooper wore a wig, the Reverend Charles Chauncy wore a wig. One wonders whether the ministers, as they looked out from beneath their borrowed locks over the wig-adorned heads of their congregations, stopped to think of their own warnings against "pride of hair," or to admit to themselves that their own surrender was a convincing evidence of the "spiritual decay" which they so deeply deplored.

Dancing, especially "mixed" dancing, the Puritans condemned as frivolous, a waste of time, and immoral. So outraged were the Boston ministers when, in 1684, they discovered that many persons were indulging in this form of diversion, that they issued a pamphlet entitled, *An Arrow against Profane and Promiscuous Dancing, drawn out of the Quiver of the Scriptures.*[49] When this failed of the desired effect they took the matter into the court. "The ministers of this town come to the court and complain against a dancing-master who seeks to set up here and hath mixt dances and his time of meeting is lecture-day," wrote Samuel Sewall. "Mr. Moodey said 'twas not a time for New England to dance." [50] Later the instructor, Francis Stepney, was "ordered not to keep a dancing school," and was forced to give bond for compliance.

Yet dancing, like wigs, gradually established itself, and though the clergy continued to frown upon the practice, the drawing rooms of the mansions of the wealthy merchants frequently echoed to the strains of the minuet. "For dancing-schools, we cannot commend the time and cost often thrown away on them, but greatly disapprove them, looking on them as hurtful to the interests of serious piety among our young people," [51] declared the Boston ministers. Nonetheless, in 1723 a dancing-master so far

---

[49] Justin Winsor, *The Memorial History of Boston,* II, p. 191.

[50] "Diary of Samuel Sewall," Massachusetts Historical Society *Collections,* Fifth Series, V, p. 112.

[51] *A Testimony against Evil Customs,* p. 3.

SAMUEL SEWALL

COTTON MATHER

defied them as to advertise in a local newspaper, apparently without molestation.[52]

Thus, long before the end of the seventeenth century, it had become evident that many young people were rebelling against the strict code of conduct which the Church tried to impose upon them. For this the clergy blamed not only the parents but those neighbors who closed their eyes to what was going on or refused to report it. "There are families that do not pray to God constantly morning and evening and many more wherein the Scriptures are not daily read," they declared. Parents were sinfully indulgent to their children, unmindful of the judgment this would bring upon their family just as it had done with Eli's family and David's family.[53] That similar conditions existed in Connecticut we learn from a report of the Associated Churches deploring the lack of Bibles in some families, the laxity of "domestic government" and the neglect of catechizing.[54] No wonder William Hubbard declared that there were few "hopeful buds springing up among the rising generation."[55]

The sailors who manned the numerous sloops, brigs and ships which were constantly entering and departing from the New England ports constituted an especial problem for the ministers. These men could not be forced to remain on board the entire time that their vessels were tied up at Old Wharf or Scarlett's Wharf or were undergoing repairs at Thorton's shipyard, yet when they came ashore they became a corrupting influence. And it was a grief to the ministers that the sailors, when they were upon the high seas or in some foreign port, were entirely removed from their jurisdiction. If a Mather or a Norton, when passing a water-front tavern, heard sounds of revelry, they could report it to the officers of the law, but they were helpless when the men fiddled or drank or sang lewd songs in the middle of the Atlantic or in the bawdy-houses of London.

Cotton Mather, who was especially concerned over this leak

[52] Justin Winsor, *The Memorial History of Boston*, II, pp. 322, 480.
[53] *Necessity of Reformation*, p. 5.
[54] William B. Weeden, *Economic and Social History of New England*, II, p. 549.
[55] William Hubbard, *The Happiness of a People*, p. 52.

in the roof of New England's moral structure, tried to remedy it with his pen. Since he could not corral the sailors into the North Church to reprove them for their drunkenness, profanity, gambling, quarreling and fighting, he preached a short sermon which he published under the title *The Religious Marriner—A Brief Discourse Tending to Direct the Course of Sea-men in those Points of Religion which may bring them into the Port of Eternal Happiness.* Nine years later he followed with a volume which he called *The Sailours' Companion—An Offer of Considerations for the Tribe of Zebulan: Awakening the Mariner to Think and to Do Those Things that may render his Voyage Prosperous.* This little book, designed to warn "the unregenerate sailour out of his dangerous condition" by "admonitions of piety, fetched out of the various objects and actions aboard," he placed in the cabins of the vessels entering and departing from the chief New England ports. "Who can tell what may be done?" he asked. "Whether some of the elect of God may not be found out upon the waters?"

Mather makes it clear that the "sea-faring tribe" of colonial New England were not less addicted to strong drink than those of other ages, and he warned them that intemperance was destroying both the bodies and souls of many of them. "My friend, six foot water in the hold of the vessel would not more endanger it than the pouring in the cups of intoxication will endanger thy soul. . . . Every time a sailor makes himself drunk the Devil keelhauls him." How much better it would be for the sailors to pray than to howl out those foolish and filthy songs "which only too often were in their mouths." They should "abhor those wretched songs," and substitute holy psalms which would be a melody to the Lord.[56]

It seems strange that the man who wrote a book to establish the reality of witchcraft should deplore the prevalence of superstition among sailors. It is probable, however, that he condemned the sorcery practiced to bring a prosperous voyage not because he thought it futile, but because it was an appeal to evil rather than holy powers. As for the horrid baptisms used among sailors in passing the equator, they were "black defiances of Heaven, better for Devils than Christians." He urged the sailors, also, to abhor

[56] Cotton Mather, *The Sailours' Companion,* p. 37.

all invocations to St. Andrew, St. Clement, St. Nicholas, St. Michael, St. Christopher and St. Barbara as vanities introduced by those "new gentiles, the Roman Catholics." [57]

The proneness of sailors to curse and swear aroused Mather's indignation. They ought to be as loath to take "obscene, smutty, baudy talk" into their mouths as to swallow "so much filthy bilge water." If shipwreck or other disaster should drive them to make a prayer to God, how could such a blaspheming mouth do so? "For a sailor to be a swearer, or to have a mouth full of cursing or to scoff at religion, how unreasonable is such foaming madness." It was as though some horrible devil had taken possession of their tongues.[58]

Mather urged the sailors to avoid gambling in any form. "It occasions broils and quarrels, it wastes time and consumes wealth and induces sloth, inadvertency and neglect of business. And what's still worse, it usually indisposes men for their devotion and all serious thought. . . . There is much pleasanter entertainment in ingenious discourse, in many pleasant and useful histories and in other divertive books." [59]

Although he did not blind himself to the necessity seafaring men were under of working on the Lord's Day during sea voyages, he urged them to do just as little as possible, utilizing the leisure thus gained to read books of piety.[60]

For those guilty of unnatural vice, Mather threatened divine wrath. Perhaps many a vessel had been lost at sea, he thought, because of uncleanness aboard. "God will have those dogs to be drown'd; thro' the water they must pass to the vengeance of eternal fire." As for those who visited disreputable houses ashore, they not only made fools of themselves and squandered their wages, but ran the risk of ruining their health.[61]

In conclusion the good minister advised the sailors, as they traveled over the wide sea, to observe the numberless and surprising works of God and to praise Him, who did whatever He pleased in Heaven, on earth and in the ocean. But praise should

[57] Ibid., pp. 6, 7.
[58] Ibid., pp. 38, 39.
[59] Ibid., pp. 41, 42.
[60] Ibid., pp. 9, 10.
[61] Ibid., pp. 39, 40.

be accompanied by fear. "When that work of nature, the thunder, which you often meet withal, is making its rapid peals over your heads, let it awaken you to think, 'This is the voice of God' . . . and add, 'Let me always be afraid of offending the great God, who can when he pleases thunder-strike the disobedient.' " [62]

Apparently Mather's efforts to reform the seafaring men did not meet with success, for years later, in a moment of despondency, he spoke bitterly of their ingratitude. He had done his best for them, he said, "in prayers for them, in sermons to them, in books bestowed upon them"; and yet there was not a man in the world "so reviled, so slandered, so cursed among the sailors." Especially irritating was the indignity cast upon him by a lieutenant on a man-of-war by naming his Negro slave Cotton Mather. [63]

It was September 10, 1679, that the elders and ministers of the churches met in Boston to consider "what are the evils that have provoked the Lord to bring his judgments on New England." As they took their seats, elected John Sherman of Watertown and Urian Oakes moderators, and proceeded with their deliberations, all the congregations throughout Massachusetts sent up their prayers for the success of the synod. Earnestly and anxiously the members debated the evils of the times, the decay of the Churches, the laxness of morals. New England had indeed fallen from the high estate in which the founders had left it. One member contended that there was a visible decline in godliness, another declared that "the pride that doth abound in New England" was only too obvious; another spoke of the many breaches of the Second Commandment; a fourth deplored the frequency with which the name of God was taken in vain; another declared there was too much Sabbath-breaking; another condemned parents for the laxity of home discipline; another dwelt on the many "sinful heats and hatreds, and that amongst Church members"; still another spoke of the prevalence of drunkenness. In the face of such evidence as this could anyone wonder why God had punished His people with the terrible Indian war, with pestilence and fire?

Finally a committee was appointed "to draw up what did ap-

[62] *Ibid.*, pp. 52, 53.
[63] "Diary of Cotton Mather," Massachusetts Historical Society *Collections*, Seventh Series, VIII, pp. 663, 706.

pear to be the mind of the Assembly." When their report was presented to the synod it was read twice as all listened intently, and then, after some further debate, unanimously adopted.

It was a great and high undertaking of their fathers, they said, when they ventured themselves and their little ones upon the rude waves of the vast ocean to follow the Lord into New England. To find a parallel one would have to go back to ancient history, to the journey of Abraham from Ur, or that of the Israelites from Egypt. In the American wilderness the Puritans had been the recipients of God's peculiar mercies. He had turned the desert into a fruitful land, He had cast out the heathen. "Our fathers neither sought for, nor thought of great things for themselves, but did seek first the Kingdom of God and his righteousness."

But now, after many years of the Lord's favors, His people were forgetful of the errand upon which He had sent them to America. No wonder, then, that He was not only withholding His favors, but was "turning to do them hurt." There were a number of precious souls in every congregation who had not defiled their garments with the sins of the times, but the present generation as a whole was far short of those who built God's temple in New England. Their iniquities were the more inexcusable, since they were fortunate in having greater "light" than other peoples. It was high time for the synod to make "an impartial scrutiny" as to the cause of God's displeasure and suggest the proper remedies. If New England remembered whence she had fallen and heeded the synod's warning there was still hope. But if this, together with the other efforts of the Lord to reclaim them was unheeded, they dreaded what would follow. "What God out of his soveraity may do for us, no man can say, but according to his wonted dispensations, we are a perishing people if we reform not." [64]

The report was put into the form of a communication to the General Court. When the Court had read it and "commended the same to the serious consideration of all the Churches and peoples," it was published under the title of *Necessity of Reformation* and circulated throughout New England.

This document is a landmark in the history of the Bible Com-

[64] *Necessity of Reformation*, Epistle Dedicatory.

monwealth, hardly less significant than the loss of the charter. While the latter brought to an end the autonomy which was essential for the religio-political structure of society established by the Puritans in Massachusetts, the former is a confession that the moral standards upon which it was based had greatly deteriorated. Sainthood for all God's people had been the ideal of the founders, but the picture which the Synod of 1679 draws of conditions existing at the time of their sitting shows how far it was from realization.

The Puritan leaders were learning that you cannot run away from sin. The people who had left their homes in England to follow the pillar of light into the New World were for the most part pious, good men and women; but they were ordinary human beings with ordinary desires and instincts. These desires and instincts they might hold in subjection, but they could not eliminate them nor prevent their children from inheriting them. And the children, lacking the religious zeal which comes from original discovery and persecution, tempted to self-indulgence by increasing prosperity, failed to uphold the original standards. As Eleazer Mather put it, they had grown cold in religious power, decayed in godliness.

Chapter VII

MORE OF THE WORLD, LESS OF HEAVEN

THE PURITAN fathers in founding New England were but dimly aware of the effect of local conditions upon their great venture. Yet, as they looked out from the decks of their little vessels upon the safe harbors in which they cast anchor, or noted the great schools of cod and herring which swarmed offshore, or explored every nook of Massachusetts Bay, Buzzards Bay and Narragansett Bay or peeped into the mouths of the Thames, the Connecticut and other rivers; as they examined the sandy soil of southeast Massachusetts, the boulder-covered uplands of the interior and the ancient mountain ranges to the north and west; as they viewed the vast reaches of the forests, they must have realized that these things would have a profound influence, not only upon their lives, but upon the future of the theocratic society it was their purpose to found.

If so, they were comforted by the thought that it was God Himself who had selected this region as the future home of His people, so that it must be in every way suitable. The abounding fish of the ocean had been placed there for their use, the noble harbors had been especially fashioned for their ships, the forests had been planted so that they might have wood for building houses and vessels, the soil had purposely been made rather infertile so that they would not forget religion for the quest of wealth. The Lord had led the Children of Israel into a land flowing with milk and honey, and it was to be expected that in the new Canaan He wished His people to enjoy the good things He had provided for them.

The ideal Puritan State was a very delicate plant, requiring not only constant care, but the most favorable conditions of soil and climate. It demanded isolation from the rest of the world lest it wither under the impact of new ideas, new discoveries and

new ideals; the concentration of the people in centers of population so that they would not escape the ministrations and admonitions of the preachers and elders; an even distribution of wealth
that there might be no influential group whose authority did not
have its roots in religion; political sovereignty, so that no outside
power might reach across the Atlantic to overthrow its laws and
break down its safeguards against heresy. Exacting demands these,
so exacting that Massachusetts and her sister Commonwealths
were to find it impossible to meet them.

The town with its agricultural village was the ideal economic
and social unit for the Puritan State, and had it continued un-
changed the forces of disintegration would have been greatly re-
tarded. But when thousands turned from agriculture to commerce,
shipbuilding and fishing, when many villages grew into thriving
cities, and when the farm began to replace the common field,
the effect upon the established order was decidedly unfavorable.
The "fathers," as we have seen, showed remarkable foresight in
making the agricultural village the center of life in every community, but their vision did not extend beyond the first generation, for the typical town contained from the first the germ of
disintegration.

It was land-hunger which proved the undoing of the original
scheme. In England where great areas were held by the aristocracy
and where tenantry was so widespread, the ownership of land
in fee-simple was the ambition of every agricultural worker. It
was the promise of land, not an acre or two, but scores, perhaps
hundreds, of acres, which brought many of the first settlers to
America and which later drove thousands of pioneers westward
until the frontier had been wiped out. Had the founders of New
England so restricted the size of each town that no point within
its bounds lay more than two or at most three miles from its
center, the course of New England history might have been different. But with each group of newcomers clamoring for land,
and pointing eagerly to the vast unoccupied reaches, it seemed
unreasonable for the government to be niggardly. So they usually
set out for their new home bearing with them a charter for a tract
far larger than they or their sons after them could hope to put
under cultivation.

This was not a matter of serious concern during the first generation, for the town committee, after laying out the village and dividing the land adjacent to it, left the outlying tracts as common property to be held by the proprietors for future use. But its effects became apparent when the sons of the original settlers came of age, married and demanded land of their own, for the setting off of new divisions three, four or perhaps five miles from the village, made it imperative that the owners should organize their holdings as farms and erect on them dwellings and barns. The most conservative of selectmen, the most earnest minister, could not insist that a young proprietor reside in the old "center," when it would force him to go so great a distance to and from work, taking his farm implements with him and perhaps driving his ox team.

Consequently the more distant parts of the town were usually divided, not into strips of land within a field, but into farms. This all-important development may be traced in the records of scores of towns in Massachusetts, Connecticut, New Jersey and other colonies. The case of Enfield was typical. The original grant, embracing as it did a wide expanse of land in north-central Connecticut, was far too large for the first settlers to put under cultivation, and many square miles of good land was left in common. But in 1697 it was decided to make a new division, allotting each proprietor extensive holdings east of a north-south line four miles from the village.[1] Most of these new lots lay idle for years, but gradually the owners' sons, as they grew to manhood, cleared away the trees from limited areas and put them under cultivation. It is probable that in some cases these young men continued to live in the village, making the trip to the fields only when plowing or harvesting, and erecting crude shacks in which from time to time they could spend the night. The first settler in what is now Somers, one Benjamin Jones, lived on his land only during the summer. But in time many proprietors moved out permanently, built houses and established themselves as farmers.

Thus was the original plan of the founders undermined. While the village of Enfield, with its system of fields and lots continued for many more decades, it had ceased to be the place of residence for an ever-increasing part of the people. In 1729 the number of

[1] Francis O. Allen, *History of Enfield, Conn.*, I, pp. 289–308.

families in the eastern part of the town had become so numerous that they were permitted to have their own school. The establishing two decades later of a school system for the entire town, with buildings in the northern, southern, northeastern and southeastern parts, shows how widespread the farm system had then become.

The Enfield ministers must have viewed with dismay the dispersal of their congregation over so wide an area. No longer was it possible for them, as in the old days when their entire flock lived within the village, to catechize the children, visit all the sick, watch over the wavering and admonish the wayward. When the roads were blocked by snow or washed by heavy rains, they knew that there would be many vacant seats during the Sunday sermon. Even though they did their best to hold the congregation together, riding out to the outlying farms to catechize the children and visit the sick, the effort was a severe one and the results unsatisfactory. So they made no serious objection when, in 1723, the farmers in the most distant part of the town set themselves off as the East Precinct, or when, four years later, they drew up their covenant as a separate Church, or when, in 1734, they broke off completely from Enfield and established their own town.[2]

The experience of Enfield was repeated by town after town. In Woodbury, when a new community was formed known as the Upper Farms, the good people living there retained their membership in the parent Church for years, trudging from four to seven miles every Sunday in winter and summer to the village meeting-house, carrying with them their fire-arms as protection against the Indians. But at last, when they begged the Assembly to have mercy on their souls by permitting them to establish a Church of their own, that body, after long delays, constituted them into the parish of Roxbury. Still later another group, living in what was known as the North Purchase, "near ten miles distant from the first society," established a third Church.[3]

Even more instructive is the story of the Church of South Hadley. When the people south of Mount Holyoke, tired of walking eight miles over mountain paths to attend Sabbath services, gained permission to have their own ecclesiastical society, they

[2] *Ibid.*, I, p. 344. The new town was named Somers.
[3] William Cothren, *The History of Ancient Woodbury, Conn.*, pp. 239–257, 273–276.

began plans to erect the meeting-house. But now a bitter controversy arose over its location. If it were placed in the east part of the precinct, the farmers in the west would still have to cover miles of bad road to reach it; if in the west part, the eastern farmers would suffer. When at last the western group won and actually began construction, some of the others under the cover of night cut off the plates and pushed over one end of the frame. After this act of vandalism, so inconsistent with the "brotherly sweetness" urged by the ministers, the two parts of South Hadley were divided into separate Churches, so that each could have its own meeting-house.[4]

It was perhaps inevitable that the first village to be founded in New England was also the first to suffer from the transition to rural life. The Pilgrim fathers, toiling upon their infertile soil, found it difficult to supply themselves with the bare necessities of life. But with the Great Migration came a decided change, for the demand for grain and cattle, which sent prices soaring, brought sudden and unexpected prosperity. This in turn influenced the people to make new clearings for pastures and corn-fields, which, in many cases, were at such a distance from the village that the owners were forced to reside upon them. "There was no longer any holding them together," complained Governor Bradford, "but now they must of necessity go to their great lots. And no man now thought he could live except he had cattle and a great deal of ground to keep them, all striving to increase their stocks. By which means they were scattered all over the bay quickly and the town, in which they had lived compactly till now, was left very thin, and in a short time almost desolate."[5]

The Governor did not begrudge the people their sudden prosperity, but he bewailed the effect of this dispersal upon religion, which turned benefit into hurt and "accession of strength to their weakness." For the scattering of the settlers was followed by the dividing of the Church so that "those that had lived so long together in Christian and comfortable fellowship must now part and suffer many divisions. First, those that lived on their lots on the other side of the bay (called Duxbury) they could not long

[4] Sylvester Judd, *History of Hadley*, pp. 289 n., 395–401.
[5] William Bradford's *History of Plymoth Plantation* (Boston, 1899), pp. 361–362.

bring their wives and children to the public worship and Church meetings here, but with such burden as, growing to some competent number, they sued to be dismissed and become a body of themselves, and so they were dismissed . . . though very unwillingly." [6]

Warned by this experience, the town tried an experiment which it was hoped would prevent the further disintegration of the village. Some especially desirable land at Green Harbor, which had remained in common, was now laid out in farms and granted to certain persons who were "likely to be helpful to the Church and commonwealth," on the express condition that they reside in Plymouth, leaving their cattle and cornfields under the supervision of servants. In this way the land was to be "tied" to the village. "But alas! this remedy proved worse than the disease, for within a few years those that had thus got footing there rent themselves away, partly by force, and partly wearing the rest with importunity and pleas of necessity . . . and others still, as they conceived themselves straitened . . . break away under one pretence or other." [7]

When the Indians, in King Philip's War, laid waste town after town and brought sorrow to hundreds of New England families, the Reverend William Hubbard placed the blame in part upon this movement. "The first that came over hither for the Gospel could not tell what to do with more land than a small number of acres, yet now men more easily swallow down so many hundreds and are not satisfied," he said in the election sermon of 1676. If they were but a "little straitened," they thought it necessary to move, even though by so doing they parted with "a good neighborhood and the beautiful heritage of Church communion, or Gospel worship, to pitch with Lot in the confines of Sodom. . . . Is it a wonder then that we find war at our gates? God is knocking the hands of New England people off from the world and from new plantations, till they get them new hearts resolved to reform this great evil." [8]

As late as 1705 the Reverend Joseph Easterbrooks was bewail-

[6] *Ibid.*, p. 362.
[7] *Ibid.*, pp. 362, 363.
[8] William Hubbard, *The Happiness of a People*, pp. 58, 59.

ing the fact that men were no longer living together in compact communities where they could enjoy the religious instruction of learned clergymen, but were going out to remote places "for worldly conveniences." "By that means [they] have seemed to bid defiance, not only to religion, but to civility itself, and such places thereby have become nurseries of ignorance, profaneness and atheism." [9]

In Massachusetts Bay when the movement from the villages to the farms began to gain headway, the founders attempted to put a stop to it by law. In September, 1635, the General Court ruled that thereafter no dwelling should be built more than half a mile from the meeting-house without especial leave, "in any new plantation granted at this Court." The order applied to "Ipswich, Hingham, Newbury and Weymouth, as well as to all towns to be established in the future," [10] and the next year it was extended "to all the towns in the jurisdiction." But the General Court was no match for economic law, and the pressure from those who had experienced the inconvenience of dwelling at one place and conducting a farm at another was so great that in 1640 they rescinded the order. [11] Four decades later Increase Mather complained: "People are ready to run wild into the woods again and to be as heathenish as ever, if you do not prevent it." [12]

The change from the unified economy of the agricultural village to the farm system constituted a revolution which was not the less profound because usually so gradual. No longer was it possible for the minister and the elders to know their parishioners with the old intimacy so that they could admonish them for every breach of the Sabbath or for every exchange of gossip. If there were vacant seats at the Sunday's sermon, the absentees might reasonably plead the great distance of their farms from the meeting-house and the badness of the roads. And in winter, when heavy snows blocked the roads, the farmer was practically cut off from the rest of the world despite his sled or his snowshoes.

The ecclesiastical character of the town meeting, so vital in

[9] Perry Miller and Thomas H. Johnson, *The Puritans*, p. 17.
[10] Nathaniel B. Shurtleff, ed., *Records of Massachusetts Bay*, p. 157.
[11] *Ibid.*, p. 291.
[12] Increase Mather, *A Discourse Concerning the Danger of Apostasy*, second edition, 1685, p. 104.

the old scheme of things, might have survived the transition to farm life, had the splitting off of territory from an old town to form a new one preceded and not followed the organization of the new Church. There would then have been but one "society" in each of the separated territories, so that the old meeting could have retained its ecclesiastical functions and the meeting of the new town assumed them the moment the new Church was organized. As it was, the pleas for Gospel preaching were so urgent and so reasonable that Church dismembership almost invariably antedated civil dismemberment, and when the voters of the new town assembled for the first time, their ecclesiastical society had already been in existence for years, perhaps for decades.

The old unity within the town which had resulted from the singleness of purpose of the people was weakened, also, by the gradual breakdown of the laws against the admission of strangers. When Master Dawson, the blacksmith, or Goodman Calkins, the tanner, or Parke, the cooper, needed an apprentice, it seemed a hard case if the Selectmen refused to permit them to look beyond the town limits in case the sons of the original settlers were busy with their own affairs—opening new fields, building barns, planting orchards, caring for their livestock. Moreover, when after years of hard labor, a degree of prosperity had come to some of the families, so that they could afford to employ a servant or a field hand, the community was not inclined to balk them. Nor did it seem reasonable to exclude a "foreigner" from some other part of New England or even from old England when he presented letters from well-known Puritans, attesting to his orthodoxy and his good conduct.

In time, as the number of newcomers increased, a sharp division was drawn between them and the families of the original settlers. Since it was the founders who had endured the hardships of frontier life, who had taken the risks, who had purchased the land from the Indians, they and their descendants contended that all undivided land belonged to them rather than to the town as a whole. On the other hand, the newcomers protested violently against being excluded, so that the little meeting-houses resounded to the speeches of the contending factions. In the end the old planters usually won the day. In Milford, for instance, the town-meeting decided in 1713 to give over the proprietorship of all common land "to those persons and their heirs forever which are in the present public list of estates to be proportioned to or by the said list." [13]

Enfield had taken similar action two years before, when the proprietors of the common lands met in Sergeant James Pease's house "to regulate some things that may be just grounds of dissatisfaction respecting commonage and undivided lands." Hereafter it was this group, meeting as a distinct body having their own moderator and records, and not the town-meeting, which had the authority to grant and sequester land, to lay out grants for "foreigners," orphans and others, to confirm grants formerly made by the town and to employ persons to defend their rights in the courts. [14]

In some of the towns the victory did not rest entirely with the original planters, since many late comers were included in the lists of proprietors. Milford, for example, decided to draw the line at 1688, excluding all who had been admitted to the town since that date save those whom their committee should deem it reasonable to except. Since the completed list contained 197 names as compared with 134 in the division of 1687, it is evident that a large proportion of newcomers had been added. [15]

The proprietors were more active in safeguarding their rights and conserving the commons than had been the town-meeting. It had become the custom for the inhabitants to cut timber, gather stones for building, and to pasture their cattle in undivided tracts, but with wood becoming scarce and land more valuable, the proprietors took steps to exclude trespassers. They also kept a vigilant eye on squatters.

In Milford the situation was complicated by the purchase from the Indians of two large tracts which extended the northern boundary of the town to Waterbury, twenty miles from the village. In each case the money was raised by selling shares, so that one tract was known as the "Two Bit Purchase" and the other

---

[13] Leonard W. Labaree, "Milford, Conn.," Tercentenary Commission, *Historical Publications*, Nos. 1–10.

[14] Francis O. Allen, *History of Enfield, Conn.*, I, pp. 315, 680–685.

[15] Leonard W. Labaree, "Milford, Conn.," Tercentenary Commission, *Historical Publications*, Nos. 1–10.

the "One Bit Purchase." In each case the shareholders constituted themselves into a body of proprietors to hold the tract in common and to make divisions and grants. Although the two groups were interlocking, they were quite distinct from each other, one comprising 195 names, the other 178 names. Since a proprietary body had been created for sequestered lands as early as 1688, there now existed in Milford no less than four separate bodies each distinct from the town-meeting and each exercising certain functions which in a democratic community should have belonged to the government.

Thus did local forces change the character of the original New England town. It must have saddened the founders as they saw the beginnings of this transformation; it would have caused them deep apprehension had they lived to witness its later stages. Unity had been the key word in the organization of the old town, a unity marked by the identity of Church members and freemen, of town and proprietors, a unity sealed by the agricultural village embracing as it did within its narrow bounds the entire population. Now all was quite different. For an increasingly large part of the people farm life superseded life in the village; the town had surrendered its function as an ecclesiastical society so that no longer did all the people belong to one single congregation; to the village school had been added other schools in different parts of the town; the common land belonged not to the people of the town but to a single privileged group.

This revolution within the town should not be overemphasized in explaining the ultimate failure of the experiment of the Bible Commonwealth. A farmer might, despite the remoteness of the meeting-house and the badness of the roads, be as ardently religious as his father who had lived in the village. But when Cotton Mather, Increase Mather, Urian Oakes and other leading preachers bemoaned the decay of religion and pointed out the growth of levity, immorality, drunkenness, skepticism, indifference, profanity, Sabbath breaking, vanity in dress, pride, etc., they had every right to lay the blame in part upon changed conditions within those foundation stones of the religious-political states—the towns.

The spread of farm economy was accompanied by the transformation of many coastal villages into commercial cities, and the development of trade as the mainstay of the entire region. It was a change not wholly unwelcome to the founders, since it brought prosperity and wealth to New England and gave them evidence that God was showering favors upon His chosen people, yet it loosened new influences which many feared would in the end undermine the structure of Church and State. Edward Johnson gave vigorous voice to both points of view. He gloried that the Lord had in so brief a time converted that "remote, rocky, barren, bushy, wild-woody wilderness, a receptacle for lions, wolves, bears, foxes . . . and all kind of wild creatures," into a world mart, "Holland, France, Spain and Portugal coming hither for trade, shipping going on gallantly." But he was no less emphatic in expressing his disapproval of those who were "so taken up with the income of a large profit that they would willingly have had the commonwealth tolerate divers kinds of sinful opinions to entice men to come and sit down with us, that their purses might be filled with coin, the civil government with contention and the Churches of our Lord Christ with errors." [16]

It had been the hope of the fathers of New England that the region would afford some staple product for which there would be a ready market in England and which would place their venture upon a solid economic basis. Some even went so far as to predict what that staple would be. "How serviceable this country must needs be for provisions for shipping, is sufficiently known already," wrote John White in *The Planters Plea*. "At present it may yield planks, masts, oars, pitch, tar and iron, and hereafter, by the aptness of the soil for hemp, if the colony increase, sails and cordage." With this opinion, Thomas Morton, however much his religious views differed from those of the pious White, was in full accord. The forests of New England would produce many needed products, he pointed out, chief among which were "resin, pitch, and tar," commodities so essential to England that were they not imported from foreign countries, England's navigation would decline.[17]

[16] J. Franklin Jameson, ed., *Johnson's Wonder-Working Providence*, p. 254.
[17] Thomas Morton, "New England Canaan," Peter Force, *Tracts and Other Papers*, II, No. 5, p. 44.

Unfortunately, this expectation was disappointed. The great forests, extending hundreds of miles inland, stood ready to yield their products, the English merchants were eager to buy, but the toil expended in felling trees, splitting and sawing timbers, producing tar was so heavy and the cost of labor so high that the profits did not justify the venture. So the settlers began to look elsewhere for the promised staple, some of them hopefully, others with skepticism. Edward Johnson tells us that for a long time the great fear of many, "and those who were endued with grace from above also," was that New England "would be no place of continued habitation for want of a staple commodity." [18]

Eventually they found what they were looking for, not in the soil, nor in the mines, but in the waters which washed New England's shores. It was Captain John Smith who had predicted that fish would become the staple of the region. "Let not the meanness of the word fish distaste you," he said, "for it will afford as good gold as the mines of Guiana and Potassie with less hazard and charge, and more certainty and facility." [19] King Charles, in the Massachusetts Bay Company's charter, had promised that nothing should "hinder our loving subjects whatsoever to use and exercise the trade of fishing upon that coast of New England" nor to erect stages and houses "necessary for the salting, drying and packing their fish."

It was the Dorchester men, many of them from Dorset and Devon, who were "the first to set upon the trade of fishing in the bay," but Marblehead, Gloucester and other places were quick to follow. Before the end of the third decade of the seventeenth century scores of little sloops and ketches, each manned by a crew of three, could be seen offshore from Cape Cod to Maine, their sails furled and lines cast out. Later, as the fishermen grew bolder, they ventured out to the dangerous waters off Sable Island, and then to the Grand Banks. [20]

With the advent of longer and more dangerous voyages, the open boat gave way to the pinkie, of ten to twenty tons, decked over and carrying two fore-and-aft sails, a foresail and a mainsail.

[18] J. Franklin Jameson, ed., *Johnson's Wonder-Working Providence*, p. 246.
[19] John Smith, *Works* (Edward Arber, ed.), p. 784.
[20] Wm. B. Weeden, *Economic and Social History of New England*, I, p. 132.

The men wore a hat of canvas laid over with tar, a thick knitted jersey, heavy cowhide boots and a leather apron. Voyages to the Grand Banks lasted from ten to twelve days, but the catch, which usually was excellent, was ample compensation provided the vessel was not wrecked in the perilous shoal water. It was no unusual thing to return so heavily laden with cod that the seas swept over the decks. These early fishermen set out their lines chiefly for cod, although they also valued bass and alewives. Mackerel, in colonial times, served mainly for bait.[21]

The life of the fisherman was not necessarily unfavorable for religion, since he lived usually in the village within easy reach of the meeting-house. In fact, many were sincerely devout, and it was the practice for the skipper to take his Bible with him so that, when the weather was rough or the fish were not biting, he could read passages from it to the crew. Nor would he permit fishing on Sunday, even when the run was at its best and delay might mean failure for the entire voyage. Some, however, were not so scrupulous, and it was with a touch of envy as well as stern disapproval that the Bible-reading skipper watched on a Sabbath morning his rivals haul in cod after cod while his own lines were idle.[22] Cotton Mather states that when a Massachusetts minister was exhorting the congregation of a certain fishing village to remain steadfast for religion, since it had been the main end of their coming to America, "a well-known person there in the assembly cried out, 'Sir, you are mistaken—our main end was to catch fish.' "[23]

The New Englanders were not long in discovering that in fish they had a commodity greatly desired by other peoples. Portugal and Spain wanted fish, the Canaries wanted fish, Barbados wanted fish, southern France wanted fish. So the fishermen doubled and tripled their catch, split and salted the cod on shipboard, rinsed them in salt water on shore, spread them to dry on stages or hurdles, packed them in barrels and shipped them off to market. In 1641 no less than 300,000 were exported and the number grew with the years. The best grade was sold to the countries of south-

[21] James B. Connolly, *The Port of Gloucester*, p. 11.
[22] *Ibid.*, p. 14.
[23] Cotton Mather, *Magnalia* (Hartford, 1820), I, p. 62.

ern Europe; the middling grade of dried codfish, because it was easy to keep, was sold in large quantities to the colonial farmers, while the lowest-grade fish and pickled bass, mackerel and ale-wives fed the slave populations of the West Indies.[24]

The merchants, when their vessels came to anchor in the ports of southern Europe or of the Caribbean islands, were quick to dis-cover that their customers had many valuable products stored in their warehouses ready for exchange. So when they turned their prows back toward New England their holds were usually filled.

The trade thus started, with fish as its original incentive, re-ceived new impetus with the advent of the English Civil War and the consequent falling off in immigration. For more than a decade there had been a constant stream of vessels from English ports bringing large supplies of manufactured goods, together with hundreds of newcomers, all eager purchasers of corn, wheat, cattle and whatever else they had been unable to bring with them. But when the flow of settlers was cut off hard times followed. "All foreign commodities grew scarce and our own of no price," wrote Governor Winthrop. "Corn would buy nothing; a cow which cost last year £20 might now be bought for 4 or £5. . . . These straits set our people on work to provide fish, clapboards, plank, etc. . . . and to look out to the West Indies for trade."

The traders did not turn to the mother country as a market for their goods because they had very little to offer which she stood in need of. Fish she had in plenty, brought by her own bold fishermen from the waters off Iceland, Greenland and New-foundland; she considered it unwise to import grain and meat to the discouragement of her own farmers; American naval stores and timber, after transportation costs had been paid, proved too costly.

On the other hand, England eagerly purchased all the furs which the colonists could send over. The Plymouth settlers dis-covered the value of the fur trade several years before the coming of the main body of Puritans, and by keeping a constant supply of wampum on hand, secured large quantities of beaver from the Kennebec region for export to England. Nor were other towns long in following their example. Trading posts were established

[24] Samuel E. Morison, *The Maritime History of Massachusetts*, pp. 13, 14.

on the more important rivers, to which the Indians brought their beaver and other furs in exchange for wampum, knives, blankets and, only too often, for firearms. From these posts the peltry found its way to the commercial centers, where it was bought up by the exporters. John Hull, the Boston merchant, was a constant dealer in furs and more than once tells us of his losses, when his cargoes were taken by enemy warships or went down in a ship-wreck. [25]

Yet New England was not destined to be a great fur-trading region comparable to Canada or New Netherlands. The supply within her own territory was limited, and dwindled rapidly with the advance of the frontier and with the Indian wars. At the same time she lacked any great waterway comparable to the St. Lawrence, or the Hudson and the Mohawk, leading to the vast fur-bearing regions around the Great Lakes. No doubt the clergy were well satisfied that the number of New Englanders who were exposed to the debauchery of life at the trading posts was small, but the Boston and Salem merchants regretted deeply the scarcity of furs to throw into the balance of trade with England.

A glimpse at the lading of the *America*, a 300-ton vessel sailing in 1692 from Portsmouth, shows that by that date the emphasis for exports to the mother country had shifted from furs to naval stores and barrel staves, for it included 18 masts, 9 bowsprits, 13 yards, 11,400 feet of oars, 2,900 feet of wood, 25,000 staves, 46 spars and but 84 pounds of beaver and 130 small furs.[26] John Hull was especially active in the trade with England.

In contrast to the English trade the interchange of goods with the West Indies became more and more extensive.[27] The keen New England merchants, once they cast anchor in the ports of Antigua, or Jamaica, or Barbados, were not long in noting that fish was not the only commodity which they could supply for which there was a lively demand. Before long they were back again with a part of their cargo space filled with dried beef, pork, wheat and pease, or perhaps with staves for sugar or molasses barrels or for wine pipes; perhaps with horses for the sugar mills, or with

[25] "Diary of John Hull," American Antiquarian Society *Transactions and Collections*, III, p. 148.
[26] *Provincial Papers of New Hampshire*, II, p. 80.
[27] William B. Weeden, *Economic and Social History of New England*, I, p. 56.

timber for the framing of houses.[28] Edward Johnson could boast
that the Lord, "whose promises are large to his Sion," had turned
everything in the country into a staple—"wheat, rye, oats, pease,
barley, beef, pork, fish, butter, cheese, timber, mast, tar, soap,
plankboard, frames of houses, clapboard and pipestaves." [29]

Having discharged their cargoes at the wharves of Bridgetown,
or Kingston, or St. John, the New England masters loaded their
holds with West Indian products—barrels of molasses, barrels of
sugar, packages of cotton or tobacco or indigo, perhaps a few
Negro slaves. Back in New England they could dispose of these
goods to advantage, for what could not be consumed there was
re-exported and brought excellent returns. The sugar and molasses
were welcome on every table, while the rum into which much
was converted was welcomed not only by lumbermen and fishermen, but by the mass of the people. Newport had twenty-two
"still-houses" at one time and it was estimated that the Massachusetts stills consumed 15,000 hogsheads of molasses yearly.
However, the larger part of the fiery liquor went, not down the
throats of the New Englanders, but to Africa as an important item
of exchange. The tobacco, too, was in part sold in the local
markets, for, if we may judge from the number of pipes imported,
the people must have been inveterate smokers. Nor were the
slaves left on the hands of the merchants, since servants were always in demand and even the clergy looked upon it as no sin to
purchase them. When some of the members of Cotton Mather's
congregation presented him with a slave he rejoiced at Heaven's
smile,[30] while Reverend Ebenezer Bridge considered it a "sore
providence," when his "negro servant Venus died of the throat
distemper." [31]

The vessels which left New England with cargoes of fish and
staves for La Rochelle, Bordeaux, Marseilles, Bilboa, Lisbon,
Malaga, Barcelona, Leghorn and other southern European ports
brought back pipes and butts full of wine to grace the tables of
the well-to-do; salt, so essential to the fishing industry; fruits, oil,

[28] Charles M. Andrews, *Colonial Period of American History*, I, p. 516.
[29] J. Franklin Jameson, ed., *Johnson's Wonder-Working Providence*, p. 247.
[30] "Diary of Cotton Mather," Massachusetts Historical Society *Collections*,
Seventh Series, VII, p. 579.
[31] *Diary of Ebenezer Bridge*, MSS. II, p. 265.

soap, raisins and many other products.[32] This trade, which yielded so much profit to the merchants and such luxuries to the people, was, however, subject to losses from shipwreck in the long voyage across the Atlantic or from capture by hostile raiders in time of war. "The Lord brought all the vessels I was concerned in this year in safety," wrote John Hull in 1671. "But, upon 23d of 9th, John Harris, with his ketch, being gone out to sea . . . came back . . . but could not reach the harbor and was put on shore. . . . One half of the vessel and cargo was mine."

Not content with their European and West Indian trade, the New Englanders made themselves at home in every port of the American North Atlantic. As early as 1634 we find them in Virginia waters and we know from Winthrop that both Plymouth and Massachusetts Bay "had oft trade" with the Dutch in the Hudson River. In the Chesapeake Bay region the Yankee skippers became unpopular when they sent rowboats up the creeks at night to trade with the slaves for stolen goods. Yet they found the planters and storekeepers quite ready to trade tobacco, corn, beans and meat for West Indian sugar and molasses. The voyage of the *Orataro*, of Rhode Island, from Barbados to Virginia with a cargo of rum, molasses and brown sugar for exchange for wheat, corn, beeswax, leather, pork, beef and staves, although made in 1740, was typical, even for the mid-seventeenth century.[33]

Nor did the New Englanders scruple to take on a cargo of Virginia or Maryland tobacco, bring it to Boston or Newport or Salem and then sail with it directly to the continent of Europe in defiance of the Acts of Navigation. In 1679 Robert Holden, a British collector of customs, reported that six Boston merchants received regularly the larger part of the Albemarle Sound tobacco crop and shipped it to Ireland, Holland, France and Spain "under the notion of fish and such goods." English merchants complained that "New England men did carry much tobacco and other commodities of the growth of the plantations to New England and from thence did carry them to foreign nations, whereby they could undersell them."[34] Parliament responded

[32] Charles M. Andrews, *Colonial Period of American History*, I, p. 517.
[33] T. J. Wertenbaker, *Norfolk—Historic Southern Port*, p. 38.
[34] George L. Beer, *The Old Colonial System*, I, p. 80.

with the Navigation Act of 1673, placing a duty on the shipment of tobacco and other commodities from one colony to another, but the traders found various ways of evading it.

Edward Randolph, writing in 1676, gives an instructive account of the commerce of New England. The native products suitable for exportation he lists as "all things necessary for shipping and naval furniture," especially the trunks of pines "for masts the best in the world," but also pitch, tar, hemp, and iron; various kinds of timber products, such as "clapboards, pipestaves, planks and deal boards"; "horses, beeves, sheep, hogs and goats"; the furs or skins of "beaver, otter, moose, deer, stags, foxes," etc.; "also plenty of wheat, rye, barley, oats, and peas"; several kinds of fish, "especially cod, mackerel and herring, which are very large and fat."

To Virginia, Maryland and Jamaica, the merchants sent "beef and pork salted, pease, flour, biscuit and malt, codfish and salt mackerel"; to Barbados, Nevis and St. Christopher the same commodities together with horses, dealboards, pipestaves and "houses ready framed"; to Spain, Portugal, Madeira and the Canaries "fish, timber, pipestaves and dealboards"; to England "masts and yards for ships, fir and oak planks, with all sorts of peltry." The exports to Europe were not confined to the products of New England, but included those of other colonies, while the return cargoes were made up of goods "vendible either in New England or in any other of his Majesty's dominions in America—as brandy, Canary, Spanish and French wines, bullion, salt, fruits, oils, silks, laces, linnen of all sorts, cloth, serges, bays, kersies, stockings and many other commodities." It was the great care of the merchants to keep their ships in constant employ, which made them "try all ports to force a trade." [35]

Among the trading centers of New England Boston early took the lead, partly because of her fine harbor, in which several hundred vessels could lie at anchor in good depth of water, partly because of the enterprise and ability of her merchants. As early as 1640 we find the town government encouraging the building of wharves and supervising storage. Along the irregular water front of the Boston peninsula one might see long lines of wagons

[35] "Hutchinson Papers," II, *Publications of Prince Society*, pp. 230, 231.

and, tied up to the jetties, scores of small vessels all laden with
country produce, while the countinghouses and storage houses
were crowded with busy traders. At the larger wharves were
sloops, ketches and ships, their sailors heaving at barrels and
crates as they unloaded their cargoes of sugar, molasses, or European goods, or took on fish, meat, breadstuffs and tobacco. Conspicuous was the dock at the foot of Dock Square, and the market
place, which was famous for its great hoisting crane.[36]

Boston, in 1664, was reported to have 14,300 souls, and its
growth continued throughout the colonial period. Its merchant
fleet, numbering no less than 300 vessels, plied back and forth
from the West Indies, the Chesapeake, Madeira, etc., while its
numerous fishing craft brought in tons of cod and mackerel from
Cape Sable waters.[37] "Boston may be esteemed the mart town of
the West Indies," stated Edward Randolph.[38] The interchange of
goods was carried on almost exclusively in New England-built
vessels, many of them Boston built, for from a very early date
the banks of the Back Bay and the Mystic were dotted with the
frames of ketches, sloops and ships. In 1700 Bellomont, after going
through the registers, sent word to the British government that
the town could boast of 25 ships of from 100 tons to 300, 39 of
about 100 tons or under, 50 brigantines, 13 ketches, and 67 sloops.

Edward Johnson gloried in the prosperity of Boston as a signal
evidence of God's indulgence to His chosen people. "The chief
edifice of this city-like town is crowded on the sea-banks and
wharfed out with great industry and cost, the buildings beautiful
and large, some fairly set forth with brick, tile, stone and slate
and orderly placed with comely streets, whose continual enlarge-
ment presages some sumptuous city. . . . But now behold the
admirable acts of Christ; at this His people's landing the hideous
thickets in this place were such that wolves and bears nursed up
their young from the eyes of all beholders, in those very places
where the streets are full of girls and boys sporting up and down,
with a continuous concourse of people. Good store of shipping is
here yearly built, and some very fair ones. . . . This town is the

[36] Charles M. Andrews, *Colonial Period of American History*, I, p. 514.
[37] *Calendar of State Papers, Colonial, America and West Indies*, 1665–68,
p. 532.
[38] "Hutchinson Papers," II, *Publications of Prince Society*, p. 231.

very mart of the land; French, Portugals and Dutch come hither for traffic." [39]

But the ministers and elders were not quite so positive as Johnson that the growth of commerce in New England was entirely the Lord's doing. They feared that all this bustle and stir in the ports, this constant attention to business affairs, this eager desire for profits, this discussion of markets and prices, this bringing in of a rough seafaring element, most of them frequenters of the taverns rather than of the meeting-houses, this creation of a wealthy merchant class, would turn the face of the people away from religion. Like Jefferson they considered agriculture the ideal vocation, not because, like Jefferson, they were concerned with its influence upon democracy, but because they thought it the best foundation for a religious commonwealth. And, like Jefferson, they were powerless to prevent the growth of another form of economic life, when the force of natural conditions dictated it. Had they declared an embargo on trade as a kind of "peaceful coercion" against irreligion, it would have failed just as, a century later, Jefferson's embargo failed to keep the United States out of the Napoleonic wars.

But though the religious leaders accepted the growth of commerce as inevitable, they battled fiercely against the evils which followed in its wake. In the election sermons and in every local pulpit the ministers warned the people that they must not substitute Mammon for the true God. "It concerneth New England always to remember that originally they are a plantation religious, not a plantation of trade," pleaded John Norton in the election sermon of 1657.[40] Four years later John Higginson echoed his words. "My fathers and brethren, this is never to be forgotten that New England is originally a plantation of religion, not a plantation of trade. Let merchants and such as are increasing cent per cent remember this, that worldly gain was not the end and design of the people of New England, but religion." [41] Eleazer Mather, pastor of the Northampton Church, asked whether in the first years of settlement, when there had been "less of the world," there had not been more of Heaven. "Less trading, buying,

[39] J. Franklin Jameson, ed., *Johnson's Wonder-Working Providence*, p. 71.
[40] John Norton, *The Heart of New England Rent*, p. 58.
[41] John Higginson, *The Cause of God and His People in New England*, p. 11.

selling, but more praying, more watching over our hearts, more close walking, less plenty and less inequity?" [42]

The ministers were especially concerned at the development of the merchant aristocracy, for they realized that it would inevitably become a rival of the aristocracy of religion. In the train of successful sea ventures came wealth, and wealth brought power. The merchants of Boston, Salem, New Haven and other New England ports built handsome residences and filled them with fine furniture and silver, became the acknowledged leaders in social life, frequently played important roles as selectmen, deputies, judges and commanders of the militia, contributed generously to charity or to public works, added a touch of rationalism to an atmosphere supercharged with religion.

Their absorption in acquiring worldly riches rather than heavenly riches was especially displeasing to the clergy. The founders of New England had come into the wilderness, not in search of great estates, they reiterated, but to enjoy the pure worship of God after the apostolic manner. But now their descendants were deserting the good old ways, were forgetting that they were God's chosen people, in their eager search of profits. "Some there are, and not a few, that are so engaged in their own interests that, let the cause of God and his people sink or swim, they care not, so their own ends be compassed," complained John Wilson and Samuel Whiting. "We have been changing in our main fundamental interests," Samuel Torrey warned; "we have been deserting our own religious interest and espousing another, a worldly interest; we are turning from God after the world; the world is becoming the main interest of New England." "When men have property, outward riches, and know not what to do with them besides making gods of them, this is a sign that God's gracious presence is not among a people, when men lose religion in the world, and what they get in temporals they lose in spirituals," pointed out Eleazer Mather. "Outward prosperity is a worm at the root of godliness, so that religion dies when the world thrives." [43]

Yet many of the merchants were men of religious lives and

---

[42] Eleazer Mather, *A Serious Exhortation.*
[43] Eleazer Mather, *A Serious Exhortation.*

ardent supporters of the established order in Church and State. Typical was John Hull, who reveals himself in his *Diary* as an interesting amalgam of the astute businessman and the religious devotee. When a ketch was cast ashore on Cape Cod and lost with part of her cargo, he jotted down: "One half the vessel and cargo was mine. The Lord give me spiritual and heavenly treasure when he taketh from me earthly, and that will be a good exchange." On June 17, 1672, he wrote: "This winter the ships that went home to London were many of them taken by the Dutch capers. I lost in Master Hilton, Master Jonas Clark and Thomas Moore six hundred and forty pounds. God mixeth His mercies and chastisements." [44]

At times Hull seems to have had misgivings as to the effect of his success in business upon the welfare of his soul. On one occasion he wrote that he would "more and more affect and embrace opportunity of getting out rather than running into the business of this world, specially foreign traffic, as desirous to be more thoughtful of launching into that vast ocean of eternity whither we must all shortly be carried that so I might be in a prepared posture for my Lord's coming." [45]

Edward Johnson found it difficult to explain why pious merchants and masters were permitted to perish with the sinful. "The Lord was pleased to command the wind and seas to give us a jog on the elbow by sinking the very chief of our shipping in the deep and splitting them in shivers against the shore; a very goodly ship, called the *Seaforce,* was cast away and many New England people put to hard shifts for their lives, and some drowned, as the godly and dearly beloved servant of Christ, Mr. Thomas Cortmire, a very able seaman and a good scholar, one who had spent both his labor and estate for the helping on of this wilderness work. As also another ship set forth by the merchants of New Haven, of which the godly Mr. Lamberton was master, neither ship, person nor goods ever heard of. . . . This seemed the sorer affliction to these New England people, because many godly men lost their lives." [46]

<hr/>

[44] "Diary of John Hull," American Antiquarian Society *Transactions and Collections,* III, p. 160.
[45] *John Hull Letter Book,* quoted by W. B. Weeden, *Economic and Social History of New England,* I, p. 249.
[46] J. Franklin Jameson, ed., *Johnson's Wonder-Working Providence,* p. 253.

Prominent among the seventeenth-century merchants was Philip English of Salem. Coming to the colony from the Isle of Jersey, he rose in the world until he became one of the richest men in New England. Out from his wharf and warehouses went goods in his own vessels for Bilboa, Barbados, St. Christopher's and elsewhere. His mansion on Essex Street, known as English's Great House, a large frame structure whose overhanging second story and steep roof proclaimed it a typical example of East Anglian architecture, stood for a century and a half as a reminder of his wealth and influence. Like Hull a man of piety, English constantly interlined his business records with references to God and the Bible. "Shipped by the Grace of God . . . in the good sloop called *Mayflower* whereof is master under God for the present voyage John Swazey . . . and by God's grace bound for Virginia or Maryland . . . twenty hogsheads of salt. . . . And so God sent the good sloop to her desired port in safety. Amen." [47]

English's power, influence and religious life did not suffice to save him and his wife from being "cried out upon" as witches in the "epidemic" of 1690. Mrs. English, a woman of education and piety and a loving wife and mother, was accused first, when the High Sheriff, deputy and other officers came at night to arrest her. When six weeks later her husband, also, was taken into custody, they were both removed to Boston. They would no doubt have perished on the gallows had not two ministers, more practical than some of their fellows, urged them to flee. Finding a safe refuge in New York, they waited there until the witchcraft craze had run its course, and then quietly returned to Salem. [48]

Prominent among the Salem merchants was Captain George Corwin. Merchant and shipbuilder, the owner of wharves, warehouses, ships and farms; honest, shrewd and energetic, though inclined to be cold and unrelenting; devoting much time to the public service as selectman, captain in the militia and deputy to the General Court, he was little inferior in wealth and influence to English. Of similar stamp, but of a kinder and more charitable disposition was William Browne, Sr., a successful merchant and shipbuilder. Devoutly religious and interested in the advancement

[47] R. D. Paine, *The Ships and Sailors of Old Salem*, pp. 23, 24.
[48] *Ibid.*, pp. 26, 28.

of education, he made large gifts to Harvard, to the Salem school, to the poor and to the Salem meeting-house.[49]

It must have been with perplexity and perhaps alarm that men of the type of John Hull, Philip English and William Browne, as they sat in their prominent seats in the meeting-house, listened to the ministers' warnings of the evil influence of wealth. Ardent supporters of the established order in Church and State, they gladly devoted their influence, their time and their money to its support, and were convinced that in return the way to salvation would be opened to them. True, the Bible stated that it was easier for a camel to pass through the eye of a needle than for a rich man to enter Heaven, but they would not admit to themselves that their property, valued perhaps at £10,000, perhaps at £8,000 or £6,000 would exclude them. After all, was not their prosperity the result of God's will and a clear evidence of His favor to His chosen people?

Nor was it to be expected that these men should realize the broadening influence which contact with the outside world was having upon them. The ministers might reiterate that God had led his people into the wilderness to protect them from contamination, but the effects of isolation were in part lost when the Yankee traders sailed their little vessels into every port along the Atlantic seaboard and swarmed in West Indian, Spanish, Portuguese and British waters. When they learned to their surprise that the Roman Catholic Spaniard, the Anglican Marylander or Virginian, the Quaker Pennsylvanian had many good qualities, were often honest, kindhearted, industrious, they weakened in their belief that they were all headed for damnation. Nor was it unusual for outsiders, no doubt because of their friendship for individual merchants, to make protracted visits to New England. "Mr. Tho. Smith from Barbados brings the Honorable Francis Bond, one of his Majesty's Council for that island, and of great estate, also one Middleton: former comes to recover his health," wrote Samuel Sewall in his *Diary* in 1685. A few months later he added: "This day Mr. Morgan, his lady and family arrived from Barbados intending to dwell here some time." [50]

[49] James D. Phillips, *Salem in the Seventeenth Century*, pp. 261–62.
[50] "Diary of Samuel Sewall," Massachusetts Historical Society *Collections*, Fifth Series, V, pp. 71, 97.

Of the merchants themselves, a large proportion had migrated to New England decades after the first founding, many of them from foreign countries. The Devereux, Delano, Faneuil and Bowdoin families came from France; Patrick Tracy from Ireland, Casper Crowninshield from Germany, John Wendell from Holland.[51] Some came for religion's sake, to escape persecution in their native lands, or because they were in sympathy with the reformed Church established in Massachusetts; but others migrated to take advantage of the opportunities for lucrative trade. However sincerely they tried to adjust themselves to the Puritan State, they could not fail to become an element of disunity. John Hull was surprised and outraged when, in 1662, "sundry young merchants and others, being non-freemen, boldly offered their votes to the freemen, when they were together for nomination of magistrates."[52] Even more significant was the petition of the Boston merchants in 1645 against the law restricting the entertaining of strangers and the statute for banishing Anabaptists.[53] And later, during the Salem witchcraft delusion, it was the merchant Robert Calef who had the common sense to see the folly of the inquisition and the hardihood to ridicule the great Cotton Mather for his share in it.

The theory of economic determinism, which has led so many writers to overemphasize commerce, industry and agriculture in interpreting the great movements of history, is quite inadequate as a full explanation of either the rise or the fall of the New England Zion. Unless we weigh also the forces of religious zeal, of political developments, of the advance of science, of the growth of rationalism, we secure an incomplete picture with a distorted perspective. Yet it would be equally incorrect to minimize the importance of the decline of the agricultural village, the growth of the farm, the development of a wealthy merchant class and the multiplying of the number of seafaring men in hastening the "decay" of the old order.

[51] Samuel E. Morison, *The Maritime History of Massachusetts*, p. 21.

[52] "Diary of John Hull," American Antiquarian Society *Transactions and Collections*, III, p. 207.

[53] William B. Weeden, *Economic and Social History of New England*, I, p. 80.

Chapter VIII

JERICHO'S WALLS

IN 1679 CHARLES II wrote to the Governor of Massachusetts, criticizing the provincial government for the persecution of those who did "not agree in the Congregational way," a thing which he thought the more to be wondered at in that liberty of conscience had been one principal motive in the migration to those parts.[1] That the King should so have misinterpreted the purposes of the leaders of the Great Exodus is understandable, but surely Sir Richard Saltonstall's memory must have failed him when in 1651 he wrote to John Cotton and John Wilson that in persecuting the Quakers they were pursuing the very course they had gone so far to prevent.[2]

It must be reiterated that the Puritans in leaving England fled not so much from persecution as from error. They were afraid to remain in a country where the way of worship and of Church government "plainly set forth in God's Word," was neglected and discouraged; where they and their children might be led astray by false prophets; where God's chosen people were a minority. So, when they turned their backs on their homes, their relatives, their native land, to set out for the wilderness, it was not because of peril to their bodies, but of peril to their souls.

We gain an insight into the overwhelming fear of error which gripped the minds and hearts of thousands of deeply religious men and women, of error which might cast them into Hell and doom them to eternal torture, through the experience of Edward Johnson with the Anne Hutchinson heresy. When Johnson first came to Massachusetts in 1630 his soul rejoiced that he had found a retreat safe from false doctrines. So, when he had arranged his affairs, he returned to England with a light heart to bring over

[1] Prince Society, *Hutchinson Papers*, II, p. 259.
[2] *Ibid.*, p. 128.

his family. What then was his horror on his return when he found Boston resounding to the Antinomian controversy, with opposing factions denouncing each other as heretics and threatening each other with damnation. When old friends approached him to draw him over to this side or that, he reflected with agony of mind that they might be luring him on to his doom. On the other hand, how could he be certain that they were not God's messengers, sent to guide him safely along the road to Heaven.

One day, wishing to be alone in the midst of his perplexities, he set out along a narrow Indian trail, where "none but senseless trees and echoing rock made answer to his heart." At last, emerging from the forest, he heard the beat of a drum, which was summoning the people to religious services, and entered the meeting-house with the others. Breathlessly he listened to the minister, the Reverend Thomas Shepard, denounce the Antinomians and expose the falsity of their views. At last Johnson was satisfied. God had conducted his footsteps to this place, he was sure, so that he might know the truth. With bowed head and streaming eyes, "his heart crying aloud to the Lord's answer," all doubts and fears were swept away.[3]

With eternity at stake, then, the Puritans were not inclined to temporize with error. When the Quakers invaded Massachusetts, demanding toleration for their doctrines, Urian Oakes exclaimed: "They may as well ask liberty to destroy us! . . . Boundless liberty will expose us to great danger." Liberty of conscience he denounced as liberty for a man to destroy himself and others, "a liberty of perdition."[4] John Norton was even more emphatic. "Monsters in nature are eye sores. The face of death, that king of terrors the living man by instinct turns his face from. An unusual shape, a satanical phantasm, a ghost or apparition affrights the disciples. The vision of sin into a spiritual eye is an object of much more abhorrence than the former. But the face of heresy is of a more horrid aspect than all the aforenamed put together, as arguing some signal inlargement of the powers of darkness, as being in a high degree diabolical, prodigious and portentous. Heretical doctrine is not only a sin, but profession of

[3] J. Franklin Jameson, ed., *Johnson's Wonder-Working Providence*, pp. 133–136.
[4] Urian Oakes, *New England Pleaded With*, p. 55.

a doctrine which is both all sin and a way of sin, the speaking of
lies against the Lord and his truth, destructive ˙of the souls of
men." [5]

No one who had the slightest doubts concerning the correct-
ness of his own beliefs could express such extreme views as these.
It was the intensity of faith of Norton and others like him which
made them persecute. The present-day view that religious toleration is vital to the welfare of mankind has gained such wide acceptance that we often forget that in other times thousands of
kindly, pious men would have none of it. Toleration stems from
weakness—weakness of faith or physical weakness—which par-
alyzes the hand of the persecutor. If we believe with burning intensity, if we have no shadow of doubt concerning the heretic's
error, it is logical that we should persecute. It would be a dark
stain on our consciences to permit misguided persons to scatter
the poison of error broadcast, to wither men's souls and send
them to eternal damnation.

Caesar of Heisterbach reports that in the Albigensian crusade
of 1209, when the barons were about to storm the city of Béziers,
the Abbot Arnold of Citeaux gave the order to exterminate the
inhabitants. When it was objected that there were some orthodox
Catholics within the walls, he replied: "Slay all; the Lord will
know His own." [6] Whether or not this story is true, it illustrates
the spirit in which the New England clergy and magistrates persecuted. To them it seemed far better that a few Baptists and
Quakers should suffer imprisonment or mutilation or even death,
than that any of the faithful should be led astray.

"Who can make question but that a man that hath children
and family both justly may and in duty ought to preserve them
. . . from the dangerous company of persons infected with the
plague of pestilence, or other contagious, noisome and mortal
diseases?" asked the Massachusetts General Court in 1659. "Can
any man doubt but that in such case the father of the family, in
defense of himself and his, may withstand the intrusion?" And
should he in self-defense "slay the assailant and intruder, his blood
would be upon his own head. And if private persons may . . .

[5] John Norton, *The Heart of New England Rent*, p. 46.
[6] J. H. Warner, *The Albigensian Heresy*, II, p. 50.

shed the blood of intruders, may not the like be granted to them that are the public keepers and guardians of the common-wealth?"[7]

To the ministers and elders the structure of Church and State in New England was a thing of beauty, a temple of which God was the architect. John Higginson declared that had he the power to depict it in all its glory, "according to its divine original and native beauty, it would dazzle the eyes of angels, daunt the hearts of devils, ravish and chain fast the affections of all the saints." For anyone to attempt to undermine or deface it was the most hideous of crimes. Therefore the laws which had been made by the civil government to defend it and to eradicate heresy, Higginson was sure, would be "a glory to New England so long as the Sun and Moon" endured.[8]

So when the Baptist and Quaker invaders attacked the foundations of the Wilderness Zion its leaders were angered and alarmed. "The destructiveness of the doctrine of the Quakers unto Christian states appeareth from the nature of the object they single out immediately to fight against, viz. the Scriptures as the rule of life . . . with power in matters of religion; ecclesiastical as instituted in the Gospel," stated John Norton. It was highly dangerous, he thought, for them to deny that "the visible-political Churches, Church officers, Church worship and administration were Gospel institutions instituted by Christ" to continue to the end of the world. As to the Quakers' pretense of direct divine guidance, without respect to the Churches, it was destructive of all. Their "diabolical zeal" in so bad a cause he likened to "so much hell-fire," which it was the duty of good men to quench. "The very light of nature teacheth all nations that madmen acting according to their frantic passions are to be restrained with chains."[9]

"Do not wrong and mar an excellent work and profession by mixing and weaving in spurious principles and practices, as those of Separation, Anabaptism, Morellian (Anarchical) confusion and licentious toleration," warned Jonathan Mitchell.[10] Other leaders

[7] *Records of the Governor and Company of the Massachusetts Bay*, IV, Part I, pp. 388, 389.
[8] John Higginson, *The Cause of God and His People in New England*, p. 12.
[9] John Norton, *The Heart of New England Rent*, pp. 30, 38.
[10] Quoted by Samuel Torrey, *An Exhortation Unto Reformation*, p. 1.

denounced the heretics as "seducers from the Holy Trinity, the Lord's Christ, our Lord Jesus Christ, etc., the blessed Gospel and from the Holy Scriptures as the rule of life, open enemies of government . . . malignant and assiduous promoters of doctrines directly tending to subvert both Churches and State. . . ." [11]

If there had been any further incentive to persecution it could have been found in the invincible belief of New Englanders that they were God's chosen people, whom He had singled out to carry on his design for a Zion in America. For them to permit false doctrines to filter in to thwart His purpose would be a betrayal of trust which might bring upon them the punishment meted out to the Children of Israel. Cotton Mather and other ministers emphasized this point when in 1719 they issued an appeal for reformation, explaining that the covenant of God which made them a "peculiar people" set aside from the sinful world, obligated them not to sleep as others did, but "to watch and be sober." [12]

But persecution in New England was purely defensive, not aggressive. This was in keeping with the whole conception of the Wilderness Zion to which the Puritans fled rather than stay in England to continue the struggle to establish their principles throughout the kingdom. It was their concern for their own souls which made them take to the lifeboat of America, leaving the remainder of the crew to go down to perdition with the sinking ship of Britain. They were of stern stuff, the New England settlers, and many among them would have died without flinching rather than yield one iota of their religious beliefs, but they lacked the crusader's zeal, there was no Peter the Hermit among them. They were content to leave the wicked world to its fate, so long as God had singled them out for salvation and prepared for them a place of refuge.

So when heresy showed its frightful face in this refuge, they were concerned to expel it rather than to destroy it. "All Familists, Antinomians, Anabaptists and other enthusiasts shall have free liberty to keep away from us," declared Nathaniel Ward. [13] The

[11] *Records of the Governor and Company of the Massachusetts Bay*, IV, Part I, p. 451.
[12] *A Testimony against Evil Customs*, p. 3.
[13] Nathaniel Ward, *Simple Cobbler of Aggawamm*, pp. 3–12.

ministers and magistrates alike were agreed in offering heretics the opportunity to depart in peace. It was only when they refused to go, or, when expelled by force, insisted upon returning, that they resorted to sterner methods. "In case of heresy incorrigible, in conjunction with endeavors to seduce others thereunto, and tending to the disturbing of public order, we acknowledge it to be the pious wisdom of the magistrates to proceed gradually . . . by restraint in the prison until an opportunity of shipping them away," explained John Norton. "The wolf which ventures over the wide sea out of a ravening desire to prey upon the sheep, when landed, discovered and taken, hath no cause to complain, though for the security of the flock he is penned up, with the door opening into the fold fast shut, but having another door purposely left open, whereby he may depart at his pleasure." [14]

But when the heretic refused to accept banishment, because he wished to remain to attack the established Church and wean the people from it, the ministers and magistrates showed him no mercy. "If any Quaker or Quakers shall presume, after they have once suffered what the law requireth, to come into this jurisdiction," stated the Massachusetts law of 1656, "every such male Quaker shall for the first offence have one of his ears cut off and be kept at work of correction till he can be sent away at his own charge, and for the second offence shall have his other ear cut off . . . and every woman Quaker . . . shall be severely whipt and kept at the house of correction at work till she shall be sent away . . . and for every Quaker, he or she, that shall a third time herein again offend, they shall have their tongues bored through with a hot iron." [15] At last, if all other measures failed and the heretics, after repeated banishments, continued to return, they were to be put to death. [16]

The New Haven laws also were severe. "If after they have suffered the law . . . and shall presume to come into this jurisdiction again, every such male Quaker shall for that second offence be branded on the hand with the letter H, be committed to prison and kept to work till he can be sent away at his own charge, and

[14] John Norton, *The Heart of New England Rent*, p. 54.
[15] *Records of the Governor and Company of the Massachusetts Bay*, IV, Part I, p. 308.
[16] *Ibid.*, p. 383.

every Quaker woman that hath suffered the law here and shall presume to come into this jurisdiction again, shall be severely whipt . . . and for every Quaker, he or she, that shall a fourth time again offend, they shall have their tongues bored through with a hot iron." [17] The Connecticut government, in keeping with the more tolerant spirit introduced by its founder—Thomas Hooker—was milder. It was merely ordered that when any person was suspected of heresy, he was first to be examined by the elders, and if found guilty was to be sent to prison or banished. Later it was decided to "leave it to the discretion of the magistrates or assistants . . . where any such person shall be found fomenting their wicked tenets . . . to punish the said heretics by fine or banishment or corporal punishment as they judge meet." [18]

To the criticisms coming from England that all this was inconsistent with the principles and spirit of toleration, the Puritan leaders answered by emphatically denying that they had ever intended to permit freedom of belief and worship. " 'Tis Satan's policy, to plead for an indefinite and boundless toleration," declared Thomas Shepard.[19] "The loud outcry of some is for liberty of conscience that they may hold and practice what they will in religion," states Urian Oakes. "I look upon an unbounded toleration as the first born of all abominations . . . I make no question but our Lord Jesus . . . will remember and remunerate . . . the kindness and good affection of our pious and faithful rulers in that they preserved and secured him, with respect to his truth, ordinances, interests and concernments of his kingdom, from the insolences and encroachments of erroneous and unruly persons." [20]

"We both dread and bear witness against liberty of heresy, liberty to blaspheme the blessed Trinity, the person and office of Christ, the holy Scriptures, the tabernacle of God and those that dwelt in Heaven," declared John Norton. "It is a liberty . . . to answer to the dictate of error of conscience in walking contrary to

[17] *New Haven Colonial Records,* 1653–1665, p. 239.
[18] *Colonial Records of Connecticut,* 1636–1665, pp. 303, 324.
[19] Lindsay Swift, "The Massachusetts Election Sermons," Colonial Society of Massachusetts *Publications,* I, p. 400.
[20] Urian Oakes, *New England Pleaded With,* pp. 54, 56.

rule. It is a liberty to blaspheme, a liberty to seduce others from the true God, a liberty to tell lies in the name of the Lord." [21] Increase Mather rebuked the "hideous clamors for liberty of conscience," while Samuel Torrey, although more moderate, thought that error, propagated "in open opposition to truth, the true churches, worship and ordinances of Christ," should not be tolerated.[22] Even the mild William Hubbard declared that the "civil power may and ought to nonlicentiate him that shall take upon him as a physician to prescribe to the people poisonous drugs instead of wholesome food or physick." [23]

The ministers admitted that God had given conscience to man as a guide to conduct, but they made a subtle distinction between obeying conscience in truth and obeying conscience in error. In other words, they accepted conscience as an ally, but rejected it as an enemy. "Distinguish between conscience, properly so called, and the error of conscience," said John Norton. "Conscience is God's vice-regent in the soul. . . . Liberty of conscience is a freedom from all impediment in respect to man, as to the following of the dictates of conscience in acting according to rule. But liberty of error or liberty of the error of conscience is falsely called liberty of conscience, being indeed the opposite thereto." [24]

So the battle began. It proved to be a long-drawn-out, tragic struggle, marked by angry passions, by heroism, by fanatical zeal, by fear and hope and pity, by patient suffering, by bloodshed, torture and death. The ministers and magistrates were convinced that if it went against them, if heresy gained a foothold in their Zion to divide and undermine it, the venture for which they had sacrificed so much would prove futile. To them it seemed that all was at stake—the Churches, the Christian State, their own power and influence, the purity of worship, Heaven itself—so they would not, could not yield.

The first serious trouble came from within, when one of the ministers delivered an assault upon some of the most vital tenets of the Bible commonwealth. Among the passengers of the ship

[21] John Norton, *The Heart of New England Rent,* pp. 51, 53.
[22] Samuel Torrey, *An Exhortation unto Reformation,* p. 21.
[23] William Hubbard, *The Happiness of a People,* p. 40.
[24] John Norton, *The Heart of New England Rent,* p. 51.

Lyon which arrived at Nantasket in February, 1631, was the Reverend Roger Williams,[25] "a man godly and zealous, having many precious parts, but very unsettled in judgment." Since John Wilson, minister of the Boston Church, was absent on a visit to England, the congregation called Williams to fill his place. But he immediately found himself in disagreement with Cotton and others over two points—their refusal to repent for having had communion with the Churches of England and their recognition of the right of magistrates to punish breaches of the law in points of conscience.[26]

So vital did the differences seem that when the Salem Church called Williams to be their teacher, they drew down upon themselves the censure of the General Court. It seemed to the Court preposterous to maintain that "a Church might run into heresy, apostacy or tyranny and yet the civil magistrate could not intermeddle." [27] They were the more deeply displeased when, in 1633, Williams wrote a treatise in which he denied the right of King James to grant the lands of Massachusetts Bay to the settlers, because all New England belonged to the Indians, and charged him with telling a solemn lie. To attack the charter, the very foundation of the Bible Commonwealth, was just as dangerous as denying the authority of the State to enforce the decision of the Churches in religious matters, and the Governor and Assistants agreed that Williams should be held to account. Yet when he appeared at the next General Court, expressed penitence, offered his treatise to be burnt and gave assurances of his loyalty, the matter was "passed over." [28]

But a man of such strong convictions could not long keep silence. So, in November, 1634, when the news reached Boston that Williams was again denouncing the charter, and had fallen into still another dangerous error by declaring that a magistrate ought not to tender an oath to an unregenerate juror since this forced him to take the name of the Lord in vain, he was summoned

<hr/>

[25] *Winthrop's Journal, "History of New England,"* ed. by J. K. Hosmer, I, p. 57.
[26] *Ibid.*, pp. 61, 62.
[27] *Ibid.*, p. 154.
[28] *Ibid.*, pp. 116, 118.

before the Governor and Magistrates. Although he was "clearly confuted" by the other ministers, he remained obstinate.

In the meanwhile sentiment was rapidly crystallizing against the Salem minister. He had become so disturbing a factor and had delivered so many blows against the very citadel of the Puritan society, that many were reluctantly coming to the conclusion that his expulsion was necessary, even though the little colony could ill spare so learned and pious a man. At the General Court of July, 1635, he was charged with "divers dangerous opinions," which were adjudged by all, Magistrates and ministers alike, "to be erroneous and very dangerous." But before pronouncing sentence they gave him time to meditate over his "error" so that he could recant. At the same time they gave the Salem congregation a hint of what might be the consequences of disobedience, by refusing to grant their town title to certain lands in Marblehead Neck to which they laid claim. As for Williams, he now became defiant, and wrote two letters, one to the various Churches complaining of the injustice and oppression of the Magistrates, and the other to his own congregation advising them to renounce communion with the other Churches.[29]

This proved too much. When the General Court met in October, 1636, the ministers, "being desired to be present," made their way over the paths leading through forest and fields to New Town[30] to join them. When the Governor, Assistants, Deputies, ministers and teachers had assembled in the crude little meetinghouse and other matters had been disposed of, the Court asked Williams whether he was ready to disavow his two letters. Upon his refusal they appointed Thomas Hooker to dispute with him. But Williams himself was an able debater and Hooker's best efforts could not reduce him from his errors. He was ready, as he stated upon another occasion, "not only to be bound and banished, but to die also." Thereupon, with the approval of all the ministers save one, the Court sentenced him to depart out of their jurisdiction within six weeks.[31]

[29] Roger Williams, *Mr. Cotton's Letter Examined and Answered*, p. 5.
[30] Cambridge.
[31] *Winthrop's Journal, "History of New England,"* ed. by J. K. Hosmer, Vol. I, p. 163.

Later the time was extended to take effect in the spring, provided Williams should refrain from spreading his opinions. But when it was reported that not only had he continued to preach in his own house, but had drawn around him more than twenty persons with whom he was planning to found a colony on Narragansett Bay, the Court became seriously alarmed. Such a colony on the flank of Massachusetts could become a source of grave danger, since from it "the infection would easily spread." Thereupon they sent Captain Underhill in a pinnace to Salem to arrest him and take him aboard a ship which was riding at Nantasket, there to await his sailing for England. But when the captain, with his soldiers, came to Williams' house, they were informed that three days previously he had fled into the wilderness.[32]

Thus was the first great threat to the New England Zion averted. It is misleading to contend, as certain historians have done, that Williams was banished, not because of his religious views, but merely because of his disobedience to the civil authorities. The troublesome minister's unpardonable offense was his assault upon the union of Church and State. "The prosperity of Church and commonwealth are twisted together," Urian Oakes declared. "Break one cord, you weaken and break the other also." [33] Two centuries later millions of men took up arms in defense of the political union of the American people because it seemed to them a sacred cause upon which hinged their future welfare. In like manner the New England Puritans believed that their distinctive type of union was necessary for the welfare of their souls. In their eyes Williams was a "secessionist" whose misdirected energies were threatening their newly erected Temple of God.

It was perhaps inevitable that the colony in its infancy should be shaken by theological disputes, since they brought division with them from England itself. Even though the majority accepted the tenets of William Ames and Paul Baynes, others dissented from this point or that and maintained their positions with characteristic stubbornness. In some cases, when "dissenters" reached New England, they fell under the influence of the pre-

[32] *Ibid.*, p. 168.
[33] Urian Oakes, *New England Pleaded With*, p. 49.

vailing group and in good time "saw the light." But when they persisted in their views and tried to win converts to them, they became an element of danger. Such had been the origin of the Roger Williams controversy and such was the origin of the still more serious Anne Hutchinson heresy which followed close behind it.

Mrs. Hutchinson and her husband arrived in the colony in 1634, and established themselves in a house opposite that of Governor Winthrop, almost in the shadow of the meeting-house. Mistress Anne is described as a woman "of a nimble wit and active spirit and a very voluble tongue, more bold than a man." She was also possessed of ambition, magnetism and determination. Consciously or unconsciously she craved leadership, and leadership in the infant colony meant influence over the minds of men and women in theological matters. Had fate placed her in a later age she would have been an active suffragette or a member of Congress. As it was she tried to unhorse the New England clergy from their seat of power so that she herself could occupy it.

She began by holding a series of gatherings in which she recapitulated and explained the sermons of John Cotton and other clergymen. The ministers beamed their approval, for at first it looked like a revival, an awakening. But when the good woman began delivering sermons of her own, in which she often expressed views at variance with those of the established order, some began to have serious misgivings. When Adam and Eve violated the terms upon which the Creator had given the earth to them and their seed, it put an end to the Covenant of Works, Mrs. Hutchinson contended. But God, in His mercy, had made a new agreement, the Covenant of Grace, under which not all mankind, but only such as He elected, should be saved.

With this the clergy would probably not have quarrelled had not Mrs. Hutchinson taken it upon herself to decide who was under the Covenant of Works and thus destined to damnation and who under a Covenant of Grace and so among God's elect. This vital decision they had reserved for themselves as the very foundation of their power. And when Anne actually pronounced some of the clergy themselves, men who were revered as models of piety, among the unelect, resentment was deep.

The anger of the clergy increased when it was rumored that she taught that those living in a Covenant of Grace were set aside from the unelect by the dwelling within them of the spirit of the Lord, or an Inner Light which sanctified and guided them. In this she came very near the position of the New Lights of a century later, when Theodorus Jacobus Frelinghuysen, George Whitefield and others preached that a religious experience or inner manifestation of God's spirit was necessary to salvation. But Mrs. Hutchinson went much further than Frelinghuysen and Whitefield when she claimed direct messages from God in the same manner as Abraham and other Biblical prophets. This it was which finally brought her downfall.[34]

But for a time, in her own town, Anne seemed to be carrying all before her. "It was a wonder," wrote Governor Winthrop, "upon what a sudden the whole church of Boston (some few excepted) were become her new converts, and many also out of the church, and of other churches also; yea! many profane persons became of her opinion."

This great success is explained in part by the support which the influential John Cotton gave her. Strength was added also with the arrival of Sir Harry Vane in October, 1635, and of the Reverend John Wheelwright in April, 1636, both of whom became her warm advocates. Vane was a deeply religious, winning young patrician, the son of a member of the Privy Council and thus possessed of influence at Court which might be used to the great benefit of the infant colony. Wheelwright was an ardent Puritan who had been deprived of his living in England for nonconformity. By nature a controversialist, he would probably have sided with Mrs. Hutchinson under any circumstances, but the fact that he had married her sister-in-law made the bond doubly close.

On the other hand Anne incurred the hostility of Governor Winthrop and the undying hatred of the minister of the Boston church—John Wilson. Though she failed to unseat Wilson, she humiliated him by having him censured by his own congregation in his own meeting-house. It must have been with deep resentment

[34] Charles Francis Adams, *Three Episodes of Massachusetts History*, I, pp, 401–406.

that this stern, bigoted man listened to the reproachful words of those to whom he had ministered. "It was strange to see how the common people were led by example to condemn him," stated Winthrop, "and that such as had known him for so long and what good he had done for the Church should fall upon him with such bitterness." [35]

It was inevitable that in a Bible Commonwealth a religious controversy of such import as that brewed by Mistress Hutchinson should become involved with political affairs. The side which won the support of the government could brand their opponents as factious or as heretics and subject them to the full weight of the law. Thus the election of 1637 assumed unusual significance. Vane, who had been chosen Governor in 1636, was seeking reelection, with the support of Wheelwright, Cotton and the freemen of Boston; Winthrop was the choice of most of the ministers and freemen of the other towns. Amid scenes of great excitement in which angry words and even blows were exchanged, the vote was taken. The result showed that the conservative party had won an overwhelming victory, not only electing Winthrop but a majority of the magistrates. [36]

This sealed the doom of the Hutchinson faction. Vane left the country; Cotton saved himself by renouncing his "heresies." When Wheelwright persisted in his opinions he was brought before the court on a trumped-up charge of sedition and sentenced to banishment. Shortly afterwards he preached a farewell sermon to his congregation and, turning his face northward, made his way through the snowdrifts to New Hampshire. One member of the General Court was expelled, disfranchised and threatened with banishment; another was expelled and driven out of the colony. Other ardent followers of Mrs. Hutchinson were forced to recant on pain of having their arms and ammunition confiscated.

The last act of the drama came with the trial of Mistress Anne herself. Though there could have been no doubt as to the outcome, the court weighed the evidence carefully. Their task was

---

[35] *Winthrop's Journal, "History of New England,"* ed. by J. K. Hosmer, I, p. 205.

[36] *Ibid.,* pp. 261–263.

made easier by Anne's inability to bridle her tongue. The most damning charge laid at her door was that she claimed to be above the clergy, a prophetess to whom God spoke directly, and this she admitted readily.

"It was revealed to me that they should plot against me," she declared to the Court. "The Lord bade me not to fear, for that he delivered Daniel and the three children, his hand was not shortened. And, behold! this scripture is fulfilled this day in my eyes. Therefore take heed what ye go about to do unto me. You have power over my body, but the Lord Jesus hath power over my soul. . . . I fear none but the great Jehovah, which hath foretold me of these things, and I do verily believe that he will deliver me out of your hands. . . . For this you go about to do to me, God will ruin you and your posterity and this whole State."

At this point one of the court enquired: "How do you know that it is God that did reveal these things to you, and not Satan?"

"How did Abraham know that it was God that bid him offer his son, being a breach of the sixth commandment?" was the rejoinder.

"By an immediate voice," replied Dudley.

"So to me by an immediate revelation."

This was enough. The court found her guilty and sentenced her to banishment "as being a woman not fit for our society." When she said, "I desire to know wherefore I am banished," the Governor answered, "Say no more; the Court knows wherefore and is satisfied." [37]

The Massachusetts leaders have been severely criticized for their ruthless suppression of freedom of thought. With the banishment of Mrs. Hutchinson the voices which pleaded for toleration, civil liberty, the religion of love were silenced. But the colony had not been founded on the principles of toleration, liberty and civil rights, but upon those of the Puritan State, with its emphasis upon conformity and suppression of error. When Anne Hutchinson made an open assault upon the very foundations of this structure, it was to be expected that the men who had sacri-

[37] Charles Francis Adams, *Three Episodes of Massachusetts History*, Vol. I, pp. 499–502.

ficed so much for the ideal of a Wilderness Zion should fight back with every weapon at their command.

But as ministers and deputies rode home after the trial, through the forests and fields, many sobering thoughts must have come to mind. They had won the victory, but the struggle had been hard, the outcome for a time had been doubtful. Could they be certain that error would not raise its head again? Would not others of the stripe of Roger Williams and Anne Hutchinson enter the colony to plant new heresies and bring new discords to the State? And, if so, would fines and imprisonment and banishment be adequate to crush these new errors? In other words, was it humanly possible to make all men think alike? Would it be necessary to cleanse their Zion over and over, to repair its walls again and again?

But the Massachusetts leaders seem to have had little fear of what proved to be the most serious result of their intolerance— the deadening of men's minds, the quenching of religious enthusiasm, the fostering of hypocrisy. The man who makes a discovery for himself, either by searching the pages of the Bible or by what he believes to be a direct message from the Maker, is inspired with burning zeal; he who must take his beliefs secondhand from the pulpit is often lukewarm. If we are forced to relinquish our own convictions at the demand of Church or government, we relinquish also sincerity and perhaps true piety.

But it was only with the advent of the second generation that the ministers and magistrates realized that conformity was useless if it served only to cloak indifference or secret dissent. Then it was that they raised their voices in protests against the "religious decay" which their own policies had fostered. "It is a general concession amongst us that we are in a declining, apostasizing state," warned Samuel Torrey. "You who are of the passing generation . . . who have seen with your eyes and told us what works God did in your days . . . have also seen and observed the gradual declension and defection of these Churches." [38] Five years later the General Court sent out an *Epistle* echoing Torrey's words: "It may be feared that there is in too many, spiritual and heart apostasy from God, whence com-

[38] Samuel Torrey, *An Exhortation to Reformation,* p. 36.

munion with him in the ways of worship, especially in secret, is much neglected and whereby men cease to know and fear and love and trust in him." "You are Christians, ah! but cold, but dead, but lifeless," declared Eleazer Mather. "What hopes that the next generation will ever enjoy much of the presence of God's grace and power of Godliness, if you see it dead and buried before you go to your graves?" [39]

But with the banishment of Anne Hutchinson the policy of intolerance seemed for the moment to be successful. When Presbyterianism gained the ascendancy in England during the Commonwealth period, there was some concern in Massachusetts lest it reach across the Atlantic to unhorse the established order there. But on the whole quiet reigned, and the people, when they assembled in the little square meeting-houses, listened in respectful assent as the ministers interpreted the Bible, explained the soundness of the established order and exhorted them to be worthy of their high position as God's chosen people.

Perhaps it was inevitable, then, that the next attack should come from outside the colony. The Massachusetts leaders had long regarded Rhode Island as a potential source of danger, for the heresies which Roger Williams sheltered there might at any moment cross the border. So when, in 1651, three members of the Baptist church of Newport arrived at Lynn, the ministers and magistrates were greatly alarmed. Yet it is probable that the intruders—John Clarke, Obadiah Holmes and John Crandall— would not have been molested had they kept their views to themselves. But this their religious zeal would not permit them to do. So they held a meeting in a private house, where they preached to some of the people, declaring the "institution of the Church" contrary to the Gospel, denouncing infant baptism and administering the Lord's Supper. Later they created a disturbance in the Lynn meeting-house by keeping their hats on during worship until they were removed from their heads by force.[40]

The denial by the Baptists of the validity of infant baptism was especially distasteful to the ministers, for it implied that their "Churches were no Churches" and rendered their "worship a

[39] Eleazer Mather, *A Serious Exhortation.*
[40] Massachusetts Historical Society *Collections,* Fourth Series, II, pp. 44, 47.

nullity." William Hubbard thought that it was "morally impossible to rivet Christian religion into the body of a nation without infant baptism." [41] So it was with frowns of disapproval that the court, before which the three Baptists were brought, listened as John Clarke affirmed "that a visible believer or disciple of Christ Jesus, that is, one that manifesteth repentance towards God, and faith in Jesus Christ, is the only person that is to be baptised." [42]

The court fined Holmes £30, Clarke £20 and Crandall £5, in default of which they were to be whipped. Upon the pronouncing of these sentences, Holmes exclaimed: "I bless God I am counted worthy to suffer for the name of Jesus." At this John Wilson could not contain himself. "The curse of God, or Jesus, go with thee," he exclaimed, stepping up to Holmes and striking him.[43] And so the heretics were taken back to prison. Crandall and Clarke escaped the whipping post, the latter because some sympathizer paid his fine for him, but Holmes refused either to pay or to permit anyone else to pay for him.

"The night before I should suffer according to my sentence, it pleased God I rested and slept quietly," he related afterwards. "In the morning many friends came to visit me. . . . When I heard the voice of my keeper come for me, even cheerfulness did come upon me, and taking my Testament in my hand, I went along with him to the place of execution. . . . There stood by also one of the magistrates, by name Mr. Encrease Nowell. . . . After a while Mr. Nowell bad the executioner do his office. Then I desired to speak a few words, but Mr. Nowell answered, 'It is not now a time to speak. . . .'

"And as the man began to lay the strokes upon my back I said to the people though my flesh should fail and my spirit should fail, yet God would not fail. . . . I brake forth, praying unto the Lord not to lay this sin to their charge, and telling the people that now I found he did not fail me . . . for in truth, as the strokes fell upon me, I had such a spiritual manifestation of God's presence as the like thereunto I never had, nor felt, nor can with fleshly tongue express, and the outward pain was so

[41] William Hubbard, *The Happiness of a People.*
[42] Massachusetts Historical Society *Collections,* Fourth Series, II, p. 36.
[43] *Ibid.,* p. 47.

removed from me, that indeed I am not able to declare it to you, it was so easy to me that I could well bear it, yea in a manner felt it not, although it was grievous, as the spectators said, the man striking with all his strength, yea, spitting on his whip, giving me therewith thirty strokes." [44]

The magistrates had thought that the punishment of Holmes would serve as a warning to those who witnessed it, but his patient suffering and his religious exaltation not only won sympathy, but convinced some that the Lord was on his side. When the lashing was ended several persons rushed up to the victim with expressions of sympathy, and two, John Hazell and John Spur, grasped his hand, Spur exclaiming, "Blessed be the Lord!" For this the pair were brought before the magistrates and fined forty shillings each, in default of which they were to be whipped.

The clergy and the government had not long enjoyed this doubtful victory over the Baptists when they were assailed by an even more determined and zealous group of invaders. It was in July, 1656, that two Quaker missionaries, Mary Fisher and Anne Austin, arrived at Boston from Barbados. The alarm could not have been greater had Satan himself appeared with his traditional pitchfork. George Bishop, the Quaker historian, asked why "two poor women arriving in your harbor so shook you . . . as if a formidable army had invaded your borders?" [45] In fact, the Puritan leaders would have been less afraid of an army. The people were well armed; many of them were of the stamp of Cromwell's Ironsides; the enemy would have encountered a fierce resistance. But Mary Fisher and Anne Austin struck where the established order was most open to attack—at the Puritan dogmas, at the power of the clergy, at the Church covenants.

John Hull writes in his *Diary*: "This summer two women called Quakers came from Barbados, intending to oppose the ministry and also to breed in people contempt for magistracy, but were cut short of their intents, being kept in prison until opportunity were of sending them whence they came. They were persons uncivil in behavior, showing no respect to any, ready to censure and condemn all; themselves would be thought the only

[44] *Ibid.*, pp. 47, 49, 50.
[45] George Bishop, *New England Judged by the Spirit of the Lord*, Part I, p. 8.

knowing persons and their spirit infallible, carrying a semblance of humility, but extremely proud." [46]

In the absence of Governor Endicott, Deputy Governor Richard Bellingham took charge of the case. Officials went aboard the ship which had brought the two women to Boston, to search their chests and trunks. Here they found about a hundred "heretical" books and papers which they turned over to the common hangman to be burned in the market place. Bellingham summoned the magistrates who were within call to come in all haste, and after some debate it was decided to imprison the two heretics until means presented itself of sending them out of the country. So they were locked up in the jail, forbidden to speak with anyone, denied ink and paper, and even deprived of their candles after dark. So fearful were the magistrates that they might gain proselytes that they boarded up their window "that none might visit them." They also subjected the women to examination for witch marks, which, had they been found, would undoubtedly have sent the two missionaries to the gallows. After five weeks they were placed on board a vessel bound for Barbados, and the colony, for the moment, escaped contagion. [47]

But the respite was brief. The two women had been gone but a few days when eight more of their sect, four men and four women, arrived on a ship from London. They were immediately imprisoned and examined "singly and apart" so as to trap them into damning admissions. John Endicott warned them: "Take heed ye break not our ecclesiastical law for then ye are sure to stretch by a halter." When they requested to see a copy of the laws it was denied them. The Quakers were kept in confinement for eight weeks, after which Robert Lock, master of the ship which brought them in, was forced at his own charge to take them back to London. [48]

At its meeting in October, the General Court denounced the Quakers as a "cursed sect of heretics lately risen up in the world" against whom the government must take defensive measures. It

[46] "Diary of John Hull," American Antiquarian Society *Transactions and Collections,* III, p. 178.
[47] George Bishop, *New England Judged by the Spirit of the Lord,* Part I, pp. 5 ff.
[48] *Ibid.,* p. 9.

seemed monstrous to them that the Quakers should claim "to be immediately sent of God, and infallibly assisted by the spirit to speak and write blasphemouth opinions, despising government and the order of God in Church and commonwealth, speaking evil of dignities, reproaching and reviling magistrates and ministers, seeking to turn the people from the faith and gain proselites to their pernicious ways." [49] Statutes were enacted by which masters of ships bringing Quakers to the colony were to be fined heavily; the Quakers themselves to be severely whipped, and closely confined in the house of correction. Any person concealing or circulating books or "writings concerning their devilish opinions" was to be fined five pounds for "every such book or writing," while to defend the Quakers or their beliefs was punishable with fine, imprisonment or banishment.[50]

It now became evident that the Quaker invasion of Massachusetts was not the effort of a few isolated individuals, but a concerted movement to win converts and to break down the Puritan wall of orthodoxy. No sooner had one group been punished and expelled than another made their appearance. The severe penalties inflicted upon masters of ships who brought Quakers into the province proved no serious deterrent, since the heretics found easy access by way of Rhode Island. And though the other colonies sent the government at Newport a request to expel the Quakers so that the contagion might not spread, and backed it with threats of force, Williams and his colleagues refused to comply.[51]

The Rhode Island answer is a landmark on the stony road of religious freedom in America, revealing as it does the innate weakness of the fortress of intolerance. "We find that in those places where these people . . . are most of all suffered to declare themselves freely, and are only opposed by arguments in discourse, there they least of all desire to come, and we are informed that they begin to loath this place for that they are not opposed by the civil authority, but with all patience and meekness are suffered to say over their pretended revelations and admonitions, nor

[49] *Records of the Governor and Company of the Massachusetts Bay,* Vol. IV, Part I, p. 277.
[50] *Ibid.,* p. 278.
[51] *Acts United Colonies,* II, pp. 180 ff.

are they like or able to gain many here to their way; surely we find that they delight to be persecuted by civil powers, and when they are so, they are like to gain more adherents by the conceit of their patient sufferings than by consent to their pernicious sayings." [52]

Unfortunately, this wholesome advice fell on deaf ears. When Nicholas Upshall, a weak old man of "sober and unblamable" life, protested that the severe punishments inflicted on the Quakers might bring a judgment upon Massachusetts, he was imprisoned and then banished. When he sought refuge at Sandwich, Governor Bradford of Plymouth gave orders that none should offer him hospitality. An Indian chief who sheltered him from the winter cold exclaimed: "What a God have the English who deal so with one another about the worship of their God!" [53]

Yet the invaders continued to arrive. Mary Dyer, a Quakeress from Rhode Island, was imprisoned, and released only when her husband gave bond to take her home, and promised not to lodge her in any town in Massachusetts and not to permit her to speak to anyone. Mary Clark, who entered the colony to deliver "a message from the Lord," was given twenty lashes on her back with a whip of three cords "laid on with fury" and, after an imprisonment of about twelve weeks, turned out in the bitter cold.[54]

With the arrival at Salem of Christopher Holder and John Copeland, matters took a serious turn. These two zealots, who had been "moved by the Lord" to minister to the Puritans, soon succeeded in gathering an audience and making converts.[55] The ministers and magistrates were determined to stamp out this spark lest it set the whole colony on fire. In fact, the Quakers might well have gained a real foothold in this town had they been content to work in secret instead of insisting upon "testifying" in public. It was to "testify" that Holder and some of his companions one Sabbath day attended services at the meeting-house. They sat

[52] *Rhode Island Records*, I, pp. 376 ff.
[53] George Bishop, *New England Judged by the Spirit of the Lord*, Part I, pp. 31–33.
[54] *Ibid.*, p. 40.
[55] *New England's Ensign—It being the Account of Cruelty, the Professor's Pride and the Articles of their Faith*, London, 1659. Written at sea by Quakers.

quietly listening to the sermon until the minister was done, and then Holder rose to speak. He had uttered but a few words when he was seized by the hair and pulled backwards from his feet, while a glove and handkerchief were thrust in his mouth. A few days later he and Copeland found themselves in the Boston jail, where the hangman gave them thirty lashes each with a knotted whip, "fetching his strokes with the greatest strength . . . he could to cut their flesh and to put them to suffering." [56]

But suffering was not enough to restrain the Quaker missionaries. In April, 1658, Thomas Harris, of Barbados, who had gained access to Massachusetts by way of Rhode Island, rose in the Boston meeting-house to warn the people that their pride and oppressions would bring upon them the "dreadful, terrible day of the Lord." He was hustled out of the building and lodged in jail. At his hearing Governor Endicott asked: "Why did you come here?" "In obedience to the Lord," replied Harris. "In obedience to the Lord! In obedience to the Lord! In obedience to the Devil!" retorted the Governor. "He deserves to be hanged," broke in the Deputy Governor. Though he was not hanged, his punishment was by no means light, for the very next day he was lashed until his body was a mass of cuts and bruises.[57]

And so the persecution continued. William Brend, for holding a Quaker meeting in Salem, was put in irons, "one on each thigh and another about his neck," and the three fastened together with a "horse lock," with "no more room betwixt the irons than the lock allowed," and kept in this agonizing position for sixteen hours. Since this did not suffice to break his spirit, the jailer in a rage secured a stout whip and rained blows upon him until "his flesh was beaten black as into a jelly." When Brend fell unconscious to the floor someone in alarm notified the Governor, who sent a physician to revive him. In the meanwhile a large crowd had assembled outside the jail, and as the doors were opened to admit the physician they rushed in with him. Gathering around the victim, their faces gave evidence of their horror until the Reverend John Wilson assured them that no injustice had been

[56] George Bishop, *New England Judged by the Spirit of the Lord*, Part I, p. 40.
[57] *New England's Ensign*, p. 74.

done since Brend had tried to beat the Gospel ordinances black and blue.[58]

When these harsh measures proved unavailing, the General Court sought to immunize the people by the publication of a treatise exposing the fallacy of the Quaker doctrines. The Reverend John Norton, who was chosen for this important task, entered upon it with enthusiasm. His treatise, which he entitled *The Heart of New England Rent at the Blasphemies of the Present Generation,* lashed out furiously at the Quaker claim of direct guidance by God. Such a doctrine made the authority of ministers and magistrates alike unnecessary, he pointed out. Their dictates are presented by them both as infallible and divine. "Because of the pretense of their infallibility they must not be questioned. By reason of the pretense of their divinity they must be obeyed. What can be super added to the destructive tendency of fanatical notions armed with the persuasion of the indispensable necessity of God's own command? . . . That these persons canonize themselves as the saints of the most high is a strong delusion. And if they also by virtue of a forged saintship be heard intitling themselves unto the Kingdom and thereby unto the dignities and estates of all who are not of their mind, it will be found more than satanical."

Mr. Norton did not conceal his fear that the Quakers might gain converts. "Their doctrine carryeth meat for its followers in the mouth of it, so that its contageous influence in a short time upon the tumultuous nature of the discontended and irregenerate multitude needs not so much to be discovered as to be antidoted. . . . How potent a temptation, the opening of an opportunity to the . . . multitude of exchanging places with their superiors and possessing themselves with their power, honors and estates, when this temptation is managed in a way of duty, and that duty also insinuated from the highest nature, principle, etc. viz. saintship of the highest form, inspiration divine and infallible, a super-scriptural reformation guilded over with specious pretences of the exaltation of Christ and the extirpation of Babylon."

In protecting the Church and State from this peril, Mr. Norton

[58] George Bishop, *New England Judged by the Spirit of the Lord,* Part I, p. 53.

thought the Christian magistrates indispensable. Their duty was the "vindication of the name and truth of God from the dishonor done thereunto by heresy and blasphemy." In them reposed the hope of curing the offenders, of putting away evil from Israel, of preventing infection, of saving the people from the wrath of God. Nor ought they to shrink from inflicting severe punishment, for did not the Bible say: "And he that blasphemeth the name of the Lord, he shall surely be put to death, and all the congregation shall certainly stone him"? [59]

Thus egged on, the magistrates proceeded to the next step in the persecution of the Quakers—mutilation. Christopher Holder and John Copeland were picked up at Dedham in June, 1658, and brought to Boston. When Endicott saw them he blurted out: "You shall be sure to have your ears cut off," and sent them off to the house of correction. In the meanwhile John Rous, who "was commanded of the Lord to go to Boston," had also been arrested, and on July Seventh the three were brought before the Court of Assistants,[60] where ensued an interesting debate between the magistrates and prisoners. Since the entire conflict was for ascendency over men's minds, and argument might be a more potent weapon than imprisonment and mutilation, the Puritan leaders tried to discredit the Quakers before the assembled crowd by confounding them in argument.

But they found the Quakers no weak antagonists. When someone asked: "Why came ye thither?" they answered: "The Lord God, whose law is just and equal, required us to come." To the query "whether every man is not master of his own house?" they retorted: "The Lord God is master of Heaven and earth and can send whither He will and whom He will." When Endicott reproached them for showing contempt for authority by keeping their hats on in court and addressing him by name rather than by his title, they declared that love is the honor which is due unto all men. They challenged the court to prove that "ever any magistrates that are spoken of in Scripture required any to put off their hats." This the Governor parried with the assertion that hats

---

[59] John Norton, *The Heart of New England Rent*, pp. 38, 40, 49, 50.
[60] George Bishop, *New England Judged by the Spirit of the Lord*, pp. 71, 73.

were not worn in Biblical days. Thereupon the Quakers produced a Bible and turning to Daniel, Chaper III, verse 21, put him to rout.

Someone then spoke up saying it was clear that the prisoners were deluded. "If we are deluded . . . you have more need pity us and not do as you do." "We pity you as we punish you," was the reply. The Governor interposed, "You come in a show of love and humility and the spirit of meekness, but you are such as Christ spake of, who have outwardly sheep's clothing, but inwardly are ravening wolves." It took brave men to come back with the retort: "Christ then spake of a people very like yourselves." [61]

Three days later the prisoners were called before the court to receive sentence and the battle of words was resumed. Deputy Governor Bellingham stood up and said: "These men have been here formerly and have been sent away, and though they knew the law, yet they are come again in contempt to revile magistrates and ministers and to break all order in Churches and to deceive the people, and so whatever comes upon them, whether loss of ears or loss of life, their blood be upon their own heads." The prisoners denied that they had done anything worthy of punishment. "If we suffer loss of members or loss of life our blood be required at your hands, for the Lord hath sent us hither." After further argument Endicott "in great bitterness passed his sentence" as follows: "It is the sentence of this Court that you three all have each of you his right ear cut off by the hangman." [62]

So, on July 16, the marshal with a company of men came to the prison and, admitting a few selected witnesses, closed the door on the throng outside. When the order for the execution of the sentence had been read Rous pleaded for delay until their appeal to England could be heard. But the marshal replied that he had nothing to do with that. When Holder complained because their mutilation was not to be done in public, one of the witnesses said: "We do it in private to keep you from tattling." Thereupon the executioner took hold of Christopher Holder "and when he had turned aside his hair" proceeded to cut off his ear. He and the

[61] *New England's Ensign*, pp. 86–88.
[62] *Ibid.*, pp. 88–90.

other victim "suffered joyfully," declaring that they would have freely given not only one member but all if the Lord so required.[63]

In their conflict with the Quakers it is surprising that the Puritan authorities did not think of the concentration camp. Had they herded the missionaries and their converts off to some remote spot on the frontier and kept them under strict guard where they could not "testify" before the people, they might have had more success in preventing "infection." But either this device for strangling free thought and free speech, so familiar to modern times, did not occur to them, or they were deterred by the expense it entailed. They could think of nothing better than inflicting ever more severe penalties in the hope that the Quakers would eventually abandon hope and leave New England.

In this they were disappointed. When the death penalty was threatened for repeated offenders, it opened a welcome opportunity to those who believed that God had singled them out for martyrdom. For this we have the words of Marmaduke Stevenson himself, one of those who were hanged in Boston. Having received a message from the Lord that he had been ordained a prophet to the nations, he had gone to "testify" in Barbados. Here he received another command. "I heard that New England had made a law to put the servants of the living God to death . . . and as I considered the thing and pondered it in my heart, immediately came the word of the Lord unto me saying: 'Thou knowest not but that thou mayest go thither.'" And thither he went.

Arriving in Rhode Island, he crossed the Massachusetts border in company with William Robinson, a Quaker merchant from London. They were immediately arrested and lodged in the Boston jail, where they found themselves in the company of Mary Dyer. Mrs. Dyer, it seems, had once more been "moved" to enter the colony despite the prospect of the gallows which awaited her there. The three were released with the warning that if they were found within the province after a certain date they would suffer death. Mrs. Dyer left, but Robinson and Stevenson remained in order to try the "bloody law unto death." So they retired to Piscataway, and spent their time there "in the service of

[63] *Ibid.*, pp. 92, 93.

the Lord" until they were again apprehended. In the meanwhile Mary Dyer, whose family's tearful entreaties did not suffice to keep her from returning a third time, had been found standing at the window of the prison where Christopher Holder was confined. So she, too, was seized.[64]

On October 18, 1659, the three prisoners were brought before the court. The Governor addressed them: "Neither whipping, nor cutting off ears, nor banishment upon pain of death will keep ye from among us. I desire not your death." Robinson asked permission to read a paper giving the reasons for their defiance of the laws, but Endicott exclaimed: "You shall not read it, nor will the Court have it read!" After the prisoners had been found guilty, the Governor read their sentence: "You shall go from hence to the place from whence you came, and from thence to the place of execution and there hang till you be dead."[65] When he had concluded, Stevenson exclaimed: "The Lord hath said . . . the same day ye put his servants to death shall . . . you be curst for evermore. . . . Therefore in love to you all I exhort you to take warning before it be too late."[66]

On October 27, as the congregation was leaving the meeting-house after services, the roll of drums was heard, and Captain James Oliver with one hundred soldiers armed with pipes and muskets marched to the prison. When the door was opened and Edward Michelson, the marshal, summoned the condemned trio, they bade their friends farewell "full of the joy of the Lord." As they emerged they attempted to address the people, who thronged around them, but Oliver ordered the drummers to drown out their voices. When they arrived at the training field, hand in hand, Michelson asked Mrs. Dyer whether she was not ashamed to walk so between two men. "It is the greatest joy and honor I can enjoy in this world," she replied. The Reverend John Wilson "fell a taunting at William Robinson and shaking his hand in a light scoffing manner, saying: 'Shall such Jacks as you come in before authority with your hats on!'"

[64] George Bishop, *New England Judged by the Spirit of the Lord*, Part I, p. 91.
[65] *Records of the Governor and Company of Massachusetts Bay*, Vol. IV, Part I, p. 383.
[66] George Bishop, *New England Judged by the Spirit of the Lord*, Part I, p. 91.

Robinson then ascended the ladder, which apparently was placed against the limb of a tree, and addressing the people who pressed close around the ring of soldiers, declared that he and the other two suffered not as evildoers, but as those who testified and manifested the truth and that this was the day of their visitation and therefore desired them to note the light that was in them, the light of Christ. But Wilson exclaimed: "Hold thy tongue, be silent, thou art going to die with a lie on thy mouth." So Robinson and Stevenson were turned off.

As Mary Dyer stood watching their bodies swinging before her, the executioner bound her arms and legs, covered her face with a handkerchief borrowed from Mr. Wilson, made her ascend the ladder and placed the halter about her neck. At this moment, when she had prepared herself for death, she was told that she had been reprieved. When the rope was removed and her limbs freed, she still hesitated to descend, as though rebelling at being thus cheated of martyrdom. Thereupon the people cried out, "Take her down," and rushed to the ladder to assist her. But the marshal, brushing them aside, took her down and back to prison. When life was extinct in the bodies of Robinson and Stevenson the ropes were cut so that they crashed to the ground. Their clothes were then ripped off and the naked bodies dragged by the legs to a hole in the earth which served as their grave.[67]

Soon after these tragic events Mary Dyer was forced to mount a horse and, despite her protests, was conducted back to Rhode Island. But again the entreaties of her family could not restrain her and once more she returned to Massachusetts. When she was brought before the court and a second time condemned to death she denied the validity of the law, declaring that she had come to bear witness against it. On June 1, 1660, at about nine in the morning, she was conducted to the place of execution and there hanged.[68] George Bishop, the Quaker historian, declares that Mary, despite her "double death," came out the victor in her conflict with the Puritan leaders. "Your bloody laws were snapt asunder by a woman," he told them, "who, trampling upon you

[67] Ibid., Part I, p. 93; Part II, p. 27.
[68] Records of the Governor and Company of Massachusetts Bay, Vol. IV, Part I, p. 419.

and your laws and your halter and your gallows and your priests, is set down at the right hand of God." [69]

The Quakers accepted the executions of Robinson, Stevenson and Mrs. Dyer as a challenge and so redoubled their efforts to breach the walls of the New England Zion. As one was banished or executed several others would cross over from Rhode Island to take his place. Among the most determined was William Leddra. Leddra had visited Massachusetts several times, only to be whipped, half starved and driven out again. When he once more was found within the colony he was chained to a log of wood, which became his constant companion by night and day, even when he was brought before the court. During his hearing one of the magistrates asked him whether, if he were released, he would "go for England." "I have no business there," Leddra replied. "Then you shall be hanged." "I appeal to the laws of England," said the prisoner. But the court held that England had no jurisdiction in the case, and after sentencing him to death sent him back to prison.

At his execution the guard formed a circle around him to prevent his speaking to his friends. At the foot of the ladder, however, as the officers were pinioning his arms, he called out: "For bearing my testimony for the Lord against deceivers and the deceived am I brought here to suffer." So visibly moved were the spectators by his calmness in the face of death, that a minister who was present thought it necessary to explain: "People, I would not have you think it strange to see a man so willing to die. . . . The apostle sayeth that some should be given up to strange delusions and even dare to die for it." As they turned the prisoner off the ladder he exclaimed, "Lord Jesus, receive my spirit." [70]

In the meanwhile Wenlock Christison, who had entered Massachusetts during the trial of Leddra to warn against "the shedding of any more innocent blood," was brought before the court. But by this time some of the leading men in the colony were beginning to doubt the wisdom of an unlimited number of executions, and several of the judges now refused to vote for a

[69] George Bishop, *New England Judged by the Spirit of the Lord*, Part I, p. 118.
[70] *Ibid.*, pp. 24, 25.

verdict of death. This so angered the Governor that he exclaimed: "I could find in my heart to go home!" When a second vote was taken and some still held back, he stood up, saying, "You that will not consent, record it. I thank God I am not afraid to give judgment." After listening to the sentence of death Christison took it upon himself to give the court some very good advice "Do you think to weary out the living God by taking away the lives of his servants? What do you gain by it? For the last man that you put to death here are five come in his room; and if you have power to take my life from me, God can raise up the same principle of life in ten of his subjects and send them among you in my room, that you may have torment." [71]

Yet Christison was not executed. Word had reached Massachusetts that the monarchy in England had been restored and grave fears arose that Charles II might call the validity of the charter in question. It would hardly strengthen an appeal from the Massachusetts leaders for a confirmation of their privileges to have the Quakers complaining to the King of imprisonments, whippings and hangings. So one day Christison and the twenty-seven other Quakers in prison with him were surprised to have the marshal enter to read them an order recently passed: "The Court judgeth it meet to declare that all the Quakers now in prison shall forthwith have their liberty to go for England. . . . And for such as will not go for England, they shall have liberty forthwith to depart this jurisdiction within eight days." [72] So the jail doors were thrown open and the prisoners driven out of the colony, two, who probably refused to go of their own volition, being tied to a cart's tail and whipped through the streets of Boston on their way to the frontier.

In the meanwhile, an English Quaker, Edward Burrough, had secured an audience with the King to tell him of "the vein of innocent blood opened in his dominions." Charles listened sympathetically, and calling to his Lords to hear it, remarked sarcastically: "Lo, these are my good subjects of New England." Then he added, "I will put a stop to them and grant appeals to England."

[71] *Ibid.*, pp. 34, 35.
[72] *Records of the Governor and Company of Massachusetts Bay,* Vol. IV, Part I, p. 433.

So he gave instructions to the Lord Chancellor to prepare a letter to the Governor of Massachusetts instructing the government there to put an end to the persecution. The Quakers, finding that no ship was booked to sail immediately, themselves hired one and sent the letter over. Several weeks later Samuel Shattuck, who had been expelled from the colony several years before, appeared before the stern Endicott to bring him the missive. It must have been with chagrin and resentment that the Governor read: "I do hereby require that if there be any of those people called Quakers amongst you, now already condemned to suffer death or other corporal punishment or that are imprisoned . . . that you forthwith send the said persons . . . over into this our Kingdom of England." When he had finished, Endicott said, "We shall obey his Majesty's command." [73]

In alarm the Court sent John Norton and Simon Bradstreet to London to justify to the King the colony's severity in defending its religious and political structure against the assaults of the Quakers. "Such was their dangerous, impetuous and desperate turbulency, both to religion and the State civil and ecclesiastical," the envoys pleaded, "as that, how unwillingly soever . . . the magistrate at last, in conscience both to God and man, judged himself called, for the defence of all, to keep the passage with the point of the sword held towards them." [74] Norton, as he stood bowing to the King and the Archbishop, denied that he was personally responsible for the mutilations and hangings, but John Copeland, who was present to display the scar where once had been his right ear, contradicted him. Yet the victory this time remained, not with the persecuted, but the persecutors. Charles stated that it was not his intention to grant any indulgence to the Quakers, whose principles were inconsistent with any kind of government. "We have found it necessary by the advice of our Parliament here to make a sharp law against them, and we are well contented that you do the likewise there.[75]

[73] *Calendar of State Papers, Col.* 1661–68, pp. 55, 56; George Bishop, *New England Judged by the Spirit of the Lord,* Part II, p. 38.

[74] *Records of the Governor and Company of Massachusetts Bay,* Vol. IV, Part I, p. 451.

[75] *Clarendon State Papers, New England,* 1664, p. 11, Bodleian Library, Oxford.

The Massachusetts authorities needed no further encouragement. Though there were no more hangings, the persecution of the Quakers was renewed with great severity. When Ann Coleman, Mary Tomkins and Alice Ambrose were found holding Quaker meetings at Dover, in Maine, the deputy marshal tied them to a cart's tail, and lashing them cruelly on their bare backs, drove them from town to town. Through the deep snow they trudged, the blood streaming from their backs, singing hymns in the midst of their suffering. "The white snow and crimson blood . . . and the tender women . . . was a hard spectacle to those who had in them anything of tenderness." When they were set free they at once returned to Dover, only to face new sufferings. While they were in the midst of prayer at a Quaker meeting two deputies entered and, seizing Alice Ambrose by the arms, dragged her through the snow and over stumps to a house where she was locked up. They then returned to arrest Mary Tomkins. The next morning the two women, despite the bitter cold, were thrown into deep water and drawn along at the tail of a canoe, until they were in danger either of drowning or freezing.[76]

By this time some of the Quaker converts had been aroused to a high pitch of fanaticism, quite in contrast to the usual mildness and gentleness of members of their Society. When Deborah Wilson "was constrained to go through the Streets of Salem naked as a sign," it is not surprising that she was arrested and whipped.[77] And it is easy to imagine the anger of the Boston congregation at the boldness of Thomas Newhouse in coming into their meeting with a bottle in each hand and, as he smashed them together, crying out "That so they should be dasht to pieces."[78] In July, 1677, Samuel Sewall wrote in his *Diary:* "In sermon time there came in a female Quaker, in a canvas frock, her hair dishevelled and loose like a periwig, her face black as ink, led by two other Quakers, and two others followed. It occasioned the greatest and most amazing uproar that I ever saw."[79] In June, 1685, he adds: "A

[76] George Bishop, *New England Judged in the Spirit of the Lord,* Part II, pp. 61–65.
[77] *Ibid.,* p. 74.
[78] *Ibid.,* p. 113.
[79] "Diary of Samuel Sewall," Massachusetts Historical Society *Collections,* Vol. V, Fifth Series, p. 43.

Quaker comes to the Governor and speaks a message which was to show the great calamities of fire and sword that would suddenly come on New England. Would fain have spoken in the meeting-house, but was prevented." [80]

Although these outbursts probably won far fewer converts than the patient, even joyful suffering of the Quakers under persecution, their numbers continued to increase. In 1664 King Charles II had sent to New England a commission, headed by Colonel Richard Nicolls, with instructions to reestablish the royal power there. In the midst of the protracted contest which ensued, the Puritans dared not go to extremes in crushing the Quakers. The commissioners told them plainly that it was most surprising that when they themselves were granted full liberty of conscience they should deny it to others, especially when the King had forbidden them to do so. Their laws should be so modified, they advised, that the Quakers might "quietly pass about their lawful occasions." [81]

Thus the Puritan leaders found themselves in a serious dilemma. Whenever two or three met, after Church services, or on the street, or when visiting each other, the treatment of heretics and the dangers involved in ignoring the King's wishes were earnestly weighed. If the Quakers and Anabaptists were permitted to spread their doctrines, religious disintegration was inevitable; if they were again subjected to mutilation and death, it might cost Massachusetts her charter. The scene which Samuel Sewall describes in his *Diary* was no doubt typical. While several friends were visiting Sewall's father, the Reverend Thomas Shepard joined them and began to talk about the need of reformation, especially concerning the "disorderly meetings of Quakers and Anabaptists." If the magistrates and ministers would only come to an agreement in the matter, he thought both groups could be suppressed. "As to what it might injure the country in respect to England, trust God with it." [82]

But the leaders could no longer agree upon a policy of ruthless

[80] *Ibid., p.* 83.
[81] Clarendon MSS., Bodleian, *Negotiations between Massachusetts and His Majesty's Commissioners,* pp. 17, 55.
[82] "Diary of Samuel Sewall," Massachusetts Historical Society *Collections,* Vol. V, Fifth Series, p. 30.

suppression. In 1674 the Quakers were bold enough to set up a meeting in Boston itself, and, despite bitter protests, were permitted to remain. "Some of the magistrates will not permit any punishment to be inflicted on heretics as such," wrote John Hull. in 1697, after the overthrow of the charter and the granting of toleration, the Society of Friends signalized their final victory by erecting a substantial brick meeting-house on Brattle Street.[83] The walls of the Wilderness Zion apparently lay in ruins; "heresy" had triumphed. But after the Quakers had weathered the storms of persecution and were reasonably secure in the right to worship and make converts, their influence began to wane. At the opening of the American Revolution their numbers had been greatly reduced, and soon after the turn of the nineteenth century they ceased to hold regular meetings. By that time it must have become obvious to all that the strength of the Quakers in Massachusetts had been a direct consequence of their sufferings. Had the ministers and magistrates heeded Roger Williams' remarkable observation that persecution gained more adherents for the Quakers than all their arguments, the sect would probably at no time have embraced more than a handful.

Years later some of the leading Massachusetts ministers themselves became convinced that Williams had been right. In his election sermon of 1676, William Hubbard declared that dissenters in religion were much like rebels in the State, "who by fair means may be gained, but by too much severity are apt to run into uncurable opposition and obstinacy." Cotton Mather was of the same opinion. "A great clamor hath been raised against New England for their persecution of the Quakers," he wrote, "and if any man will appear in the vindication of it, let him do as he please; for my part I will not. I am verily persuaded these miserable Quakers would in a little while (as we have now seen) have come to nothing, if the civil magistrate had not inflicted any civil penalty upon them." [84]

Persecution it was, also, which kept alive the Baptist spark in the colony. "It is highly probable that the late severities exercised towards our brethren in this jurisdiction set many to examining

[83] Justin Winsor, *The Memorial History of Boston*, I, p. 195; II, p. 196.
[84] Cotton Mather, *Magnalia* (London, 1702), Book VII, p. 23.

their principles," wrote David Benedict. "Certain it is that the Baptists now began to be more numerous."[85] Thomas Gould, of Charlestown, was the leader of the movement. Harassed by the ministers, elders and even Deputy Governor Richard Bellingham, because he would not bring his infant child to the meeting-house for baptism, he decided to organize a congregation of his own. He was joined by Thomas Osburn, of Charlestown, by Richard Goodall, William Turner and Robert Lambert, all of whom had recently come over from England, and by four others.[86] They were immediately haled into court, condemned as heretics, fined and imprisoned.

In the midst of these repressive measures the authorities gave the Baptists a rare opportunity to advertise their doctrines by arranging for them a public debate with six leading ministers. So, on April 18, 1668, the little group of illiterate Baptists, seated in the Boston meeting-house, in the presence of the Governor and the magistrates, pitted their arguments against those of such learned men as Thomas Shepard, John Allen, Thomas Cobbet, John Higginson, Samuel Dansforth and Jonathan Mitchell. But the "heretics" were not to battle alone, for the Newport Baptists sent three of their ablest members to assist them. Unfortunately we have no full account of this remarkable meeting, but it seems that the Baptists were browbeaten, threatened and reviled as enemies of the Churches and the government. At the end of the second day Mitchell closed the proceedings by reading from Deuteronomy: "And the man that will do presumptuously and will not hearken unto the priest, that standeth to minister there before the Lord thy God or unto the judge, even that man shall die, and thou shalt put away the evil from Israel."[87]

Yet the magistrates at this time dared not proceed to such lengths. Gould, Turner and John Farnum were brought into court, and charged with organizing a pretended Church without the approbation of the authorities, "to the great grief and offence of the godly orthodox." Their denial of the validity of infant

[85] David Benedict, *History of the Baptist Denomination in America*, I, p. 380.
[86] "Diary of John Hull," American Antiquarian Society *Transactions and Collections*, III, p. 219.
[87] David Benedict, *History of the Baptist Denomination in America*, pp. 391, 392.

baptism made the members of the regular Churches unbaptised persons, it was stated, and so tended to undermine all the congregations, the ministry and the ordinances, to nullify Church discipline and open the door to all sorts of abominations. The court therefore sentenced them to banishment. When the three men refused to go, they were lodged in jail and kept there many months.[88]

But sentiment against religious persecution was growing and protests began to pour in from Puritans, both in Massachusetts and England. When a group of sixty-six men, some of them prominent in the life of the colony, pleaded for the Baptists, the ministers and magistrates were angered and not a little alarmed. The petitioners, for their contempt of authority, were fined and forced to apologize. But the court could not fine Robert Mascall, of Finsbury, England, when he wrote expressing his grief that dear New England should persecute. "What principles is persecution grounded upon?" he asked. "Domination and infallibility. But are we infallible and have we the government? God made none, no not the apostles, who could not err, to be lords over faith; therefore what monstrous pride is this! At this rate any persuasion getting uppermost may command and persecute them that obey them not. We blush and are filled with shame and confusion of face, when we hear of these things." [89]

Nor was the persecution of the Baptists any more successful than of the Quakers. The little heretic group who believed in immersion and condemned infant baptism received fresh accessions —Isaac Hull, Jacob Barney, John Russell, and others. For some years they held their meetings on Noddle's Island in Boston harbor, but in the summer of 1674 they rented a house from a Mr. Symond Lind in the town, and five years later erected a meetinghouse of their own.[90] Thereupon the Court passed a law making all houses of worship built without legal permission liable to confiscation. The doors of the little building were nailed up and a notice posted warning all persons not to hold religious services

[88] *Ibid.*, pp. 393, 394.
[89] *Ibid.*, p. 396.
[90] "Diary of John Hull," American Antiquarian Society *Transactions and Collections*, III, p. 238; Justin Winsor, ed., *Memorial History of Boston*, II, p. vi.

there "without licence from authority." Thereupon the congregation met for worship in the yard and soon after erected a shed to protect them from the cold and rain. Finally the Court relented, fearing to go too far in defiance of the King, and opening the doors, relinquished the little church to its rightful owners. The Baptists had won their battle, and had rooted themselves in Massachusetts soil despite all the magistrates could do.[91]

Bitter though this was to the supporters of the old order, it caused less heartburning than the intrusion of the Church of England. To such men as Samuel Sewall, Cotton Mather and John Norton it seemed calamitous that the use of the Book of Common Prayer and the Church ceremonial should follow them to their Zion in America. Yet with the restoration of the monarchy they must have realized that this was inevitable. They could not hope for the King's protection while prohibiting his subjects in Massachusetts from worshiping according to the rites of the established Church of England.

In 1664 the King's commissioners brought this to the attention of the Governor and the General Court in no uncertain terms. It was the King's desire, they reported, "that such who desire to use the Book of Common Prayer may be permitted to do so, without incurring any penalty, reproach or disadvantage . . . it being very scandalous that any person should be debarred the exercise of his religion according to the laws and custom of England by those who by indulgence granted have liberty left to be of what profession in religion they please to be." [92] In alarm the Court sent a reply which, despite its vagueness, was both a protest and a refusal to obey. They would never have left their dear native country could they have seen in the Word of God any warrant to perform devotions in that way, they answered. "To have the same set up here we conceive it is apparent that it would disturb our peace in our present enjoyments." [93]

Despite the indignation of the commissioners at this reply, for the time being the Puritans had their way. Since there were few Anglicans in Massachusetts to arouse the King by their com-

[91] David Benedict, *History of the Baptist Denomination in America*, p. 400.
[92] *Clarendon MSS.*, Bodleian, p. 41.
[93] *Ibid.*, pp. 50, 54.

plaints, and since Charles had troubles enough at home, the matter was allowed to slumber. But it awoke with a start in June, 1676, with the arrival in Boston of the King's messenger, the energetic Edward Randolph. When Randolph reported to Secretary Coventry that persons of the Anglican faith were still discriminated against and that the Puritans dreaded the introduction of episcopacy more than another Indian war, the Lords of Trade were deeply offended.[94] In July, 1679, the King wrote that he expected obedience to his command "in respect of freedom and liberty of conscience, so as those that desire to serve God in the way of the Church of England, be not thereby made obnoxious or discountenanced from their sharing in the government, much less . . . subjected to fines and forfeitures." [95]

When news of this order spread in Boston, the Anglicans, hoping that the hour of deliverance was at hand, sent a petition to the King "that a Church might be allowed them for the exercise of religion according to the Church of England." This request Randolph seconded in two letters to the Bishop of London. "In my attendance on your Lordship I often exprest that some able ministers might be appointed to perform the offices of the Church with us . . . and we will contribute largely to their maintenance." As though doubtful whether this would be adequate, he added, "One thing will mainly help, when no marriages hereafter shall be allowed lawful but such as are made by the ministers of the Church of England." [96] When a report reached Boston that the Bishop had promised to send over a minister, it gave great satisfaction to many whose children had not been baptized and who had never received the sacraments since leaving England. Randolph wrote joyfully: "He will be received by all honest men with hearty respect and kindness, and if his majesty's laws be of force with us, we could raise a sufficient maintenance for divers ministers out of the estates of those whose treasons have forfeited them."

But there were many delays, probably because of the difficulty

[94] *Calendar of State Papers, Colonial, America and West Indies,* 1675–1676, pp. 406–408.
[95] Prince Society, *Hutchinson Papers,* II, p. 259.
[96] *Ibid.,* p. 271.

of finding a man who was willing to commit himself to such
hostile territory and with such dubious financial backing. But in
1686 Randolph returned to Massachusetts after a visit to England,
bringing with him the Reverend Robert Ratcliffe, "a sober man,
recommended by my Lord of London." Mr. Ratcliffe was forti-
fied with a letter from the Board of Trade to the colonial authorities "for their countenance and encouragement in the discharge
of his office." But all the encouragement he received was black
looks and denunciations from the pulpit as "Baal's priest," whose
prayers were "leeks, garlic and trash." Randolph secured a small
room in the town house for the Anglican services, but it proved so
inadequate that Mr. Ratcliffe moved to the Exchange. There he
delivered his sermons and baptized all who came to him, some
infants, some adults, and held prayer meetings on Wednesday
and Friday mornings.[97]

Not content with breaking through the Puritan's defenses by
thus introducing the Anglican tenets and ceremonials, Randolph
now sought to make them contribute to the support of the
Anglican minister. Against this injustice the Congregationalists
were quick to protest, forgetting that it had always been their
own custom to demand the payment of tithes from non-Church
members. A scant seven years had elapsed since the General Court
had declared that the Scriptures were "express that not only members of Churches but all that are taught in the word" must contribute, and if any refused, the magistrate was to force them to do
their duty.[98] But they told Randolph that the Anglicans, now that
they had brought in a minister, must maintain him at their own
expense.

How few Anglicans there were in the colony Randolph makes
clear by his complaint to the Archbishop of Canterbury that it
was not to be expected that Mr. Ratcliffe should be supported by
himself and "some few others." [99] "I humbly represent to your
grace that the three meeting houses in Boston might pay twenty
shillings a week apiece out of their contributions towards the
defraying our church charges," he said. He suggested, also, that

[97] *Ibid.*, pp. 291, 292.
[98] *Necessity for Reformation*, p. 11.
[99] Prince Society, *Hutchinson Papers*, II, p. 292.

£2000, which had been set aside for converting the Indians, might be appropriated to the erection of a church and a school, so that the youth of Anglican persuasion "might no longer be poisoned" with the seditious principles of the country.

With the revoking of the charter and the arrival of Sir Edmund Andros, the King's Governor, with about sixty redcoats, the Puritans realized that they must expect many encroachments on their ancient rights. But it seemed hard indeed when they were commanded to share one of their meeting-houses with the Anglicans. At a gathering of all the Boston ministers together with four laymen from each of the congregations, it was agreed that they could not, with a good conscience, consent that the building be used for "the common-prayer worship." Nonetheless, Andros had his way, obtaining the key of the South Meeting-house from the sexton and taking forcible possession.[100]

Now followed a series of clashes between the two congregations over the hours of services. The alternate use of the building was maintained until Whitsunday, 1687, on which day both groups wished to hold communion. When Andros told the Congregationalists that he would expect them to leave off by noon and not return again till they heard the bell ring, they gave way and decided to hold communion some other day. The following year Andros, complaining of the interminable length of the Puritan services, asked that the hour of meeting be altered. When Samuel Sewall and a Captain Frary called on him to discuss the matter, reminding him of an alleged promise to worship elsewhere on the day of the Lord's Supper, the Governor lost his temper. He had made no such promise, he said; the legality of the title to the meeting-house was questionable; the New Englanders had separated from the Church of England contrary to the wishes of the government; he would force obedience with his soldiers; the Puritans were derelict in their duty in not contributing to the support of the Anglican minister. Seward retorted that they had left their homes in England to avoid ceremonials and the Book of Common Prayer, so that it was unreasonable to expect them to aid in bringing them over to Massachusetts now. Finally Andros

[100] "Diary of Samuel Sewall," Massachusetts Historical Society *Collections,* V, Fifth Series, p. 141.

agreed that the Anglican services should begin at eight in the morning, by candlelight, if necessary, and end by nine, and so the discussion ended.[101]

A few years later further controversy concerning the South Meeting-house was rendered unnecessary when the Anglican congregation moved into their newly erected King's Chapel. But the presence of this building in which surpliced ministers read from the Book of Common Prayer and devout worshippers knelt before the altar, was gall and wormwood to Sewall, to Increase Mather, to Cotton Mather, to William Stoughton and other staunch upholders of the old order. It was a visible sign that the walls of Zion had been breached, and that the hosts of evil had rushed in. When Sir William Phip's expedition to Canada in 1690 proved a failure, many attributed the disaster to God's anger at the intrusion among His people of the Anglican congregation.

Yet King's Chapel remained, and together with the Quaker and Baptist meeting-houses, gave ample evidence that the sixty-year-old conflict of the Puritan leaders to maintain complete ascendency over men's religious beliefs had ended in failure. We can see now that failure was inevitable. The essence of Calvinism was individualism, the refusal of men who could think for themselves to accept unquestioningly the thoughts and interpretations of others. This it had been which had made revolutionists of Calvin's followers, crusaders for what their own investigations had convinced them was God's command; and it was not to be expected that they could succeed in stemming the very forces which had moulded them and their beliefs. They might have foreseen that heretics would arise among them—a Roger Williams, an Anne Hutchinson, a John Wheelwright. They might have foreseen, also, that hundreds of less zealous men and women, refusing to close their minds at the ministers' dictates, would form opinions of their own which they would keep to themselves for fear of incurring the frowns of elders and magistrates. But they resolutely closed their eyes to the fact that repression and the insistence upon uniformity were quenching the fires in which their own minds and characters had been moulded, in which New England itself had been moulded.

[101] *Ibid.*, p. 217.

It was in vain, also, that the Puritan leaders sought to isolate their Zion, erecting around it a wall against the invasion of ideas from the world outside. They might pass laws for the exclusion of strangers, they might arrest and banish incoming Baptists and Quakers, they might burn heretical books in the market place; what men were thinking and doing in England or on the continent of Europe, or in Virginia, or in the West Indies became known in Boston and Salem and left its imprint. Whenever a ship from England drew up at Dock Square, or when a Cotton Mather read the works of Newton, or Harvey, or Boyle, or when a letter arrived from a Saltonstall or a Mascall, or when new immigrants arrived from London, another wooden horse had penetrated the walls of Israel.

The New England historian, Justin Winsor, speaks of the Puritan commonwealth, compacted of souls united in faith and doctrine, in which Church and State were substantially one, as a "noble vision," and rejoices that it lasted long enough to impress on the community a marked character which two centuries had not been able to efface.[102] Yet one questions whether Massachusetts really benefited from the suppression of thought in the early years of her existence, whether it did not cost her dear by the drying up of the springs of inspiration. Cotton Mather, who became the acknowledged leader of the old order, sought to make himself an exact replica of the migrating generation, of John Cotton and the others, but he failed completely because they had been the product of a creative era, he of a static society. There were many creative minds in the New England of Mather's time, but they were the intellectual rebels, the men who broke the chains of religious conformity, not those who strove to fasten them on more securely.

But whether or not the experiment was noble, it is most instructive, for it illustrates well the action of the forces which created American civilization. We watch the transit of the conception of a community which was certain it had attained ultimate truth and so wished to retain that truth by excluding "erroneous" ideas and ideals; we see its beginnings in the wilderness, its desperate efforts to defend itself against enemies within and

[102] Justin Winsor, *The Memorial History of Boston*, I, p. 160.

without, its ultimate failure, and realize that men's control over the forces which shape their destinies is limited indeed. It was Ames and Baynes and Winthrop and Cotton who planned the New England Zion; it was the great currents of world thought, the soil and climate of the region in which it was founded, the innate longing of mankind for freedom, especially freedom of thought, which ultimately brought it down in ruins and reshaped the civilization of the region.

Chapter IX

THE INVISIBLE WORLD FADES

WHEREAS THE New England leaders tried desperately to close the doors of their Zion to heresy, they threw them wide open to philosophy and science. They accepted knowledge as an ally; had no fear of it as an enemy, since scientific truth could not clash with revealed truth. So the ministers and other educated men sent to England for the latest works of Newton, Halley, Kepler, Boyle and other great thinkers, and not only accepted their findings but sought to use the new light which they shed on the wonders of God's world to buttress Christian faith. They seem to have been unaware that the advance of science was transforming thought both in Europe and New England, their own thought as well as that of the layman, to some extent even the uneducated layman, and weakening the entire structure of the Bible community.

The world which the Puritan fathers left when they led their people to the American wilderness was divided into two distinct and yet closely associated realms—the visible or natural realm and the invisible or supernatural realm. They brought both with them to become as much a part of their Zion as was the charter, or the Church covenant or the Bible itself. When the head of a Massachusetts household sat down for his evening meal he could see his wife and his children at the tableboard around him, he could see the cold pork, the brown bread and the mugs of beer, he could hear the crackling of the flames in the great fireplace and see the flickering light they cast on the oak ceiling beams; these things gave him no concern, for they were visible, audible, natural. But he shuddered at the thought that there were other things in the room which he could not hear nor see nor feel, spirits good and evil, the one intent on doing him harm, the other sent by God to protect him. If one of his children became ill, or if the blast ruined his wheat, or his cow broke her leg, he saw in it the work of imps of Satan; if he harvested an abundant crop, he gave thanks to God for sending His angels to bless him. When Cotton Mather lost the manuscript of three lectures, he thought that "spectres, or agents in the invisible world" had robbed him; the death of his infant he was certain was the work of a demon.[1] The people of Massachusetts, like their fathers of the Old World, believed that comets were set in the heavens by God as a sign of his displeasure and as a warning of dire things to come—death, wars, pestilence, drought. Did not the very shape of these bodies, their resemblance to fiery swords, indicate what their mission was? In a sermon entitled "Heaven's Alarm to the World," Increase Mather declared that the comet of 1680 presaged some great calamity. "For the Lord hath fired his beacon in the heavens among the stars. . . . O! pray unto him that he would not take away stars and send comets to succeed them."

In an age when the belief that sickness was caused by evil spirits, and when Martin Luther declared that "pestilence, fever and other severe diseases are naught else than the devil's work," it was inevitable that similar opinions should prevail in New England. "'Tis the destroyer, or the Devil, that scatters plagues about the world, pestilential and contagious diseases," declared Cotton Mather, "'tis the Devil who does oftentimes invade us with them." In their appeal for religious reformation in 1679, the General Court warned the people against pride of apparel, pointing out that for that sin the Lord had threatened to visit transgressors with "loathsome diseases." Six years later the Court appointed a day of humiliation and prayer in the hope of staying "the threatening hand of God," shown by "the spreading of that infectious disease of the smallpox."[2]

In New England as in Europe mental disease was mistaken for demoniacal possession. Meric Casaubon, in his treatise on *Supernatural Operations*, published in London in 1672, noted how frequently "natural melancholy" was attributed to a devil, and how much the disease was "increased and made incurable" as a

[1] "Diary of Cotton Mather," Massachusetts Historical Society *Collections*, Seventh Series, pp. 171, 204.
[2] "Diary of Samuel Sewall," Massachusetts Historical Society *Collections*, Fifth Series, V, p. 127.

consequence.[3] In Boston, when a poor woman, Mary Hacker, "was taken with a kind of raving and madness," making doleful noises, and "taking no care of or content or pleasure in anything . . . men knew not the human cause." Some thought that this affliction came as the result of notorious sin, others that Satan had taken advantage of a spirit of discontent to afflict her.[4]

The malignity of evil angels was seen in a thousand incidents. When Cotton Mather wrote his defense of the Salem witchcraft trials, he expected "not a few or small buffetings from evil spirits" for his pains. Baxter, in his preface to another of Mather's books, explains why New England, a place of as serious piety as any under Heaven, should be so troubled with evil spirits, by pointing out that it was to be expected that the devil should show the greatest malice to the land which was most devoted to God. And so, Mather adds, "an army of devils is horribly broke in upon the place." These demons dragged people out of their chambers to "carry them over trees and hills for divers miles together." They destroyed others with "lingering, spreading, deadly diseases." They took the form of imps and suckled infants; they held ghostly meetings marked by sacrilegious rites and by plots against God's people; they summoned up the spirits of murdered people.[5]

Although Satan and his minions were the direct cause of these enchantments, they could do nothing without God's permission. So war or disease or hurricanes or shipwrecks were accepted as signs of the Lord's displeasure. During the witchcraft visitation at Salem, Cotton Mather, admitting that the Devil would not have been permitted to descend on New England had not God been angry, asked in supplication what had caused his displeasure. "Are all the other instruments of vengeance too good for the chastisement of such transgressors as we are? Must the very devils be sent out of their own place to be our troublers?"[6] Increase Mather, in his *Cases of Conscience,* echoes his son's words: "The awful hand of God now upon us, in letting loose of evil angels

[3] P. 29.
[4] "Diary of John Hull," American Antiquarian Society *Transactions and Collections,* III, pp. 181, 182.
[5] Cotton Mather, *The Tryals of Several Witches* (London, 1693), pp. 9, 13, 16, 34, 35.
[6] *Ibid.,* p. 18.

among us to perpetrate such horrid mischiefs and suffering of Hell's instruments to do such fearful things as have been scarce heard of, hath put serious persons into deep musings." [7]

Since it was God who had made the laws by which the universe was governed, he could at will countermand them; he could cause the sun to stand still, or the waters of the Red Sea to open that his people might pass, or he could blow up a hurricane. John Cotton declared that it was the providence of God which determined every event, even the weather, while Cotton Mather stated that "as the world was at first created, so it has ever since been preserved, by the immediate hand of God." He had only to move this hand and the so-called laws of nature were no longer operative. [8] When a man was struck by lighning, or was lost at sea, or fell a victim to the plague, it was thought that he was the object of a chastising providence. Sometimes these acts of God were hard to interpret. In 1668 John Hull wrote in his diary: "A man at Ipswich repeating a sermon, and, because it was darkish, stood at a window, as a flash of lightning stunned him, but not hurt. His Bible being under his arm, the whole Book of Revelation was carried away, and the other parts of the Bible left untouched." [9] Had it been a contention of the ministers that Revelation had been included in the Bible by mistake, this incident would have been heralded as a confirmation from God himself; but since they all accepted the book as a part of God's Word, it became merely an "inscrutable" providence. But crystal clear was the case of Henry Bull and the wicked crew of his vessel, who derided the "Churches of Christ" with a mock ceremony, after which a tempest drove them on shore where they were slain by Indians. [10]

The people of New England believed that God had swept the Indians, Satan's subjects, from about Plymouth and Massachusetts bays by a deadly epidemic just before the Pilgrims sailed, to prepare the region for their reception. The Puritan New England, they were sure, was God's vine, which he planted after "casting

[7] Increase Mather, *Cases of Conscience Concerning Evil Spirits Personating Men*, p. 2.
[8] Cotton Mather, *Manuductio ad Ministerium*, p. 52.
[9] "Diary of John Hull," American Antiquarian Society *Transactions and Collections*, III, p. 231.
[10] *Ibid.*, pp. 169, 231.

out the heathen and preparing a room before it and causing it to take deep root." [11] In like manner when the Indians fell upon the settlements to kill and burn and torture in the terrible war of 1675, it seemed God's way of reproving the elect for their growing neglect of religion. "If enquiry be made . . . whereby God hath been provoked to let loose the rage of the heathens thus against us, it is not hard to give an answer," wrote William Hubbard, of Ipswich. "The Sovereign Ruler of the World need never pick a quarrel with any sort of men . . . or seek of a ground why to bring a scourge upon them . . . the best of his servants at all times giving him just occasion of controversy with them because of their pride, luxury, inordinate love of the world, etc." [12] Hubbard was less certain of his ground in reporting certain miraculous warnings of what was to come—"the noise of guns heard in the air in sundry places" and the prophecies of a dying Indian.[13]

The influence of the supernatural in upholding the hands of the clergy can hardly be exaggerated. If the people were becoming apathetic, if they were "secure," if they were too fond of worldly pleasures, if the preacher found it difficult to arouse them, it needed only some unusual phenomenon to bring them back to a consciousness of danger. On the night of October 29, 1727, the people of Boston were aroused by "an horrid rumbling like the noise of many coaches together, driving on the paved stones," attended by "a most awful trembling of the earth, which did heave and shake so as to rock the houses." With the coming of dawn the church bells pealed out a summons to the people to send up to Heaven "the supplications which the solemn occasion called for." As they sat down, with solemn, frightened faces, the ministers thundered out their warning:

"Be now at length effectually alarmed, O inhabitants of Boston. . . . A few months ago how fearfully did we see the Heavens blazing over us with coruscations that filled people with a fearful expectation of the fiery indignation which is anon to devour the adversaries of God. And how frequently did hot thunder bolts fall where many objects felt the force of an arm which what can

[11] Cotton Mather, *The Tryals of Several Witches*, p. 12; Samuel Torrey, *An Exhortation unto Reformation*, Mather's Introduction.
[12] W. Hubbard, *A Narrative of the Troubles with the Indians*, p. 76.
[13] *Ibid.*, pp. 81, 82.

stand before? After this the stormy wind which fulfills his word, came rushing down upon us. We saw a horrible tempest. A storm came which tore up the trees of our fields by the roots, tore down parts of our houses, yes, wounded and killed some of our people. . . . And now, after the wind an earthquake. Oh! let it not be said, the Lord was not in the earthquake. Our God says, 'Now surely they will fear me and they will receive instruction, that I may not proceed unto a more dreadful extremity.' " Then looking out at his audience triumphantly, the minister continued: "I see none asleep at this time. 'Tis a congregation of hearers that I am this time speaking to. . . . Now, sirs, you have an earthquake to give you a push like that of the goads given of old . . . for the awakening of drowsy sleepers." [14]

The clergy were quite aware that the invisible world was their own especial field of activity. If the farmer busied himself with clearing the stumps from his fields, or with building a barn, or with putting out his crop of wheat or rye, he could expect no especial help or guidance from the ministers; if the Boston merchant was in search of the best place to purchase sugar or tobacco, or was undecided whether to invest in a ship or a brig, he saw no reason to consult John Cotton, or John Wilson, or Cotton Mather. But if a drought dried up the farmer's crop, or a storm flattened it, or if disease decimated his cattle; if the merchant's ship were lost at sea or if fire consumed his warehouse, it was easy to see the hand of God at work, and the need for interpretation from the pulpit became obvious. From witches, demons, hurricanes, from blights, wars, pestilence, shipwrecks, demoniacal possession, the only protection was God, working through his Churches.

If then the invisible world began to fade, if it obtruded less upon human consciousness, if phenomena which formerly were ascribed to the supernatural now were shown to be subject to natural law, the power of the clergy would decline. Meric Casaubon, while not going so far as to say that those who did not believe in the existence of devils and spirits, sorcerers and witches were atheists, thought that it could not be denied that their views were "very apt to promote atheism." With this Cotton Mather was in

[14] C. Mather, *The Terror of the Lord*, pp. 1, 2, 10, 13, 17, 19.

full sympathy. "The old heresy of the sensual Sadducees, denying the being of angels either good or evil died not with them," he wrote. "How much this fond opinion has gotten ground in this debauched age is awfully observable; and what a dangerous stroke it gives to settle men in atheism is not hard to discern." [15]

It is strange, then, that the Puritan ministers were unaware that it was the advance of science which was undermining the invisible world, an advance in which they gloried and in which they even took an active part. We would have expected them, instead of accepting the Copernican system, to have denounced it as contrary to revelation; instead of agreeing with Newton, Kepler and Halley that comets are natural bodies, obeying natural law, to have denounced these great scientists as atheists who were trying to take God's weapons out of the heavens; instead of themselves observing lunar eclipses, or investigating the causes of disease or storms or lightning, to have insisted that these things were guided by the inscrutable hand of God.

Cotton Mather makes their position clear in the Introduction to his *The Christian Philosopher*: "The essays now before us will demonstrate that [natural] philosophy is no enemy, but a mighty and wondrous incentive to religion. . . . The works of the glorious God in the creation of the world are what I now propose to exhibit. . . . Chrysostom, I remember, mentions a twofold book of God; the book of the creatures and the book of the Scriptures. God having taught first of all us by his works, did it afterwards by his words. We will now for a while need the former of these books, 'twill help us in reading the latter. They will admirably assist one another. . . . Glorious God, I give thanks to thee for the benefits and improvements of the sciences, granted by thee unto these our later ages." [16]

In his *Manuductio ad Ministerium,* Mather sounds the same note. "What we call natural philosophy is what I most encourage you to spend much more time in the study of. Do it with continual contemplations and agreeable acknowledgments of the infinite God. . . . Be sure the experimental philosophy is that in which alone your mind can be established. For that purpose, be-

[15] *Memorable Providences,* "Address to the Reader" (Boston, 1689).
[16] Pp. 1, 8, 19.

sides your more occasional conversing with such things as our *Philosophical Transactions* and several communications of our illustrious Boyle, and of Hook, and of Grew, and Cheyne and Keil . . . I would commend unto you *The Christian Philosopher* of the admirable Nieuwentyt and what has been communicated by the illustrious Ray and our ingenuous Derham, who still nobly serve religion as well as philosophy." [17]

For these views Mather had the authority of other Puritan leaders, both in England and America. William Ames had spoken of the possibility of natural religion, while in every dissenting academy, those nurseries of Puritan thought, science was emphasized. "Go into the world and view the height of its glory and then conclude if the creature be thus excellent, what must the Creator be," said Thomas Hooker. John Cotton, while more cautious than some others, thought "to study the nature and course and use of all God's works" a duty "imposed by God upon all sorts of men." [18]

The study of nature was, of course, part of the revolt against scholasticism. Had John Cotton or Hooker or Cotton Mather lived in the age of Abelard they would have gone to the Bible or to Aristotle to solve every problem of nature, and if neither authority made it clear, would have found some passage relating to it, however remotely, and then resorted to deduction to reach a conclusion. It is true that the Puritans accepted the Bible as the fountainhead of all true knowledge, to which they turned for guidance and for a rule of life. And they took God's Word literally, accepting it without reservation whenever it pronounced on any subject whatsoever. But they did not twist its meaning to make far-fetched deductions from this passage or that to explain the phenomena of nature.

The Puritans, like others in the sixteenth and seventeenth centuries, fell under the influence of the Renaissance. It was the recovery of the Greek language and the renewed interest in Greek civilization, the discovery of the printing press, the opening of a new world by Columbus, which blew away the clouds of scholas-

[17] Pp. 47, 50.
[18] Perry Miller and T. H. Johnson, *The Puritans,* p. 731; Perry Miller, *The New England Mind,* pp. 208-210.

ticism and prepared men's minds for a more natural view of the world and the universe of which it is a part. The experiments of that strange genius Roger Bacon, the discoveries of Leonardo da Vinci, the epoch-making work of Copernicus, the educational reforms of Colet, the assault of Petrus Ramus on Aristotle, the *Principia Philosophiae* of Descartes, the inductive method of Baconian investigation gave a new meaning to the sun, the air, the water, the earth, the stars, to light, heat and gravity, and the relationship of these things to man.

If one had visited the home of a Massachusetts minister of the seventeenth century to inspect the titles of the leather-bound or parchment-bound volumes which lined the shelves of the book-cases in his study, one would have found among them the works of the greatest humanists and scientists of the age. Here is Francis Bacon's *Natural History* and his *De Augmentatione Scientiarum*; this much-thumbed volume is Newton's *Principia Mathematica Naturalis Philosophiae,* the ones next to it his *Optics* and his *Astronomy*; here are Boyle's *Philosophical Essays, Natural Philosophy, Experiments Physico-Mechanical Touching the Air, Of Forms and Qualities,* and other works; here is Halley's *Synopsis of Comets;* here Hugenius's *Discovery of Coelestial Worlds*; there Kepler's *On the Loadstone;* there Hevelius's *Machinae Coelestis* and his *Cometographia.*[19]

It was books such as these which had freed the Puritan mind from the deadening force of scholasticism. To Cotton Mather, Aristotle was no magic name. "It is indeed amazing to see the fate of the writings which go under the name of Aristotle. . . . They were for a long while hid underground, where many of them deserved a lodging. . . . The torn or worn manuscripts were anon fetched out and imperfectly and unfaithfully enough transcribed and conveyed to Rome where copies were in like manner made of them. The Saracens by and by got them . . . and brought [them] over into Spain. . . . When learning revived under Charlemagne all Europe turned Aristotelian. . . . With . . . the head of the Church at Rome, this muddy-headed pagan divided the empire over the Christian world. . . . Though

---

[19] T. G. Wright, *Literary Culture in Early New England,* pp. 129, 179, 184–185, 237–263, 272–293.

Europe has, with fierce and long struggles about it, begun to shake off the shackles . . . no mortal else had such a prerogative to govern mankind as this philosopher, who after the prodigious cartloads of stuff that have been written to explain him, remains in many things . . . unintelligible and in almost all things unprofitable." [20]

Despite their interest in science it was not to be expected that the New Englanders should contribute greatly to its advancement. The vital task of the settlers was to expand the borders of civilization, rather than to add to it new facts and new ideas. Yet both ministers and laymen made many scientific observations of the fauna and flora and the climatic conditions of America, and interested themselves in astronomy, medicine, metallurgy, chemistry and physics.

One of the most distinguished, as well as earliest, New England scientists was John Winthrop, Jr. A student of Trinity College, Dublin, and at the Inner Temple, and widely travelled, he had an intense interest in science which the frontier could not stifle. It was an epoch-making event when, in 1663, he brought over from England the first telescope ever to search the heavens from what is now the soil of the United States. Though it is a long cry from this little three-and-a-half-foot instrument to the 200-inch reflector at Mount Palomar, Winthrop's observations with it were of no little assistance to Sir Isaac Newton in arriving at his laws of gravitation.

In March, 1670, the *Philosophical Transactions* of the Royal Society of London published extracts from one of Winthrop's letters.[21] "I know not whether I may recommend some of the productions of this wilderness as rarities or novelties, but they are such as the place affords." He then proceeds to describe a species of oak so low that hogs could pick off the acorns. With the letter he sent a box of specimens—some pieces of bark containing "a liquid matter like turpentine," the pods of a vegetable called "silk-grass," a branch of the cottonwood tree, a "strange kind of fish" its "main branches resembling a star, and the dividing of the branches the plant missel-toe."

[20] Cotton Mather, *Manuductio ad Ministerium,* pp. 47–49.
[21] Vol. V, pp. 1137–1153.

262 THE PURITAN OLIGARCHY

A great distincton it was for this early American to be chosen
a member of the Royal Society, and an even greater distinction
to be on terms of friendship with some of the foremost scientists
of the age—Newton, Boyle and others.[22] Winthrop was deeply
interested in medicine, and though some of his remedies seem
today to be a hodge-podge of superstition and ignorance, we
should in justice ascribe this to the backward state of medical
science. Of more practical value were his researches in chemistry
and metallurgy, which he pursued partly in the hope of establishing mines and industries.[23] The breadth of Winthrop's interests
is shown by his correspondence, not only with English scientists,
but with the chemist Johann Rudolph Glauber, the astronomers
Johann Hevelius, the younger Johann Kepler and other distinguished Germans.[24]

That some of the early New England clergymen stole time
from their theological studies to delve into chemistry or astronomy
we know from their libraries and their correspondence. Peter
Bulkeley, the founder of Concord and the first pastor of its church,
was not only a poet and a Biblical scholar but a chemist as well.
In the Walter R. Steiner Medical Library at Hartford is the
manuscript collection of the Bulkeley family in thirty-five volumes, crowded with excerpts from books, laboratory notes and
chemical, medical and theological notes from sources not as yet
identified. How much of this was the work of Peter Bulkeley,
and how much of his sons Gersham and Peter, is not certain, but
the father seems to have been the author of the manuscript entitled *Prolegomena de Arte in Genera* and perhaps of several
others. Certainly Cotton Mather was fully justified in stating that
Bulkeley "was a most excellent scholar" and "a very well-read
person." [25] No doubt, if we could go through the papers of other
clergymen of the first days of New England, we would find some
who were not less interested in science.

Occasionally this interest was stimulated by the arrival from
England of some scholar who had drunk deep at the well of

[22] Perry Miller and T. H. Johnson, *The Puritans*, pp. 734, 739.
[23] T. J. Wertenbaker, *The First Americans*, pp. 82, 167–169.
[24] H. S. Jantz, *German Thought and Literature in New England*, 1620–1820,
p. 7.
[25] Cotton Mather, *Magnalia* (London, 1702), Book III, pp. 96–98.

knowledge. Such a one was Samuel Lee. A student at Magdalen, Oxford, and later a Fellow of Wadham and All Souls, he won a wide reputation for his *Orbis Miraculum* and other works. He came to New England in 1686, where he did much to arouse interest in new scientific discoveries. Lee turned his back upon scholasticism, declaring that it took only a few simple experiments to make all its finely spun distinctions seem ridiculous. Fired with enthusiasm for the new learning, he was the prophet of the marvels it would eventually accomplish. "What the admirable sagacity of future ages may compass as to thousands of problems within the circle of sciences, or in that most noble art of chemistry or the analysis of the three kingdoms of nature, the tubes and glasses of our present inventions give us no sufficient prospect." Lee himself was an able chemist and physicist, and his large library contained many books on these subjects. "If learning ever merited a statue, this great man has as rich a one due to him as can be erected, for it must be granted that hardly ever a more universally learned person trod the American strand," wrote Cotton Mather.[26] Lee's *The Joy of Life,* published in Boston in 1687, in which he magnifies God's glory through the works of nature, was influential in popularizing the conception of the philosophical religion.[27]

The merchant class was well represented among the scientists by Thomas Brattle, member of a wealthy family and chief organizer of the liberal Brattle Street Church. Graduating from Harvard, he travelled extensively before settling down to his mercantile pursuits and to his astronomical investigations. Serving his Alma Mater well as treasurer for twenty years, he served her even better by bringing her distinction through his observations of Halley's comet, of eclipses of the sun and moon and of variations of the magnetic needle. Some of his data was used by Newton in his *Principia.* Brattle contributed articles to the almanacs and the account of his observations of the solar eclipses of June 12, 1692 and November 27, 1703 and of the lunar eclipse of April 5, 1707, were published in the *Philosophical Transactions* of the Royal Society.[28] Upon receiving word of his death in 1713 the

[26] *Ibid.,* Book I, p. 223.
[27] Merle Curti, *The Growth of American Thought,* p. 88.
[28] *Philosophical Transactions,* XXIV, p. 1630; XXV, p. 2471.

Society sent a request for his "manuscripts relating to astronomy, music and other parts of the mathematics."

The readers of the *Philosophical Transactions* were even better acquainted with the researches of Paul Dudley, of Roxbury. Among his contributions were articles on maple syrup, on the moose, on the "poison-wood-tree," on "a new sort of molasses made of apples," on the rattlesnake, on earthquakes in New England, and on beehives. Another article on "the natural history of whales with a particular account of the ambergris," attracted especial interest in Europe.[29] Dudley's conclusions were in part the result of personal observations, in part of conversations with Indians. He was one of the first to advance the theory that earthquakes are caused by the motion of the earth's crust.

It is a tribute to the intellectual honesty and to the clear thinking of the Puritan scientists that in most cases they would not let preconceived religious interpretations or belief in supernatural occurrences interfere with their observations or falsify their conclusions. But how easy it was for them to be led astray is shown by Cotton Mather's letters to John Woodward and Richard Waller, extracts from which were published in the *Philosophical Transactions*. The discovery of huge bones in New York, which Mather concluded were human, convinced him that a race of giants, possibly those mentioned in the sixth chapter of Genesis, at one time inhabited the American continent. The black acacia he thought might be identical with the shittim wood used in the construction of the ark of the covenant. Observing the flights of wild pigeons, he suggested that they might be on their way to or from some "undiscovered satellite, accompanying the earth at a near distance." The venom of the rattlesnake was so strong, he wrote, that in one instance some of it on the edge of an axe changed the color of the steel, and when the axe was used at the very first stroke "the so discolored part broke out, leaving a gap" in it.[30]

But though Mather was not himself a careful observer or an able experimenter, he was indefatigable in following the work of

[29] *Ibid.*, XXXI, XXXII, XXXIII, XXXIV.
[30] *Ibid.*, XXIX, pp. 62–71.

leading European scientists. He has only praise for "the admirable Sir Isaac Newton, whom we now venture to call the perpetual dictator of the learned world," the "industrious Mr. Ray," the "inquisitive Mr. Derham," the "acute" Cheyne, the "learned Hugens," the "great Hevelius," the "acute and accurate Mr. Halley." He does not question Hugen's statement that light is a million times swifter than a cannon ball; he follows Boyle's experiments with keen interest; he is grateful to Newton for his discovery of the laws of motion; he accepts the latest findings concerning the distance of stars, the size of the sun, the influence of the moon on tides, etc.[31]

It is remarkable that the Copernican system found acceptance in New England while the controversy which it blew up was still raging in Europe. When first made known to the learned world this startling theory of the Polish astronomer was received with incredulity, and in hundreds of pulpits, clergymen both Catholic and Protestant denounced it as ridiculous. If it should prove correct, what became of the "firmament on high," of "the circle of the heavens," of "the windows of heaven"? If the sun did not move, why did God command it to stand still? Galileo, whose investigations lent support to the new astronomy, was imprisoned and forced on his knees to "abjure, curse and detest the error and the heresy of the movement of the earth." Europe was flooded with sermons, tracts and books refuting the Copernican system as repugnant to the Bible, which always speaks of "the earth as at rest and the sun and moon as in motion." [32]

Yet two decades after Galileo's humiliation, a young Harvard graduate was writing an article for a New England almanac, showing his sympathy with the Copernican view of the universe. Later still Samuel Lee could write: "The learned of this age wonder at the denial of the motion of the earth, though now the truth of it appears clear." Cotton Mather took Copernicus to his heart, rejoicing in the glory which the vast mechanism of the solar system cast upon its Creator. "The arguments that prove the stability

[31] Cotton Mather, *The Christian Philosopher.*
[32] Andrew S. White, *The History of the Warfare of Science and Theology,* I, pp. 15, 140–148.

of the sun and the motion of the earth have now rendered it indisputable," he writes. "It is impossible to account for the appearances of the planets and their satellites and the fixed stars in any tolerable manner without admitting the motion of the earth." [33]

With the acceptance of the new astronomy in New England the belief in comets as instruments of divine wrath slowly faded. When it was proved that these bodies were subject to natural law, that some were periodic in their journey around the sun, so that their return could be accurately predicted, it became more and more difficult to associate them with epidemics or wars or the death of great men. But how slowly and with what reluctance the New Englanders accepted the inevitable is shown by an article in the Almanac of 1665, by Samuel Danforth, in which, though he holds that comets are natural phenomena, he clings to the traditional theory that they are "portentous signals of great and notable changes." So late as 1680 Increase Mather took the same stand, in his sermon on "Heaven's Alarm to the World," pointing to the "fearful sights and signs in the heavens" which God had placed there to give warning that great calamities were at hand. "For the Lord hath fired his beacon in the heavens . . . and his scythe whereby he doth shear down multitudes of sinful creatures."

But his son some years later in his *Manuductio ad Ministerium* [34] explicitly repudiates the old belief. "There may be some need for me to caution you against being dismayed at the signs in the heavens, or having any superstitious fancies upon eclipses and the like occurrences. . . . Yea, I am willing that the cometomancy which has hitherto so much reigned even in the most honest minds, be laid aside with you; and that you be apprehensive of nothing portentous in blazing stars." Some years later he wrote an "Essay on Comets," in which he subscribed fully to the findings of Newton, Hevelius, Cassini, Bernoulli, Kepler, Halley, Cheyne and other scientists.[35]

But the strange mixture of theologian and scientist which ex-

[33] Cotton Mather, *The Christian Philosopher*, p. 75.
[34] Pp. 54, 55.
[35] Cotton Mather, *Essay on Comets*, Boston, 1744.

plains so much in the career of the younger Mather led him into conjectures as irrational as those of his father. "These blazing stars seem not designed for the habitation of animals in a state of happiness. . . . Most likely they are the ministers of divine justice, sending out baneful streams from their long trains upon the planets. . . . From them we may learn that the divine vengeance may find a seat for the punishment of his disobedient creatures without being put to the expense of a new creation. When I see a comet blazing and rolling about the immeasurable ether, I will think, Who can tell, but I now see a wicked world made a fiery oven in the time of the anger of God!" [36]

Yet the man who could indulge in a fancy such as this, a man who believed in demoniacal possession and who looked upon epidemics of yellow fever and smallpox as visitations of evil angels, played an important role in one of the great advances of medical science. In April, 1721, the dread spectre of smallpox laid its hand on Boston, in the next few months striking down nearly six thousand persons and bringing death to hundreds. In the midst of the universal dismay and of the prayers for mercy, Mather recalled that he had read in the *Philosophical Transactions* that the transmission of a mild form of smallpox as a protection against the more virulent forms, had long been practiced at Constantinople with marked success.[37] When he wrote and circulated among the Boston physicians a paper asking them to give this new treatment a trial, Zabdiel Boylston was the only one who would do so. Boylston, despite criticisms and threats, inoculated his own children and servants. When the word spread that the experiment had been successful, others came to him for immunization until in a few months he had treated 241 persons. Of these only six died. In the meanwhile, however, the fear that Boylston would spread the epidemic by the new treatment created such fear and anger that both he and Mather were in danger of their lives. A mob swarmed around their houses and one man actually hurled a bomb through a window into Mather's study. Mather defended himself in a war of pamphlets in which Benjamin Colman and Increase Mather came to his support and Dr. William Douglas led the opposi-

[36] *Ibid.*, pp. 6, 7.
[37] *Philosophical Transactions*, XXIX, pp. 22–76, 393.

tion. In the end the inoculators won the victory and a bill to make the transmission of smallpox illegal was defeated.[38] Later, reports on "the way of proceeding in the small-pox inoculated in New England" were published in the *Philosophical Transactions,* and had a decisive effect on British opinion and practice.[39]

Of the growth of rationalism in New England we have an excellent illustration in Cotton Mather himself. One wonders whether he was conscious of the change in his mental outlook which his reading of the works of the great scientists of his time gradually brought about. No one was more prone, even eager, to grasp at every phenomenon for which there was no ready rational explanation, as evidence of the existence of a supernatural world. But the borders of this world became narrower and narrower for him as he learned the true nature of eclipses, comets, the stars, the planets, the tides, light and heat, and gained some insight into lightning, epidemics, and earthquakes. When science confessed itself baffled, however, he instantly, joyfully fell back upon a supernatural explanation. Thus he contended that the force of gravity, since it was "insolvable by an philosophical hypothesis," must "be religiously resolved into the immediate will of our most wise Creator, who, by appointing this law throughout the material world, keeps all bodies in their proper places and stations." [40]

Despite Mather's slow retreat before the advancing forces of rationalism, he lagged far behind certain other New England intellectual leaders—Thomas Brattle, William Brattle and Benjamin Colman—in clearing away the cobwebs of superstition. On the other hand, he was far ahead of the more ignorant masses. Superstition in New England, as elsewhere, did not die in the seventeenth and eighteenth centuries, nor the nineteenth century either. Yet rationalism was winning victory after victory. The farmer, the shoemaker, the fisherman, the shopkeeper who read in his almanac essays on the nature of eclipses, or on the movements of comets, or exposures of the folly of astrology, or heard Cotton Mather in one of his sermons accept fully the Copernican system,

[38] Similar bills became law in Virginia and elsewhere in the colonies.
[39] Vol. XXXII, p. 33; Vol. XXXIII, p. 67; Perry Miller and T. H. Johnson, *The Puritans,* p. 737.
[40] Cotton Mather, *The Christian Philosopher,* p. 82.

could not fail to take a more rational view of the world and the universe.

It was in 1681 that a group of eminent New England clergymen, after a discussion of the dangers to religion from the growth of rationalism, decided to combat it with proofs of the supernatural. So they set themselves the task of gathering and publishing every instance they could find of "divine judgments, tempests, floods, earthquakes, thunders as are unusual, strange apparitions, or what ever else shall happen that is prodigious, witchcrafts, diabolical possessions, remarkable judgments upon noted sinners, eminent deliverances and answers to prayer." [41] In 1684 Increase Mather completed his part of the project and gave it to the public under the title *An Essay for the Recording of Illustrious Providences*. This work was widely read. Around the hearth with the logs blazing in the great fireplace, or while at work in the fields, or over mugs of beer in the tavern, people spoke with awe of the magicians and witches, of the imps and changelings which the eminent author held before them. The *Illustrious Providences* planted seed which soon sprouted into the rankest harvest of witchcraft in the history of New England.

The first outcropping came when the children of a Boston mason named Goodwin were taken with fits, "which the most experienced physicians pronounced extraordinary and preternatural." "Sometimes they were deaf, sometimes dumb, sometimes blind." "Their tongues would be drawn down their throats and then pulled out upon their chins to a prodigious length." It was a triumph for the ministers of Boston when, after they kept a day of prayer and fasting at the Goodwin house, "the youngest of the four children was immediately, happily, finally delivered from its persecutors." An old, half-insane laundress was accused, brought before the court where her incoherent answers were accepted as evidence of guilt, and led forth to the gallows. [42]

But this did not end the trouble, for evil spirits continued to torment the three older children. "They barked at one another like dogs, and then purred like so many cats. They would complain that they were in a red-hot oven, and sweat and pant. . . .

[41] Increase Mather, *Illustrious Providences,* Preface.
[42] Cotton Mather, *Magnalia* (London, 1702), Book VI, pp. 71, 72.

They would complain of blows with great cudgels laid upon them . . . of being roasted on an invisible spit, and lie and roll and groan as if it had been sensibly so, and by and by shriek that knives were cutting of them. They would complain that their heads were nailed unto the floor, and it was beyond an ordinary strength to pull them from thence." [43]

Had not the ministers and elders taken this affair so seriously, had they not welcomed it as a refutation of Sadducism, had they ignored the antics of the children and advised their parents to try the efficacy of a few sound spankings, the evil spirits would have vanished. But the temptation to continue to be the objects of profound interest to the great of the community proved too much for the children. When Cotton Mather took the oldest girl into his own home for observation, the child quite naturally, though perhaps unconsciously, played the part expected of her. She complained of chains on her legs, of a noose about her neck, she would mount an invisible horse and simulate its paces, "sometimes ambling, sometimes trotting, sometimes galloping very furiously." She would lie "exactly with the stiffness and posture of one that had been two days laid out for dead." All this Mr. Mather noted with intense interest, even calling in outsiders to witness for themselves this convincing evidence of the reality of the supernatural. Later he presented his findings in a sermon which was published under the title *Memorable Providences*.[44] When a second edition was printed in London, Richard Baxter wrote for it a preface in which he pronounced Mather's evidence so convincing that "he must be a very obdurate Sadducee that will not believe it."

That thousands in New England were convinced by it, in large measure explains why within three years the colony was shaken to its foundations by an outbreak of witchcraft unparalleled in America, in which scores of persons were accused of selling their souls to the devil, many sentenced to death and nineteen executed.[45]

The trouble began in the household of the Reverend Samuel

[43] *Ibid.*, p. 72.
[44] *Ibid.*, p. 73.
[45] Robert Calef, *More Wonders of the Invisible World*, p. 152.

Parris, of Salem Village, when his daughter of nine and niece of eleven listened with fascinated eagerness to the stories of witchcraft and magic told them by two West Indian slaves, John Indian and his wife Tituba. The girls from listeners proceeded to being themselves bewitched, accusing the specter of Tituba of pinching them and otherwise tormenting them. "Sometimes they were taken dumb, their mouths stopped, their throats choked, their limbs racked and tormented."

Again the clergy were called in, and again the enormous importance which they attached to the pranks of overwrought children fanned the flame of terror. The ministers in the Salem neighborhood gathered at the Parris house for a fast and prayer to God "that he would rebuke Satan." This was followed by a public fast by the people of the village; this by a service of humiliation by several local congregations; and this in turn by a fast throughout the colony at the order of the General Court.[46] The effect of all this in aggravating the evil it was intended to remove was soon obvious. Just as the holy processions and services held in the Middle Ages as antidotes to epidemics often spread the disease, so the gatherings and fasts and sermons in colonial Massachusetts broadcast the infection of the witchcraft frenzy. Soon others than the Parris children began to complain of being bewitched, and gradually the numbers increased until about forty had been "afflicted with horrible torments by evil spirits." [47]

It would be unjust to accuse the ministers of insincerity. Their satisfaction at the blow which the mounting evidence of the reality of evil spirits had struck at rationalism was tempered by their dismay at God's evident anger. Nor is there any reason to doubt that the judges at the trials of the witches made a conscientious effort to be just. Cotton Mather tells us that they followed the best precedents, consulting such well-known books as Keeble's *Common Law,* Sir Matthew Hale's *Trials of Witches,* Bernard's *Guide to Jurymen,* etc. But they were under the pressure of an excitement which warped their judgment and blunted their sense of fair play.

Sir William Phips, the Governor, with the "loud cries and

[46] Cotton Mather, *Magnalia* (London, 1702), Book VI, p. 79.
[47] Increase Mather, *A Further Account of the Tryals,* p. 9.

clamors of the friends of the afflicted" resounding in his ears, turned to the clergy for advice. So the two Mathers drew up a paper advising him how to proceed, "which twelve ministers concurrently presented." They were thankful to the merciful God for the success of "the sedulous and assiduous" efforts of their rulers in detecting the abominable witchcrafts committed in the colony. They recommended "the speedy and vigorous prosecution" of such as had "rendered themselves obnoxious, according to the direction given in the Laws of God, and the wholesome statutes of the English nation, for the detection of witchcraft."

But to their credit it must be added that they gave a note of warning, which if it had been heeded during the trials, not only by the judges, but by themselves, would have prevented much of the suffering which ensued. "We judge that in the prosecution . . . there is need of a very critical and exquisite caution, lest by too much credulity for things received only upon the Devil's authority, there be a door opened for a long train of miserable consequences." Conviction should be based upon evidence far more trustworthy "than barely the accused person being represented by a spectre unto the afflicted." [48]

The Lieutenant Governor, William Stoughton, and others in high positions, added their voices to the demands for a vigorous prosecution, so at last Phips gave a commission to a court of oyer and terminer, "for discovering what witchcraft might be at the bottom." [49] After the trial of the first witch, which began June 2, 1692, the Governor left for the Maine frontier to take command of the forces there, and so knew nothing of the subsequent proceedings until his return in October. In his absence the court, with Stoughton acting as chief judge, sent one group after another to the gallows—on July 19 five old women, on August 19 four men and one woman, on September 22, two men and six women. Miles Corey, who refused to plead, was pressed to death. Eight others were condemned but were never executed. [50]

In these trials spectral evidence was freely admitted. When asked to name their tormentors the "victims" cried out that they

[48] Increase Mather, *A Further Account of the Tryals*, Postscript.
[49] George L. Burr, *Narratives of the Witchcraft Cases*, p. 196.
[50] C. W. Upham, *Lectures on Witchcraft*, pp. 25–31.

PORTRAIT OF WILLIAM STOUGHTON, ARTIST UNKNOWN

could see Goodwife this or Master that choking them or pinching them. Thereupon these unfortunate persons would be brought into court, subjected to mental torture in an effort to secure confessions, and put on trial. The evidence in most cases showed that the devil had appeared to them in the form of a small black man who pressed them by terrible threats and torments to sign a spectral book, giving over their souls to him in return for supernatural powers, and that when they had signed they were at once released from all their miseries. It was testified that the specters had the power of "clothing the most substantial and corporeal instruments of torture with invisibility," though the wounds inflicted with them were "the most palpable things in the world"; that the witches held ghostly meetings in which they had diabolical sacraments and in which devils were assigned them to aid them in destroying Christ's kingdom in New England;[51] that the accused persons had been searched by a jury who found preternatural growths for suckling Satan's imps.

The trial of the Reverend George Burroughs as related by Cotton Mather shows the nature of the proceedings. "This G.B. was indicted for witchcraft and . . . accused by five or six of the bewitched as the author of their miseries; he was accused by eight of the confessing witches as being an head actor at some of their rendezvous and one who had the promise of being a king in Satan's kingdom. . . . He was accused by nine persons for extraordinary lifting and such feats of strength as could not be done without a diabolical assistance. . . . One of the bewitched persons testified that in her agonies a little black haired man came to her saying his name was B. and bidding her set her hand to a book which he showed unto her and bragging that he was a conjurer above the ordinary rank of witches. . . . But he inflicted cruel pains and hurts upon her because of her denying to do so.

"Others of them testified that in their torments G.B. tempted them to go unto a sacrament, unto which they perceived him with a sound of trumpets, summoning of other witches who quickly after the sound would come from all quarters unto the rendezvous.

[51] Cotton Mather, *The Tryals of Several Witches* (London, 1693), pp. 13, 15, 16, 34.

"It cost the court a wonderful deal of trouble to hear the testimonies of the sufferers, for when they were going to give in their depositions they would for a long time be taken with fits that made them uncapable of saying anything. The chief judge asked the prisoner who he thought hindered these witnesses from giving their testimonies? And he answered he supposed it was the Devil. That honorable person replied, 'How comes the Devil then to be so loathe to have testimony borne against you?' Which cast him into great confusion . . .

"Several of the bewitched had given in their testimony that they had been troubled with the apparitions of two women, who said they were G.B.'s wives, and that he had been the death of them. . . . Moreover, it was testified the specter of G.B., threatening the sufferers, told them he had killed, besides others, Mrs. Lawson and her daughter Ann. And it was noted that these were the virtuous wife and daughter of one at whom this G.B. might have a prejudice. . . . And that when they died, which was long since, there were some odd circumstances about them which made some of the attendants there suspect something of witchcraft, though none imagined from what quarter it should come. Well, G.B., being now upon his trial, one of the bewitched persons was cast into horror at the ghosts of B.'s two deceased wives then appearing before him and crying out vengeance against him. . . . But he, though much appalled, utterly denied that he discovered anything of it." [52]

This naive account is evidence enough of the dishonesty or the delusion of the witnesses, the prejudice of the judges, the unfairness of the prosecution, which sent this good man to his doom. But Robert Calef gives us additional details. Mr. Burroughs was so far from being feeble, as Mather stated, that "all who ever knew him spoke of his remarkable strength." As for those feats which were alleged to be supernatural, he brought in witnesses to prove that they had been duplicated by others. But the court contended that this must have been done by the devil in human form and so ruled out the evidence.[53]

[52] *Ibid.*, pp. 34, 35.
[53] Robert Calef, *More Wonders of the Invisible World* (London, 1700), p. 4.

There could be no doubt of the verdict and Mr. Burroughs, in company with four other unfortunate persons, was led out to his execution. Among the throng who came in from the surrounding countryside to witness the tragedy were the Reverend John Hale, of Beverly, the Reverend Zachariah Symmes, of Bradford, the Reverend Samuel Cheever, of Marblehead, the Reverend Nicholas Noyes, of Salem, Cotton Mather and other prominent men. When Mr. Burroughs's turn came he made a brief statement asserting his innocence with such earnestness as to bring conviction to many. As he concluded with the Lord's Prayer there was a movement in the crowd as though some would hinder the execution, but Mather spoke up, explaining that it was easy to simulate innocence through the devil's promptings, and so the condemned man was turned off.[54]

An interesting though by no means unique feature of the trials was the large number of confessions, a score or more persons admitting that they had signed the devil's book. To the prosecutors this seemed final. Cotton Mather admitted that it was possible that "the delusions of Satan" might "be interwoven into some circumstances" of the admissions, but thought that "all the rules of understanding human affairs" must be discarded "if after so many voluntary, harmonious confessions, made by intelligent persons of all ages, in sundry towns, at several times," their evidence had to be thrown out. If innocent people could be made to unite in confessing a crime, it was "a thing prodigious beyond the wonders of former ages." [55]

In his *Magnalia* Mather gives us an example of the confessions, written and signed in prison by one of the accused. When the devil had appeared before him in the form of a black man, the victim stated, he had set his name to the spectral book. He heard the blast of the trumpet calling the witches to assemble at Salem Village and witnessed the mock sacrament, though not himself a participant, "being carried over all upon a stick." Later, when he had been at work with his cart in the field, the devil brought his

[54] "Diary of Samuel Sewall," Massachusetts Historical Society *Collections*, Fifth Series, V, p. 363.
[55] Cotton Mather, *The Tryals of Several Witches* (London, 1693), p. 12.

shape to Salem to torment two persons. "The design was to destroy Salem Village, and to begin at the minister's house, and to destroy the Churches of God and to set up Satan's Kingdom." [56]

That the confessions were not quite so voluntary as Mather represents is shown by the explanation of some of the confessors who repudiated their statements after the charges against them had been dropped. "Our understanding, our reason and our faculties were gone, we were not capable of judging our condition; as also the hard measures they used with us rendered us uncapable of making our defense, but said anything and everything which they desired, and most of what we said was in effect a consenting to what they said. . . . And indeed that confession that it is said we made was no other than what was suggested to us by some gentlemen; they knew it, and they knew that we knew it, which made us think that it was so. . . . Our nearest and dearest relations, seeing us in that dreadful condition, and knowing our great danger, apprehending there was no other way to save our lives . . . persuaded us to confess." [57]

Mr. Mather would have been indignant had someone suggested that the plight of these unfortunate persons was similar to that of the squirrel which he describes in a letter, parts of which were published in the *Philosophical Transactions*. "Rattlesnakes . . . frequently lie coiled at the bottom of a great tree with their eyes fixed on some squirrel above in the tree; which though seeming by his cries and leaping about to be in a fright, yet at last runs down the tree and into the jaws of the destroyer." [58] It is obvious that it was mental torture which forced the "witches" of New England, like those of other lands and other ages, into self-destroying confessions.

In the midst of the frenzy and suspicion which the accusations, the trials and executions aroused, there were some who saw clearly that the whole affair was a delusion. Of these, Thomas Brattle, the merchant-scientist, had the courage to speak out, and in a paper entitled, "A Full and Candid Account of the Delusion Called Witchcraft which Prevailed in New England," which was

---

[56] Cotton Mather, *Magnalia* (London, 1702), Book VI, p. 81.

[57] George L. Burr, *Narratives of the Witchcraft Cases*, pp. 374, 375; Samuel G. Drake, *Annals of Witchcraft* (Boston, 1869), pp. 206, 207.

[58] Vol. 29, p. 67.

passed from hand to hand in Boston in manuscript form, pleaded for a return to sanity.

"This Salem philosophy some men call the new philosophy," he wrote, "but I think it rather deserves the name of Salem superstition and sorcery, and it is not fit to be named in a land of such light as New England is." The spectral evidence he derided, holding that if it meant anything it meant that the afflicted children had held correspondence with Satan. "The reasonable part of the world, when acquainted herewith, will laugh at the demonstration, and conclude that the Salem gentlemen are actually possessed, at least with ignorance and folly.

"I must admire that Mr. Nicholas Noyes, the reverend teacher at Salem, who was educated at the school of knowledge, and is certainly a learned, a charitable and a good man, . . . should cry up the above mentioned philosophy after the manner that he does. . . . With respect to the confessors, as they are improperly called, . . . there are now about fifty of them in prison, many of which I have again and again seen and heard; and I cannot but tell you that my faith is strong concerning them that they are deluded, imposed upon." [59]

As for searching the prisoners for preternatural excrescences, Brattle wondered what person there was, man or woman, on whom some mark could not be found which could be so termed.

"Some of the Salem gentlemen are very forward to censure and condemn the poor prisoner at the bar because he sheds no tears," he continues, "but such betray great ignorance in the nature of passion, and as great heedlessness as to common passages of man's life. Some there are who never shed tears; others there are that ordinarily shed tears upon light occasions and yet for their life cannot shed a tear when the deepest sorrow is in their hearts." [60]

He then proceeds to level his guns at the spectral evidence. "I cannot but admire that the justices, whom I think to be well-meaning men, should go so far as to give ear to the Devil as merely upon his authority to issue out their warrants and apprehend people. Liberty was evermore accounted the great privilege

[59] George L. Burr, *Narratives of the Witchcraft Cases*, pp. 172, 173.
[60] *Ibid.*, p. 175.

of an Englishman; but certainly, if the Devil will be heard against us and his testimony taken, to the seizing and apprehending of us, our liberty vanishes.[61]

"What will be the issue of these troubles, God only knows; I am afraid that ages will not wear off that reproach and those stains which these things will leave behind them upon our land."

In the meanwhile the colony was seething with excitement and fear. Neighbor accused neighbor; children, their parents; pastors, pious and beloved members of their flocks. Every day one or more claimed that the devil's agents were tormenting them, until the number of "sufferers" rose to about fifty. And when the constable was seen entering the house of some prominent citizen to arrest him or his wife or his son, there was consternation as well as astonishment. Could it be that Satan was deceiving the "afflicted" and the judges in order to destroy God's servants? Many who had witnessed the executions had been deeply impressed with the earnest protestations of innocence of the victims. [62]

Skepticism increased when the girls "cried out" against one of the Magistrates, Dudley Bradstreet, and against the proud and aristocratic wife of Philip English, the leading merchant of Salem, while the accusing of the Reverend Samuel Willard, the beloved minister of the Old South Meeting and Mrs. Hale, the pious wife of the Reverend John Hale, of Beverly, was greeted with angry incredulity. Mr. Willard, from the first, had criticised the manner in which the trials had been conducted, but Hale had been unrelenting in clearing the community of the devil's agents. He saw the light, however, when his wife was thus branded, and turned about face to oppose the storm and to do his utmost to save other men's wives from the fate that had threatened his. The final mistake of the "afflicted," so it was openly stated in Boston, was to brand as a witch the wife of Governor Phips. That Lady Phips was accused seems not unlikely since we know that she took it upon herself during her

---

[61] *Ibid.*, p. 182.

[62] Cotton Mather states that not one of those who had confessed was executed. See *Magnalia* (London, 1702), Book VI, p. 82.

husband's absence to issue an order for the release of one of the accused. It gives, also, a ready explanation for the determined vigor with which Sir William turned against the judges to put a stop to the persecutions. In explaining this step to the British government, Phips wrote, "Some were accused of whose innocency I was well assured and many considerable persons of unblameable life and conversations were cried out upon as witches and wizards. . . . I have now forbidden the committing of any more . . . accused without unavoidable necessity, and those that have been committed I would shelter from . . . the least suspicion of any wrong to be done unto the innocent." [63]

For the defenders of the invisible world this was a severe blow. It was a public announcement that the chief executive of the colony considered all or most of the testimony brought out at Salem false or at best a delusion—the evil angels, the tortures, the devil's book, the riding through the air on sticks. Would not this react harmfully on religion and strengthen the hands of the rationalists?

On September 20, we find Cotton Mather writing to Stephen Sewall, clerk of the court at Salem, for weapons with which to fight the Sadducees. "That I may be more capable to assist in lifting up a standard against the infernal enemy, I must renew my most importunate request that you would please quickly . . . give me a narrative of the evidence given in at the trials of half a dozen, or if you please a dozen, of the principal witches. . . . Also some of your observations about the confessors and the credibility of what they assert. . . . Imagine me as obstinate a Sadducee and witch advocate as any among us; address me as one that believed nothing reasonable; and when you have so knocked me down, in a spectre so unlike me, you will enable me to box it about among my neighbors till it come, I know not where at last." [64]

In the meanwhile the Governor left Boston for another visit "eastward," and in his absence there were earnest discussions

[63] George L. Burr, *Narratives of the Witchcraft Cases*, pp. 197, 198; Charles W. Upham, *Salem Witchcraft and Cotton Mather*, pp. 55, 59.
[64] Quoted by Charles W. Upham, *Salem Witchcraft and Cotton Mather*, p. 44. See Literary and Historical Society of Quebec, *Transactions*, of 1831, II, pp. 313–316.

among ministers and judges as to the possibility of defying his orders. Sewall tells us that the Reverend Samuel Torrey seemed to be of the opinion that the trials should continue, with the judges amending "anything that may have been amiss when certainly found to be so." This in itself would be a damaging admission that something had been very amiss indeed with the trials, but it would put the judges and the clergy in a better light than would a complete collapse of the prosecutions.

Accordingly, when the matter came before the General Court, amid intense excitement, a bill was introduced to summon a convocation of ministers to advise the government of the "right way as to witchcraft." Yet so many were opposed to yielding and wished to defy the Governor by going on with the trials without any change of procedure that the issue hung in the balance. When the vote was taken the ayes were found to number 33 and the noes 29. Even this slender margin of victory would have been impossible had it not been for the votes of those who themselves had been accused of witchcraft, or who had one or more relatives who were suspected or had been condemned.

The Governor, upon his return, gave no indication of yielding. When Sewall asked the Council whether the court should meet, the silence which prevailed seemed to say, "Do not go." A Mr. Russell argued with the Governor for the continuing of the court but received for his pains the curt reply, "It must fall." [65]

When the convocation of ministers met, the more ardent witch hunters remained at home, no doubt as a protest against the expected compromise, so that the proceedings were dominated by such moderates as William Hubbard, Samuel Willard and John Wise. Their first step was to draw up a letter addressed to Increase Mather, asking for his opinion upon the validity of spectral evidence and giving a strong hint of what they expected his answer to be. The principal plea to justify spectral evidence had been "the wisdom and rightfulness of God," which it was imagined would fail "if such things were permitted to befall an innocent person," but which they thought was a bold "usurpation" of God's authority. "God doth sometimes suffer such

[65] "Diary of Samuel Sewall," Massachusetts Historical Society *Collections*, Fifth Series, V, p. 368.

things to evene, that we may thereby know how we are beholden to Him for that restraint which he lays upon the infernal spirits who would else reduce a world into a chaos."

Mather was willing to do his part. "I am desired to express my judgement . . . whether it is not possible for the Devil to impose on the imaginations of persons bewitched and to cause them to believe that an innocent, yea, that a pious person does torment them, when the Devil himself doth it, or whether Satan may not appear in the shape of an innocent and pious person as well as a nocent and wicked person to afflict such as suffer by diabolical molestations? The answer must be affirmative."

All had heard certain persons declare that the accused were most certainly guilty, he continued, only soon afterwards themselves or some near relative to be impersonated by the Devil and cried out against. Such rebukes as this should make men careful how they joined with Satan in condemning the innocent. "It is certain both from Scripture and history that magicians by their inchantments and hellish conjurations may cause a false representation of persons and things."

Having thus pronounced spectral evidence inadmissible, he hastened to add a word of praise for those who had used it to send so many persons to their deaths. He hoped that none would think him unfair to the judges, who were good men, acting with fidelity according to their light. Yet he thought it better that ten witches should escape than one innocent person be condemned. Thus did the clergy make their first great surrender to the forces of rationalism. They could, and did, claim that this opinion constituted no real retreat, since the letter of advice given the Governor by several of their number in June had warned against "too much credulity for things received only on the Devil's authority." But recommending caution in the use of spectral evidence was quite different from ruling it out entirely. Mather knew, the fourteen ministers who penned the queries knew, the judges knew, that the Sadducees had won an important victory over the defenders of the invisible world.

The Governor, who had no desire to discredit either the ministers or the judges, his only design being to put an end to injustice, suffering and turmoil, was willing to accept the compromise. "Whereas Mr. Increase Mather and several other divines did give it as their judgment that the Devil might afflict in the shape of an innocent person, and that the look and the touch of the suspected persons was not sufficient proof against them, and upon this consideration I permitted a special Superior Court to be held at Salem." [66]

This court met on January 3, 1693, with Lieutenant Governor William Stoughton, Thomas Danforth, John Richards, Wait Winthrop and Samuel Sewall on the bench. Restricted by the debarment of spectral evidence, the judges, even the stern Stoughton, found it difficult to secure convictions. True bills were found against less than half of the fifty-two persons indicted, and of these all were acquitted save three. Two of these three were so "senseless and ignorant" that apparently they trapped themselves, while the other had formerly confessed and now was not so stiff in her retraction as to convince the jury. Fearful that his prey might escape him, Stoughton signed a warrant for the "speedy execution" of eight persons, five who had been condemned at the previous court and the three unfortunates just convicted. But when the graves had been dug and all was in readiness, a messenger from the Governor arrived with reprieves for all eight.[67]

Word of this act of mercy and justice reached the court as it went into session at Charlestown on January 31. It was applauded by thousands in the colony, but it filled the implacable Stoughton with "passionate anger." [68] Rising, he said that they had been in a way to have cleared the land of witches. Who it was that obstructed the execution of justice or hindered the court's proceedings, he knew not, but thereby the kingdom of Satan was advanced. The Lord have mercy on the country. Thereupon, he left the court. This was fortunate, since Phips tells us that Stoughton had "from the beginning hurried on these matters with great precipitancy," not only by sending men and women to the gallows, but having their property seized and disposed of

---

[66] George L. Burr, *Narrative of the Witchcraft Cases*, p. 200.

[67] Robert Calef, *More Wonders of the Invisible World*, p. 141; George L. Burr, *Narratives of the Witchcraft Cases*, p. 201; Increase Mather, *A Further Account of the Tryals*, p. 10.

[68] George L. Burr, *Narratives of the Witchcraft Cases*, p. 201.

without the Governor's consent.[69] In his absence Danforth acted as chief judge, and in the next few days five or six were acquitted and several more cleared by proclamation. When the jury brought in a verdict of not guilty for an old woman named Sarah Daston, Danforth admonished her: "Woman, woman, repent, these are shrewd things come in against you." After the trial one who had been present gave it as his opinion that the evidence did not warrant this rebuke, even though it was more damaging than that which had sent others to the gallows at Salem.[70]

It was only in April, however, that a stop was put to the prosecutions. At a session of the court at Boston, with Lieutenant Governor Stoughton back in his accustomed seat, Mary Watkins, a servant girl who suffered from melancholia, was indicted for witchcraft. When the grand jury found "no bill," the court sent them out again to reconsider the case. But the jury, who no doubt reflected the general reaction against the witchcraft delusion, stuck to their guns and again returned "no bill." "About this time the prisoners in all the prisons were released."[71]

This should have ended the matter and no doubt would have done so had not the clergy, deeply concerned at the flood of rationalism which the reaction against the Salem affair loosened, seized the first opportunity to stir up renewed excitement and fear. Under any circumstances there would be suspicion of witchcraft here and there, just as there were charges of witchcraft in other colonies, even in far-off Virginia. But these were latent dangers. It was only when persons in high places, ministers and magistrates, took some idle tale seriously, accumulated evidence and prayed with the "afflicted," that the embers broke into flame.

Thus it is probable that the case of Margaret Rule would have been lost in the obscurity it deserved, had not the two Mathers seized upon it in a renewed effort to combat Sadduceeism. It seems that this girl of seventeen claimed that she had been assailed by eight cruel specters, who brought her a great, red book, long but not broad, and ordered her to sign it. When she refused "they

[69] *Ibid.*, p. 201.
[70] Increase Mather, *A Further Account of the Tryals*, p. 10; Robert Calef, *More Wonders of the Invisible World*, pp. 141, 142.
[71] Robert Calef, *More Wonders of the Invisible World*, p. 142.

fell to tormenting her in a manner too hellish to be sufficiently described." She would have her jaws pulled open and invisible, but scalding, brimstone poured down her throat.[72]

Immediately the Mathers, father and son, appeared at Margaret's house, followed by about thirty or forty persons who crowded in behind them. The girl lay in bed very still. Increase Mather sat on a stool, while his son seated himself on the bed to conduct the examination. "Margaret Rule, how do you do?" To this there was no answer. "Do there a great many witches sit upon you?" "Yes," the girl replied. She then had a convulsion, after which Mather continued, "Don't you know these is a hard master." After another fit, "Who is it that afflicts you?" "I know not, there is a great many of them." "You have seen the black man, haven't you?" "No." "Now the witches scratch you and pinch you and bite you, don't they?" "Yes." Then Mather put his hand on the cover and declared that he felt a living thing, like a rat, but invisible. Increase Mather also felt. "Don't you feel the live thing in the bed?" "No." "That is only fancy," retorted Mather.[73]

Cotton Mather later denied the accuracy of certain details in this account, but he did not deny what was essential, that he had asked leading questions and that the examination had been conducted in public. It is true that at one stage he had requested the throng to leave the room, but when one woman said, "I am sure I am no witch, I shall not go," and the others also held their ground, he proceeded as before. Certainly, he could have had privacy had he so desired, if necessary by calling for the constable to clear the room. But what he wanted was publicity so that people would convince themselves of the reality of the invisible world. That this might lead to another frenzy of fear and suspicion and to new trials and hangings did not outweigh the benefits of confounding the Sadducees. In order to reach a wider audience he wrote an account of the Margaret Rule case entitled "Another Brand Pluckt out of the Burning," but since Governor Phips had wisely forbidden the publication of anything relating to witch-

[72] Cotton Mather, "Another Brand Pluckt out of the Burning," in Robert Calef's *More Wonders of the Invisible World*, pp. 4–6.
[73] Robert Calef, *More Wonders of the Invisible World*, pp. 13, 14.

craft, he had to content himself with passing it from hand to hand in manuscript form.

But now he ran into opposition from an unexpected quarter. Robert Calef, a Boston cloth merchant, had been deeply shocked at the Salem tragedy, which he attributed to the activities of the clergy, especially to the publication of the *Memorable Providences* and the *Illustrious Providences*. When the report of Margaret Rule's "possession" reached him he visited her room to be a witness of the Mathers' examination. On his return to his home he wrote an account of what he had heard and seen, which he later showed to a number of people. When word of this reached Cotton Mather he called Calef "one of the worst of liars," denounced him from the pulpit and sent him word that he would have him arrested for slander. Whereupon Calef sent him a copy of his account, together with a severe rebuke. "Sir, after the sorest affliction and greatest blemish to religion that ever befel this country. . . . and after his Excellency had put a stop to executions, and men began to hope there would never be a return of the like [I found your proceedings], to contain in them something extraordinary." [74]

Calef hoped to have a meeting with Mather to argue the matter, but instead he found himself arrested and bound over for the Court of sessions. But Mather thought better of his intention of putting him on trial, so that when Calef waited on the Court no one appeared against him. Nor was he to be intimidated. He kept plying Mather with letters to drive home his points, show the absurdity of the witchcraft charges and the unreliability of the evidence. "I find coals are fresh blown up, I being supposed to be represented in your late manuscript, 'More Wonders, etc.' as travestying your discourse in your faithful discharge of your duty, etc. and such as see not with the author's eyes rendered Sadducees and witless." [75]

Mather now took a different tack. If he could not intimidate Calef, he would overcome his skepticism by irrefutable evidence. So he sent him an affidavit signed by one Samuel Ames that he had seen Margaret Rule "lifted up from her bed, wholly by an invisible force, a great way towards the top of the room where she

[74] *Ibid.*, p. 15.
[75] *Ibid.*, p. 18.

lay . . . I have seen her thus lifted, when not only a strong person hath thrown his whole weight across her to pull her down, but several others have endeavored with all their might to hinder her from being so raised." [76] To this Calef replied contemptuously: "I suppose you expect I should believe it."

It would be wrong to assume that Calef by his battle of letters with Cotton Mather singlehanded prevented another witchcraft frenzy. The Governor would not have permitted a repetition of the Salem trials; public opinion would have condemned it. But that the Margaret Rule case might have caused serious trouble had it not been for Calef's efforts does not admit of a doubt. He is deserving of all praise rather than the contempt which has been accorded him by so many historians. It was a brave thing to stand up for what he believed right, and we know today to be right, against the "magistrates, ministers and people, . . . men of the highest profession of Godliness," who reviled him as a troublemaker and atheist.[77]

It has often been assumed that the collapse of the trials put an end to the witchcraft controversy, but such was not the case. The real battle, which from the first had been fought not in the courtrooms but in men's minds, continued for some years more. It continued in the pulpit as certain ministers told of new manifestations of the invisible world and warned the people against the devil's agents; it continued as two or more neighbors, conversing over the garden fence or on the street corner, argued as to whether the "bewitched" had lied in their evidence during the trials, or had been deluded, or had actually been tortured by demons. The clergy, so far from admitting defeat, as late as March, 1694, resumed the offensive, when the President and Fellows of Harvard, clergymen all of them save John Leverett, sent out "certain proposals" to the reverend ministers of the Gospel in the several Churches of New England:

"To observe and record the more illustrious discoveries of the Divine Providence . . . all unusual accidents in the Heavens, or earth or water. All wonderful deliverances of the distressed, mer-

[76] *Ibid.*, pp. 22, 25.
[77] *Ibid.*, p. 14.

cies to the Godly, judgments on the wicked . . . with apparitions, possessions, enchantments and all extraordinary things wherein the existence and agency of the invisible world is more sensibly demonstrated.

"It is therefore proposed that the ministers throughout the land would manifest their pious regards unto the works of the Lord and the operation of his hands by reviving their cares to take written accounts of such remarkables, but still well attested with credible and sufficient witness.

"It is desired that the accounts thus taken of these remarkables, may be sent in unto the President or Fellows of the College, by whom they shall be carefully reserved for such a use to be made of them as may by some fit assembly of ministers be judged most conducting to the glory of God and the service of his people." [78]

When a copy of this paper fell into Calef's hands he took it upon himself to send in to President Increase Mather a few "remarkables" which must have made him wince. The sudden death of one of the witchcraft judges, the death of two sons of another, the fall of a man while raising the new bell which was soon to ring out at the death of the "child of him, who by printing and speaking had had a great hand in procuring the late actions," [79] the bursting of a gun at Salem which rent to pieces "that furious marshal and his father," all of these Calef thought providences worthy of recording.

More effective than Calef's sarcasm in combatting the efforts of the clergy to revivify the fading invisible world was the burning memory of that tragic summer in Salem. More and more it dawned upon men that the Reverend George Burroughs, Rebecca Nourse and many others had been guiltless of any crime when they went to their fate on the gallows, that the tortures of the "afflicted" were either imaginary or were wilful deceptions, that much of the evidence had been idle gossip magnified out of its true proportion, in short that there had been no witchcraft at Salem, but in place of it a ghastly delusion, marked by supersti-

[78] *Ibid.*, pp. 39–41.
[79] Clearly Cotton Mather.

tion, injustice, fear and cruelty. Relatives of the executed, the imprisoned, the accused could not conceal their resentment against the chief actors in the drama.

The Reverend Samuel Parris was driven out of his parish at Salem for his part in the prosecution; Ann Putnam, the most active of the "afflicted" children admitted her guilt and asked forgiveness. Samuel Sewall, who had sat on the bench during all the trials, wrote out his confession and gave it to the Reverend Samuel Willard to read to the congregation of the South Church. As he commenced Sewall stood with bowed head. "Samuel Sewall . . . being made sensible that as to the guilt . . . at Salem, he is upon many accounts more concerned than any that he knows of, desires to take the blame and shame of it, asking pardon of men and especially desiring prayers that God . . . would pardon that sin." [80]

The clergy were well aware that all this reflected seriously upon their leadership, but they could still contend that they had done no more than their duty in combatting the forces of evil. The excesses at the trials, the dissembling of the "afflicted," the false confessions, the injustice and severity, they had not been responsible for.

They were thoroughly aroused, then, when they learned that a vessel had arrived in Boston harbor with a number of copies of a book by Robert Calef in which he placed the responsibility squarely on their shoulders, especially the shoulders of the two Mathers. Calef had incorporated under one cover Cotton Mather's "Another Brand Pluckt from the Burning," his own account of the Mathers' visits to Margaret Rule, the "Proposals" of the Harvard Fellows, and his reply, an account of some of the later trials, a stinging criticism of the whole witchcraft prosecution, and other papers. *More Wonders of the Invisible World,* he called it. "Mr. Cotton Mather was the most active and forward of any minister in the country in those matters," Calef stated in this work, "taking home one of the children and managing such intrigues with that child, and after, printing such an account of the whole in his *Memorable Providences,* as conduced much to

---

[80] "Diary of Samuel Sewall," Massachusetts Historical Society *Collections,* Fifth Series, V, p. 445.

the kindling those flames that . . . threatened to devour the country." No printer in Boston had dared publish this book, but Calef had had the work done in London. Over at Cambridge, Increase Mather had a copy burned in the Yard. A committee of Cotton Mather's Church published a reply under the title of *Some Few Remarks on a Scandalous Book,* in which they denounced Calef and stigmatized his charges as false.

But this served only to advertise Calef's book and to make people the more eager to read it. No doubt some of the members of the North Church itself took it home under their coats to read by candlelight in the privacy of their chambers. To most of the facts recorded in it all men had been witnesses. That it had been the zeal of the clergy in broadcasting supernatural happenings and in encouraging the "afflicted" which had "blown up" the Salem frenzy could not be denied; the inference that the whole affair from the first had been a tragic delusion was now widely accepted. Just as Tom Paine's *Common Sense* crystallized public opinion for a declaration of independence during the American Revolution, so Calef's *More Wonders* crystallized opinion in condemnation of the witchcraft trials.

It is quite erroneous to say, as some have done, that this affair brought the downfall of the Massachusetts "theocracy." The clergy remained a power in the colony and the State for a full century after the blaze in the Harvard Yard from Calef's burning volume had died out and the repentant Sewall had ceased his fastings and his prayers for forgiveness. Yet they emerged from the battle of demons at Salem with diminished prestige and influence. People were not so ready to turn for advice and guidance to the men who had had so large a part in that miserable mistake, asking in bewilderment: "Is this the best that learning, godliness and traditional leadership can produce?"

More important than the discomfiture of the clergy was the effect of the witchcraft craze upon the growth of rationalism. As a visible demonstration of the reality of the invisible world, the Salem witchcraft incident had ended in complete failure. The stunning realization that the "witches" had been the only sufferers, and that the "afflicted" had been deluded or had dissembled their tortures, cast doubt upon the whole structure of the supernatural world, with its devils, witch meetings, specters and midnight rides through the air. New England was no more ready than other parts of the world at this time for the rationalistic interpretation of all phenomena, but Salem is an important milestone on the road leading away from the Invisible Kingdom. Yet it was only a milestone, only an incident in a struggle which had been going on for centuries and was to continue for many decades to come.

It was Copernicus, Newton, Galileo, Halley who produced the tide which swept the brooms of the *Illustrious Providences* and the *Memorable Providences* from the hands of the Mathers, and this tide would have continued to advance even had there been no witchcraft trials in Massachusetts.

In time the clergy became somewhat reconciled. Even though the invisible realm of witches and demons should fade, even though it should become obvious that the universe was governed by natural law, it did not follow that God's power was limited. So they fell back upon the doctrine of intervention. Natural laws were God's laws which He had made for the governing of the world, but He himself was not bound by them. Cotton Mather wrote: "The influences of one thing upon another in the course of nature are purely from the omnipotent and omnipresent God, actually forever at work, according to his own laws, and putting his laws in execution, and as the universal cause producing those effects, whereof the creatures are but what one may call the occasional causes." [81] God could, therefore, withhold His hand and all the laws of nature would cease to function. Yet that He seldom did withhold His hand they were more and more forced to admit. The sun did not stand still, comets obeyed the law of gravity, even earthquakes and hurricanes had natural causes.

The clergy could, moreover, point out that science had by no means explained the mystery of the universe. Scientists might know the law of gravity; they could not, by power of reason, know whence it came nor in what its mysterious power consisted. Therefore to assume that because science had explained so much in nature it could, if man had the wit to fathom it, explain all things, was illogical. Many decades after the discoveries of New-

[81] Cotton Mather, *Manuductio ad Ministerium*, p. 52.

ton and Kepler, the Reverend James Allen, of Beverly, pointed
out that philosophers themselves knew only the outskirts of
God's works. There was no justification, therefore, for their
assumption that nothing is true "but what is capable of solution,
like one of their problems." [82]

But the invisible world of eighteenth-century New England
was to be more remote, more spiritual, less real, less vivid than
that of the seventeenth century. Evil spirits there were, but they
belonged rather to the next life than to this. The sinner could no
more escape their clutches than could the sinners of the time of
John Norton, or Urian Oakes or Increase Mather, but he had
less fear of what they might do to him in his carnal form through
disease or witchcraft. And, despite the doctrine of intervention,
how greatly this change weakened the hands of the clergy is obvious. The growth of rationalism must take its place beside the
growth of commerce, the disintegration of the agricultural village and the intrusion of heresy, in undermining the old Bible
Commonwealth for which John Winthrop and the other fathers
risked their all.

[82] James Allen, *The Danger of Philosophy* (1852).

Chapter X

THE ELECT LOSE THE FASCES

ERESIES, as we have seen, breached the walls of the Bible Commonwealth, scientific discoveries changed its character, the growth of commerce widened its horizons, the transition from the agricultural village to the farm weakened it; but the threat to its political foundations was perhaps the most serious of all.

From the infancy of New England the founders had to face the possibility of interference by the mother country. When they departed from England they left behind them a hostile King and a hostile Church. Sooner or later Charles would learn that they had taken with them the charter he had granted to a trading company, so that they could found upon it a semi-independent government, and then he might revoke it and reduce them to the status of a royal colony. Would Archbishop Laud be content to have them set up in America the form of worship and Church organization he denied them in England? Might not the day come when they would have to defend their new homeland against the armed forces of the old?

The danger was made the more acute by the fact that the colonists themselves knitted more closely the tie which bound them to England by basing their economic life so largely upon commerce. The trade which brought them prosperity, built up their ports, provided an outlet for their goods, doubled and tripled their wealth, was carried on chiefly within the British Empire. It was as British colonists that they were permitted to send their ships to the Somers Islands, the Bahamas, Barbados, Antigua and England itself; the government at London had only to exclude them and ruin to their economic life would follow. With this threat hanging over their heads, Massachusetts and her sister colonies could not assume an attitude of defiance.

Nor dared they dispense with the protection of the English navy. Planted on the St. Lawrence and in Acadia on their northern flank were the French, accompanied by the hated Jesuits. An independent New England would have to reckon with them, with the possibility of French warships athwart the trade routes and even French troops on the shores of Massachusetts Bay. The threat of a clash with Spain also was not to be ignored, while to the west the Dutch at New Amsterdam and Fort Orange were cutting them off from the fur-bearing region of the Great Lakes and edging eastward on Long Island and in Connecticut.

The Puritan leaders were thus faced with the problem of remaining independent of English governmental and religious control, while enjoying English naval and economic protection. But in the game which followed, a game of procrastination, intrigue and veiled threats, not all the high cards were in the King's hand. The mother country had need of New England, not only as a bulwark against the French, but as a source of timber, masts, cordage and other naval stores. Even had not the lack of funds and the threatening political situation in England made the prospect of a military and naval expedition to subdue the colonists most unwelcome, the King and his ministers would have been reluctant to drive them into rebellion.

Nonetheless, the New Englanders had either to be in or outside the British Empire, and if they decided to be in, they had to accept a measure of control incompatible with the ideal of their Bible Commonwealth. Yet they were fortunate in postponing the issue for decades, at first because of England's preoccupation with revolution and civil and foreign wars, and later by a policy of evasion and delay.

Paralleling this struggle, and equally important, were the efforts of the Church members to retain all power in their own hands in the face of the constantly increasing numbers of the non-elect. As the years passed the fear of the magistrates and ministers that at least some of this group might demand and gain the right to participate in the government became ever more apparent. The Wilderness Zion would be safe only so long as its destinies remained in the hands of those who were its zealous supporters, only so long as all voters, magistrates, deputies, military officers, schoolteachers were Church members. If others wished to live in the colony, they must submit to the rule of this group. The Puritan leaders were deeply concerned, then, when they found that this undemocratic system was threatened in three ways—by the premium it put upon hypocrisy, by petitions to the English government for its overthrow, and by open revolt.

Of these the most insidious and perhaps the most dangerous, though not the most obvious, was the first.[1] The privileges of Church membership were so great, the penalty for exclusion so heavy, that only the most stubborn skeptic or the most convinced heretic could be indifferent to it. It was the door, not only to bliss in the next world, but to power and privilege in this. To fool the elders with a pious front was not easy, perhaps less easy than to fool oneself; but there must have been many who made the attempt. And each insincere member admitted added an element of weakness to the Churches. One could attend services regularly, assume an outward piety, fill one's conversation with Biblical quotations or with references to God's providence, and yet be lukewarm in upholding the ideals of the Wilderness Zion. When the ministers in their sermons complained of the general decay of godliness, the "declension and defection in religion," the indifference of Church members, a little reflection might have convinced them that at least one principal cause lay in the very foundations of their political society.

To the danger from England, however, they were keenly alive. The King would certainly resent the disfranchising of his subjects in New England for refusing to relinquish the form of worship prescribed by the Church of England. Nor could he ignore the complaints which from time to time reached his ears that one group had monopolized power, that the traditional liberties of Englishmen were denied to a large part of the people, and that thousands had no certain means of protection for their property and their lives. Sooner or later the order would come for a more equal distribution of rights, for an extension of the franchise and the admission to office of all properly qualified men.

---

[1] "Though they cannot keep hypocrites from their sacred fellowship, yet they go as far as they can to render and preserve themselves Churches of saints," said Cotton Mather. *Magnalia* (London, 1702), Book II, p. 46.

At the same time the possibility of revolt against the established order was not to be ignored. Even though this might take the form of a revolution in public sentiment rather than an armed rising, it was not the less to be dreaded. So the ministers threw the full weight of their influence against change. In their election sermons they lauded the established government as the best and purest in the world, and the magistrates as godly men who had done nothing to merit "the murmurings of discontented people." "They that are wea y of and disaffected to this government that God hath established among us and shall betray and give up the civil interest of New England, will have more to answer for than they are aware of," declared Urian Oakes. "He is a madman that will hope for the continuance of our spiritual liberties if the wall of our civil government be once broken down. Those that break down the hedge of our civil government do not design, or do it merely because they are angry with the hedge, but because they would break in and devour all that is precious and dear to us. The change of our government will inevitably introduce a sad change in our Churches." [2]

In the early years of the Bible Commonwealth it was the threat from England which caused the greatest apprehension. If Charles I were unaware that a semi-independent State had been established in Massachusetts and that the charter on which it was based had been taken out of the country, there were many to inform him. The territory granted under the charter conflicted with grants made previously to Sir Ferdinando Gorges and John Mason, and immediately upon the arrival of the Puritan settlers a bitter quarrel ensued. Gorges, who was a prominent member of the Council of New England, and Mason, an ardent royalist and friend of the Duke of Buckingham, laid their case before the King, with a round of abuse of the Puritans to back their plea.[3] The colonists had cast off all dependence on England, they said; had refused to obey the laws of Church and State, and "did continually rail against . . . the bishops." [4] But the friends of the colony on their part rallied to its support, Sir Richard Salton-

[2] Urian Oakes, *New England Pleaded With*, p. 49.
[3] *Winthrop's Journal*, "History of New England," ed. by J. K. Hosmer, I, p. 99.
[4] *Ibid.*, p. 102; *Acts Privy Council, Colonial*, I, p. 183.

stall and others reminding the Privy Council that if England wished to profit from the New England naval stores she must be indulgent in the matter of religion and autonomy. Their arguments proved so convincing that the Council and the King not only decided in favor of the colonists but even rebuked Gorges and Mason for abusing them.[5]

But with the accession of Bishop Laud to the see of Canterbury and his appointment to head the newly created colonial office, styled the Lords Commissioners for Plantations in General, the attack on the colony was resumed. In February, 1634, this body informed Matthew Cradock, former Governor of the Massachusetts Bay Company, that since many persons who were resorting to New England were dissatisfied with the conduct of affairs there, both civil and ecclesiastical, they would like to examine the charter.[6] But when Cradock sent to America for it, the Governor and Assistants put him off with the reply that they could do nothing until the meeting of the next General Court three months later.[7]

In the meanwhile things in England were going from bad to worse. Gorges, from under the cover of the Archbishop's robes, renewed his attack, advising the division of New England among certain members of the old Council, the appointment of himself as Governor of the entire province and the revoking of the Massachusetts charter. The Commissioners for Plantations accepted this program and, instituting *quo warranto* proceedings against the charter, secured a verdict against the patentees. It seemed that the Bible Commonwealth, which the emigrants had made such great sacrifices to found, was to be overthrown even before it had been firmly planted.

When this dire news reached New England, the ministers were called together at Boston to advise the Governor and Assistants as to the proper course of action should Gorges arrive to assume his office. The clergymen were for defying the King, if necessary by force of arms. Thus, while Gorges busied himself

[5] Winthrop's Journal, "History of New England," ed. by J. K. Hosmer, I, p. 101.
[6] Acts Privy Council, Colonial, I, p. 199.
[7] Winthrop's Journal, "History of New England," ed. by J. K. Hosmer, I, p 129.

in England raising a force to subdue the colony, the little Puritan army of "Ironsides" was drilling and practicing "divers sorts of skirmishes" in preparation to resist him. Fortunately, the expedition never left England. The King failed to back Gorges with funds, the Governor's flagship broke at the launching, and finally the rumblings of approaching civil war brought things to a standstill.

In the meanwhile the Lords Commissioners for Plantations wrote the colonists a letter "wherein they straightly required the patent to be sent home by the first ship." But again the stiff-necked Puritans would not obey. Instead they drew up and sent over "an humble petition," praying that they might enjoy in peace the privileges the King had granted them. The Lords Commissioners replied that they had no intention of interfering with the liberties of the colonists, but once more peremptorily demanded the return of the charter, with threats of punishment in case of disobedience.[8]

But the threats were never carried out. Events in England were moving swiftly—the rising in Scotland, the Short Parliament, the Long Parliament, the impeachment and execution of the Earl of Strafford, the Grand Remonstrance, the flight of Charles I from London, the opening of the Civil War. From across the Atlantic the New Englanders watched the tragic panorama with alternating hopes and fears. For them a victory for the King would bring imminent danger; the success of Parliament meant the triumph of Calvinism. Yet when some Puritans in England advised them to put themselves under the protection of Parliament, they declined to do so, not wishing to surrender their autonomy to any power in England, however sympathetic. Nonetheless, they were overjoyed to hear that the judgment of the court annulling the charter had been set aside. On September 2, 1641, a thanksgiving service was held in each little meeting-house throughout the colony because of "the good success of the Parliament in England."[9]

The war between King and Parliament was still raging when an incident occurred in Boston harbor which made it necessary

[8] *Ibid.*, p. 301.
[9] *Ibid.*, II, p. 42.

for the colony to decide definitely whether it wished to place itself at last under the jurisdiction of Parliament. A hundred-ton ship from the royal port of Bristol was anchored off Charles-town, when a London ship under a Captain Stagg, armed with twenty-four pieces of ordnance, came beside her and took her prize. A crowd assembled on Windmill Hill in expectation of a battle between the two vessels and some who had goods aboard the Bristol ship began to raise a tumult. But the Governor dispersed the crowd, and then wrote Captain Stagg, demanding to know upon what authority he had acted. Thereupon the captain produced a commission from Parliament authorizing him to take vessels bound from or to Bristol, Barnstable and other hostile ports.

A few days later Stagg laid this commission before a meeting of elders and magistrates then in session at Salem. An earnest debate ensued. If the captain were forced to surrender his prize, it would be an open defiance of Parliament and a virtual declaration of independence; if the colony refused to interfere, it would be an admission that final authority rested, not on their royal patent, but upon Parliament.

Some argued that the seizure of the ship had violated the liberties of the people, that a commission could not supersede a patent, that they were subject to no power but themselves. But this group was voted down, the majority choosing the course of prudence. Since Massachusetts had already incurred the King's displeasure it would be rash indeed to repudiate the protection of Parliament, it was pointed out. It would be time enough to fall back on the doctrine of *salus populi* should Parliament, which was now so friendly, ever turn against them.

Yet the course of events in England was already giving the magistrates and elders grave concern. Parliament had concluded an alliance with "their brethren of Scotland," and in September, 1643, had subscribed to a Solemn League and Covenant to bring the Churches in both kingdoms "to the nearest conjunction and uniformity." An assembly of English divines, peers and commoners had met with commissioners from Scotland in Westminster Abbey to reform the Church upon the Presbyterian model. The Westminster Confession, which emerged from this conference, had not been ratified by Parliament, but the system of Presbyterian Church government was accepted in theory, though not put into operation on a national scale. It seemed to the New Englanders a hard turn of fate that at the moment of triumph, when they had been freed of the fear of the bishops, they should have to face the possibility that a Presbyterian Parliament might meddle in their affairs or undertake to reshape their Churches and their civil government.

They were in no mood, then, to deal leniently with a group of discontents who threatened to appeal to Parliament to bridle the power of the elders and magistrates. On May 19, 1646, a petition, signed by Dr. Robert Child and six others, was presented to the Assistants and the General Court, complaining of the suppression of liberty and the exercise of arbitrary authority by the colonial government. It was the greedy lust for power, they thought, which accounted for the "illegal commitments, unjust imprisonments, taxes, . . . unjustifiable presses, undue fines, unmeasurable expenses . . . non-certainty of all things . . . whether lives, liberties or estates. . . .

"There are thousands in these plantations of the English nation, free-born, quiet, peaceable men, righteous in their dealings, forward with hand, heart and purse to advance the public good, known friends of the honorable and victorious Houses of Parliament, lovers of the nation, etc., who are debarred from all civil employment, not being permitted to bear the least office, no, not so much as to have any vote in choosing magistrates, captains or other civil or military officers. . . . Whence issue forth many great inconveniences, secret discontents . . . also jealousies of too much unwarranted power and dominion on the one side, and of perpetual slavery and bondage to them and their posterity on the other. . . . We therefore desire that civil liberty and freedom be forthwith granted to all truly English, equal to the rest of their countrymen. . . .

"There are divers sober, righteous and godly men," they continued, "members of the Churches of England, not dissenting from the late and best reformation of England, Scotland, etc., yet they and their posterity are detained from the seals of the covenant of free grace, because they will not take these Churches'

covenants. . . . Notwithstanding, they are compelled, under a
severe fine, every Lord's day to appear at the congregation . . .
and in some places forced to contribute to the maintenance of
those ministers, who vouchsafe not to take them into their flock."
They therefore humbly sued for permission to join the congregations, or to set up Churches of their own "according to the best
reformations of England and Scotland." [10]

The authorities were angered and alarmed. From pulpit after
pulpit the ministers denounced the petition as a seditious document "full of malignancy, subversive both to Church and commonwealth," whose authors were "sons of Belial, Judases, Sons
of Corah." So they were haled into court and fined ruinously—
one £50, one £40, four £30 and the other £10. When word
reached the magistrates that Child had drawn up a petition to
Parliament and was making preparations to sail for England to
present it, he was arrested, together with another of the petitioners, their trunks searched and the petition confiscated.

However, Thomas Fowle, another of the group, succeeded in
getting away on a ship bound for London, with copies of both
the paper addressed to the General Court and of the petition to
Parliament. On board with him were several persons who had
heard John Cotton declare in his Tuesday lecture that if any
ship carried complaints against God's people the paper would,
like Jonah, be the cause of great storms. So, when a storm did
actually threaten during the voyage, they crowded around the
master clamoring for the Child petition to be thrown overboard.
To appease them Fowle surrendered a copy of the petition to
the General Court, of which he had several. Although many
hours passed after this paper touched the water before the wind
subsided, some of the passengers on reaching England spread the
report that a miracle had been performed.[11]

In the meanwhile the General Court once more took up the
matter of the status of Massachusetts in relation to England, and
after a long debate turned to the elders for advice. As before, the
majority were in favor of playing the game both ways by re-

[10] Peter Force, *Tracts and Other Papers,* IV, "New England's Jonas Cast
up at London," pp. 8–14.
[11] *Ibid.,* pp. 18–20.

pudiating the control of the mother country while enjoying its naval and economic protection. Allegiance was due to England, it was argued, because the charter, the foundation of all their privileges, had been granted by England; because the tenure of their lands depended on England; because it would be unwise to renounce the protection of England. Yet they could still be independent in respect to government in the same way as Normandy and Gascoyne had formerly been independent of the Crown of France, even though the kings of England did homage to the French kings for them.[12]

The constantly shifting scene in England greatly influenced them in this decision. At one moment they had had to deal with the King and the bishops, the next they had been faced with the possibility that Parliament might try to force Presbyterianism upon them; now Cromwell and his army might demand that they become Separatists and grant toleration to all Protestants.

In order to present a determined front many thought it advisable to publish an official statement of the "New England way." But when it was proposed that the General Court call a synod for this purpose, serious opposition arose. The Presbyterians protested violently. Was it wise for the colonists to put themselves on record as opposed to the Westminster Confession? they asked. Would it not anger Parliament? Would it not leave New England in dangerous isolation? And when, after long debate, the resolution was passed, and the synod had actually assembled, the congregations of Boston, Salem and Hingham refused to send representatives. After waiting two weeks in a vain effort to persuade them to yield, the synod adjourned.[13]

When they reassembled at Cambridge on June 15, 1648, the Reverend John Allen, of Dedham, preached a "learned" sermon, in which he gave the cue for the Congregationalist platform and refuted the "errors, objections and scruples" of those who opposed it. While he was holding forth a snake entered the meetinghouse. Some who were near the door sprang aside, but one of

[12] *Winthrop's Journal, History of New England,* ed. by J. K. Hosmer, II, pp. 290, 291.
[13] *Ibid.,* II, pp. 278–282.

the elders, "a man of much faith," trod on it and held it with his foot and a staff until it was killed. Winthrop thought that "the Lord discovered somewhat of his mind" in this incident. The serpent was the Devil who had been overcome by the synod "in the midst of his attempt to bring confusion to the Churches of Christ." Thus encouraged, the elders turned vigorously to their task. They began by declaring themselves in full agreement with the Westminster Confession in matters of faith. After which they explained how they differed from it in the relationship of Church to Church and of the Churches to the civil government. The Cambridge Platform, the document which they drew up, came to be called.[14] Thus did New England proclaim to the world its complete independence of England in matters ecclesiastical. If King or Protector or Parliament or the bishops disapproved, they would find it a troublesome matter indeed to force her to recede from her "established order."

Moreover, for a full decade England was so engrossed in her own troubles that there was no opportunity to interfere. In quick succession came the execution of Charles I, the conquest of Ireland, the war with Scotland, the Dutch war of 1654, the dissolution of the Rump Parliament, the appointment of Cromwell as Lord Protector, the war with Spain, the death of Cromwell and the succession of his son. It was with deep concern that the people of New England followed these tragic events, knowing full well that their own fate was involved. Might not continued disorders finally convince England that a King alone could restore peace and prosperity? So they were not surprised, however greatly alarmed, at the news of the landing of Charles II at Dover, on May 25, 1660, and his restoration to the throne. "Our private meeting kept for a day of humiliation at our house for the state of our native country," John Hull wrote in his *Diary,* "it being like to come . . . under the bishops; the Church countenancing the old liturgy, and formalities again to be practiced."[15]

Shortly afterwards the arrival at Boston of Edward Whalley and William Goffe, two of the regicides who had fled from the

[14] *A Platform of Church Discipline.*
[15] Nov. 21, 1660, p. 151.

vengeance of the new King, was a vivid reminder that the day of Puritan supremacy in England had passed. The fugitives were taken to Governor Endicott, who embraced them and lodged them in Harvard College, where they held prayer meetings and where they were visited by many of the magistrates and ministers. When a certain Captain Breedon criticized the colony for this warm welcome, he was summoned before the Governor and denounced as a "malignant." The marshal grinned in his face, with the threat, "Speak against Whalley and Goffe if ye dare, if ye dare, if ye dare." [16]

Nonetheless the authorities deemed it necessary to recognize the monarchy. "After our ordinary lecture," wrote John Hull, on June 8, 1661, "the soldiers being all in arms, viz., our four companies and the country troop, the magistrates mounted on horseback, the ministers being present, and a multitude of people, King Charles II was proclaimed by Mr. Edward Rawson, Secretary of State, all standing bare, and ended with 'God save the King!' and a shout, sundry volleys of shot from the soldiery, all the guns in the castle and fort and town and ships. All the chief officers feasted that night at the charge of the country." [17]

"May it please your Majesty," wrote Governor Endicott in the name of the General Court, "now . . . that you are King over your British Israel, to cast a favorable eye upon your poor Mephibosheth . . . we mean New England, kneeling with the rest of your subjects before your Majesty as her restored King." He then craved protection in the continuance of their civil privileges and religious liberties according to the patent granted by his father. "Our liberty to walk in the faith of the Gospel was the cause of our transporting ourselves, with our wives and little ones and our substance from that pleasant land, over the Atlantic ocean into this vast and waste wilderness." Concerning any charges laid at their door, he requested that nothing be done until their answer had been heard.[18]

[16] *Calendar of State Papers, Colonial, America and West Indies*, 1661–1668, pp. 15, 16, 27.
[17] "Diary of John Hull," American Antiquarian Society *Transactions and Collections*, III, p. 203.
[18] *Calendar of State Papers, Colonial, America and West Indies*, 1661–1668, pp. 8–10.

To this the King sent a noncommittal reply. Their letter had been very acceptable, he said, and he would extend his protection to all his subjects there. But when he added that he was confident that the good people of New England would make a right use of the promises of liberty and moderation to tender consciences expressed in his declarations, the concealed threat was not lost on Endicott.

Once more the General Court took under consideration the relationship of the colony to England, and, despite their professions of loyalty, reasserted the old claims to autonomy. This they backed by a declaration that against any who should attempt the "destruction, invasion, detriment or annoyance" of their government, they would defend themselves by force of arms.[19] The fortifications on Castle Island were rushed to completion, while a little army of 400 foot and cavalry was kept in readiness for action. At the same time, they sent Simon Bradstreet and the Reverend John Norton to England to plead their cause at Court and to "take off all scandal" from the colony.[20]

"Scandal" there was in full measure. Ferdinando Gorges, grandson of Sir Ferdinando Gorges, complained to the King that Massachusetts, "taking advantage of the late rebellion" in England, had without any color of right encroached on his province of Maine.[21] John Dand, who had been fined, imprisoned and forced to make "his humble submission" for his part in the Child affair, now with twelve others came forward with a list of grievances. Multitudes of the King's subjects had been imprisoned, fined, fettered, whipped, their ears cut off, their estates seized, he asserted, all contrary to the laws of the colony and of England.[22] The Quakers handed in a mass of papers, detailing their sufferings at the hands of the New England authorities. Captain Breedon reported that when a stranger arrived in Massachusetts some time before, he had been mistaken for the King and put under arrest; that the distinction between freemen and non-freemen and between Church members and non-members

[19] *Massachusetts Records,* IV, pt. 1, p. 25.
[20] *Ibid.,* p. 37.
[21] *Calendar of State Papers, Colonial, America and West Indies,* 1661–1668, p. 22.
[22] *Ibid.,* p. 16.

was as famous as between Cavaliers and Roundheads and would become as odious. The warm welcome to Whalley and Goffe was recited in detail.[23]

All this convinced the Council for Foreign Plantations that the Massachusetts authorities "had strayed into many enormities." They had exceeded their powers in enacting laws repugnant to those of England, in imposing unequal restraints in matters of conscience and divine worship and in ignoring the laws for trade. It was obvious, the Council thought, the government there intended to suspend their obedience to the King's authority.[24]

While waiting for the colony to present its defense, the Council sent a letter to all the New England governments, instructing them to proclaim Charles II, reminding them that their constitutions and governments were derived from the Crown, and warning them that they must be obedient if they were to enjoy the benefits of the Act of Oblivion.[25]

In the meanwhile Bradstreet and Norton arrived in London with the address and petition of the General Court. They must have made a convincing case for the colony, for on June 28, 1662, the King wrote the Massachusetts government, confirming the patent, excusing their straying from the Crown by the "licence of late times," and pardoning all not attainted by Parliament. But he required them to take the oath of allegiance, declared void laws contrary to those of England and ordered them to permit the use of the Book of Common Prayer. Most important of all, he directed that the franchise be granted to all freeholders of competent estates and not vicious in conversation, whether or not they were members of a Congregational Church.[26]

At the last of these commands the General Court stood aghast. It was like Aladdin's demand for the roc's egg. It was an order to the Puritan oligarchy to commit suicide. After long and earnest deliberation it was decided to make a pretence of compliance, but in fact to yield nothing. The Court began by repealing the law which restricted the right to vote to members of the Churches. But they at once substituted for it another which was

[23] *Ibid.*, pp. 15, 16, 32, 54.
[24] *Ibid.*, p. 25.
[25] *Ibid.*, p. 22.
[26] *Clarendon State Papers* (Bodleian Library, Oxford), pp. 10–12.

equally effective in placing all power in the hands of the clerical party. Any settled inhabitant, twenty-four years or more of age could petition the General Court for the right to vote, provided he could present a certificate under the hand of the local minister and another from the selectmen certifying that he was orthodox in religion, not vicious in his life and rateable to the sum of ten shillings. Even then the General Court was under no obligation to admit him. The restrictions were not applicable to Church members.[27]

Not only did this law leave the selection of the electorate exactly where it had been before, in the hands of the elders, but it relieved them of the need of passing on any of the non-church members save a mere handful. As was later pointed out, in many towns not three persons could be found who paid taxes amounting to ten shillings. And even these three would have to run the gauntlet of the minister, the selectmen and the General Court, any of whom could reject them if they considered them unsympathetic to the established order, under the pretext that they were unorthodox or vicious in conduct.[28] Edward Randolph, writing twelve years later, testified that the old restrictions were in full force and that no person was admitted to be a freeman or have a vote in any election "but church-members who are in full communion and approved by the General Court."[29]

So the conflict between colony and King continued, a conflict marked by procrastination, stubbornness, evasion and pretended humility on the one side, and by threats of economic and military coercion veiled by paternal solicitude on the other. Finally the Committee of Plantations decided to take the offensive. The Duke of York had been granted a patent to the vast region between the Connecticut and the Delaware, and in 1664 an expedition under Colonel Robert Nicolls was sent over to wrest it from the Dutch. This was an opportune time, the Committee thought, to press the King's demands upon the New Englanders. With

[27] *Ibid.*, pp. 13, 14.
[28] *Ibid.*, p. 55; C. H. Hayes, "Representation and Suffrage in Massachusetts," John Hopkins *Studies in History and Political Science*, 12th Series, VIII–IX, pp. 56–59.
[29] *Hutchinson Collection*, p. 477.

English warships and English soldiers in America, the colonists might be more reasonable. So a Commission consisting of Colonel Nicolls himself, Sir Robert Carr, George Cartwright and Samuel Maverick was appointed to go over in the fleet to beard the Puritan lion in his lair.

The Commissioners received two sets of instructions, one to be shown the New Englanders and the other to be kept secret. By the former they were to assure the Massachusetts government of the King's good intentions, to examine the administration of justice, to see that no one was debarred from the exercise of his religion according to the laws of England, to enforce the Act of Navigation and to apprehend persons attainted of high treason. The secret instructions required them to report on conditions in New England, to win the good will of the principal inhabitants, to examine the Massachusetts charter and to lead the people to desire its renewal, to build up the King's party in the General Court, but not "to appear solicitous to make any change in the matter of religion." [30]

Nicolls also brought a letter from King Charles to the Governor and Council. He was sending the Commissioners over to extinguish the malicious calumnies that the people of the colony did not submit to his government but looked upon themselves as independent of England and English law, the King said; to inform them that he had not the least intention of infringing their charter nor of restraining their liberty of conscience; to confer with them concerning their reply to his letter of June 28, 1662, which did not answer his expectations nor the promises made by their agents.[31]

It was with outward deference, but with ill-disguised resentment, that the Governor and Assistants received the Commissioners when they arrived at Boston in July, 1664. It was especially galling that Samuel Maverick, whom they had fined for his part in the Child petition, and whom they now termed their "known and professed enemy," should be one of the four persons sent over to inquire into their affairs, curb their freedom and report

[30] *Calendar of State Papers, Colonial, America and West Indies,* 1661–166' pp. 200, 201.
[31] *Ibid.,* pp. 201, 202.

directly to the King. But as little could be done until Nicolls had
completed the conquest of New Netherlands, they contented
themselves with a letter of protest to the King.

"This people did at their own charge transport themselves,
their wives and families over the ocean, purchase the lands of
the natives, and plant this colony with great labor, hazards, costs
and difficulties," they pleaded. But now with what affliction of
heart they found that their adversaries had persuaded his Majesty
to send a commission empowered to determine complaints and
appeals and to proceed in all things according to their discretions.
Whereby, instead of being governed by rules of their own choice,
which was the fundamental privilege granted in their patent,
they were like to be subjected to the arbitrary power of strangers.
They would either be forced to seek dwellings in some other
part of the world, "or sink and faint under burdens" that would
be intolerable. They willingly acknowledged their dependence
upon the King, but it was a hard case to have no other alternative offered them than to yield up their liberties which were far
dearer than their lives.[32]

The taking over of New Netherlands proved an easy matter
despite all that Governor Stuyvesant could do, so that early in
1665 the Commissioners were in Boston, ready to come to grips
with the Puritans. They began by going over to the courthouse
to address Deputy Governor Bellingham, the Magistrates and
the Deputies, and to deliver the King's letter and other papers.
They denied the report that they had come to annul civil and
religious liberties or to impose taxes, and stated that their mission
was to bring the King's command that Massachusetts observe
the Navigation Acts and grant full rights of citizenship to persons using the Book of Common Prayer.

After the General Court had read the papers they sent word
to the Commissioners that the instructions which they contained
greatly infringed the patent. The Commissioners came back with
a request for a committee with whom they could confer to make
clear that the patent was "not in the least infringed." But the
committee, when it met with the Commissioners, proved as stub-

[32] *Clarendon State Papers* (Bodleian Library, Oxford), pp. 15–20; John G.
Palfrey, *History of New England*, II, pp. 588–590.

born as the General Court itself. The charter gave the colonial government absolute power to make laws, to put them into effect, and to administer justice, they contended. To permit appeals to England would be an insufferable burden, a breach in the walls of government which would be "an inlet of much trouble." They would prefer to return to England "to live under his Majesty's wing," than be under the heels of arbitrary commissioners.[33]

A few days later the Commissioners gave the General Court a stinging rebuke. The fact that they valued their own conceptions more than the wisdom of the King and Council showed either that they distrusted his Majesty or thought him an incompetent interpreter of the charter. It was strange, the Commissioners said, that though the King had ordered them to sit as a court of appeals, they should be told that to do so would violate the charter.[34]

"You propose you prize the King's favor and yet in the same paper you refuse to do what the King enjoins." In defiance of his command that all should take the oath of allegiance, they had made provisos and curtailed the oath. They would not administer justice in the King's name; had refused to grant liberty of conscience upon a "vague conceit" that it would disturb their enjoyments; they had tried to deceive the King by a false pretense of obeying his command to remove the religious restrictions on the franchise. These answers, so far from satisfying the King, would highly offend him. "We have thought it necessary to reduce our discourse into one question and expect a positive answer: Whether do you acknowledge his Majesty's Commission, wherein we are nominated Commissioners, to be of full force?"[35]

But the General Court was not to be trapped. "Why you should put us on the resolve of such a question we see not the grounds thereof?" they said evasively. And when the Commissioners repeated their demand they replied that it was not their function to pass on the validity of the Commission.[36]

To this the Commissioners rejoined that since after some days' debate and delay they had given such a dubious answer, they

[33] *Clarendon State Papers* (Bodleian Library, Oxford), pp. 44–49.
[34] *Ibid.*, p. 53.
[35] *Ibid.*, pp. 53–55.
[36] *Ibid.*, pp. 55, 57.

would proceed to carry out their instructions to act as a court of appeals by meeting in Captain Thomas Breedon's house to hear the complaint of Thomas Deane against the Governor and Company. Thereupon the General Court declared that this would be inconsistent with the laws and authority of the colony, and that they would announce publicly to the people that they could not consent to it. As good as their word, they proclaimed "by the sound of the trumpet" that the General Court was the supreme court of the colony and that the attempts of the Commissioners to hear appeals was a breach of their privileges. "By which they silenced about thirty petitions for justice against them." [37]

Balked in this effort, the Commissioners told the General Court that since they persisted in using the authority granted by the King to oppose the King, they would waste no more time on them, but would refer the whole matter to his Majesty, not doubting that he could force obedience in all his dominions. [38]

They next turned their attention to the code of laws, to determine in what particulars they were inconsistent with the status of Massachusetts as a colony within the empire. The laws should declare the King the fountain of their authority, they thought; all writs should be in his name; "his Majesty's colony" should be substituted for the word "Commonwealth"; the King's arms should be set up in all courts of justice; the militia ought to carry the colors of England; the people should celebrate Guy Fawkes day, the King's birthday and the Restoration; members of the Church of England should not be fined for non-attendance upon Congregationalist services; the penalty for celebrating Christmas should be abolished; an end should be put to the minting of the pine-tree shilling.

Though the Commissioners left Boston with a sense of frustration, they wrote the Governor and General Court of Massachusetts a letter which touched the heart of the controversy and sounded a warning which the colony would have done well to heed. "The King did not grant away his sovereignty over you,

[37] *Calendar of State Papers, Colonial, America and West Indies,* 1660–1668, p. 344.
[38] *Clarendon State Papers* (Bodleian Library, Oxford), p. 61.

when he made you a corporation," they wrote. "When his Majesty gave you power to make wholesome laws and to administer justice by them, he parted not with his right to judge whether those laws were wholesome. . . . When his Majesty gave you authority over such of his subjects as lived within the limits of your jurisdiction, he made them not your subjects. . . . 'Tis possible that the charter which you so much idolize may be forfeited until you have cleared yourselves of those many injustices, oppressions, violences and blood for which you are complained against." [39]

In December, 1665, the Commissioners sent a report to the English government admitting that they had failed in their mission, and stating that the colony still regarded themselves as autonomous. They had pointed out many things in their laws derogatory to the King's honor, but nothing had been done about it. The Governor and Magistrates hoped to tire the King, the Lord Chancellor and the Secretaries, and boasted that they could easily spin out seven years by writing, before the end of which time a change of government might come in England. The situation of the many loyal subjects in the colony, who desired obedience to the King but were overawed by the ruling faction, was comparable to that of the royal party in England in Cromwell's time. [40]

There can be no doubt that Charles II was highly displeased with the defiance of the Massachusetts government, and that he was determined, when the opportunity presented itself, to force their submission. But the moment had not yet arrived. England was in the midst of a war with Holland; the plague, which had carried off 70,000 persons in 1665 in London alone, was still sweeping over the southern and eastern counties; in September, 1666, the heart of London was destroyed by fire; the bitter attacks on the Chancellor, the Earl of Clarendon, foreshadowed important changes in the administration; the King was engaged in the usual conflict with the House of Commons and was plotting to free himself from its control by building up a standing army and accepting subsidies from the King of France.

[39] *New York Colonial Documents,* III, p. 99.
[40] *New York Colonial Documents,* III, pp. 110–113.

It is in the light of these events that we must interpret the conciliatory tone he adopted to Massachusetts. In April, 1666, he wrote the Governor that he would recall his Commissioners and asked him to send agents to explain fully the colony's position. He would then make it appear how far he was from the least thought of infringing their charter.[41] So, for the moment, victory rested with the colonial government.

In the meanwhile a movement within the Churches which made the requirements for membership less rigid was extending the franchise and so widening the support for the established order. Many persons had long held that all baptized persons "not scandalous in life" ought to be considered members of the Church, even though not admitted to the Lord's Supper, and by 1657 their numbers had grown so large that the General Court called a synod to meet in Boston to advise on the matter. This synod, despite bitter opposition from the more conservative ministers, decided that persons who had been baptized in infancy and had led exemplary lives and "would own for themselves their baptismal vows" should be regarded as members and "allowed to present their children for baptism." This recognition of a partial church membership for persons who had made no formal profession became known as "the Half-Way Covenant." In 1662 another synod reaffirmed the decision and the General Court "commended the same unto the consideration of all the Churches." How many men were admitted to the franchise by this loosening of the religious list there is no way of determining, but the bitterness of the opposition seems to indicate that hundreds were affected.[42]

Some of the more conservative Churches rejected this liberalizing measure, while in others it occasioned bitter strife and heartburning. When the Reverend John Davenport, of New Haven, who had placed himself at the head of the reactionary party by publishing a treatise against "the Half-Way Covenant," was appointed minister of the First Church of Boston, a part of

[41] *Calendar of State Papers, Colonial, America and West Indies, 1660–1668,* pp. 372, 373.

[42] C. H. Hayes, "Representation and Suffrage in Massachusetts," Johns Hopkins University *Studies in History and Political Science,* 12th Series, VIII–IX, p. 54.

the congregation withdrew and established a Church of their own. The old Church refused to have fellowship with them, and, if we may believe Edward Randolph, actually had some of the seceders imprisoned. "We have in Boston one Mr. Willard, a minister," wrote Edward Randolph. "He is a moderate man and baptizeth those who are refused by the other Churches, for which he is hated. . . . There was a great difference between the old Church and the members of the new Church about baptism." [43] It was only at the near approach of the dreaded Episcopacy that differences were reconciled. [44]

In the meanwhile the rights of non-freemen had been broadened in other ways. In 1647 the General Court, "taking into consideration the useful parts and abilities of divers inhabitants amongst us which are not freemen, if improved to public use, the affairs of this commonwealth may be easier carried out," voted that those of good character might act as jurymen, vote in town meetings and act as town officers. These were important concessions which must have made local government more democratic than the provincial government. [45]

But the large group of non-freemen were not satisfied. They saw no reason why loyal Englishmen and good citizens should be denied the right to vote for Governors, Magistrates and Deputies, and excluded from military and civil offices, merely because they could not satisfy the religious test imposed by the elders. They had no voice in the making of laws which they were required to obey, in the appointing of judges who sat in judgment over their property and lives, in the appropriating of public funds to which they were forced to contribute, in the appointment of ministers to whom they had to listen every Sabbath; they were forced to serve in the trained bands in which they could not hold office. As time passed the complaints of the disfranchised became louder and louder, their denunciations of the ruling group bolder.

The clergy's fear that the flood of discontent might sweep away the old order is reflected in Urian Oakes's election sermon

[43] Prince Society, *Hutchinson Papers,* II, p. 272.
[44] Justin Winsor, *The Memorial History of Boston,* I, pp. 193–195.
[45] C. H. Hayes, "Representation and Suffrage in Massachusetts," Johns Hopkins University *Studies in History and Political Science,* 12th Series, VIII–IX, p. 55.

of 1673, in which he glorifies the magistrates and elders and denounces those who were demanding a greater share in the government. "It is the hard condition of magistrates and ministers that they must bear all the murmurings of discontented people and be loaded with all the obloquies and injurious reproaches that can be. They had need be men of great meekness and patience, able to bear much, that are pillars of the Church and commonwealth. . . . Nothing is more advantageous to the designs of innovators than the right knack of kindling and fermenting jealousies and fears in the minds of men concerning magistrates and ministers. Such men are wont to make and improve false alarms of danger that people may believe that religion and liberties are at stake. . . . And that men are generally disposed to receive such impressions and suspect evil of their superiors and leaders, is but too manifest . . .

"Here is a great cry in the country at this day about our civil liberties, these and those, in the frightful imaginations of some men, are about to rob us of our liberties. . . . Take heed what you do. Outcries for liberty are popular and plausible . . . but . . . commonly they that raise the loudest outcry against governors for robbing the peoples of their liberties, either design or eventually prove to be the greatest oppressors of them, when they come to be masters. . . . When you have pious rulers, of whose faithfulness you have had experience, do not easily suspect them. . . . There is no greater engine to embondage and enslave a people than such causeless outcries for liberty. In popular states the great danger is of a licentious, factious, ungovernable spirit, that kicks and spurns at authority." [46]

Oakes seems to have had little success in convincing the nonfreemen that liberty consisted in a passive submission to the ruling group or that it would be dangerous for them to have a voice in the government. That they continued to demand their rights is obvious since the ministers, in sermon after sermon, condemned their efforts and depicted the ruin which would follow should they succeed.

In the election sermon of 1674 Samuel Torrey resumed the attack. "We must be careful to exercise our Christian liberty in

[46] Urian Oakes, *New England Pleaded With*, pp. 51, 52.

a way of Gospel order," he warned. "Liberty and order are inseparable. . . . Those therefore that do plead for liberty unto the subversion of order are libertines and dangerous enemies of liberty. We must also exercise and improve our Christian liberty in a way of full subjection unto the power, rule and government of Christ." [47]

In 1676, William Hubbard, in his election sermon, exhorted the Magistrates to stand firm against innovation. "It is possible you may be importunately molested with the clamors of these or those to make this or that change in your course, to gratify particular men's humors, of which you need take no more notice than the skilful pilot at the helm uses to do of the cries of the unskilful, fearful passengers that think that course will ruin the vessel, which is the only way to preserve it. . . . I humbly conceive you cannot do better than to let things be as they have been heretofore, so to countenance and encourage those that fear God and work righteousness, but sharply to rebuke and timely to repress whatever is contrary to sound doctrine." [48]

At first sight it would seem strange that the disfranchised should not have taken more vigorous measures to gain their rights. Edward Randolph declared that the Church members constituted "not more than a sixth of the whole," and though this is probably an underestimation, they seem to have been decidedly in the minority. But they had the charter in their hands and the law on their side, while every important officer in the militia was of their number. The first rumors that the "disaffected" group were creating an organization for resistance would have been the signal for arrests and perhaps executions.

So the non-freemen based their hopes upon intervention by the King. There had been bitter disappointment at the failure of the Commission in 1664, and though some, who had been helpful to Nicolls, were subjected to "hard usage," [49] others continued to lay their complaints before the Board of Trade and Plantations. When Charles II, instead of showing resentment against the Massachusetts government for their defiance, thanked them in

[47] Samuel Torrey, *An Exhortation unto Reformation*, p. 26.
[48] William Hubbard, *The Happiness of a People*, Epistle Dedicatory.
[49] *Calendar of State Papers, Colonial, America and West Indies*, 1677–1680, p 248.

a conciliatory letter for the gift of a ship's load of masts, the royal party in the colony "despaired of relief." "I will not trouble you with the sad complaints which frequently come from them, for you know in what bondage they live," wrote Samuel Maverick to Colonel Nicolls in October, 1659. Captain Wyborne, of H.M.S. *Garland*, reported in 1675 that some of the principal merchants and others had told him that if the King would send over a Lord Lieutenant, not only would the people welcome him, but would build him a noble palace.[50]

Both the ruling party and the royal party, realizing that events in England would have a profound influence upon the King's attitude to the colony, followed the course of political intrigue with intense interest. The English dissenters wrote regularly to the Massachusetts leaders, now with elation at some favorable turn of the wheel of fortune, now in alarm lest the machinery of persecution be turned against them or the Roman Catholics gain the ascendancy. And the magistrates, ministers and other freemen reflected their emotions, not only because of sympathy with the Puritans of England, but from a consciousness that their own fate was involved. And when a ship came into Boston harbor from London or Bristol, the master was at once surrounded by questioners who wanted to know the latest news about the Declaration of Indulgence, or the Test Act, or the "Popish Plot," or the fall of Danby, or the persecution of the Covenanters.

For a full decade and a half after the Restoration, Charles II was not in the humor to come to grips with the Massachusetts government. His need of money was too great even to consider laying out thousands of pounds for a military and naval expedition to subdue the stubborn colonists; he was too bent on securing toleration for the Roman Catholics in England to enforce strict conformity to the tenets of the Anglican Church; he was too deeply involved in his perennial conflict with the House of Commons and the intrigues in his Court to be very much concerned with the affair of the little colony on the fringe of the American wilderness. The snubbing of his Commissioners and

[50] *Ibid.*, 1675–76, p. 307.

the flouting of his authority in 1664 no doubt angered him, but he realized that the time to force obedience had not yet arrived.

In 1671, when Ferdinando Gorges once more began to urge his claims, the Council of Plantations momentarily shook off its lethargy. Cartwright was called in and questioned, the Massachusetts charter was read and plans were made to send over another commission.[51] But with the outbreak of another war with Holland the whole matter was once more left in abeyance.

The appointment of the meticulous Sir Joseph Williamson as Secretary of State in June, 1674, once more brought New England affairs to the foreground. Arlington, "who loved his leisure," had been content to "let sleeping dogs lie," but not so Williamson. In his *Note Book* the latter wrote down various queries concerning the New Englanders. Did they coin money? Did their Governor take the oath to enforce the Navigation Acts? How stood the Church of England in the colony? [52]

He was deeply concerned over the evasions of the Navigation Acts. These laws had been designed to create an interdependent empire, an economic planetary system with England the sun and the colonies the satellites. The latter were to produce the things England needed and send them only to England; they were to use the things England produced and purchase only from England; and all trade within the empire was to be carried on in English or colonial vessels.

The Council of Plantations listened with indignation, then, when a certain Captain Wyborne testified before them that the Navigation Acts were constantly evaded in Boston and other New England ports. The colony had, in fact, become an entrepôt for both European and American goods, he said. The people regarded themselves as a "free State," not interested in England's differences with other nations and not subject to Parliamentary restrictions on their trade. When he had suggested the seizing of an Ostend vessel which had defied the Navigation Acts by entering the port of Boston, the Massachusetts authorities refused

[51] *Ibid.*, 1669–1674, pp. 208, 232, 244.
[52] *Ibid.*, 1675–1676, p. 154.

on the grounds that they were the King's vice-admirals and would do as they liked. He had been lucky, he added, to escape injury at the hands of a mob.[53]

A group of merchants who had been to New England were next called before the Lords of Trade, and though "some were shy to unfold the mystery," others fully bore out Wyborne's accusations. At that very moment, they declared, several vessels were taking on goods in Holland for delivery in New England whose masters had no intention of stopping at England to pay the duty prescribed by law. In this way they could undersell the English merchants by twenty per cent and still make a large profit.[54]

After some deliberation the Lords of Trade and Plantations, no doubt recalling the humiliating failure of Colonel Nicolls and his colleagues in 1664, gave up the plan for another commission. Instead they decided to send a special messenger with a letter from the King commanding the Massachusetts government to appoint agents to come to England. Edward Randolph, who was the man chosen for this mission, now became the chief instrument of the English government in its assault upon the Bible Commonwealth. For this thankless task he was admirably suited. A sincere advocate of imperial control, sympathetic with the disfranchised party in the colony, possessed of untiring energy and tenacity, he fastened upon the Massachusetts rulers with a grip they could not shake off. A very large part of his time was spent upon the water, for he made nothing of crossing the Atlantic in the slow little vessels of the day to take a letter from the King to the Governor, or of rushing back to report on the "disobedience" of the colony or to give the lie to their agents. When in New England he bombarded the Lords of Trade with letters filled with complaints of the disobedience of the colonists; when in England he was always on hand to answer questions or to give advice. With such a man to keep the pot boiling the Lords of Trade found it impossible to let the Massachusetts matter slumber; and the colonists found that their old policy of evasion and procrastination was no longer effectual. It is little

[53] *Ibid.*, pp. 306, 307.
[54] *Ibid.*, p. 379.

wonder that they accused Randolph of "going up and down seeking to devour them." [55]

He was greeted with frowns and snubs upon his arrival at Boston on June 10, 1676. As soon as he had shown his commission and delivered the King's letter, Governor Leverett suggested that if he had nothing further to communicate he might take the next ship for London. But Randolph was not so easily to be got rid of. He had received orders to inquire into conditions in the colony— the structure of government, the number of Church members, the enforcement of the Navigation Acts, etc.—and he was not the man to take this duty lightly.

He seems to have discovered much in an incredibly short time, for he had been in Boston only a week when he wrote the Lords of Trade, pouring out a catalogue of the colony's transgressions. They still gloried in their affronting the King's Commissioners in 1664, he said. They were adepts at "that old trade of inventing and spreading false reports"; the Governor had freely declared that they were not subject to the Navigation Acts; they refused to permit appeals to the King; no one could vote save Church members, confiding men, who had signally expressed their affection for their government; the clergy, with the exception of a few who were free of "the hypocricy of their pharisaical Sanhedrin," were proud and inclined to sedition; many of their laws were at variance with those of England; the observance of Christmas Day was forbidden; non-attendance at Congregational services was punishable by fine.[56]

The present, while the colony was still staggering from the blows of King Philip's War, he thought an opportune time to reduce them to "due obedience." True, they could put in the field a formidable force of 6000 foot and twelve troops of horse, while the channel to Boston was guarded by a fort of "38 guns and a battery of six." But there were many persons in the colony who favored the King and were kept from declaring themselves only by force. Moreover, his Majesty had in his hands the weapon of economic coercion. Three frigates of forty guns, with three ketches, stationed off Boston harbor with orders to seize all

[55] John Hutchinson, *History of the Colony of Massachusetts Bay*, I, p. 319.
[56] *Publications of the Prince Society, Edward Randolph*, II, pp. 205-209.

shipping to and from the port, would do more to bring the colonists to terms in one week than all the orders from the King and Council in seven years.[57]

In the meanwhile the General Court, together with a number of elders, met in session to draw up an answer to the King's letter. The ministers advised the sending of agents empowered to answer the charges of Mason and Gorges, but not to represent the colony in other matters. Accordingly, William Stoughton and Peter Bulkeley[58] were appointed and in July, 1677, appeared before the Lords of Trade and Plantations.

They found that Randolph had been there before them with a long list of charges which the Lords now asked them to answer. This they attempted to do, insisting, however, that they spoke merely as private citizens and not as representatives of Massachusetts. The Lords must have listened with impatience as they evaded one charge after another, or resorted to unconvincing excuses. The colony had issued warrants for the arrest of Whalley and Goffe in 1660, but they had managed to escape; they had been forced to coin money by the needs of commerce; Quakers had been put to death, not for religion's sake, but for defying the law under which they had been banished; it was true that some merchants had violated the Navigation Acts, but the loss to the royal revenue was inconsiderable; the substance of the oath of allegiance was required of all officers.[59]

Long and serious were the debates which followed in the Committee on how to bring "those people under a more palpable declaration of their obedience to his Majesty." Had the Massachusetts Bay Company, which was no more than a corporation, been empowered to make laws extending to life, member and banishment? they asked each other. Had they not committed treason by coining money? Was not their law requiring that marriages be performed only by magistrates repugnant to English law?[60] In April, 1678, Attorney General Southall and the Solicitor General were directed to give their opinions as to whether

[57] Ibid.
[58] John Hutchinson, History of the Colony of Massachusetts Bay, I, p. 311.
[59] Calendar of State Papers, Colonial, America and West Indies, 1677–1680, pp. 124, 125.
[60] General Laws of Massachusetts Colony, 1658, p. 52.

the Massachusetts charter was not void because of the *quo warranto* brought against it in 1635; and if not, whether the corporation had not forfeited it by maladministration.[61] Three months later they reported that "many transgressions and forfeitures" furnished ample grounds for declaring the old one void.[62]

The case for the agents was made worse by a letter from a certain Robert Holden exposing the means by which traders to Boston eluded the Laws of Navigation. They often brought tobacco in from North Carolina, entered it in the customs as fish, and then shipped it out to Ireland, Holland, France and Spain. They would often put in at the Canaries, with which trade was forbidden, to load up with wine, and then go to Madeira, from which imports were legal, to add a few casks of wine which they placed in the hatchway. At Boston the local officers would ask, "Whence your ship?" "From Madeira with wine," would come the reply. Thereupon the officers would draw off a taste from the upper casks, and pass the whole cargo. The trade with Scotland was carried on by the like "legerdemain juggles." [63] How deeply concerned the Committee was at these revelations is made clear by a letter from Stoughton to the Massachusetts government: "The country's not taking notice of these acts of navigation to observe them, hath been the most unhappy neglect that we could have fallen into, for, more and more every day, we find it most certain that without a fair compliance in that matter, there can be nothing expected but a total breach."

In the colony every congregation took to fasting and prayer for the divine blessing and the continuance of the charter, while the General Court appointed November 21, 1678, as a day of humiliation.[64] When the news arrived that the Lords of Trade had decided to leave the process against the charter in abeyance because of the confusion and terror caused by the machinations of the notorious Titus Oates, it seemed that God had not been deaf to the appeals of his people.[65]

[61] *Publications of the Prince Society, Edward Randolph*, II, pp. 289–298.
[62] *Calendar of State Papers, Colonial, America and West Indies*, 1677–1680, p. 280.
[63] *Ibid.*, p. 372.
[64] John Hutchinson, *History of the Colony of Massachusetts Bay*, I, p. 324.
[65] *Calendar of State Papers, Colonial, America and West Indies*, 1677–1680, pp. 377, 378.

But there were no laurels awaiting Stoughton and Bulkeley upon their return to Boston on December 23, 1679. They had yielded too much, had not been staunch enough in defending the colony's rights, people said. And when it became known that they brought with them a stern letter from the King, and that their old enemy, Edward Randolph, had been appointed royal Collector of Customs for New England, much of the blame was placed at their door. It seemed hard indeed that this man Randolph, of all others, should be placed in their midst, to interfere with their trade, spy on their activities and to bombard the Lords of Trade with reports and letters and suggestions for the curtailing of their privileges.

The Governor, General Court and the ministers were in no mood for "appeasement." To yield anything would yield all, they thought, and would bring down the political and ecclesiastical structure of their State in ruins. It was in vain that Stoughton and Bulkeley, who had experienced the temper of the Court and realized that the present lull was temporary, pleaded with them for moderation. When Randolph arrived he found them "acting as high as ever." It was in every man's mouth that they were not subject to the laws of England, he reported. A *quo warranto* was the only remedy, and then they would beg on their knees for what now they would not even thank the King for.[66]

In the execution of his duties as Collector, Randolph found himself resisted and balked on all sides. When he seized the pink *Expectation,* from Cork, the master sued him in a local court for £800. His servant, whom he had posted in a warehouse to inspect the goods landed from a ketch just in from Bilboa, had been set upon and beaten. His deputy had been threatened and driven out of town. He, himself, when he attempted to seize the *James,* of Londonderry, which was preparing to sail with 100 hogsheads of tobacco, was warned that if he came on board he would be knocked on the head. The Commissioners of Customs should write to the West Indies and to every port in England, he thought, to exclude any vessel from New England that did not bring a certificate of clearing from his office. For the King to

[66] *Publications of the Prince Society, Edward Randolph,* III, pp. 56–61.

write more letters would do no more good than the sending over a copy of the *London Gazette*.[67]

Perhaps the New Englanders would not have been so bold had they not received encouraging news from the English dissenters. The new Whig Party, with Shaftesbury at its head, had won a majority in the recent elections, had passed a bill to exclude the Roman Catholic Duke of York from the succession and was trying to force Charles' consent by withholding appropriations. Shaftesbury had built up a private army in London. Randolph wrote that the "fanatics at home" were trying to "keep up the minds" of their friends in the colony by all sorts of scandalous papers, and suggested that something be done to dissolve the "conspiracy" between the factious parties in both Englands.[68]

But neither the English dissenters nor the Massachusetts leaders knew what was going on behind the scenes in London. Charles, in order to shake off the financial fetters with which the Commons bound him, had made a secret agreement with Louis XIV, by which he was to receive large sums from the French treasury. A new election had confirmed the Whig majority, so that in March, 1681, when Parliament assembled in Oxford, they swarmed into town over Magdalen Bridge in high spirits. The Lords sat in the Bodleian tower, where Charles joined them, his robes of State, which he wore for a dissolution, following in a sedan chair. These he donned secretly, and suddenly appearing before the Lords, summoned the Commons from the Convocation House. Across the library quadrangle they came and up the spiral steps of the tower, laughing and chatting and confident that at last the King would have to yield to their demands. But upon crowding in they were struck with dismay to see the King in his robes of state and to hear his dismissal. Fearing a royal *coup d'état*, they fled from Oxford with "dreadful faces and loud cries."

And so began the Second Stuart Despotism. Shaftesbury fled to Holland, where he died in January, 1682; the persecution of

[67] *Calendar of State Papers, Colonial, America and West Indies*, 1677–1680, pp. 544, 545.
[68] *Ibid.*, 1681–1685, pp. 31, 249.

dissenters was resumed; two of the Whig leaders, Lord William Russell and Algernon Sidney, perished on the scaffold. *Quo warranto* writs were brought against the charters of London and other cities. Whether or not the cities defended their rights in court, or surrendered without a fight, the result was the same— the old charters were replaced by new ones in which the Whigs were excluded entirely or in part from the franchise.

The King's triumph had an immediate effect upon colonial affairs. It was not to be expected that after reducing England to obedience, he should leave the colonists all their old privileges. And though his death in February, 1685, defeated his purpose of curtailing or perhaps destroying representative government in America, his successor James II, took up the task where he left off. In Virginia Charles and James tried to deprive the Lower House of Assembly of the right to initiate legislation, challenged their control over taxation, and annulled their laws by proclamation; while in New York, Maryland, everywhere, they made equally vigorous attacks upon the rights of the people. So the time was ripe for the settling of old scores with Massachusetts.

Not aware of what was in store, Governor Bradstreet, in June, 1680, wrote to the Earl of Sunderland in the old evasive, unyielding style. Though freedom of worship had been a chief design in the founding of New England, he took for granted that the King did not intend that "a multitude of notorious errors, heresies and blasphemies" should be tolerated there; the religious test for the franchise had been abolished; they had not sent over agents in compliance with the King's command, since they had heard that his time was taken up with matters of greater importance.[69]

This letter served no other purpose than to anger the Lords of Trade. The Massachusetts authorities had not taken the least notice of certain material parts of his Majesty's commands, they reported to the King;[70] they still excluded Church of England men from a share in the government, they still coined money, they still obstructed the enforcement of the navigation laws in

[69] *Ibid.*, 1677–1680, p. 549.
[70] *Ibid.*

every possible way, they had not repealed the laws repugnant to English law.

Charles waited until October, 1681, when his triumph over his enemies in England seemed assured, and then wrote the Governor a severe and threatening letter. He reminded him that so early as 1635 complaints against the Massachusetts government had made it necessary to issue a *quo warranto* against their charter; that upon his restoration to the throne, despite their protestations of loyalty, they had harbored two of his father's murderers; that there had been complaints of their oppression of his subjects; that they had coined money, constantly broke the acts of trade, made laws repugnant to English law. He charged them to send agents within three months, if they desired to defend their charter.[71]

When, on the heels of this letter, came the dire news that a *quo warranto* had been brought against the charter of the city of London, the General Court realized that it might be their turn next. They had appointed Stoughton and Joseph Dudley as their agents in 1681, but Stoughton had refused to go and the matter had been left in abeyance. Now, in February, 1682, they named Dudley and John Richards, but with instructions to plead that they were not empowered to take definite action if anything was proposed tending to infringe upon the charter.[72] Their departure was marked throughout the colony with fasting and prayer.[73]

Their mission, difficult enough under any circumstances, was made almost hopeless by reports from Randolph telling of continued infringements of the laws of navigation and continued obstruction of his attempts to put a stop to them. Governor Bradstreet and a majority of the Magistrates had tried to uphold Randolph in carrying out his duties as Collector, but Deputy Governor Thomas Danforth, with six Magistrates and a majority of the Deputies, contended that no one had a right to seize ships in their ports save colonial officers. So they proceeded to appoint

[71] *Publications of the Prince Society, Edward Randolph,* III, pp. 110–113.
[72] *Calendar of State Papers, Colonial, America and West Indies,* 1681–1685, pp. 198, 199.
[73] John Hutchinson, *History of the Colony of Massachusetts Bay,* I, p. 335.

one Russell as naval officer, and when Bradstreet refused to swear him in, the Deputy Governor swore him.

So the smuggling continued. The *Swallow*, of Salem, brought Scotch goods into Boston harbor, and when Randolph's deputies boarded her they were driven off. The *Johanna*, of Piscataqua, smuggled ashore fruit and Spanish wine. At the trial of the Scotch master of the *Susanna*, the "evidence was conveyed away," and a verdict of acquittal returned. The case of the *Hope* had a similar result. The owners of the ketch *Newbury* were awarded £307 damages against one of Randolph's agents and when he could not produce so large a sum the court threatened to sell him into bondage.[74]

In February, 1683, Randolph sailed for England to be on hand for the proceedings against the charter. Before his departure Danforth sent him a letter which was both an appeal and a threat. "God hath made you an eye and ear witness of the sincere desire of this poor people . . . to serve God and honor the King; resolve not, therefore, to be an enemy to them, who have done you no wrong."[75]

In the meanwhile Dudley and Richards had arrived in England. But when the King discovered that they had nothing to offer but the time-worn evasions and excuses, and had not been empowered to negotiate concerning the charter, he told them that unless they secured full authority without further delay he would proceed with the *quo warranto*. The agents, duly alarmed, wrote to the General Court that his Majesty was "greatly provoked," and asked them to consider whether it was best to hazard all rather than satisfy him by submitting to the laws of trade and obeying his commands in other matters.

When this letter reached Massachusetts, submission or non-submission became the burning question. In this great crisis, which involved the entire structure of the Bible State, they turned to the ministers for advice. To yield meant the breaking down of the clerical control over the franchise, and everyone knew that this control was essential for the maintenance of the order which

[74] *Publications of the Prince Society, Edward Randolph*, III, pp. 216, 239, 254, 255, 273.
[75] *Ibid.*, pp. 227, 228.

their fathers had sacrificed so much to establish. After many arguments and much prayer the ministers gave it as their opinion that it was better to die by the hands of others than by their own. So the agents were ordered to make no concessions.[76]

When this news reached England, the Lords of Trade directed the Attorney General to proceed with the *quo warranto*. At the same time the King sent Randolph back to Boston with a final offer of compromise. Should the Governor and Assembly make "a full submission and entire resignation," he promised not to destroy the charter, but merely regulate it for his service and the good order of the colony.[77]

The day after Randolph reached Boston a fire broke out which destroyed a large part of the town, and it was whispered about that the hated emissary was responsible. But when both the fire and hot heads had cooled off, the General Court assembled. The next day[78] they spent in fasting, after which they, together with the ministers of the colony, began the debate over the King's letter. And throughout the colony, wherever two or more people met together, the all-important question was the topic of discussion. At a town meeting in Boston, in which two of the Magistrates and two leading ministers were present, someone read aloud his Majesty's offer. Thereupon Samuel Nowell, one of the Magistrates, stood up and suggested that those who favored delivering up the charter and with it their right to the country should hold up their hands. Not a freeman held up his hand. "The Lord be praised!" someone shouted. The Reverend Increase Mather then rose to exhort them to remain firm. If they yielded what their fathers had purchased so dearly, even as Ahab required Naboth's vineyard, their children would curse them.[79]

Emboldened by the support of the freemen, the Deputies and most of the ministers held out for resistance. But the Governor and a majority of the Magistrates, seeing the handwriting on the wall, thought it better to assent to the alteration of the charter than to have it declared void. So they proposed a letter from the General Court to the King declaring that since he merely in-

[76] John Hutchinson, *History of the Colony of Massachusetts Bay*, I, p. 337.
[77] *Publications of the Prince Society, Edward Randolph*, III, pp. 245–247.
[78] Nov. 8, 1683.
[79] *Publications of the Prince Society, Edward Randolph*, III, pp. 283, 285.

tended to regulate the charter, they would not presume to contend with him in a court of law. But the Deputies, by an overwhelming vote, refused to concur. In the end, after weeks of debate, Deputy Governor Danforth and five Magistrates united with the Deputies in a vote to employ Robert Humphreys, of the Inner Temple, to defend the charter and to supply him with a credit of £3000 to cover costs.[80]

The bitterness aroused by this struggle was slow to die out, and in the next annual election Dudley and some of the other Magistrates failed of reelection. But that there was strong support for the policy of submission is shown by the fact that when Bulkeley and Stoughton resigned in protest, about seventy leading citizens, many of them wealthy merchants, mounted their horses and escorted them to their homes outside Boston.[81]

Upon receipt of the news that Massachusetts intended to defend the charter, the Attorney General proceeded with the *quo warranto*. But when he ran into some unexpected legal difficulties, he advised resorting to a *Scire Facias*.[82] On April 16, 1684, the *Scire Facias* was directed to the Sheriff of Middlesex, and after some further delay judgment for the King was entered on June 18, 1684.

When this news reached Boston, the adherents of the old order were cast into gloom. Ever since Winthrop and his colleagues had secured possession of the charter and smuggled it over to the colony, it had been considered the very foundation of the Bible State. Upon it was based the right to government by God's elect, the right to exclude "error," the right to an established Church. "Keep to your patent," Urian Oakes had warned in his election sermon of 1673. "Your patent was a royal grant indeed befitting a great prince to make and that which our worthies that are gone to rest have many a time blessed God for; and it is instrumentally your defense and security. Recede from that one way or other and you will expose yourselves, for aught I know, to the wrath of God and rage of men. Fix upon your patent and stand for the liberties and immunities conferred

[80] *Ibid.*, p. 599; *Calendar of State Papers, Colonial, America and West Indies, 1681–1685*, pp. 563, 599.

[81] *Ibid.*, p. 669.

[82] *Publications of the Prince Society, Edward Randolph*, III, p. 297.

upon you therein and you have God and the King with you." [83] But now the patent was gone and the elect looked anxiously to an uncertain future.

The loss of the charter made Massachusetts a royal colony, so that henceforth the Governor would not be selected by the voters, but by the King, and would represent, not the freemen, but the Crown. He might be a complete stranger to New England, he might be an Anglican who looked upon all Congregationalists as dissenters, he might veto legislation vital for the upholding of the old order. With such an officer placed over the colony to defend the royal prerogative and keep a watch on every move by the General Court or the ministers, the old alliance between Church and State, considered the very essence of the Puritan experiment in the New World, would be seriously weakened, if not entirely destroyed.

Even more damaging would be the effects upon the franchise. Henceforth the right to vote would rest upon property rather than upon membership in a Congregational Church, so that no longer would the government be of the elect, by the elect, for the elect. Who could say that laws would not be passed which were not in accord with the ideals of the founders, or perhaps in direct conflict with them? Could it be expected in the future that the Assembly would consult the elders on all important policies, civic as well as religious? Would they listen respectfully to their praises, or admonitions, or scoldings in the interminable election-day sermons? Would not Massachusetts cease to be a Bible State?

On the other hand, though the fasces were struck from the hands of the ministers, much influence and power remained to them. They could still proclaim themselves the champions of the order established by the founders; they could still exalt these founders as God's lieutenants, the equals of Abraham or Aaron; they still enjoyed the prestige with which tradition and half a century of leadership had invested their order; despite the gradual emergence of a lay group of intellectuals they remained on the whole the most learned and mentally active men of the colony; they were now, as before, the spiritual guides of an intensely

[83] Urian Oakes, *New England Pleaded With*, p. 50.

religious people. Thus the loss of the power to shape the electorate did not prevent their wielding a powerful influence over political affairs. A century or more after the loss of the charter the Jeffersonian liberals in Massachusetts were demanding that the ministers cease trying to govern and confine themselves to preaching.

But to Increase Mather, John Ward, Samuel Torrey, William Hubbard and many others, this half loaf seemed almost worse than none. A pamphlet, supposed to have been written by Mather and the Reverend Samuel Moody, intimating that "the colony would not abide by the judgment against their charter, but stand up to defend their liberties," was circulated in Massachusetts and even in England.[84] But the people, most of whom realized the folly of resistance, devoted their efforts to sending up prayers to God to deliver his people. He had led them into the wilderness, had brought them prosperity, had saved them from many perils in the past; would he desert them now? But it seemed that God had indeed forsaken them when the terrible news arrived that Charles II had died and that the Roman Catholic James, Duke of York, had succeeded him.

Then came a ray of hope. It was announced that the Duke of Monmouth had landed in Dorset, had promised to deliver England from "popery" and tyranny and had proclaimed himself King. Once more the sermons in the little New England meeting-houses rang with a note of triumph. The prayers of the ministers had been answered, the "time of their deliverance was at hand."[85] Anxiously they waited for the arrival of the next vessel from England, which, they were confident, would bring the news of James's overthrow. Deep was their disappointment, then, when they heard that James had triumphed. "Jno. Gardener came in late last night," Samuel Sewall wrote in his Diary. "This morning the news he brings runs through the town, viz. that James, late Duke of Monmouth, was beheaded on Tower Hill on the 15th of July last. Argyle drawn, hanged and quartered. Neighbor Fifield brought me the news, who had it from the crier of fish."[86]

[84] *Publications of the Prince Society, Edward Randolph*, IV, p. 12.
[85] *Ibid.*, p. 101.
[86] "Diary of Samuel Sewall," Massachusetts Historical Society *Collections*, Fifth Series, V, p. 89.

This was bad enough, but when it became known that Colonel Percy Kirke, whom Charles II had selected to be Governor General of New England, had proved himself both brutal and venal, by executing scores of Monmouth's unfortunate followers without trial and sparing only those from whom he could extort money, Massachusetts was thrown into despair.[87] It was Randolph who saved the colony from the clutches of this man. The situation would be hopeless, he told the English government, if the people were "condemned to that misery to have Coll. Kirke to be their Governor," and as for himself, he would "rather have £100 a year in New England under a quiet, prudent Governor than £500" under Kirke.[88] In the end the appointment went to Sir Edmund Andros, formerly Governor of New York, whose administrative career, though far from ideal, had won for him the reputation of a man of honesty and ability.

Randolph urged that since the revoking of the charter had left Massachusetts without a legal government, a temporary body be appointed to take charge until Andros should arrive.[89] Accordingly a commission was granted to a Council made up of some of the most prominent men in the colony, with Dudley as its President. This body had extensive administrative and judicial powers;[90] far too extensive, in fact, had its authority been permanent.

It was a tragic moment for the members of the old order when Dudley appeared before the Magistrates and Deputies, whom he addressed as "some of the principal gentlemen and chief inhabitants of the several towns," to show them his commission. "The old government draws to the north side," Sewall relates. "Major Dudley, the President, Major Pynchon, Captain Gedney, Mr. Mason, Randolph, Captain Winthrop, Mr. Wharton come in on the left . . . Major Dudley made a speech that he was sorry he could treat them no longer as Governor and Company; produced the exemplification of the charter's condemnation, the commission under the broad seal of England." After the others had gone, Sewall and three others lingered to "speak their

[87] *Publications of the Prince Society, Edward Randolph,* IV, p. 40.
[88] *Ibid.,* IV, p. 29.
[89] *Ibid.,* p. 12.
[90] *Ibid.,* p. 51.

minds." Someone proposed a protest, but Sewall objected, pointing out that "the foundations being destroyed," the righteous were helpless.[91]

Yet the members of the former Assembly did send a protest to Dudley and the Council. "There is no certain determinate rule for your administration," they said, "and that which is, seems to be too arbitrary, that the subjects are abridged of their liberty as Englishmen, both in the matter of legislation and in the laying of taxes, and, indeed, the whole unquestioned privilege of the subject transferred upon yourselves, there being not the least mention of an Assembly." [92] Of those named for the new Council, former Governor Bradstreet, Nathaniel Saltonstall and Dudley Bradstreet refused to take office. The interregnum proved as stormy as it was brief. Dudley, formerly trusted and admired, was now regarded as little better than a traitor, while he incurred Randolph's animosity by refusing to encourage the Church of England or to enforce the Navigation Acts. Randolph himself was thoroughly hated. "The ministers quarrel for my bringing in the Common Prayer," he complained, "the old Magistrates and freemen for vacating their charter . . . the merchants for putting the acts of trade in full execution." [93] He longed for the arrival of Andros.

But the Governor General, who had set sail from England in the *Kingfisher,* a frigate of 50 guns, had gone out of his way to stop at Bermuda, and arrived only on December 20, 1686. "I heard a gun or two, as I supposed, which made me think Sir Edmund might be come," wrote Sewall. Later in the day Andros stepped ashore at Governor Leverett's wharf, where President Dudley and members of the Council met him. Together they proceeded through streets lined with soldiers to the Town House, where part of the Governor General's commission was read aloud.[94] Andros then took the oath of allegiance, and stood with his hat on while eight members of his Council were sworn in.

[91] "Diary of Samuel Sewall," Massachusetts Historical Society *Collections,* Fifth Series, V, pp. 138, 139.
[92] *Publications of the Prince Society, Edward Randolph,* IV, pp. 75, 76.
[93] *Ibid.,* p. 105.
[94] "Diary of Samuel Sewall," Massachusetts Historical Society *Collections,* Fifth Series, V, p. 159.

Four days later, sixty redcoats landed at Pool's Wharf and marched through the town to their quarters at Fort Hill. The new regime, the imperial regime of the Second Stuart Despotism, had begun.

Among the crowds which viewed curiously the royal frigate at anchor in the harbor, or looked on as the Governor came ashore, or lined the streets while the British soldiers marched past, were many who rejoiced that the hour of their deliverance had come. No longer would they be refused the right to vote, no longer fined for not attending meeting, no longer subjected to laws not of their own making, no longer excluded from civil and military offices.

Training day was marked by real enthusiasm. Among the crowd which cheered as the eight companies went through their exercises, were many who had fastened red paper crosses to their hats in token of their loyalty to the King. When the Governor rode out to review them, the troops saluted him with several volleys, which were echoed by three salvos from the *Rose*. That night bon-fires and fireworks lit up Fort Hill, while the air resounded to loud huzzas.[95]

But the people, even the old royal party, were not long in discovering that they had little to cheer about. Nothing more had been effected than a change of masters. In fact, under the arbitrary rule of Andros they had fewer rights than under the old government by "God's elect." They could not vote for members of the Assembly because there was no Assembly. The Governor, with the advice of a Council, governed like an Eastern despot, promulgating laws, levying taxes, appointing military and civil officers, placing men under arrest and denying them the right of *habeas corpus*.

Great was the indignation throughout the colony when the Governor and Council levied a tax on all estates of a penny in the pound, together with a poll tax of twenty pence, an import duty of a penny in the pound and an excise on liquors. The town of Ipswich led in resisting. The Selectmen resolved: "That inasmuch as it is against the privilege of English subjects to have money raised without their own consent in an Assembly or

[95] *Ibid.*, p. 173.

Parliament, therefore they will petition the King for liberty of an Assembly before they made any rates." For this, the Reverend John Wise and others of "the principal persons" were thrown into jail, denied the *habeas corpus,* tried in Boston by a packed jury and fined heavily.[96]

The people, sullen and resentful over the loss of their liberties, suddenly awoke to the realization that they faced also the loss of their property. Since the charter had from the first been illegal, argued Sir Edmund, all patents for land issued under its authority were of no force. If owners wished to validate their rights they must apply for new patents, paying ruinous prices. If we may believe Cotton Mather, all the personal property in the province would not have sufficed to redeem the patents and satisfy "these crocodiles." "The Governor caused the lands of particular persons to be measured out and given to his creatures."[97] Other favorites laid claim to the commons in several towns, and when the towns appointed agents to defend their rights, the latter were forced "to answer as criminals at the next assizes."[98]

"It would take a long summer's day to relate the miseries which were come . . . in upon poor New England by reason of the arbitrary government then imposed on them," says Cotton Mather. The town meetings were to be held only once a year; exorbitant fees were charged for all legal papers, probates of wills costing no less than fifty shillings; prominent men were arrested on slight pretexts, and hurried out of their own counties to be tried by packed juries. "The foxes were made the administrators of justice to the poultry."[99]

In their distress the people had no other recourse than to complain to the King, even though they must have realized that the King himself was their real oppressor. Plymouth petitioned that they might be "quieted in the possession of all property both in houses and lands" and that all titles be confirmed; "that no laws be made nor monies raised there without the consent of a General Assembly, as it is in other plantations; that all townships

[96] Cotton Mather, *Magnalia* (London, 1702), Book II, pp. 43, 44.
[97] *Ibid.,* p. 44.
[98] *Ibid.,* p. 43; John Hutchinson, *History of the Colony of Massachusetts Bay,* II, pp. 357–369.
[99] *Ibid.,* p. 368.

have liberty to assemble and manage the business of their several precincts."[100]

In the meanwhile Increase Mather, disguising himself to escape detention, had slipped out of the colony on a ship bound for England. Upon his arrival there, he joined with Samuel Nowell and Elisha Hutchinson, two former Massachusetts magistrates, in a petition to the Lords of Trade. They prayed that all titles to land be confirmed, that the town meetings be permitted to transact business by the vote of the freeholders, that courts be set up in every precinct where probates of wills could be made, that no laws be enacted and taxes levied upon the people save by a General Assembly elected by the freeholders, that no man be taxed to support a religion other than his own.[101] The Lords received this petition favorably, but the opposition from above was too strong for a favorable outcome. It is said that Lord Sunderland with his own hand struck out the clause for the restoring of the Assembly.[102]

Back in New England, when a few Indians launched isolated attacks in New Haven, on the upper Connecticut and in Maine, the wildest rumors spread throughout the colonies—the Governor had told the Indians that he expected them, in company with Irish Catholics, to take possession of Boston; the King had promised the Pope that he would establish Catholicism in the English colonies; he was planning an Irish colony on their borders.[103] So when, at eleven o'clock on the night of August 16, 1688, Boston awoke to the ringing of bells, the beating of drums, the reports of cannon and loud huzzas, people sprang from their beds ready to defend themselves. Nor were they greatly relieved upon learning the occasion of the din—a prince had been born to James II, thus assuring a Roman Catholic succession to the throne.[104]

It was in April, 1689, that rumors began to filter into New

[100] Ibid., p. 368.
[101] Calendar of State Papers, Colonial, America and West Indies, 1685–1688, pp. 580, 581.
[102] John Hutchinson, History of the Colony of Massachusetts Bay, II, p. 366.
[103] Ibid., p. 369; Cotton Mather, Magnalia (London, 1702), Book II, p. 45.
[104] "Diary of Samuel Sewall," Massachusetts Historical Society Collections, Fifth Series, V, p. 223.

England by way of Virginia that the Prince of Orange had landed in England. Governor Andros, who was at Pemaquid at the time, hastened back to Boston. "There's a general buzzing among the people, with great expectation of their old charter, or they know not what," he wrote Anthony Brockholls in New York. When John Winslow arrived from Nevis with a copy of Prince William's proclamation, Andros demanded to see it, and upon Winslow's refusal called him a saucy fellow and committed him to jail.[105] At the same time he began preparations to put down any uprising of the people or to resist the landing of forces sent over by William.

But he was too late. On April 18, signals were run up on Beacon Hill and excited men and women began to pour into the streets. From the gallery of the quaint wooden Town House one of the leading citizens began the reading of a "Declaration" condemning the Andros regime. At its conclusion the mob responded with a shout and headed in the direction of Fort Hill, dragging several cannon with them. Realizing that he could make no effective resistance to the trained bands of the colony, Andros came forth and gave himself up. Soon after, the little garrison of fourteen men surrendered and the next day the Castle and the frigate *Rose* also yielded.[106]

In the meanwhile, in England, Increase Mather had looked on with mounting hopes as the drama of the Glorious Revolution was enacted before his eyes—the landing of William of Orange, the march on London, the flight of James II, the meeting of the Convention, the crowning of William and Mary as joint sovereigns. The time was at hand, he thought, for the restoration of the Massachusetts charter and with it the privileges of the old ruling class. In company with Sir Henry Ashurst he not only pleaded with the King, but hung around Westminster Hall buttonholing the leading members of both houses of the Convention.[107] But he was told that the judgment in chancery against the charter had annihilated it, so that to restore it would be impossible.

[105] *Andros Tract*, I, p. 75 n., pp. 77 f.
[106] *Calendar of State Papers, Colonial, America and West Indies*, 1689–1692, p. 92.
[107] Cotton Mather, *Magnalia* (London, 1702), Book II, p. 55.

Mather must have been much surprised when certain lawyers whom he consulted advised him that the charter which Massachusetts had so prized had all along been an inadequate basis for her government. It was silent in regard to a representative Assembly, it did not empower the Governor and Company to levy taxes, it did not grant to the courts power extending to life. In fact, the charter gave the government no more power than was exercised by corporations in England. In other words, for over half a century Massachusetts had been exercising powers which had no authorization from King or Parliament.[108]

So Mather now busied himself with securing a new charter which would remedy these defects and yet restore the power of the old order. When the Lords of Trade asked him whether he and the other agents would accept a charter similar to those granted to other colonies, he demurred. Since Massachusetts was overwhelmingly Congregationalist, he pleaded, and Congregationalist Churches needed the sustaining hand of the government, the people should be permitted to select their own Governor as formerly. But this was asking too much. Under the old colonial system the Governor was the chief, almost the sole, representative of the throne and so of imperial authority. King William was very anxious to satisfy the agents, but he realized that to yield to the New Englanders the privilege of electing their Governor would make them virtually independent.[109]

Mather had hardly reconciled himself to having a royal Governor in Massachusetts, when he found that the Lords of Trade wished to base the franchise on a property qualification rather than on membership in one of the Congregational Churches. Against this he protested violently. He would sooner die than consent, he said. But the Lords, at last tired out with his tenacity in demanding rights for his own group while denying them for others, replied that if he would not submit to the King's wishes he must take what would follow. So a clause was inserted in the charter providing that all freeholders whose income amounted to £40 a year and "inhabitants" owning property

[108] *Ibid.*, p. 57.
[109] *Calendar of State Papers, Colonial, America and West Indies,* 1689–1692, pp. 417, 420, 423.

worth £100 should have the right to vote for members of the Assembly.

A few years later Cotton Mather, in an effort to justify his father's course in this matter, claimed that in some respects the new charter was better than the old. "The colony is now made a province and their General Court has, with the King's approbation, as much power in New England as the King and Parliament have in England. They have all English liberties and can be touched by no law, no tax, but of their own making. All the privileges of their holy religion are forever secured and their titles to their lands . . . are now confirmed to them. If an ill Governor should happen to impose upon them, what hurt could he do to them? None. . . . For he cannot make one Councillor, or one judge, or one justice, or one sheriff to serve his turn. . . . The people have a negative upon all the executive part of the civil government as well as the legislative, which is a vast privilege, enjoyed by no other plantation in America." [110]

Cotton Mather was right. The second charter was a far better document than the first. But he does not mention the greatest advance, the point of greatest significance. The liberties and privileges which he enumerates were not to be confined to one group hand-picked by the ministers from one religious faith. True, the new government was to be far from democratic, since the property qualification debarred the poorer classes from voting, yet the gain for freedom was vital—freedom to think and worship as one chose. No longer was the penalty for non-conformity to be disfranchisement. Whatever Cotton Mather said in praise of the new charter, he knew, and his father knew, that it struck a fatal blow at that all-important feature of the Wilderness Zion, the oligarchy of the saints.

[110] Cotton Mather, *Magnalia* (London, 1702), Book II, p. 59.

CONCLUSION

PURITANISM found its truest expression, not in England, but in New England. The Bible Commonwealth envisaged by Ames, Baynes, Bradshaw and others was never established in the mother country. It was not so much the opposition of the King and the bishops which thwarted the Puritan leaders as the fact that a large part of the people, perhaps a decided majority, were not in sympathy with the reform movement. Even in their hour of triumph, when the monarchy had been overthrown by Cromwell's Ironsides, the Puritan leaders found themselves powerless to set up the government by the elect of which they had so long dreamed. The very suggestion, when made in the famous Barebones Parliament, led to the dissolution of that body and the proclaiming of the Protectorate. As for Oliver Cromwell, stern Independent though he was, his ideals were far from squaring with those of a Cotton or a Norton.

So it is to New England we must turn if we are to study the true Puritan State with all its distinctive features—congregations whose autonomy was derived from a covenant with God, a civil government in which only Church members participated, an educational system designed to buttress the orthodox religion, a rigid code of morals, the suppression of heresy. In fact, New England may be considered a laboratory of Puritan civilization.

The founders of the Massachusetts Bible State confidently expected it to endure forever. To them it was no social and religious experiment, but the carrying out of God's commands. Yet they had been in America but five or six years and were still struggling to clear the forests, lay out their meager crops and build their houses, when alarming weaknesses appeared. A few decades later the ministers were bewailing the general decline of godliness, were searching their souls for the cause of the general "decay," were warning the people that God had a controversy with them. Before the end of the seventeenth century it was ap-

parent to all who had eyes to see that the Puritan experiment
had failed.

The reforming synod of 1679, despite their earnest debates,
their fasting and their prayers, threw little light upon the causes
of decline. There had been heresy in the colony, they pointed
out, swearing and drinking to excess had become common, the
Sabbath day had been broken, love of wealth was supplanting
the love of God, parents had been lax with their children, Christian education was being neglected. But they failed to see that
these things were symptoms rather than causes. Had they looked
deeper they would have found behind them all human nature
itself—man's natural desire to acquire the good things of this
world, and his instinctive dislike of restraint, whether of his
personal conduct or his freedom of thought or his conscience,
or his right to have a voice in the conduct of the state.

There is no reason to doubt the sincere belief of Winthrop
and Cotton and Shepard that their Bible State was shaped according to God's directions and that in consequence it was as
near perfect as man could make it, a civil and religious Utopia.
To those who complained that this structure was undemocratic
they replied that it was intended to be so. But they would
have been indignant had one stigmatized it as a tyranny. Yet in
some respects a tyranny it was, a tyranny over men's minds, a
restriction upon one's right to think, imposed by sermons, laws
against heresy and the control of education and the press. In
early Massachusetts one disagreed with the minister at one's peril.

The ministers and magistrates would have been even more
indignant at the accusation that the structure of Church and
State was designed with the end of bestowing upon them special
privilege and power. Certainly such a charge would have been
unjust. Nonetheless special privilege and power it did give them.
And though the ministers spoke of themselves as "God's poor
servants," they valued their influence to the full and battled
fiercely to retain it. In reading the election sermons one cannot
escape the impression that a Norton or an Oakes or a Torrey took
deep satisfaction in the privilege of scolding Magistrates and
Deputies, of instructing them as to their duties and telling them
what to do and what not to do. And in his own community the

minister, even though perhaps a loving shepherd to his flock, demanded obedience as well as affection.

But the power of the few over the many, whether exercised by an aristocracy or a plutocracy or a theocracy, always is vulnerable to attack. If it is based on wealth, wealth may be confiscated; if it is based on military strength, arms may overcome arms; if it is based on ascendency over men's minds, reason may overthrow it. When the Puritans left England they fled from the things which seemed to them to threaten their souls, from a hostile King, from the bishops, from Church ceremonials, from lax morals, from disobedience to God's "ordinances"; but they could not flee from human nature, they could not flee from themselves. Upon landing on the shores of Massachusetts Bay they might fall on their knees to ask God to bless their great venture, but it was they themselves who brought the germs of failure.

As we have seen, economic conditions in New England—the expansion of foreign trade, the growth of fisheries, the shift from the agricultural village to the farm—tended to undermine the Puritan State. Yet it is doubtful whether any other place on the American continent would have been more favorable. Had the Puritans planted themselves on the banks of the Potomac they would almost certainly have established the plantation economy so unfavorable to religion, and have sacrificed the autonomy they valued so highly for a binding trade with England. Had they landed on the Delaware they would have found conditions there, too, far from ideal. It was on the Delaware that Penn tried his Holy Experiment, and, it will be remembered, the Holy Experiment failed. As for New Jersey, a Puritan community based upon the ideals of Ames, Cotton and Davenport was actually established there in 1666, but before five decades had passed it lay in ruins.[1]

Even had Winthrop and the other leaders of the Great Exodus led their followers into the very heart of the American continent to establish their Zion on the banks of the Ohio or the Mississippi, the results would not have been greatly different. Though there they might have found the complete isolation they so highly

[1] T. J. Wertenbaker, *The Founding of American Civilization, The Middle Colonies*, pp. 126–129.

valued, though no heresies from without might have filtered in, though they might have enjoyed complete political and economic independence, though the supernatural might not have grown dim before the glaring light of rationalism, the experiment would certainly have failed. It probably would have endured longer than in New England, but its ultimate fate would have been just as certain.

The temple of American Puritanism fell because it was built, had to be built, on the sands of human nature. When the pillars of the structure—political autonomy, the close alliance of Church and State, the control of education, orthodoxy, the stern code of morals, isolation—one after another began to sag, it was not so much the pillars themselves as the sand which caused the trouble. It was from beneath that came the succession of shocks which threatened the whole structure—the Roger Williams heresy, the Anne Hutchinson heresy, the Child petition, the Halfway Covenant, the demand for a wider franchise, the liberalizing of Harvard, the defeat of the clergy and magistrates in the witchcraft prosecutions, the growing laxness in morals.

In bringing to the New World a society which was largely the product of sixteenth-century thought and defending it there against change in a changing world, the Puritans attempted the impossible. As the decades of the seventeenth century passed, men's minds expanded to keep pace with new scientific discoveries, with new ideals of human rights, with new conceptions of man's relation to God. The leaders of the old order in Massachusetts might as well have attempted to interfere with the movement of the moon around the earth as to block these changes. While they were vainly trying to crystallize the Puritan spirit of the time of Winthrop and Cotton, the tide of a new civilization swept over and past them.

But failure did not bring immediate destruction. Certain features of the Puritan State survived not only the loss of the charter, the Glorious Revolution, the advance of rationalism, the weakening of the moral code, but even the American Revolution and the creation of a Federal Union. When the nineteenth century dawned New England society was still undemocratic; the clergy and the moneyed classes were still entrenched behind a barrier of statutes, patronage, election devices and traditions. In Massachusetts no atheist, no Jew, no man of meager income could be Governor; in Connecticut no Roman Catholic could be Governor. To be eligible for the Upper House in Massachusetts one must have a freehold of £300 or personal property valued at £600; in New Hampshire, a freehold of £200. "We have lived in a State which exhibits to the world a democratic exterior," one New Englander remarked, "but which actually practices all the arts of an organized aristocracy under the management of the old firm of Moses and Aaron."

It was this remnant of the Puritan oligarchy which Thomas Jefferson and his New England henchmen of the Democratic-Republican Party attacked so fiercely in the early decades of the nineteenth century. In Connecticut Abraham Bishop denounced the old charter of Charles II, upon which the government based its authority. "Let us sweep it away for a Constitution based on the will of the people," he said. The reformers denounced the clergy as a pack of privileged reactionaries who strutted around with queues and cocked hats and prated about government by the wisest and best. The conservatives fought back with every available weapon. From one pulpit after another Jefferson was denounced as an atheist, a liar, an enemy of the Churches, a Jacobin. "Let us not destroy the fabric erected by our fathers," the clergy pleaded. "The issue is clearly between religion and infidelity, morality and sin, sound government and anarchy." But they pleaded in vain. Election after election went against them, and new and more liberal Constitutions replaced the old governments. The day after the final defeat of the Connecticut conservatives, Lyman Beecher found his father seated with his head drooping on his breast. "Father, what are you thinking of?" he asked. "I am thinking of the Church of God," was the answer.

Despite the failure of the Puritan experiment it is a widely accepted belief that it was largely instrumental in moulding the character not only of modern New England, but of the entire United States. Plymouth is spoken of as the birthplace of the nation; the Puritans, it is claimed, came to America as the champions of religious freedom, they founded American democracy, they gave us the public school system, they lit the torch of learning to shine in every corner of the country, they contributed an element of stern morality.

Obviously this rests more upon fiction than reality. Plymouth was not the birthplace of the nation, for the nation was founded neither upon the ideals and institutions of the Pilgrims nor of the Puritans who followed them to New England. In fact, the use of the word "birthplace" as a metaphor to explain the origin of the country is quite misleading. When the English colonized America they established not just one beachhead on the coast, but a half dozen or more. And it was from each of these beachheads that European civilization swept westward or northwestward or southwestward to create what later became the United States. The founders of St. Mary's, Charleston, and Philadelphia were as truly founders of this nation as those of Jamestown and Plymouth.

The belief that the Puritans came to the New World in the cause of religious freedom is, of course, completely erroneous. The battle for toleration in this country was won in the face of their bitter opposition. It would have seemed to Mary Dyer, William Robinson, Marmaduke Stevenson and William Leddra, as they went to their fate on the gallows, ironical indeed that three centuries later their executioners should win applause as champions of religious freedom.

Nor did American democracy have its origin in New England. American democracy was born in England, it was defended and enlarged in Westminster Hall and upon many an English battlefield, it was brought to America by the settlers and there given a new expression, a new growth under the influence of frontier conditions. There were noble men in New England, as in other colonies, who fought the good fight for democracy, but they were rebels against the old Puritan order, not its defenders. An oligarchy of Church members has no more place in the American system than Locke's feudal system, or a slave-holding aristocracy, or a plutocracy based on big business, or a proletarian dictatorship.

As for the Puritan code of morals and the Puritan Sabbath observance, despite the many lapses in colonial New England itself they have left an imprint on life in many parts of the United States which has not yet been entirely erased. Blue-laws are often ignored, but they remain on the statute books. Yet it is in the South that blue-laws have the greatest vitality, and the Southern inheritance is Presbyterian, Baptist and Methodist, not Congregationalist.

A better case can be made for the influence of the Massachusetts school system, which was the most efficient in the colonies, the first to receive support from public funds, the first to be capped by a college. Yet the chief indebtedness of the United States is not to the founders of the Puritan educational system but to the men who so reconstructed it as to make it fit the needs of a democratic society. It was only under the pressure of Jeffersonian ideals that New England, two centuries after its founding, accepted the vital principle that public education should not be affiliated with any religious sect and should make civic duty rather than religion its chief objective.

But it is to the everlasting credit of the founders of New England that they lit and kept alive in infant America the fires of scholarship. The great importance they attached to learning, the readiness with which they accepted the findings of noted scientists, their own scientific strivings bore rich fruit for New England and the United States. The fact that eleven New Englanders were invited to join the Royal Society of London during the colonial period testifies to the intellectual activity of the region.

No truthful historian will withhold from New England the credit due her for her part in the creation and moulding of the nation. Her sons were among the most active in winning independence, they did their full share in shaping the Constitution, they were pioneers in opening western New York, northern Pennsylvania and the Great Lakes region, they gave the country its first American literature, they made noble contributions in the fields of invention, science, art, architecture. But most of the contributions were made after the fall of the Puritan oligarchy, and the men to whom the chief credit is due were not its supporters, but, on the contrary, those who rebelled against it.

INDEX

Agriculture, of manor, 3–4; of New England town, 50–54; field system, 53–54; early farms, 51–52; fruits and vegetables, 54; implements, 55–56

Aldeburgh, fishing, 2, II; shipbuilding, 10

Allen, James, opposes Church liberalism, 155

Allen, John, gives cue to synod of 1648, 301

Ambrose, Alice, persecution of, 240

America, lading of, 197

Ames, William, on Church covenant, 23; father of New England Churches, 24; career, 24; writings, 24; on Church federation, 24–25; on appointment of ministers, 25; influence, 29; *Medulla* at Harvard, 142; on God in nature, 259

Andros, Sir Edmund, takes meeting-house for Anglicans, 248; clashes with Congregationalists, 248–249; royal governor, 331; arrival, 332–333; tyranny of, 333–334; overthrow, 336; taxes illegally, 333–334; threatens property rights, 334

Anglican Church, Puritans cling to, 22; members disfranchised, 245; rights for demanded, 245; Randolph pleads for, 246; request for minister, 246; Robert Ratcliffe, 247; support for, 247–248; in South Meeting-house, 249; King's Chapel, 249

Arbella, voyage of, 88–89

Architecture, East Anglia, 13–16; medieval house, 13–15; Flemish cottage, 15–16; in New England, 106–127; Puritans reject Gothic, 107; meeting-houses not churches, 107–108; early meeting-houses, 108–109; four-square meeting-house, 109–111; meeting-house becomes church, 111–112; Wren churches, 112–115; log cabin myth, 115–116; half-timbering, 116; New England cottage, 117–118; thatch, 118–119; windows, 119–120; medieval house in New England, 120–123; the Georgian, 124–126; inheritance and development, 126–127; influence of religion, 127

Artisans, of New England town, 49–50; blacksmiths, 49; millers, 49

Austin, Anne, expelled for heresy, 226–227

Baptists, at Lynn, 224–225; doctrines, 224–225; persecution of, 225–226; whipping of Holmes, 225–226; thrive on persecution, 242–243; debate with, 243; continued persecution, 243–244; meeting-house of, 244–245

Barley, on manor, 4; in New England, 55

Barrowe, Henry, doctrines of, 20–21; on Church government, 21; execution, 21; Cotton criticises, 21–22

Bastwick, John, persecution of, 33

Baynes, Paul, on Church covenant, 23

Bay Psalm Book, evaluated, 94–95; revised, 95; musical notes omitted, 129

Belcher, Joseph, on qualification for office, 70

Billerica, meeting-house, 108–109

Bellingham, Richard, imprisons Quakers, 227; dispute with Commissioners, 308

Bishop, George, on expulsion of Mary Fisher, 226; glorifies Quaker martyrs, 236–237

Black Death, denudes manors, 6

Blacksmiths, in New England towns, 49

Boston, Cotton teacher at, 63; Sabbath in, 162, 172; fire of 1711, 172; dancing, 176; trade, 200; growth, 201; Hutchinson heresy, 219–222; Quakers, 240–241; Quaker meeting-house, 242; earthquake, 256–257; inoculation, 267–268; revolt against Andros, 336

Boylston, Zabdiel, inoculates, 267–268

Bradford, psalmody at, 132–133

Bradford, William, *The History of Plymouth Plantation,* 87–88; as historian, 87–88; on wickedness at Plymouth, 169

Bradstreet, Anne, life of, 101–102; *Contemplations,* 102–103; *The Tenth Muse,* 103

Bradstreet, Simon, mission to London, 239,

347

verts, 229–230; disputes with Endicott, 232–233; sentenced, 233; right ear cut off, 233–234

Holmes, Obadiah, at Lynn, 224–225; whipped, 225–226

Hooker, Thomas, flees to New England, 34; as preacher, 81–82; describes Hell, 82; disputes with Williams, 217; on God in nature, 259

Hopkins, Edward, bequest to education, 146

Hops, grown in Essex, 12; at Milford, 55

Hornbook, in primary schools, 157

House of Seven Gables, described, 120–121

Hubbard, William, on John Cotton's preaching, 80; preaching of, 85–87; on educational independence, 138–139; on education for civil office, 140; on Puritan founders, 169; on rising generation, 177; on dispersal of congregations, 188; on toleration, 215; thinks persecution a failure, 242; Indian was God's scourge, 256; opposes innovations, 315

Hull, John, diary of, 91–92; condemns long hair, 174; trades in wine, 199; the pious merchant, 203–204; on Quaker invasion, 226–227; describes strong "providence," 255; deplores Restoration, 302; on proclaiming of Charles II, 303

Hutchinson, Anne, Johnson on heresy of, 89–90; character, 219; doctrines of 219–220; battle over, 220–221; trial and banishing of, 221–222; meaning of incident, 222–223

Iconoclasm, in East Anglia, 17, 19

Idleness, a serious misdemeanor, 165–166

Illustrious Providences, to prove the supernatural, 269; witch hunt attributed to, 285

Immigration, restrictions on, 68; divides towns, 190–191; of merchants, 207

Implements, agricultural, in England, 3, 4, 6; in New England, 55–56

Ipswich, England, cloth industry, 2; shipbuilding, 2, 10; exports, 8, 9; the Orwell shallow, 9; fishing, 11; persecution at, 33

Ipswich, Mass., cattle drivers, 56–57; refuses taxes without representation, 333–334

James I, opposes Puritan reforms, 23; consents to Pilgrim settlement, 28

James II, despotism of, 324; overthrow

hoped for, 330; son born to, 335; overthrow of, 336

Jefferson, Thomas, attacks old order, 343

Johnson, Edward, as historian, 89–90; Wonder-Working Providence, 89–90; God's favors in commerce, 193, 197; on trade and irreligion, 193; describes Boston, 201–202; deplores losses at sea, 204; abjures Hutchinson heresy, 208–209

Johnson, Isaac, plans exodus, 30

King's Chapel, erection of, 249

Kirke, Perry, selected to rule New England, 331

Labaree, L. W., on meadow lots, 57

Land, William, represses Puritans, 27; persecution, 32, 33–34; on Sabbath observance, 33; expels lecturers, 34; heads colonial committee, 296

Lavenham, cloth industry, 2, 7; medieval houses, 14

Lechford, Thomas, on restrictions of Church membership, 67; records building contract, 117–118

Leddra, William, chained to log, 237; execution of, 237

Lee, Samuel, scientific work of, 262–263; his The Joy of Life, 263; accepts Copernican system, 265

Leigh, commerce, 9

Leverett, John, tutor at Harvard, 152–153; in Harvard Corporation, 156; president, 156; influence, 157–158

Levity, Puritans condemn, 162–163

Literature, New England, religion theme of, 78–79; sermons, 79–87; histories, 87–91; diaries, 91–93; poetry, 93–103; evaluated, 103–104; blind to beauty of nature, 106

Log cabins, none in early New England, 115

Lots, divisions of home lots, 45–48; few inequalities, 46; use of, 48; field lots, 50–54

Lynn, Meeting-house, 109

Magistrate, duty of to Church, 71–72

Magnalia Christi Americana, on character of clergy, 61; evaluated, 90–91; schoolmasters and religion, 139; on witch confessions, 275–276

Makemie, Francis, says villages advance religion, 43

Maldon, "decay" of, 9–10

exodus, 208; fear bans, 208–212; a betrayal of God's people, 212–213; ministers denounce, 214–215
Tomkins, Mary, severe treatment of, 240
Topsfield, Jacob Perkins house, 117
Torrey, Samuel, on unity of Church and State, 71; on neglect of education, 148–149; on decline of godliness, 170; on God's controversy with New England, 171; warns on earthly riches, 203; opposes toleration, 215; on decay of religion, 223; wants new witch trials, 280; on liberty, 314–315
Town, New England, grants for, 42; imitates manor, 42–43; religious considerations shape, 43; the village, 43–44, 45–46; journey to, 44; autonomy of, 44–45; economic democracy, 46–47; description, 48; self-sufficiency, 48–49; artisans, 49–50; social life, 50; division of fields, 50–54; early farms, 51–52; fishing in, 52; fences, 53; field not an agricultural unit, 53–54; fruits and vegetables, 54; grain, 54–55; hops, 55; agricultural implements, 55–56; cattle, 56–57; pasture, 56–57; meadow, 57; congregation, 58–69; town meeting, 69–70; town officers, 69; Selectmen, 69–70; dispersal of population, 184–192; growth of farms, 184–190; farms in Enfield, 185–186; dispersal of congregation, 186; Woodbury farms, 186; South Hadley farms, 186–187; dispersal at Plymouth, 187–188; laws against dispersal, 189; town unity lost, 189–190; proprietors versus "strangers," 190–192; Enfield proprietors, 191–192; Milford proprietors, 191
Tufts, John, to reform psalmody, 132

Upshall, Nicholas, persecution of, 229

Vane, Sir Harry, in Hutchinson controversy, 220–221; defeated for governor, 221
Vegetables, on manor, 4; in New England, 46, 54
Village, New England, purpose of, 43–44; plan, 45–46; description, 48; life in, 50; gardens, 54; disintegration of, 184–192; drift from to farm, 184–190; dispersal of congregation, 186; dispersal in Enfield, 185–186; Plymouth dispersal, 187–188; laws forbid dispersal, 189
Villein, of manors, 4; Black Death, 6

Vindication of New England, on services of Harvard, 137
Virginia, New Englanders trade with, 199–200

Waldon, saffron, 2, 12
Ward, Edward, on meeting-houses, 110
Ward, John, prosecution of, 35
Ward house, described, 121–122
Ward, Nathaniel, denounces foppery, 168; on Puritan profanity, 172; warns heretics, 212
Ward, Samuel, persecuted, 33
Watertown, selection of teacher, 143–144
Weatherboarding, in England, 14–16
West Indies, New England trade to, 197–198, 200; imports from, 198; visitors from, 206
Westminster Confession, New Englanders alarmed by, 298–299; synod of 1648 accepts in matters of faith, 306
Whalley, Edward, flees to New England, 302–303; Charles II hears of welcome, 30
Wheat, on manor, 4
Whitgift, Archbishop, prosecutes Barrowe and Greenwood, 20–21
Wheelwright, John, supports Mrs. Hutchinson, 220–221; banished, 221
Whipple house, lean-to, 123
White, John, founds New England Company, 29–30; on New England products, 193
Wigglesworth, Michael, God's Controversy with New England, 96–97; The Day of Doom, 97–101; influence of, 97–98
Wigs, in New England, 174–176; Sewall denounces, 174–176; Josiah Willard wears, 175; Benjamin Colman wears, 175–176
Willard, Josiah, defends wig-wearing, 175
Willard, Samuel, vice-president of Harvard, 154; resigns, 156; accused of witchcraft, 278; liberalism of, 312–313
Williams, Roger, character, 215–216; "heresies" of, 216–217; banished, 217; flight, 218; his threat to Bible State, 218; views on toleration, 228–229
Williamson, Sir Joseph, Secretary of State, 317
Wilson, John, flees to New England, 34; Boston pastor, 63; warns on earthly riches, 203; censured, 220–221; justifies torturing of Brend, 230–231; taunts